The Myths
of School Self-Renewal

The Myths
of School Self-Renewal

DAVID GORDON

**TEACHERS
COLLEGE
PRESS**

Teachers College, Columbia University
New York and London

Published by Teachers College Press, 1234 Amsterdam Avenue, New York, N.Y.
10027

Library of Congress Cataloging in Publication Data

Gordon, David, 1941–
    The myths of school self-renewal.

    Bibliography: p.
    Includes index.
    1. Education—Philosophy. 2. Educational planning.
3. Organizational change. 4. Education—Israel—Case
studies. I. Title.
LB1025.2.G625   1984   370'.1   84-2616

ISBN 0-8077-2755-5

Manufactured in the United States of America

89 88 87 86 85 84   1 2 3 4 5 6

To Jinks Beinashowitz
Without Whose Help This Book
Would Not Have Come About

Contents

Preface

Perhaps the first function of the preface of a book should be to point out the special perspective the author has adopted in writing the book. In my case this requires me to discuss the two different aspects or strands of my work—theory and case studies. With regard to theory, I suggest that readers consult the theoretical literature to which I refer in the notes. Readers will find some rather strange items from fields not usually linked to educational change — philosophy, Freudian analysis, anthropology, political science, semiotics. They will also find a lot of mention of metaphor and even reference to a work on the history of jazz. In a sense, it is this bibliographical hodgepodge that constitutes the perspective of this book.

Traditionally, planned change in organizations has been considered a sort of hybrid subfield of social psychology and organizational theory. Not only that, the perspectives derived from social psychology and organizational theory have been of a very specific sort. People have usually looked at organizational change in the way that mainstream social psychologists and organizational theorists looked at small groups and organizations in the 1950s and 1960s.

But paradigms change and the locus of academic excitement crosses old disciplinary lines. Social psychology and organizational theory underwent important changes during the 1970s. Phenomenological, humanistic, and neo-Marxist perspectives rejuvenated what had become rather tired subdisciplines. As a result, people began to look at different aspects of organizations and groups. The rituals, myths, and stories of organizational activity became interesting in themselves. In parallel, the social sciences in general began to discover how much they could use research in the humanities—literary criticism, history, and philosophy—and how, in many ways, the humanities had more to offer to social science than the revered natural sciences. This book is, from one point of view, an attempt to explore what these changes might offer the world of planned educational change and educational consulting.

Now to the second strand of the book—the case studies. The field of educational change has always encouraged the presenting of case studies. However, the style in which case studies are written has changed. At one time, cases were reported in a way similar to how meetings are summarized through minutes. In the name of scientific objectivity, the "story" side of the case study was ignored, because it was assumed that social science eschewed passion, excitement, anger, and fun, especially on the part of the social scientists themselves. Also, social science seemed unable to address people except as statistical entities or as role encumbents. All this is changing. More and more we are realizing that we can learn about general things by considering the specific in all its human detail. In this book, there are nineteen case studies, most of them related to a specific research project I will explain in chapter 1. At this point, suffice it to say that its name was the Project for the Advancement of Educational Cooperation, that it was concerned with promoting what I call school self-renewal, and that it had a project staff of six or seven people. In writing these studies I have tried to retain the people and their feelings (especially *my* feelings). Thus some of the studies are best described as vignettes rather than cases. This kind of writing is difficult. I soon discovered that experience in writing academic articles is no preparation for writing that tries to make people, including oneself, come alive. I hope that here and there I have succeeded. To the extent that I have, my accomplishment is an important justification for writing this book.

Unusual theoretical sources and descriptive case studies constitute more than the perspective used in writing this book. They are also the basis for some of its problems. Let me point out seven such problems, three relating to the theoretical sources and four to the case studies.

First is the problem of the expert reader. A colleague of mine who is an expert on Freudian theory read an early draft of the book. He pointed to a number of my interpretations regarding Freudian therapy in the second chapter that he considered a very loose way of using Freudian theory. In the end I think I managed to persuade him that, in the context of the argument I present in chapter 2, these are not loose interpretations. However, in that I use sources from many disciplines, reactions similar to those of my Freudian friend are likely to surface whenever readers who are specialists in one of these disciplines come across the passages in this book that relate to their specialties. Specialists in a field are often very wary of letting the concepts in their field be used elsewhere. They are quick to spot looseness, distortions, and inaccuracies. They forget, however, that human beings are creatures who think through metaphor. Metaphoric uses often are loose and even distorted, but nevertheless the best of them have still pushed humanity forward. Mathematicians may laugh at the social scientist's "function," and the physicists may laugh at the "energies," "fields," and "forces" discussed in social science. Yet social scientists have made quite good use of these borrowed terms, even if they have borrowed loosely.

This is one part of my reaction to the problem of the expert reader. On the other hand, I think it important to stress that in my use of different sources there almost certainly will be inaccuracies. Very few writers with a penchant for a synoptic view of things also have the erudition to use their sources as correctly as specialists. Thus inaccuracies are usually the price one has to pay for the synoptic view.

Second, eclecticism not only may encourage bold, inaccurate borrowing but also may result in a certain timidity. Several colleagues have suggested that some of my claims about educational organizations apply just as well to other sorts of organizations. Nevertheless, in this book I have not tried to enlarge the scope of my argument. My knowledge of other sorts of organizations is not very extensive, and I prefer that someone else point out the significance (if any) of some of my ideas in noneducational contexts.

Third, there is the problem of style of argumentation. Theoretical paradigms do not consist only of certain questions, concepts, and propositions. In addition, a paradigm or a discipline usually embodies a certain style of argumentation, a certain way of marshaling evidence and certain criteria for accepting or rejecting an argument. Often when writers bring a new theoretical perspective to bear on a particular topic, they retain the viewpoint of those whose academic training was in the old perspective relating to the topic. Thus they tend to present the new perspective in the old style of argumentation and marshaling evidence. This usually makes things much easier for the reader. However, I unfortunately cannot help the reader in this way. My academic background is in philosophy rather than in social psychology or organizational theory, so readers will have to come to grips with the rather close, convoluted style of argumentation that characterizes philosophical writing. I can only hope that they will find it worthwhile.

Fourth (and here I move on to the group of problems associated with the case studies), the case studies encourage what I call the "cross-cultural halo effect." All describe incidents that occurred

in the Israeli educational system. The immediate assumption on
the part of the Western reader might be that this book places educational change in cross-cultural perspective and is concerned with
how people go about changing education in an esoteric, exotic, or at
least foreign culture. For those interested in the exotic, or those
with some special interest in Israeli education, this may seem a
good thing. For those without these special interests, this emphasis
may seem to minimize the relevance of what I have to say. However, I should point out that in my view the Israeli emphasis is
irrelevant in the majority of the cases, and secondary in those cases
where cultural factors do play a part. There are four cases in chapter
3 that relate specifically to Israeli sacred cows and the limitations
the Hebrew language imposes on educational change. Three cases
in chapter 4, although not specific to the Israeli context, could only
have occurred in an educational system that is both focused vis-à-
vis implicit power talk (a term I explain in chapter 4) and bureaucratized. All other cases could have taken place in any Western
educational system.

Fifth, the fact that most of the cases relate to a specific project
invites the reader to assume the book is a report of that project. This
is not so. The book uses cases from the Project for the Advancement
of Educational Cooperation and tells part of its story. However, its
use of this project is selective. By and large, all aspects of the project unrelated to the theoretical propositions developed in the book
are ignored. Nevertheless, for those readers who are interested in
getting a reasonably full picture of an extensive attempt to promote
educational change, I have considerably expanded some of the
cases. These cases go quite a bit beyond the specific points for
which each was introduced. Thus I think that, although the book
does not tell the story of the Project for the Advancement of Educational Cooperation in a chronological sense, any reader who reads
cases I–VI, VIII–XI, XIII, XV–XVII, together with the summary of
the project's activities in chapter 1 and appendix A, should end up
with an almost complete picture of it.

Sixth, the fact that the cases relate to an intervention in schools
may create problems for those readers who themselves are inter-
ventionists or consultants. Such readers are going to be tempted to
make professional comparisons, and to say things like: "I wouldn't
have done things in that way," or "At that point I would have done
such-and-such." However, in most cases the interventionist aspect
of the story is secondary, and the case was chosen to illustrate something that would have occurred no matter what the intervention

strategy was. So I would suggest that those readers who are interventionists/consultants try to ignore the temptation to see the cases in terms of what they would have done in such situations, at least during a first reading.

Seventh, there is the questionnaire issue. It always surprises me how seriously social scientists take questionnaires. They invest such importance in them that they are often called "instruments" rather than plain questionnaires. In my experience, the presentation of a paper at an academic colloquium quite often gets bogged down when the audience requests further details about the "instruments" used. To be honest, I do not take questionnaires quite that seriously. For me, they are usually just a quick, relatively efficient means of getting the views of a group of people on some issue or question, and that is all. In the Project for the Advancement of Educational Cooperation, questionnaires also served other purposes. Often they became a means for encouraging school staffs to engage in certain types of interactive activities—the results of the filling out of a questionnaire would engender discussion, say, which would then lead to problem-solving activity and so on. Also through reacting to questionnaires, schools began to take the idea of evaluation more seriously, and as we shall see, promoting the norms of evaluation was an important component of the project's strategy. In other words, the *process* of dealing with a questionnaire was often more important than either the questionnaire itself, or the actual results obtained from filling it out. Thus we (the project staff) were encouraged whenever a school faculty rejected or modified our questionnaire, albeit drawn up according to all the professional rules laid down by experts in research methodology, and substituted a badly formulated questionnaire drawn up by the school faculty itself. Of course, we hoped they would learn to improve their formulations, but as a first step, the move towards independence seemed more important than the loss of scientific reliability.

In a number of cases in this book, this use of questionnaires is described. I think that in all such cases our process orientation is quite explicit in the description. Nevertheless, I was surprised to note how many colleagues who read a first draft of the book requested further details on our "instruments," and how school faculties reached certain conclusions from them. It seems the scientific reflex is very deeply ingrained.

Thus in writing the final version of these cases I faced a dilemma. Should I provide these details or not? If I were to do so, many readers would feel more comfortable with the cases. Yet I would be investing certain lists of questions with an exaggerated significance and would also be helping to reinforce what I regard as a ritualistic attitude to questionnaires. On the other hand, if I were not to supply the details, I would put these questionnaires in the right perspective but would run the risk of frustrating many readers. In the end, I chose the second alternative.

The seven problems raised above are mainly problems this book creates for the reader. There are also a number of problems that are probably less central for most readers but bothered me considerably as a writer. I had to struggle with the difficulties associated with anonymity in the case studies. I have used the usual methods for maintaining anonymity, such as changing names of people and places. In certain cases it also seemed important to preserve the anonymity of a school so that it would not be recognized by those from other schools who took part in the Project for the Advancement of Educational Cooperation. This was far more difficult to do, and at times impossible. Nevertheless, one tactic that seemed likely to help was to refrain from using the real names of our staff members in the cases. This raised two further problems. First at three places in the case studies, and in the general description of the project in chapter 1, I use the ideas of certain members of the staff. Academic courtesy requires that I indicate my sources, so I have mentioned two staff members by name (although not in a way that discloses the schools they worked in). I hope that other staff members understand that this does not indicate a hierarchy within the staff.

The second problem raised by such anonymity is the difficulty of hiding my own identity. I found that trying to write in the third person made my writing so stilted and artificial that I gave up the attempt. This makes it easier for teachers and principals involved in our project to identify the schools in these particular cases. However, as no problematic material surfaced and was described in these cases, it seemed that such a limited infringement of anonymity was justified.

A cursory glance at the cases will show that schools and project staff members do not all receive the same amount of attention. Specifically, in a disproportionately large number of cases I was the project staff member involved. Anonymity probably hides the fact to a certain extent, but a similar imbalance occurs with other staff members, although each is featured in at least one case. When it comes to the schools themselves, the disproportionality is even more marked, for some of the schools are not dealt with at all. I would have liked the cases to be more evenly spread among the schools and staff members, but there are good reasons why this could not be.

This book was written during my sabbatical year when the project was officially completed, and many thousands of miles separated me from most of the project staff and school faculties. In such a situation, whenever I reached a point in the writing where a particular case or type of case was called for, I could either rely on my own memory, search our records, or write to project staff members or school faculty and request certain kinds of material from them. Each of these options reinforced the disproportionality. My own memory was obviously biased towards incidents I personally participated in. Our records reflected the fact that some project staff members took the writing of detailed reports more seriously than others, and wrote more vividly than others. When I requested certain additional material from project staff and school faculty members, the same differences were apparent. And so the cases chosen came out to be those you will read in this book. I only hope that reading them will stimulate other project staff members and also school faculty members to write and publish other cases from our project.

Acknowledgments

There are four groups of persons I would like to mention and thank in particular. First, and most important, I am grateful to the principals and staffs of the schools who participated in the Project for the Advancement of Educational Cooperation. Anonymity considerations prevent me from mentioning them by name, but that cannot alter the fact that they made the three years of our work so interesting and pleasant. Many of these schools remain for me warm and exciting second homes. Second, I would like to thank our project staff: Menachem Avisar, Leah Dishon, Hava Katz, Michal Katz, Paul Shane, Batya Stein, and David Weiner. I think they would all agree that we had good and productive times together. Certainly no project leader could have enjoyed more the kind of interactions we maintained as a staff over the years. Third, I want to thank the senior officials in the Israeli Ministry of Education and Culture who dealt with high schools in general and the schools in our project in particular: David Pur (who also helped me write a section of chapter 4), Abraham Amir, Benjamin Amir, Avigdor Gonen, Abraham Green, Reuben Shapiro, and Yosef Yaron. They taught me an important lesson or rather helped me get rid of a limiting prejudice. I had always assumed that government bureaucrats were impossibly narrowminded. I discovered how wrong this view was and how committed they can be to change and innovation. Fourth, I am grateful for the intellectual stimulation of university colleagues, face to face and through letters, and to those whose comments on a final draft of this book helped me formulate my own ideas better. Specifically, I would like to mention Walter Ackerman, Chris Argyris, Terry Deal, Peter Goldstone, John Goodlad, John Meyer, Israel Scheffler, Donald Schön, and Louis Smith.

I also wish to express my gratitude to three institutions (although in chapter 2 I argue against the idea of an institution existing independently of the people in it): I thank the Faculty for Humanities and Social Sciences of the Ben-Gurion University of the Negev, Beersheba, for the grant given me in writing this book; the Israeli Ministry of Education and Culture for the research grant given to the Project for the Advancement of Educational Cooperation; and the Graduate School of Education, Harvard University, for acting as such a gracious host during the sabbatical year in which I wrote this book.

Finally I want to mention Dina, Ayellet, and Michal. Tradition has it that authors thank their families for their patience during the writing of a book. I refuse to do this. As a result of my book, Dina and the kids got a chance to spend a wonderful, eye-opening year in the United States. So I think they should thank me!

The Myths
of School Self-Renewal

1

The Road to Commitment

Over the last decade or so, the idea of planned change in schools has become very prominent. A vast number of academic educators "do" consulting in schools or school districts and their efforts are inevitably concerned with improving school functioning. In addition, national and local educational authorities, always concerned with programs for changing schools, have become more aware of the need to devote time and thought to the implementation of their ideas. The resulting variety of programs and types of consultation reflect a similar variety of theoretical approaches to planned change. However, perhaps the dominant strand of thought in the last decade has been related to the notion of transforming schools into self-renewing organizations, that is, organizations with a built-in capacity for solving their own problems or, as it is sometimes put, organizations that can learn to learn.

As the title of this book suggests, I am going to be rather critical of the idea of self-renewing schools and the literature devoted to the subject. I am, in fact, going to argue that to a large extent school self-renewal is an impossible ideal. Note that I do not call it a difficult idea to put into practice, as all believers in the ideal will readily admit, but an *impossible* ideal. Thus this book may well be regarded by many educational consultants concerned with improving organizational functioning in the schools as a pugnacious attack on their activities. If so, they will probably be correct, so let me hasten to assure them that this attack is not that of an outsider but rather of someone who, until a few years back, was a passionate believer in and proselytizer for school self-renewal. In many ways this is a very strange book. Most people who know me and know of my consulting work would probably agree with a kid to whom I once taught math. He took me aside when he completed the twelfth grade and said: "You believe in kids. You believe they

1

really want to learn. You must be the most naive person I have ever met." I *am* an optimist, probably a naive one. Nevertheless, this is a very pessimistic book. This is an uncomfortable combination but unavoidable if I want to remain honest.

This book is strange in yet another sense. On the one hand, much of the writing is very abstract. Much of the argumentation is philosophical and sociological and wanders into the upper strata of theory. On the other hand, a lot of what I have to say is very personal, because I tell part of the story of a project I lived with for three years concerned with promoting school self-renewal. The transitions from the abstract to the personal, from theory to case study, can never be totally seamless, but are unavoidable if I want to present my ideas as completely as possible.

In this chapter I wish to go back five years or so and explain how I became a believer in school self-renewal. This is both a personal history and also a review of some very powerful and convincing theories about educational change. Such an approach, combining the personal and the theoretical, clarifies better than anything else why the idea of a self-renewing school is so psychologically convincing. This will help focus the following chapters, which will be concerned with demolishing the theories about school self-renewal. So let us begin.

RESEARCH, DEVELOPMENT, AND DIFFUSION AND SCHOOL SELF-RENEWAL

The Concept of RD&D

In 1977 I chaired the teacher training department of the Ben-Gurion University of the Negev. In Israel university teacher training departments are responsible for the training of high school teachers, whereas teacher seminaries train elementary teachers. One day I received a letter from the then director of high school education in the Israeli Ministry of Education, inviting me and the chairpersons of all the other teacher training departments in Israeli universities to meet with him. The letter arrived a month after the meeting because it had been sent to the wrong address. I was furious. Seeing as I was concerned with the training of high school teachers, it was really important to me to meet the man responsible for that aspect of education at the national level. So I phoned him and requested a special meeting because I had missed the general one. A week later I traveled up to Jerusalem, weighed down with loads of material on our department, philosophy, methods, and so forth. When I entered the director's office I unloaded and began my prepared speech telling him about us and our work. However, it soon became apparent that he wasn't really listening. He made a few polite noises, but his thoughts were clearly elsewhere. When I had finished, he said, "Very interesting. Now let us talk about something else. I want to offer you a job. How would you like to be my adviser on how to change the norm of the Israeli high school system?"

Two months later I reduced my university work load and became the senior adviser to the Ministry of Education on innovations in high school education, thus beginning an activity that has dominated my professional life for the last five years. The first thing I did was to conduct a fairly exhaustive review of the literature on planned educational change.[1] As usually happens in such cases, most of this literature struck me as uninteresting and unimportant. However, early on I stumbled upon a book which remains, I think, a landmark in the field. This was Ernest House's *The Politics of Educational Innovation*. There are many reasons why this is a major work, but from our point of view, the most important chapter is "Government Policy toward Innovation—The Doctrine of Transferability" in which House mounts a devastating attack on the RD&D (research, development, and diffusion) paradigm for the diffusion of educational innovations. This was the dominant paradigm for planned educational change from the Brunerian revolution in curriculum in the late 1950s right through the 1960s.[2] It assumes that educational research should be subdivided into a quasi-linear sequence. Educational innovations will derive from research in national or regional centers far removed from the world of practitioners. These innovations will then be developed by these centers through experimentation in select classrooms and through further field testing. They will then be diffused to the entire "target system" which, it is assumed, will adopt the new ideas. House points out some of the other assumptions and characteristics of the RD&D paradigm. The most important of these are:

1. RD&D is based on a highly rational sequence of activities.
2. These activities produce a package that is then disseminated.
3. It is assumed that the practitioner is a passive consumer.
4. The innovations produced are mass-produced solutions to problems.

5. RD&D is based on a doctrine of transferability, that is, an assumption that the innovation or product will be widely accepted and have highly generalizable results in different local situations. An innovation is assumed to be almost a universal solution to some problem.[3]

House's attack on the paradigm as practiced in the United States is based on an interesting distinction which he derives from Alpert between central national goals and distributed national goals for research and development. These are explained as follows:

Central National Goals for R&D—such as leadership in the important fields of science, nuclear power, space exploration and national defense—in which the program is national in focus, sponsorship, funding and overall direction.

Distributed National Goals for R&D—such as the development of human resources, the rebuilding of our cities, water resources, and regional environments for living—in which the programs are characterized by local determinants in nature of the problems, in the approach to solution, and in their anticipated consequences.[4]

In House's view, the provision of education is one of society's most widespread national goals. Education "serves a multiplicity of interests. It is influenced locally by school boards, administrators, teachers, students, parents, and a host of others." Yet the RD&D paradigm can only work in relation to central national goals, and in fact during the 1960s federal policy in the United States, influenced as it was by the paradigm, was misguided in viewing education as a central national goal. House claims that the results of RD&D had not been very encouraging. Few innovations developed through RD&D had been successfully absorbed in the "target system":

By stripping the practitioner of initiatory power, the paradigm is justified on the basis of the belief that the practitioner is passive and will not initiate innovation on his own. The teacher is seen as slightly resistant, though someone who can be induced through persuasion to accept the new innovation. . . . When one does try to induce him to use a new innovation, one finds that the practitioner is not so passive. Being constrained is not the same as being passive. The practitioner operates in a context essentially foreign to the developer; . . . the situational constraints existing in the practitioner's home district are more important than characteristics of the innovation; . . . [and] the developer is never able to take full cognizance of the practitioner's world since the innovation process always starts on the RD&D

side. . . . The RD&D paradigm puts the practitioner immediately in the position of a consumer who is going to be sold a piece of goods which he has the option only to buy or reject. Ordinarily he uses his only remaining power—not to buy. . . . The [RD&D] paradigm assumes that the innovation will be invented on the left, developed, and passed along the chain. But even assuming a passive consumer, such a sequence of events is unlikely. The large-scale division of labor into research, development, and other interest groups almost assures it will not. . . . The paradigm is rational then only from the viewpoint of global government planners and perhaps from the perspective of researchers and developers. It imposes an orderly sequence of events on the innovation process and thereby directs attention to the planners, but it is not necessarily rational from the point of view of anyone else.[5]

House's analysis seemed to me totally convincing. Not only did it make sense in itself, it also seemed to be borne out by other analyses and by other research. The clearest support, from my point of view, came from the work of Robert Chin and Kenneth Benne, Seymour Sarason, and the Rand change agent study. Chin and Benne, in their classic review of general strategies for effecting change, identify three such strategy types. Of these, the one relevant to this discussion they call empirical-rational strategies. These assume that people are rational and will follow their rational self-interest once it is revealed to them. Thus when some person or group A proposes some change which is in their view desirable and in line with the self-interest of some other person or group B, proponents of this strategy assume that B will adopt the proposed change "if it can be rationally justified and if it can be shown by (A) that (B) will gain by the change."[6] RD&D is clearly a variant of this strategy. Although Chin and Benne attempt to maintain a neutral stance, they in effect show that RD&D in particular and empirical-rational strategies in general have been very unsuccessful in the sort of situation in which we are interested. There are many reasons for this. Perhaps the most important is that the assumption of rationality has distracted attention from the problems of dissemination.

In a similar vein, Sarason argues that the introduction of new math in American schools in the 1960s failed because the creators of these new curricula tended to ignore the fact that schools are self-contained cultural entities with unique characteristics, norms, and structural properties. In many cases, these general school norms and structural properties influenced the specific behaviors and attitudes of math teachers in ways that militated against the simple incorporation of the ideas embodied in the new curricula.[7] More generally, one of the major findings of the Rand study of federal change agent programs and especially Title III programs was that "an innovation's local institutional setting has the major influence on its prospects for effective implementation; . . . the local organizational climate and the motivations of project participants had major effects on perceived success and on change in teacher behavior."[8]

All this would probably just have remained part of the academic information I carry around in my head, if curriculum development in Israel and specifically what I personally had experienced had not confirmed these research efforts. During the 1960s Israel was probably one of the countries that embraced the curriculum revolution most completely, uncritically, and extensively. Huge sums of money were poured into a few curriculum centers staffed mainly by educators influenced by the University of Chicago school of curriculum development and by respected university professors from the scientific disciplines. Great energy was expended in the production of teacher-proof materials. During some of that time I was a junior high school math teacher in a school that was using one of these curricula in seventh grade. Also, for a period of two years, I was part of one of these curriculum centers, brought in as "someone from the field" to fill out a team writing a new ninth grade math text book. What I remember from that time is summarized in three words: contempt, anger, and irritation. I recall my contempt and anger, as one of the teachers, for the curriculum specialists who visited my school and clearly had never taught seventh-grade kids—nor for that matter, anyone else. I also recall the contempt and irritation expressed by the curriculum team for the teachers using their materials. House's analysis struck a responsive chord in me.

To be fair, it did not take long for the curriculum field in Israel to realize it was working with an oversimplified conception of curriculum development. In an important document written by Shevach Eden, the director of the main curriculum center, House and Sarason are explicitly mentioned and methods to overcome their criticisms are suggested.[9]

So if the conventional wisdom in the early 1960s was to produce teacher-proof material and disseminate it, the conventional wisdom of the 1970s seemed to be that the beliefs, values, and norms of individual teachers, schools, and local districts are central factors in determining the fate of educational innovations. How should these factors be taken into account? As I saw it, there seemed to be two possibilities. The first was to retain the RD&D paradigm but to improve it by being more sensitive to characteristics of the target population. The second was to scrap the whole idea of a "target population" altogether and to conceive of educational change as a process initiated, developed, and implemented by the schools themselves according to their needs and values. Let us consider each possibility in turn.

Improved RD&D

How can one retain the RD&D paradigm and yet improve it to take into account criticism of people like House and Sarason? Essentially, two things need to be done: First, greater emphasis must be placed on the diffusion stage. Linkages between producers and users of innovations must be strengthened, both by offering courses to teachers to instruct them in the use of the innovation and by creating the role of field instructor, someone who meets with the teachers and talks with them about their problems with the new ideas, material, or behavior embodied in the innovation. Second, the RD&D process must be transformed from a linear one to a process with feedback loops at all stages to enable and encourage the creators of an innovation to take into account the ideas and reservations of teachers. This essentially is the solution offered by Ronald Havelock in his very influential work.[10] It is also the one suggested in the aforementioned work of Eden.

The latter solution felt wrong to me from the moment I came upon it in the literature, for three reasons. First I had an emotional, gut objection to the language used for talking about RD&D. "Producers," "users," "consumers," "target population," "client system" seemed to me to be terms more suited to Madison Avenue than to the world of schools. I saw improved RD&D simply as an attempt to sell a product more efficiently after a drop in sales. Second, RD&D limited the chances that teaching could become a full, as opposed to a semi-, profession. No matter how many feedback loops are added to it, RD&D remains a process that puts the teacher in a position subordinate to the producers, developers, and disseminators of innovations. Yet one of the most important identifying characteristics of a profession is the autonomy granted its practitioners.

The third objection to improved RD&D is that it basically evades Sarason's point that schools are self-contained cultural entities. In the vast majority of cases, innovations in education are not relevant for an entire school faculty and are not intended to be so. Even in those cases which are relevant to everyone, they are rarely intended to change the way schools run in toto. So improving the linkage between the creators of an innovation and its users is almost invariably a process by which communication is set up between the center which has produced the innovation and a certain slice of school life. Thus the influence of the total school culture on the implementation of the innovation is not taken into account by improved RD&D.

The Self-Renewing School

What then about the second possible way of overcoming the criticism of "ordinary" RD&D—the concept of educational innovation as a process developed within the school itself? This requires that the school be so constituted as to be able to develop educational innovations. What sort of school could do this? The answer I found in the literature was deceptively simple—the self-renewing school. In the next chapter I will discuss the question of definition of this sort of school. Here I will merely characterize a self-renewing school as one that continually reviews its aims, methods, and achievements; is expert at identifying its problems; and suggests creative ways of dealing with them which are then implemented.

The notion of school self-renewal invites us to see the whole process of planned change in schools in a completely new light. Instead of being concerned with the diffusion of specific innovations, planned change is now linked with the implementation of one "metachange" — the transformation of ordinary schools into self-renewing ones. The assumption, of course, is that if a school becomes self-renewing then we will see a great number of specific innovations being implemented in it.

The move from the level of innovations to that of "metachange" is significant in itself, both formally and substantively. However, when I first came across the idea, what struck me most forcibly was the change in the language used to describe the promoting of self-renewal as opposed to the language of "target population," "consumers," and so forth, in the RD&D literature. However, I subsequently discovered that much of the self-renewal literature is still couched in terms similar to those used in talking about RD&D. Still, let us consider the way Mary Bentzen describes the relationship between the school and the change agent in promoting school self-renewal. She uses the analogy of the fable of Dumbo the elephant:

> Dumbo had a marvellous natural gift. He could fly. In the beginning, however, he didn't know that he could fly. His ability was due to his large ears, which could serve as wings; but since such big ears were not the usual case among elephants, Dumbo was for some time ridiculed by all other elephants. This continual put-down was devastating to Dumbo's self concept. He considered himself a failure as an elephant, until he was befriended by a mouse who spotted Dumbo's true talent. But because Dumbo was afraid to try much of anything on his own, the mouse first had to convince him to use his ears as wings. So the mouse gave Dumbo a feather, a magic feather, he said, which would enable Dumbo to fly. With the feather he began to fly and win great praise from all who watched him. One day, to his horror, Dumbo dropped the feather in midflight. As he fell he heard his friend call out, "You don't need the feather! You can fly!" Dumbo tried, and he flew. At last he believed in himself. The fable, we think, tells something important about principals and teachers in our schools.[11]

Apart from the obvious point that the change agent is described as no more than the catalyst in the change process, there are three exciting aspects to this story. First, the mouse is very small and Dumbo is very large. Second, the mouse does what he does because he loves Dumbo, not for personal gain or because of general benefits for the whole jungle community. Third, Dumbo flies not by buying a pair of wings but rather by flapping his own ears.

This description of the school not as a recalcitrant customer but as an organism genuinely wanting to improve itself and having the innate potential to do so with minimal help from its friends sold me on the idea of school self-renewal. As I saw it, here was a view of planned change that addressed itself directly to criticisms like those of House and Sarason. Here too was a conception of planned change with which I could feel morally comfortable. Change was seen not as an imposition from without but as a development from within. The question was, was school self-renewal a practical idea? Could ordinary schools become self-renewing?

The Literature on Self-Renewal

The literature on self-renewal was encouraging. First, there was the work on the project directly concerned with Dumbo's feather, reported in John Goodlad's *The Dynamics of Educational Change* and Mary Bentzen's *Changing Schools: The Magic Feather Principle*.[12] This project was based on four assumptions: (1) No ordinary school on its own has a sufficient repertoire of human resources to become self-renewing, but a league of ten to twenty varied schools, cooperating among themselves, does have; (2) If the schools are sufficiently different from one another and are made aware of and discuss these differences with the help of a group of external change agents, they will become aware of their self-renewing capacities and take steps to improve them; (3) Schools have been conditioned to rely on external experts as crutches. However, if the external change agents make it clear that they refuse to play the role of experts, but rather will limit their part in the league to being rather minor facilitators, then schools will gradually assume the responsibility for their own functioning; (4) The school principal is the central figure in determining school self-renewal. Goodlad established such a league of schools and the report in his and Bentzen's books indicates that over a period of three to five years most of the schools showed a dramatic improvement in their functioning as self-renewing systems.

A rather different approach to school self-renewal is that embodied in what is known as OD (Organizational Development) consultation. It is rather difficult to pin down exactly what OD is all about, since the term is a very broad one. My conception of OD relies substantially on the approach of Richard Schmuck and his co-workers, who have produced the definitive handbooks on OD consultation in schools.[13] Broadly speaking, the idea is that an external consultant diagnoses a particular school according to a number of dimensions considered relevant to school self-renewal. For example, how efficient is the communication between personnel in the school? How well does the school establish and define its goals? Are personal and group conflicts brought out into the open? How well are meetings run? Are the school's problem-solving procedures efficient? Having completed the diagnosis, the consultant then runs a number of training courses with members of the school staff, the purpose being to transmit the skills necessary to improve school functioning in the areas that have been found to be problematic. These training sessions tend to be very programmed and to rely a great deal on role playing and simulation games, which is the main difference between "classical" OD approaches and Goodlad's. OD consultants may also train certain members of the school staff to act as internal OD consultants in order to maintain the level of initial staff development. The OD approach struck me as being far more a case of selling Dumbo a pair of wings than getting him to flap his own ears. Nevertheless, there certainly were reports in the literature of successful OD interventions (terrible word!) in many schools and school districts.

Apart from approaches directly concerned with promoting school self-renewal, there were a number of indirect indications in the literature that school self-renewal was a viable option. For example, there were the reports (mainly European) of successful exemplars of school-based curriculum development. The notion of school-based curriculum development was clearly in line with the perspective that informs the concept of school self-renewal. Consider the following description of the term:

> School-based curriculum development is school based, community contexted, activity in which the detailed strategies for a curriculum appropriate to the needs of the individual children in the specific school, or even in the specific units of a school, are developed by a process of cooperative discussion, planning, trial and evaluation. . . . It is a process that reflects the problems of the school and its clients. . . . Above all else it is a curriculum that is achieved rather than ascribed, that is developed actively rather than received passively. In short, it is a dynamic element within the school that has been largely created therein and for which the school is collectively responsible.[14]

What the European experience seemed to indicate was that, at least in countries with decentralized educational systems, teachers were prepared to sit down and produce their own curricula, provided that some agency (either an external one or the school itself) provided a minimal amount of organizational support (such as released time, the opportunity to meet and work with teachers from other schools, and access to resources).

The Israeli educational system was in many ways different from those in which these apparently successful projects had been implemented. Nevertheless, it seemed worthwhile to try out similar ideas in our system as well. Thus my recommendation to the Israeli Ministry of Education was that for the next five years or so, most of the funds available for promoting high school innovation should be used to encourage school self-renewal projects. At the end of this period we should have a better idea of whether the notion of school self-renewal was viable within the reality of the Israeli educational system. This recommendation was accepted and put into effect in 1978.

THE PROJECT FOR THE ADVANCEMENT OF EDUCATIONAL COOPERATION

The First Year

Of all the projects for the promotion of self-renewal in schools funded by the Ministry of Education, by far the most extensive was the Project for the Advancement of Educational Cooperation. It was also the one in which I was personally involved and from which most of the illustrations of theoretical ideas to be developed in subsequent chapters will be taken. This project, developed by the Ben-Gurion University of the Negev, was to a large extent a replication in the high school setting of the Goodlad League of Cooperating Schools Project. At any rate, it was inspired by many of the same assumptions that guided the Goodlad program. Because of this similarity, I will not devote too much space here to a general description of our project; after all, two fine books have been written about the League of Cooperating Schools and films showing various aspects of the league have been produced. Many processes that we witnessed are similar to those documented by Goodlad and Bentzen; nevertheless, to give a clearer idea of the case studies I will be presenting in subsequent chapters, I will describe the general nature of the project. I propose to briefly summarize its history before turning in chapter 2 to the critical analysis of the idea of self-renewing schools. In addition, in appendix A, I will attempt to spell out the differences between our work and the Goodlad league for those interested in seeing the idea of a league of schools in cross-cultural perspective.

The initial circular to school principals about our project stressed that

1. This was a project addressed to schools that were not completely satisfied with the way they were functioning, dissatisfaction being seen by us as a virtue and not a flaw.

2. We did not believe that outside experts were of much help in solving school problems. On the contrary, we believed that a group of schools, by pooling resources, could improve their own functioning.
3. At the beginning of the project, each participating school would have to agree
   a. to allow the principal to meet once a month with the other principals and with the project staff (the latter we called the "external team"); and
   b. to allow the project staff access to all school activities.
4. As things progressed, other members of the school faculty in addition to the principal would become involved in project activities.
5. Joining the project could not be a decision of the principal alone, but must be a democratic decision reached by the entire faculty.

As a result of this circular and certain other activities described in certain of the case studies, ten schools joined the project, which operated officially for three years. Over the years another two schools joined the project, and four discontinued participation—three of their own accord and one because we suggested that it do so.

The latter case is interesting in terms of the idea of self-renewal. This was a school in a small isolated village and we discovered during the first year of the project that *the* problem the school faces is an *annual* staff turnover of about 70–80 percent! It was our view that a project of the sort we were suggesting was irrelevant in such a situation.

Regarding the other three schools that left the project, two will be described in case studies in chapters 2 and 5, and the third will be described briefly in appendix A.

Because of anonymity considerations, I will only describe the twelve schools we had contact with in the most general of terms. In the case studies themselves, the schools have of course been camouflaged. Five of the twelve schools were in large cities, four in small towns and three in agricultural settlements. Four of the schools were very large, with over 1,000 students and approximately 100 teachers. Five schools had approximately 500 students and three, approximately 250. Three of the schools offered courses in academic subjects only, the other nine schools offering vocational courses as well. Two of the schools catered to a predominantly middle-class population, two were predominantly working-class, and the other eight schools had very heterogeneous populations. Three of the schools were boarding schools.

The project staff was made up of six members, with a certain turnover over the years. In all cases, people left the project for personal reasons. Three members of the staff were highly experienced teachers; the others had experience of other sorts in working with schools and/or young people. In addition, the staff had diversified academic qualifications. Backgrounds included evaluation, political sociology, group dynamics, philosophy, the problems of the culturally disadvantaged, and psychotherapy. During the final year of the project, one staff member was to a certain extent an outsider whose main task was to evaluate the project staff's activities.

The phases of our activities fitted nicely into the yearly divisions. During 1978–79 we concerned ourselves mainly with two types of activities. First our staff met with the principals for day-long meetings once a month. These meetings were usually held at a Jerusalem hotel or at the Ben-Gurion University of the Negev in Beersheba. The agenda for a typical meeting would be planned by the project staff (which was a mistake) on the basis of developments at previous meetings and principals' suggestions. During the meetings themselves, the active participation of the staff was minimal. For the first few months, different headmasters told us about their schools, their successes and their failures, and in addition we spent much time discussing the idea of school self-renewal.

At one such meeting, one of the headmasters expressed considerable skepticism about the possibility of school self-renewal because he basically felt that he couldn't trust his teachers. As he put it: "Maybe experimental schools attract first-class teachers, but the teachers in my school are very ordinary, and I can't give them any responsibility." Predictably, the reactions around the table were rather heated. Many of the headmasters agreed with him, but others claimed that his attitude was a classic example of a self-fulfilling prophesy. The contribution of our staff was to suggest that perhaps this disagreement was a case amenable to an empirical check. As a result of this, a committee of three headmasters and two of our staff members undertook to plan an empirical investigation of some aspect of the subject. The idea they eventually came up with was to circulate a questionnaire among teachers in various schools in the league. Its purpose would be to check the school policy, as seen by the teachers, vis-à-vis grades. Was there a standard procedure in the school for determining grades or were teachers free to give grades as they saw fit? If there was a standard procedure, who had decided on it — the headmaster? the teachers themselves? someone else? Simultaneously, a similar questionnaire to students would be circulated whose purpose was to discover whether the latter generally saw their grades as fair or not.

Essentially, the idea of these two questionnaires was to check whether there was any correlation between school policy and student reaction to grades, and in particular whether students in schools where the teachers had more autonomy saw them as fair in grading. It was thought originally that positive evidence on the last question would contradict the claim that ordinary teachers should not be given responsibility. As things developed, the principals began to realize that one must also distinguish between individual autonomy and the autonomy of an entire faculty to formulate policy as a group.

The committee drew up the two questionnaires and it was agreed that they would be distributed in approximately half the schools at the beginning of the 1979–80 school year.

The second activity that dominated the project in the first year was the entry of the project staff into the various schools. Our first meetings with teachers (when the school faculty had to vote to join the project) had usually been characterized by a very tense, suspicious atmosphere, and although all of the ten school faculties had voted to join the project, we felt that the suspicions remained. I remember the comment of one teacher who looked at me when he entered the room and then loudly commented to his colleagues: "Oh, I see the private eye is here." So we devoted the first few months to getting to know the teachers and making them feel at ease in our presence. As one of our staff put it, we "drifted in." This meant that we did not hand out questionnaires or formally interview people. Instead, we sat in at meetings, chatted informally with staff, and acted as shadows of people in important administrative managerial positions.

While wandering around the schools, we were of course looking out for certain things. We were concerned with the school's initial self-renewing capacities. In this we were guided by Goodlad's and Bentzen's concept of school self-renewal. This hinged on what they call a school's DDAE, which stands for *dialogue, decision-making, action and evaluation.* According to Bentzen, these four processes occur in all schools, but in a self-renewing school their quality will be different from that of an "ordinary" school. In the former they will be characterized as follows: *Dialogue* involves interaction between principal and teachers, and between teachers and teachers; is continuing and pervasive; involves the whole staff; is substantive (that is, concerned with instruction, curriculum, and school organization); involves the staff in inquiry (that is, they look at many sources of data, formulate and examine the assumptions necessary to their educational decisions, face openly and make explicit what they accept and what they reject); involves the staff in evaluation. *Decision making* is based on staff involvement in dialogue; consideration of alternatives; weighing of evidence; selections made from among the alternatives. *Action* is such that decisions are implemented and more dialogue occurs. *Evaluation* is such that principals and teachers are comfortable with the concepts of objectives, evaluation and research; principals and teachers discuss what kind of people they want their students to become; the staff identifies the role the school should play in producing these kinds of people; attention is given to ways of assessing how well the school is carrying out its role.[15]

Our staff's observations in the schools attempted to determine the extent to which the DDAE of each school conformed to these criteria. (We found, by the way, that shadowing those in managerial positions was the most revealing way of learning this.) Having determined the DDAE of the schools as we saw them, we were prepared to give feedback to each school on our impressions and, in a few schools, we did this during this first year. However, giving feedback was not a central activity during this year.

The Second Year

In 1979–80, the project concentrated mainly on four sorts of activities: (1) feedback and evaluation; (2) teacher involvement in the project as a result of feedback; (3) sharing information; (4) the project staff acting as sounding boards.

At the first meeting, many of those principals in whose schools we had not yet given feedback were very critical and very resentful of the delay. As they saw it, they had acted as hosts to a bunch of invaders who had sniffed around their schools for a good many months and, to date, they had got nothing in return. (None of them seemed aware that up to that moment they had not asked for feedback.) In any event, the giving of feedback became a dominant activity for this year. In many cases the presentation of feedback conformed more or less to the format "invented" by one of our staff members, Michal Katz. I quote her report of the meetings at the school where she developed this format:

My intentions vis-à-vis feedback were that participation would be high; that the school faculty would be interested; that they would take my remarks seriously and regard them as believable; that they wouldn't bullshit; that I would be "on form." And with regards to the results: that a group of teachers would be formed that would act on the basis of the knowledge from the feedback, that this action would include both the checking of controversial findings and also improving what needs improving.

I decided not to give the feedback to the school's steering committee or pedagogic committee only. These are forums of a limited number of people with central positions who are very busy. Rather, the feedback would be given to the pedagogic plenum, which includes all the homeroom teachers. These are central people, very involved in the school, but without defined positions (most of them). They thus have more time for activity suggested by the feedback.

What actually happened was that on the evening scheduled for the giving of feedback, the school had to introduce some additional matter on the agenda and I only had a very limited period of time. I knew this a day before the meeting. After discussing this with Pnina [the headmistress] I decided to use this time to introduce the concept of DDAE theoretically and to have the teachers fill out a DDAE questionnaire [a simple adaptation of Bentzen's description of DDAE into question form, with the respondent being asked to evaluate each dimension of the DDAE in his own school: the principals of all the schools had filled out such a questionnaire a few months previously]. That was in fact what happened. Most of the people seemed quite interested in what I was saying (at ten-thirty at night!) and only two out of twenty-eight didn't hand back the questionnaire.

Ten days afterwards the "real" feedback session took place. It was set up for three hours, from eight to eleven o'clock in the morning. I prepared two large placards for this meeting that were hung on the wall and "accompanied" the entire discussion. One was a model of the process of problem solving (as implied by the notion of DDAE), and the second—the more interesting one—a diagram which described or summarized the teachers' answers to the questionnaire. With regards to each topic Pnina's response (as indicated by her questionnaire form of a few months back) was emphasized.

The moment this placard was hung up, the atmosphere simply became electrified. The diagram emphasized visually the polarization that exists in the teachers' conceptions of reality, and the fact that Pnina doesn't always identify with the majority opinion.

The three hours passed too quickly. The discussion was very interesting and it is difficult for me to reproduce it here. In general the tendency was to identify four types of gaps in the components of the DDAE, and to discuss their significance: the gap between what is and what should be; the gap between the majority and the minority opinion; the gap between the majority opinion and Pnina's opinion; the gap between the majority opinion and my own. I emphasized throughout that it isn't enough to talk about all this, but rather that the idea was to do something with all this information. In any event, we didn't reach the operational stage in the discussion. Pnina and I agreed that she should think about this, and discuss it with additional people before she and I next meet.

I must add that, at the conclusion, many teachers came up to me to thank me, to tell me that they had come to school on their free day and that it had been worthwhile. There was a lot of warmth and closeness expressed in looks and smiles.

If I must judge to what extent this activity realized my intentions, I will limit myself to checking to what extent the activity went off as planned. When it comes to results, it is too early to judge. It seems to me the activity went down far better than expected, and this was *because* of the constraints, i.e., the fact that I had to divide it up into two parts on different days. This turned out to be a good idea. The folks came prepared, the introduction aroused their curiosity, the filling out of the questionnaires ensured maximum participation, the fact that they had expressed their views in the questionnaire neutralized the urge to bullshit and the discussion really concentrated on the gaps and didn't diverge to individual opinions about things; the use I made of their answers focused attention and concretized things which increased their interest. It also gave their views and the whole activity a sense of importance. Apart from this—they caught me on a good day!

In most cases when we worked in this fashion, the examination of similar placards was sufficient to trigger a highly constructive discussion focusing on the differences between the perspectives of the participants. For some reason, this mode of presentation allowed these differences to be discussed without anyone feeling the need to be defensive. However, our impression was that although the faculties could discuss the findings very intelligently and openly, they were at a complete loss when it came to deciding what to do with these findings afterwards. One school in which I personally gave the feedback exemplifies this very well. All of us (faculty, headmaster, and myself) had agreed that the school had difficulty in moving from dialogue to decision making, in the sense that the decision tended to be a trivialization of the original dialogue. For instance, at one faculty meeting a rather profound discussion about teachers' self-concepts and professional pride had been going on. A fine analysis of reasons for the low self-concept of the teachers had been suggested. However, the decision reached was that all the teachers should go on a picnic together. At the feedback session all agreed that this and similar cases were examples of trivialization. The headmaster then turned to me and said with an air of bewilderment, "OK, what should we do about this?" It was quite clear to me that this was not a case of passing the buck to the external expert but that neither he nor anyone else in the room had the slightest notion how to begin coming to grips with his question.

This general impression of ours was borne out by the fate of the questionnaires about grades prepared in 1978–79. After the questionnaires had been filled out, we summarized the findings and offered to present them to any school interested in the results. In one such school (call it school A), we brought along the summary of the questionnaires filled out by their pupils and teachers and also a summary of the questionnaires filled out in school B. Schools A and B were in many respects very similar and this showed up in the questionnaires. However, in B a general policy concerning grades had been suggested by the teachers themselves and was more or less adhered to by most teachers at the school. At A, on the other hand, there was a totally laissez-faire situation vis-à-vis grades. The issue of a general policy had never been raised. On the average, the students at B were much more satisfied with their grades than at A, although the range of responses between different classes at B was very much larger than at A.

All this was deduced without any difficulty by the teachers at A from the tables we presented (without comment), but despite the fact that these findings seemed to us to suggest much further investigation and many things that could be tried out at A, A's faculty seemed incapable of seeing any way of using the information they had themselves derived from the data. They did not even ask, "What can we do with this?" In other words, they seemed to have a ritualistic attitude to information.

We of the project staff all agreed that the evaluation component of the DDAE process seemed to be weak in most schools. As a result, we came up with the following suggestion: in each school a new role would be defined—that of school evaluator—and during the third year of the project we would meet with the evaluators once a month in addition to the headmasters. We put this idea to the headmasters who were, with one exception, very enthusiastic about it. It was agreed that each school would choose its evaluator in its own way and that during the summer vacation, we would meet with them for an intensive introductory session.

Thus feedback and evaluation formed one focus of our activities in 1979–80. The second focus was directly related to it and could be called "teacher involvement in the project as a result of feedback." Following the feedback sessions in the various schools, groups of teachers in each school began meeting regularly with a member of our staff and usually the headmaster as well, to deal with some problem that arose during the feedback session. Here are a few examples: in the school in which there was the problem of the reduction of high-powered dialogue into trivial decisions, a group of teachers met in order to learn to formulate operational definitions of educational objectives and to implement them. In another school, the problem identified was the extremely limited alternatives drawn upon in pedagogic decision making. The teachers simply did not consider nonconformist methods of teaching ordinary material, although the school had a tradition of highly innovative teaching during certain short-term special projects. Here a group of teachers was selected to think of ways of developing and encouraging unconventional teaching during "normal" teaching time.

Unfortunately, our staff could not always be totally passive in the process of choosing the topics of the meetings of the various teacher groups because of the above-mentioned difficulty in using feedback. However, we tried in most cases to limit our active participation in the meetings themselves as far as possible. In fact, we viewed our becoming unimportant back-seaters as an indication of success. Take, as an example, a written report to the project staff about progress with the group trying to develop unconventional teaching methods which I circulated in the middle of the year:

> [There was] a meeting of the special teachers today. As requested by the group, I explained to them the meaning of the term "team teaching." I spoke for about ten minutes. I also brought a book on team teaching (also as requested). They listened to what I had to say with great interest, but they didn't even page through the book. In the discussion that developed they raised the question of whether they should try an exper-

iment in team teaching in the school. Most of them were in favour. In the middle of the discussion, Yossi [the principal] took control. He pushed very strongly that they try something and raised a whole lot of operational issues—in which classes, subjects, etc. . . . .

In my opinion this was a good meeting for a number of reasons. First—the enthusiasm of all the participants. Second —the fact that Yossi took control and, in fact, during the second half of the meeting I was unemployed. . . . Nevertheless, I must emphasize that we are only half-way in this process. This was a good meeting considering *when* it took place. If the meetings of this committee in another year will be similar, that will be a sign of failure, for two reasons: (1) It must be admitted that the idea of team teaching was raised by me, i.e. imported by an external expert. . . . In other words, the relationship with the "expert" hasn't been broken yet; (2) The fact that the committee wasn't prepared to read literature on the subject.

The third focus of 1979–80 brings us back to the headmasters' meetings. Much time at these meetings was devoted to the headmasters telling each other about the activities that had formed the second focus. It was perhaps symbolic that a number of the meetings took place at specific schools instead of on "neutral" hotel or university ground. Our contribution at the discussions was to stress the organizational as opposed to the substantive aspects of the teachers' activities. For example: when did the teachers meet? If during teaching hours, how did the headmaster succeed in releasing them from actual teaching? Why did he consider meetings during school hours preferable to the occasional evening meeting? How had the teachers taking part in the activity been chosen? and so on. Our stress on organizational aspects resulted from our conviction that transforming schools into self-renewing organizations entails organizational or structural changes. This will be discussed further in chapter 2.

In certain cases, as a result of such discussion at the headmasters' meetings, teachers and headmasters from one school would visit another. However, despite our project's name and rationale, which stressed cooperation between schools, this idea of mutual visits and learning never really became a central part of things. I will enlarge on this in appendix A.

The final focus of 1979–80 was for me perhaps the most pleasant aspect of the whole project. As a result of our drifting-in, nonthreatening strategy of entry, the project staff gradually came to be regarded as real friends of the schools, with a genuine interest in their welfare and with no axes of our own to grind. This led, from the middle of the second year, to our becoming school "sounding boards." School personnel (especially headmasters and vice-headmasters) seemed to enjoy sitting down with us and chatting over their new ideas and plans for the school. I stress the concept of a sounding board because it contrasts with two other, theoretically possible relationships that fortunately never materialized. We never became official approvers or vetoers of school initiatives, and we never became experts to whom the schools turned for solutions to their problems. Instead, they threw out their ideas and we engaged in a relaxed interplay of mutual reactions. As a result of becoming a sounding board, I think I made a lot of new personal friends, and I value this far beyond the success of the project itself.

The Third Year

In 1980–81, two foci of the previous academic year remained central. Special teacher groups continued to meet, and we continued to act as sounding boards. In addition, two further foci dominated this final year. First, we established the group of school evaluators and we worked with them right through the year. The monthly meetings with the evaluators usually consisted of the following: we would teach certain aspects of educational evaluation, for it must be remembered that they all came with no background whatsoever in educational theory; the group would decide on the evaluatory tasks each would undertake in his own school; and individual evaluators would report on the tasks of the previous month. The discussions around the last two steps always raised general problems associated with the idea of internal evaluators; should they work alone or should they establish a committee? Should they act as the person in the school concerned with evaluation or should they rather try to encourage the idea that evaluation is an important component of all school activity undertaken by all school staff?

Between meetings, evaluators were free to contact the staff members assigned to their specific schools. Some of them did this; others preferred to work things out for themselves. Yet all in all, the project staff probably spent more time in 1980–81 developing and thinking about the role of evaluator than on any other aspect of our work.

The final focus of the project was saying goodbye. At the second headmasters' meeting we raised the problem of our departure. As we explained it, the project was formally to end at the close of the 1981 school year. Funding would then cease, and the project staff would stop working. Yet the whole rationale of the project was that it aimed to develop school self-renewal. How would the project continue on its own steam in the future? Perhaps it would not. If the project were to continue, this necessitated taking certain steps a year before its official end. Without institutionalizing its continuance, we saw no hope of much happening.

The headmasters were very unwilling to deal with these questions and problems. Nevertheless, we did discuss them at some meetings and also with the evaluators. At these discussions, the following distinctions were drawn. First, we differentiated between cooperation between schools and maintaining the spirit of the project in individual schools. Second, both project staff and school personnel felt that continued contact between principals was different from maintaining the group of evaluators. The principals should be able to maintain the contact on their own, whereas the evaluators, it was felt, needed another year of professional advice from someone with an academic background in the field of evaluation.

In the end, the following decisions were reached: Principals and evaluators would continue to meet once a month. Each month a specific school would host these meetings and would be responsible for their content. The project staff undertook to find some evaluation specialist who would be prepared to participate in the evaluators' meetings. The schools undertook to pay for his services themselves. Regarding the spirit of the project in individual schools, school principals would meet with the members of the project staff with whom they had been associated to sketch out plans for maintaining the drive towards self-renewal in future years.

Concerning the first decision, we fulfilled our side of the bargain by contacting an evaluation specialist. Two meetings were held and then things petered out. Yet this aspect of continuance doesn't seem to me to be very important. For reasons elaborated on in appendix A, Goodlad's idea of creating a pool of resources in a group of varied schools was scrapped very early on. It seems inapplicable in the Israeli setting.

The final meetings of individual principals with members of the project staff were rather encouraging. A number of activities inspired by the project were put into practice in various schools.

They were "time-tabled" into the school calendar. Some of these activities are continuations of 1980–81 activities. Others are new activities that grew out of the recognition that some fault or other needed to be remedied. In addition, it is our impression that, in many cases, more intangible things will remain, such as an increased awareness of the importance of evaluation. Yet we obviously must wait a few years in order to see clearly what has remained and what has disappeared.

One may ask—if this is the case, why not delay writing the book until a clearer picture obtains? My answer lies in the book's title. Because our project was so extensive, with so many aims and so many varied activities, it is reasonable to assume that we had some successes. Of course, the project staff surely made serious mistakes, too. However, quite independently of successes and failures, I have slowly become convinced that the idea of a self-renewing school is far more problematic than I originally thought. In my view, there are four serious types of limits to school self-renewal. These limits are theoretical and are thus independent of the successes and failures of particular projects and the competency or lack of competency of the change agents involved (although they have been illustrated by many things that occurred during the three years in our project). Thus I feel I can write about them without waiting years to see what will happen to the schools in which we spent so much time.

AN OVERVIEW OF THE FOLLOWING CHAPTERS

Each of the four types of theoretical limitation on school self-renewal is dealt with in a separate chapter. Chapter 2 concerns certain philosophical or conceptual limitations to the notion of school self-renewal. Chapter 3 deals with limitations related to the idea of a belief system of a school faculty. The argument developed in this chapter will derive from anthropology, political science, linguistics, and social psychology. Chapter 4 is devoted to structural limits to self-renewal and is largely concerned with sociological theory. Chapter 5 is both psychological and sociological in emphasis. In this case, the limitations that will concern us are linked not to the schools themselves but rather to the change agent's role. By the end of chapter 5, I think not much of the idea of school self-renewal will remain intact. In chapter 6 I try to give some answers to the obvious question—quo vadis?

Although chapters 2–5 all deal with theoretical matters, it might be helpful to view them as occupying different points on a theoretical/practical continuum. Chapter 2 addresses the truly theoretical issues; chapter 3 is also very theoretical in orientation, but less than chapter 2; in chapter 4 we start encountering practical difficulties with the notion of school self-renewal; chapter 5 deals with the really practical, everyday difficulties.

A final word about chapter 6. My reaction to the question, quo vadis? is to examine the notion of ongoing collaboration, that is, a permanent relationship between the school and some external agency. This is very different from self-renewal, which is based on the idea of the change agent's contact with the school for a limited time. As we will see, the difference between ongoing and limited collaboration is absolutely crucial. Ongoing collaboration manages to avoid some (but not all) the difficulties I will point out in chapters 2 to 5. It also avoids the difficulties associated with RD&D which I have pointed out. So chapter 6 can be seen as suggesting an antidote to the pessimism characterizing chapters 2 to 5. However, as we will see, it is only a partial antidote and so it concludes with a discussion of the general question: is successful planned educational change really possible?

2

Conceptual Problems
THE PROBLEM-SOLVING
AND THE THERAPEUTIC METAPHORS

The format of this chapter (and the three subsequent chapters) is as follows: I will first present theoretical criticisms of the concept of school self-renewal. I will present certain case studies or vignettes taken from the Project for the Advancement of Educational Cooperation (in chapters 3 and 5, two cases not related to this project are also included). These case studies, as I stressed in the preface, are only illustrations of the theoretical arguments and cannot be construed as attempts to prove the theoretical considerations empirically. In this chapter, the cases are not gathered together in special sections but are introduced at the relevant points. In chapters 3 and 4, and, to a certain extent, in 5, there are special case study sections.

Before beginning, I would like to briefly mention two objections to the concept of school self-renewal that I will *not* be arguing for. Although often voiced, they can be rather easily dismissed. The first is the radical criticism that the concept of school self-renewal expresses a sham desire for change because it proposes working from within the system, whereas real change entails a restructuring of the entire society. It is thus committed to the system and therefore opposed to real change.

If the system is by definition evil, then radical critics win the case simply by defining their opponents out of the arena. However, such criticism may be more serious than that. They could make two arguments. (1) They could claim, as a matter of fact, that working for change from within the system cannot work. However, they must surely produce evidence for this claim. Therefore, they should see projects that attempt to promote school self-renewal as sources for evidence and not simply dismiss them, a priori. (2) They may also argue that there is a theoretical contradiction between working from within something and changing it. In one sense this is trivially true. As Wittgenstein once said: "If I want the door to turn, the hinges must stay put."[1] Those who believe in self-renewal are not trying to change the school into a leg of lamb. They assume that the school, after being transformed into a self-renewing one, still has some things in common with "ordinary" schools. Radical critics must show that these basic elements (the hinges) are more important and more in need of change than those aspects of the schools that did change (the door) as a result of self-renewal. This would be hard to do, unless they argue that the problems are those of "being a school in a capitalistic society." If objections are pitched at this level, then, as two of the most perspicacious radical critics put it: "Institutional change in education, unless itself random and chaotic, is the culmination of the coordinated activity of social classes. The politics of a revolutionary education like its philosophy are grounded in dialectics. They must proceed from a commitment to a revolutionary transformation of our entire society."[2] In other words, planned change and/or the promotion of school self-renewal are not being objected to in themselves but because they take place in capitalist society, and that society is seen as a negative one.

The second objection to school self-renewal that I will not try to develop is that the literature implicitly assumes that self-renewing schools are good schools, that the positive properties of these schools relate to the behavior of the school faculty while the behavior of students is ignored. But surely the quality of a school must ultimately depend on its effects on its students? Perhaps self-renewing schools are not effective ones, or at least, so the argument goes, the proponents of school self-renewal have not shown that they are.

This argument shows a lack of appreciation of how truly powerful a notion self-renewal really is. Let us assume that research in effective schooling[3] were to discover that in order for a school to be effective in achieving a specific educational objective, it must have characteristics $x_1, x_2, \ldots x_n$. Let us now consider a school that, according to some standard definition, is a self-renewing school. In relation to the desired objective, one can identify three possibilities. Two of these pose no problems. These are, first, that the school faculty, after careful analysis, reaches the conclusion that the objective is not educationally worthwhile. In such a case, the faculty will not regard the discovery concerning $x_1, x_2, \ldots x_n$ as relevant in guiding its educational and administrative policy.[4] In other words, this possibility shows that according to the supporters of school self-renewal, a school can be a good school and yet "ineffective" according to a particular criterion of effectiveness. As a second possibility, the school faculty sees the objective as a worthwhile educational aim and the school is effective in achieving it. Hence the school must be characterized by $x_1, x_2, \ldots x_n$.

The interesting case and the one the proposers of this objection clearly have in mind is a third one: The school faculty sees a certain objective as a worthwhile educational aim and yet the school is ineffective in achieving it. However, this case is less problematic than it seems at first. If the school is not effective in realizing the desired objective, it does not have characteristics $x_1, x_2, \ldots x_n$. However, because it is a self-renewing school it will, through intelligent surveys of the educational literature, discover the research linking the objective with $x_1, x_2, \ldots x_n$ and will then take steps to change into a school having these characteristics. Thus the third possibility, in the long run, collapses into the second. In other words, in the long run there can be no contradiction between the effectiveness of a school and self-renewal, assuming there to be independent research on what makes schools effective.

The only case in which this counterargument does not hold is when $x_1, x_2, \ldots x_n$ logically contradict the process of school self-renewal. For example, if research were to show that schools whose students achieve high grades are ones in which the faculty are contemptuous of educational research, then a self-renewing school by definition could never have the characteristics necessary to improve its students' grades. This is however an absurdly artificial example. When one considers the variables that one could reasonably expect to influence school effectiveness, it is difficult to see how these could contradict the characteristics of self-renewing schools.[5]

These then are the ineffective objections to the concept of school self-renewal. Let us now turn to those that deserve far more attention. Because of the complexity of the argument to be developed in this chapter, I will sketch out its formal structure in advance.

1. The idea of school self-renewal is based on two metaphors—the Dewey problem-solving metaphor and the Freudian analysis metaphor.
2. In order to be logically coherent, the self-renewalist must, in addition to using these metaphors, be a holist—that is, must accept the doctrine that organizations exist independently of the people who work within them.

3. The logical requirement that the self-renewalist be a holist renders the Deweyian and Freudian metaphors inapplicable as metaphors for organizations.
4. With regard to the Deweyian metaphor, there are two further difficulties:
   a. Dewey's conception of problem solving is also inadequate as a metaphor for school problem solving, because educational problems are ill-defined, whereas Dewey's notion of problem solving, if at all adequate, is only applicable to well-defined problems;
   b. One of the central rationales for school self-renewal stresses neutrality. However, Dewey's notion of problem solving is *not* neutral, and thus its use as a metaphor undercuts the neutrality of school self-renewal.
5. Regarding the Freudian metaphor, there are also two further difficulties in addition to that mentioned in (3) above:
   a. Freudian consciousness raising is a very *long* process, whereas school self-renewal implies a relatively circumscribed intervention.
   b. Freud saw raising to consciousness as effective only for repressed material. Not all consciousness raising by change agents is of this sort.
6. The idea of school self-renewal is not only based on the Deweyian and Freudian metaphors as a matter of fact, but also logically entails metaphors of this sort. Thus the difficulties the two metaphors raise for the notion of school self-renewal are unavoidably built into that notion.
7. From this we must conclude that the notion of school self-renewal is conceptually incoherent.

METAPHOR

Donald Schön has coined the phrase "generative metaphor." This is a particular kind of seeing-as or "carrying over" of a frame or perspective from one domain of experience to another, generating new perceptions, explanations, and inventions. For example, Schön tells us of how a group of product-development researchers concerned with improving the performance of a new paintbrush used the metaphor of a pump. By seeing a paintbrush as a pump, they were able to come up with productive suggestions of ways of improving the brush. In Schön's view, the use of generative metaphor is not limited to such technical matters. Our thinking in questions of social policy is also dominated by generative metaphors. In Schön's words:

> My point here is not that we *ought* to think metaphorically about social policy problems, but that we *do* already think about them in terms of certain pervasive, tacit generative metaphors; and that we ought to become critically aware of these generative metaphors, to increase the rigor and precision of our analysis of social policy problems by examining the analogies and "disanalogies" between the familiar descriptions . . . and the actual problematic situations that confront us.[6]

In similar vein, I wish to argue that the notion of self-renewing schools was generated from two specific metaphors and that, by becoming critically aware of them, we can reexamine the concept of self-renewal.[7] To be specific: (1) The self-renewing school's problem-solving activity is *seen as* analogous to the problem-solving activity of the intelligent individual as conceived by John Dewey; it has the same significance for the school that individual problem solving had, in Dewey's eyes, for personal growth. (2) The activity of the change agent helping to induce self-renewal is *seen as* analogous to the activity of the psychoanalyst.[8] These two metaphors—Dewey's problem solver and Freud's analyst—can be discovered in just about every piece of writing on school self-renewal. In most cases these are tacit metaphors. Dewey and Freud, generally speaking, are not mentioned directly, but hover in the background. Yet they have generated most of the strategies for encouraging schools to become self-renewing (including my own), as well as the idea of self-renewal itself.

Before dealing with each metaphor separately, let me once again stress that the Deweyan metaphor relates to how the school should solve problems and does not concern itself particularly with the problem-solving processes of the change agent (although, clearly, it is implicitly assumed that the good change agent also solves problems in the Deweyian fashion). On the other hand, the Freudian metaphor does relate to the change agent's work with the school.

The Dewey Problem-Solving Metaphor

I will here limit myself to indicating briefly those aspects or themes of Dewey's theory of inquiry and of growth that are relevant to our discussion. These are the following:

1. Dewey contrasts intelligent, reflective activity with activity born of blind habit.[9]

2. The need for reflective activity arises when blind habit fails, that is, when our habits stop being efficient means for our achieving our ends. When this occurs, we have a problem situation which for Dewey is an indeterminate, incomplete one. The aim of inquiry is to transform an indeterminate into a determinate situation.[10]

3. Scientific method, as Dewey conceived it, is *the* method of solving problems and can serve as a model for intelligent, everyday thinking. One can sketch five stages in both intelligent, everyday problem solving and also in scientific research. Dewey presents these in different places in slightly different ways. For instance, in *How We Think* these stages are: (i) a felt difficulty, (ii) its location and definition, (iii) the suggestion of a possible solution, (iv) development by reasoning of the bearings of the suggestion, and (v) further observation and experiment leading to its acceptance or rejection.[11] On the other hand, in *Democracy and Education* they become: (i) perplexity, confusion, doubt, due to the fact that one is implicated in an incomplete situation, (ii) a conjectural anticipation, (iii) a careful survey . . . of all attainable considerations which will define and clarify the problem at hand, (iv) a consequent elaboration of the tentative hypothesis, and (v) taking a stand upon the projected hypothesis as a plan of action [and] doing something overtly to bring about the anticipated result, and thereby testing the hypothesis.[12]

4. By solving a problem, people increase their knowledge, knowledge being for Dewey "a perception of those connections of an object which determine its applicability in a given situation."[13] This knowledge is something active. Through increasing knowledge we improve our *control* of our environment.

5. The growth of knowledge is an evolutionary process.[14]

6. The growth of the human organism is closely related to its increasing ability to control its environment and is thus linked to increased capacity for problem solving.[15]

7. Growth is an end in itself.[16]

From our point of view, (3) and (6) are the most central, the other five being background themes that flesh them out. An examination of the self-renewal literature shows that (3) and (6) are presented quite explicitly, the only difference being that they here refer to organizations (or at least groups) rather than individuals.

One can actually go further. At least four of the five background themes can also be detected in the self-renewal literature, in some cases explicitly, but usually implicitly. Let me now show this parallel through the examination of actual texts, first with regard to (3) and (6), and then the background themes.

The Five Stages of Problem Solving (Theme 3). A good place to begin is with an article by Kenneth Benne entitled, significantly, "Deliberate Changing as the Facilitation of Growth." Although the article doesn't deal with schools specifically, it is written by one of the best-known figures in the field of planned change, and Benne does mention Dewey's influence. Consider the following passage:

> The requirements of a methodology consonant with "growth" may be defined as norms of adaptive and adjustive behavior by the client-system. . . . [The first of these norms] may be stated as follows: Problem solving should be experimental. Growth cannot be achieved by a social system that is stereotyped and inflexible in its modes of response to difficulties. An experimental norm requires the construction of a problem out of a difficulty, the consideration of alternative meanings for the situation that signify alternative responses, the massing of relevant evidence regarding the alternatives, the choice among these, and the building-in of evaluation to check the success of the response in terms of hypothetical predictions, so that warranted and generalized learning follows from the experimentally chosen action.[17]

I rather think that if the word "client-system" were deleted, most experts on Dewey could be conned into believing that he himself wrote this passage.

Within the educational context, perhaps the source that presents the Deweyian concept of problem solving most explicitly is the *Second Handbook of Organizational Development in Schools*, by Richard Schmuck and his co-workers. The authors indicate seven rather than five stages in problem solving. These are: (i) identifying the problem, (ii) analyzing the problem, (iii) generating multiple solutions, (iv) designing plans for action, (v) forecasting consequences of intended actions, (vi) taking action, (vii) evaluating the actions.[18] The extra stages come from splitting up two of Dewey's stages; the basic view of problem solving is practically identical to his. Another publication by essentially the same group of research workers, *Transforming the School's Capacity for Problem Solving*, reveals another intellectual forefather. Of six problem-solving steps mentioned, one of them—consideration of facilitating and restraining forces—indicates the influence of Kurt Lewin. However, the other five steps—agreeing on the problem, generating alternative paths, prioritizing action steps, acting, monitoring, and recycling—again show the essentially Deweyian perspective of the approach.[19]

It seems to me that Goodlad's DDAE conception is also simply a variant on the five Deweyian stages, at least as they are formulated in *Democracy and Education.* The dialogue and decision making elements, with their stress on considering all points of view, looking at many sources of data, formulating assumptions, considering alternatives and the decision itself, parallel stages ii, iii, and iv of Dewey's model—tentative interpretation, careful survey of considerations that define and clarify the problem, and forming a tentative hypothesis. Action and evaluation, of course, relate to stage v—doing something overtly to bring about the anticipated result and thereby testing the hypothesis. What seems to be missing is the first stage—the incomplete situation. I will return to this in discussing theme 2.

Growth as Increasing Capacity for Problem Solving (Theme 6). We need not belabor the parallel here, because it is to a large extent definitional, if self-renewal or the process of becoming self-renewing is seen as an organizational synonym for growth. For instance, Schmuck et al. define organizational development as "a strategy aimed at helping schools to become self-correcting, self-renewing systems of people who are receptive to evidence that change is required and able to respond with innovative, integrated programs and arrangements."[20] Matthew Miles, in his "Planned Change and Organizational Health: Figure and Ground," indicates four dimensions of organizational health dealing with growth and changefulness.[21] Two of these—adaptation and problem-solving adequacy— are identical with the increased capacity for problem solving, when taken together. Goodlad's claim that the schools in the League of Cooperating Schools became more self-renewing rests on his showing that the schools' DDAE improved with time.

What is important is that the process of problem solving is linked with self-renewal and thus the conjunction of themes 3 and 6 shows up the Deweyian metaphor.[22]

The Supporting Themes: Themes 1, 2, 4, 5, and 7. Writing on the organizational parallel to blind habits is likely to be found in works concerned with the difficulties in implementing change. This leads us back to Sarason's *The Culture of the School and the*

Problem of Change, which contains a very extensive discussion of such an organizational parallel. Now it could be objected that Sarason's book doesn't belong to the literature on school self-renewal. After all, he certainly does not use the term "self-renewal." Nevertheless, I think it is legitimate to see it as part of the tradition I am considering because chapter 12 of the book is devoted to a discussion of the Dewey School. Despite Sarason's protestations that he does not intend to present the Dewey School as a "past educational paradise," it is obvious that he strongly approves of the way it was run and sees it as a contrast to what he calls the "modal" school. It is also clear that what impresses him in the description of the school in *The Dewey School* by Mayhew and Edwards is precisely the picture that develops of a self-renewing organization.[23] Dewey, it seems, used his own theory of inquiry and growth as metaphor for guiding his practice as principal. Mayhew and Edwards describe the weekly meetings of the faculty and they apparently could serve as a model for how, say, DDAE should function. This at least is what Sarason seems to derive from their description (without of course using terms like DDAE).

Thus it is interesting to turn to Sarason's explanation of why ordinary schools are not self-renewing. He introduces the concept of programmatic and behavioral regularities, such as "the fact that for every school day from first grade through high school, a child is expected to do something with or learn something about numbers."[24] Sarason sees these regularities as constituting a large part of the culture of a school, and his book is to a great extent an attempt to get us to see some of the regularities we normally take for granted. Now, each such regularity is one possibility out of a whole universe of possibilities. For instance, students could learn about numbers every alternate day, or only four times a week, or every second year. Sarason's major thesis is that schools tend to remain the same because "we have a tendency to assume the way things are is the way things should be."[25] Here, I think, we see how programmatic and behavioral regularities, or rather how people in school settings normally relate to these regularities, constitute the organizational analogue to blind habit (theme 1).

As previously hinted at regarding Goodlad's notion of DDAE, theme 2—the Deweyian conception of a problem as an indeterminate situation to be transformed by inquiry into a determinate one —is one strand of Dewey's thought that is not emphasized in the self-renewal literature. For instance, it would be pushing things a bit to see Schmuck's definition of a problem — "any discrepancy between an actual state of affairs and some ideal state to be achieved"—as reflecting the Deweyian notion. However, I think that the same thing can be said of Dewey himself when he concerned himself with problems of an extremely practical nature. Dewey tried to fit all problem situations into the same mold and he was not always successful. Consider his analysis of the case of being at 16th Street at 12:20 P.M. and suddenly remembering that one has an engagement at 124th Street at one o'clock:

> The purpose of keeping an engagement at a certain time and the existing hour taken in connection with the location are not congruous. The object of thinking is to introduce congruity between the two. The given conditions cannot themselves be altered; time will not go backward nor will the distance between 16th Street and 124th Street shorten itself. The problem is the discovery of intervening terms which when inserted between the remoter end and the given means will harmonize them with each other.[26]

This seems to me to be a ludicrously artificial way of describing this problem. On the other hand, this is precisely the type of difficulty for which Schmuck's very limiting definition of a problem is appropriate.

Concerning theme 4—the practicality of knowledge—because of the extremely concrete tasks of running a school and teaching in it, it would be most surprising if the practical nature of knowledge or, if you will, the pragmatic emphasis in Dewey's epistemology, were not stressed in the self-renewal literature. Thus it is not remarkable that it is stressed.

Theme 5 — the evolutionary as opposed to revolutionary emphasis in Dewey's writings — finds expression in the self-renewal literature in many subtle ways: the stress on problem solving as a continuous process (for example, in Schmuck et al.); the implication in Goodlad's and Bentzen's writings that the DDAE of the schools in their project improved steadily over time; the failure to mention revolutionary changes or quantum leaps of some sort or other.

Perhaps the best way of illustrating this is to point out one of the very few exceptions to this evolutionary stance. This is Argyris's and Schön's *Organizational Learning: A Theory of Action Perspective,* which deals with the self-renewing capacities of organizations in general. The term Argyris and Schön use as a synonym for self-renewal is deutero-learning (a term derived from the work of Bateson).[27] By this they mean an organization's learning how to detect and correct errors. The book attempts to develop a theory of intervention with which an external consultant can help an organization to achieve deutero-learning. The detection and correction of errors is also termed learning and it is here that Argyris and Schön adopt an emphatically nonevolutionary stance, for they differentiate between two very different types of error detection and correction. The first they call single-loop learning, by which they mean that the error detected and corrected permits the organization to carry on its present policies or achieve its present objectives. Double-loop learning occurs when error is detected and corrected in ways that involve the modification of an organization's underlying norms, policies, and objectives.[28] This distinction (in less esoteric terms, that which obtains between accumulation and revision of knowledge) is foreign to the Deweyan perspective and, to the best of my knowledge, is not developed in the self-renewal literature concerned specifically with schools.

Theme 7—conceiving of growth as an end in itself—is essentially an attempt to maintain a neutral attitude toward the direction of growth. This is clearly the way self-renewalists see themselves with regard to organizational change. The whole idea of self-renewal, one should remember, is a reaction to the externally imposed solution of RD&D. "Let schools provide their own solutions to their problems," seems the obvious organizational analogue of the Deweyan notion of encouraging children to realize their own potential, that is, to grow.

This then is my evidence for seeing Dewey's theory of inquiry and growth as a metaphor that has guided thought on school self-renewal. To me, the evidence is very convincing. As I became more immersed in the self-renewal literature, Dewey simply seemed to leap at me from every page. However, one could object that the parallel is clear, but it doesn't prove that the theories of self-renewal actually derived from Dewey, but rather that different research disciplines at times reach similar conclusions. Why not, for example, choose other thinkers much closer to the planned change tradition? Take Carl Rogers, whose emphasis on growth also parallels school self-renewal in many ways, and who is directly linked with certain of the OD theorists.[29] OD grew out of the group dynamics tradition and Rogers is one important strand of that tradition.[30]

My answer to this argument is as follows:

1. All great thinkers bequeath their ideas to future generations on two levels. First, these ideas remain academic issues to be discussed and criticized by academics. Second, they become part of the popular unconscious and in this way shape our spontaneous responses to matters the thinkers themselves never dealt with. On this second level, Dewey can be said to have contributed tremendously to the expression, articulation, and development of the pragmatic strand in American culture. It is this strand in American thought that I detect in the school self-renewal literature (which is almost exclusively American).

2. Whether school self-renewal theorists are conscious of the influence of Dewey or not, he presents the pragmatic strand in its most systematic form. He has thus been the target of the most sustained and detailed criticisms concerned with the pragmatic conception of inquiry and growth. As I too am critical, this criticism of Dewey is a useful starting point.

3. As a matter of fact, the Deweyian influence is not really unconscious. As previously mentioned, Benne is one of the central figures in the change literature, and he was influenced directly by Dewey. One of his first important projects was *The Improvement of Practical Intelligence,* which attempts to draw out the practical consequences of a Dewey-like view of a democratic society.[31] Then we have Goodlad, who in conversation with me has admitted the strong influence of Dewey on his thinking. Schön has been cited here as an anti-Deweyian, but this is really only so with regard to one aspect of Dewey's thought—the revision versus accumulation issue. In other ways the Argyris and Schön book has many Dewey-like components, as I will show in appendix B. Thus it is significant that Dewey was the subject of Schön's doctoral thesis. Finally, one should mention the appendix of Morris's *The Pragmatic Movement in American Philosophy,* which reports on a questionnaire sent to a number of eminent behavioral scientists.[32] Replies to this questionnaire indicate that Dewey's influence on American behavioral science was tremendous.

4. Concerning Carl Rogers: Dewey and progressive education preceded the group dynamics movement and Carl Rogers; I am convinced that the latter would never have "caught on" if the ground had not been prepared by the progressive movement. In addition, Rogers' conception of growth is far less cognitive than Dewey's, and school self-renewal is undoubtedly seen by its proponents as a cognitive matter.

The Freudian Analysis Metaphor

Just as our interest in Dewey is limited to one or two aspects of his thought, so only a tiny part of Freudian theory will be relevant to our discussion. This can be summarized in three themes:

1. People repress certain emotions and drives, but these continue to influence the psyche unconsciously.
2. This repressed material hinders people in solving their problems precisely because it remains at the unconscious level.
3. The job of the analyst is to help patients become conscious of this material so that they can deal with it effectively.[33]

These three themes are more closely interconnected than the seven Deweyian themes just discussed. Rather than treating each one separately, I will show how this metaphor is present in general in the writings of Argyris and Schön, Schmuck et al., and Goodlad.

Argyris and Schön describe individual consciousness in terms of what they call organizational maps—the public representations of the organizational theory that determine deliberate behavior (theory-in-use) to which individuals can refer. Organizational nonlearning can occur where there is an inconsistency in an organization's theory-in-use that remains undiscussable — the inconsistency doesn't have a place in the organizational maps. For instance, the authors refer to one organization that had a problem with corporate development and decentralization:

> The inconsistency in organizational theory-in-use had begun to take on the character of an organizational dilemma. That is, in the light of its conflicting requirements and its inability to resolve that conflict through inquiry, the organization had begun to find itself in situations of choice where all the options open to it appear equally bad. What was it about the organization that created this dilemma? One answer is that members of the organization had not reflected on and inquired into the issue. They had discovered neither the inconsistency in the requirements for development and decentralization nor the incongruity between espoused theory and theory-in-use for development. They had no map of the problem. In fact, they had treated the whole development as undiscussable. But this answer merely shifts the question. What prevented members of the organization from discussing the issue and mapping the problem? . . . Within [the organization] the norms of the behavioral world induced mem-

bers to express their diagnoses of sensitive issues in private, never in public. Public discussion of sensitive questions was considered inappropriate. It involved the risk of vulnerability to blame, and of interpersonal confrontation. Both were to be avoided. As a consequence the members . . . did not know the extent to which they held different views of their own problem. . . . Perceptions and memories of the development stories were scattered among individuals who held their views private.[34]

In other words, the company had problems because certain difficulties were "repressed" and unavailable to organizational consciousness. What is the role of the consultant? In this particular case:

When the consultant found that various members . . . held different and conflicting views of their problem, he brought them together to confront and discuss their differences. . . . The consultant then undertook and supported others in undertaking the public confrontation of different and conflicting views of the problem, the testing and exploration of differences through the construction of organizational history, the concerting of scattered perceptions of organizational events, the shared interpretation of data pertaining to development, and the joint mapping of the corporate development process. All of these interventions had the effect of reducing certain conditions of error (scattered perceptions, vague maps, ambiguous diagnoses) so that still other conditions for error (inconsistency and incongruity in corporate theory of action) might be surfaced and subjected to inquiry.[35]

The shadow of Freud is surely behind this conception of the consultant's role.

Schmuck et al. seem to be saying similar things in simpler, less theoretical language. They also are concerned with organizational conflicts remaining unconscious:

If conflicts are legitimated, compromises, trade-offs, and other negotiations can be conducted openly at problem solving meetings; more realistic educational policies can be achieved and conflict anxieties can be diminished as outcomes are more clearly foreseen. If they are not uncovered and managed, informal groups and underground networks which greatly distort the truth will arise to cope with them, often increasing destructive tension and personal hostility between conflicting parties.[36]

The OD consultant's job here is again to help in raising problems to consciousness: "OD consultants must know how to seek out conflicts, how to conceptualize them and *make them known,* and how to help school participants generate creative solutions to them." [37]

Schmuck et al. in many ways go beyond Argyris and Schön in their use of the Freudian metaphor. Instead of limiting themselves to tensions and organizational deceptions that arguably parallel the kind of repressions individual therapy deals with, Schmuck et al. see the task of consultation as raising many other aspects of school functioning to consciousness. Each section of their handbook deals with a particular skill of organizational adaptability, (such as problem solving, clarifying communication) and with each, more or less the same procedure is suggested. The OD consultant diagnoses the school in terms of this skill, then tries to raise the school's awareness of its functioning vis-à-vis this skill and only then begins training the faculty in improving their functioning.

Goodlad's project exhibits similar emphases. For instance, Bentzen talks about the notion that "a self-conscious, self-help group of schools could encourage responsible receptivity to change," [38] and characterizes one of their project's major intervention targets as "setting up interschool communication that would heighten each school's awareness of the quality of its DDAE process." [39] In fact, one of the incidents described at length by Goodlad probably expresses the therapeutic perspective at work more explicitly than any other source. The first meeting of the league's principals at the beginning of the second year of the project was a two-day retreat. The meeting opened with two presentations by project staff which were perceived by the principals as threatening and critical of their lack of activity. In Goodlad's words:

[The principals] were in a new kind of ballgame. Nothing much would happen unless they initiated and fostered it. There had been glimmers of such a realization before but, somehow, they had been put aside. Now, there was a full dawning during and after these two speeches. . . . The message got through and it was unnerving. By nightfall, the tension of self-confrontation was high. The cocktail hour was jokingly dubbed "tension reduction." But an hour was not sufficient. Rather grim, boisterous revelry picked up after dinner and continued well into the night. . . . Subsequent information and events emphasize its significance as one of several major watersheds in developing the League of Cooperating Schools. At that meeting, most of the principals sensed and several confronted the realization that "we have met the enemy and he is us." . . . That night became a benchmark toward brotherhood, a time when former strangers began to look differently at one another. And especially at themselves. They were "in it" and they were in it together. . . . There was no safe place of retreat. . . . One's life space suddenly had closed in very close to the elbows. While this was a significant—and, ultimately, very positive—development in the life of the League, it also was a potentially dangerous one. Suddenly being revealed to one's self and, to considerable degree, to others can be catastrophic. Fortunately, there is, among other things, a certain therapeutic quality in happenings such as this.[40]

Of course, as I stressed at the beginning of this section, we are concentrating on one aspect of Freudian theory which was the one taken over by most other therapeutic theories. Over and beyond this, each strategy of self-renewal seems to be using as metaphor a specific theory of therapy, and the differences between the strategies often express the differences between these metaphors. Thus the rather active consulting of Argyris and Schön is more thoroughly "Freudian" than Goodlad's "magic feather" intervention, which can perhaps be seen as an organizational analogue of Rogersian client-centered therapy. Yet the basic idea of raising to consciousness as I am using it is one Freud gave to the world; in criticising the metaphor in this chapter, I will relate to criticisms of the idea that appear in the philosophical literature on Freud. Let us now turn to these criticisms and also to criticisms of the Deweyian metaphor.

CRITICISM OF THE DEWEYIAN AND FREUDIAN METAPHORS: HOLISM

The main thrust of my argument concentrates on one aspect of school self-renewal which I have not mentioned—that anyone endorsing self-renewal must also uphold the holistic doctrine that *organizations exist independently of the people who work within them*. The self-renewalist must be a holist. The former term logically entails the latter. If self-renewal in schools only meant that the specific members of the school faculty had improved their individual capabilities for problem solving, then (to use the Dumbo fable once again) every significant personnel change in school faculty would require the mouse to rush back with his feather again. Thus, unless school faculty remained stable for a considerable period of time (which is highly unlikely in our mobile society), the mouse would have to remain as a semipermanent fixture. This

Sisyphus-like activity is obviously not what is implied by the ideal of school self-renewal. Yet the self-renewalist generally under-emphasizes holism. One of the reasons, I suspect, is that holism invalidates most of the empirical "proofs" that have been offered of successful strategies for promoting self-renewal. The moment self-renewal is associated with the school independently of the specific faculty members, then the effects of an intervention can only be judged after staff turnover has significantly altered the faculty that had been working in the school at the time of the intervention. This requires extended in-depth historical studies. I am unaware of many such studies.[41]

The holist perspective has been under attack of late in educational administration theory through the work of Thomas Greenfield, who has published a series of controversial articles arguing for a new antiholist or individualistic perspective.[42] With some justice Greenfield has complained that most critiques of his position have related to his first two articles and thus have not acknowledged the developments in his thought. Nevertheless, I limit my discussion to an early article, "Organizations as Social Inventions: Rethinking Assumptions About Change," because it is the only article of his that deals directly with the topic of educational change.

In Greenfield's view, which draws upon the phenomenological perspective, organizations are created by individuals; they are human constructs that must be sustained by individuals. Organizations and human beings are inextricably intertwined.

This view of organizations seems to derive from the philosophic position that no facts exist independently of the human being perceiving them. This, predictably enough, leads Greenfield to the claim that various members of an organization will see it in different ways because people and their definitions of social reality are different. In those cases where there is a similarity of vision, it is likely that some particular, politically powerful group or individual within the organization has succeeded in forcing others to accept a certain definition of the social reality of the organization. This brings us to the question of organizational change, which for Greenfield "requires more than structural change; it requires changes in the meanings and purposes that individuals learn within their society."[43] Thus "we should desist in our efforts to discover the 'most effective' organizational structure or the one 'best adapted to the environment' and put more effort into understanding the specific meanings, purposes, and problems of specific individuals in specific organizations."[44]

Accepting Greenfield's views must lead to a rejection of the idea of school self-renewal. However, despite my sympathy with much that he says, I note many difficulties with which he has not come to terms. The reason probably is that he has simply ignored the literature in the philosophy of the social sciences that deals with the issue of holism versus what is known as methodological individualism vis-à-vis societies and social facts.[45] Methodological individualism is very similar to Greenfield's position. However, instead of concentrating on the social construction of reality by individuals, the methodological individualist is mainly concerned with showing that statements pertaining to be about social laws and facts can be reduced to statements about the actions and dispositions of individuals. Holism (and it is from this literature that I have taken the term) denies that all such statements can be so reduced.

One of the most famous articles supporting the holist position is Ernest Gellner's "Explanations in History." The following passage from that article presents the difficulties with Greenfield's argument particularly well.

Individuals do have holistic concepts and often act in terms of them. For instance, ... de Gaulle's actions were inspired by his *idea* of France — which may perhaps have had little relation to actual Frenchmen. When the holistic ideas of many individuals are co-ordinated and reinforced by public behaviour and physical objects— by ceremonials, rituals, symbols, public buildings, etc.—it is difficult for the social scientist, though he observes the scene from the outside, not to use the holistic concept. It is quite true that the fact that X acts and thinks in terms of an holistic idea—e.g. he treats the totem as if it were his tribe, and the tribe as if it were more than the tribesman —is itself a fact about an individual. On the other hand, though the holistic term used by the observer may be eliminable, as used by the participant it is not. Are we to say that a logically impeccable explanation of a social situation is committed to crediting its subjects with nonsensical thought? Perhaps we are. On the other hand, the fact that holistic terms are ineliminable from the thought of participants may well be a clue to their ineliminability from that of observers.[46]

Greenfield is to a certain extent aware of this paradox that the observer "*responds* to [social reality] as something other than human invention."[47] But he never really follows up this line of thought, preferring to concentrate on the participants' *creation* of social reality. Also, despite his avowed support for individuals, their values, and their views, in at least one sense he ignores the individual within the organization. As previously mentioned, he stresses the differences between views of people in organizations, and when they are not so different he (as observer) infers that we have a case of someone's views being imposed on another. Yet consider the following cases: just about every faculty member in a school, let us say, affirms the statement, "Ours is a school that stresses tradition." From the point of view of the participants, the teachers, this is clearly not the same sort of statement as "Mr. Smith [the principal] doesn't allow us to try out new ideas in our classrooms." So why should we assume that the first statement is really similar to the second? However, if we do take the first statement more or less at face value, we do have a case of most of the members of an organization taking for granted that a certain belief is associated with the organization independent of themselves? Now, if in addition, we assume that they see it as their duty to inform new members of the organization of the existence of this belief, there is a good chance that it will be upheld by succeeding generations in the organization. In such cases, I see no good reason for not talking about the *organization*'s norms or ideology, rather than of the beliefs of specific individuals.

This is a very weak version of holism, but it is sufficient for the self-renewalist, although the statement "Ours is a school that stresses tradition" almost certainly would not characterize a self-renewing school. Let us thus formulate this both more generally and more explicitly: Self-renewal in an organization depends on the following:

a. Most members of the organization accept a set of sentences of the form, "X is a characteristic of our organization" (where X is a characteristic relevant to self-renewal).

b. By virtue of (a), most members of the organization see themselves as obligated, as members of the organization, to act according to or to believe in particular Xs.

c. Because of (b), most members of the organization see themselves as obligated to getting new members of the organization also to accept the set of sentences mentioned in (a).[48]

I assume that it is an empirical fact that beliefs like (b) and (c) often characterize human behavior in the organizational setting. Thus in order to decide whether self-renewal is a viable concept or not, it seems we have to first determine whether there does exist a set of Xs which the organization's members believe characterize their organization. To return to our discussion of the Deweyian and Freudian metaphors: these should supply us with a list of possible Xs. In the following sections I will identify the items that would make up such a list and then ask, with regard to each X-candidate, whether it makes sense to assume that organizational members could accept the statement "X characterizes our organization." To the extent that this search is successful, school self-renewal would appear to be a meaningful concept. Unfortunately, most of the X-candidates fail dismally. What in effect I am going to show is that, despite its conceptual flaws as a general thesis, Greenfield's analysis does seem to work pretty well in the specific case of self-renewal. Let us see this by examining the Deweyian and Freudian metaphors separately.

The Deweyian Metaphor

On the face of it, Dewey's conception of problem solving seems to create no difficulty. It supplies us with one general X-candidate—the norm of experimental empiricism—and a number of more specific ones — the institutionalization of the different stages of problem solving as norms. This is what Goodlad, for example, tried to do in his project—to institutionalize the belief that DDAE is important and also a number of more specific norms associated with good dialogue, decision making, action, and evaluation.

However, it seems to me that this way of looking at things oversimplifies what Dewey meant when he suggested his five-stage process of problem solving. In a reply to a critique of his book *How We Think,* Dewey wrote:

> In speaking of steps [of thought] it is perhaps natural to suppose that something chronological is intended, and from that it is presumably a natural conclusion that the steps are taken in a temporal sequence in the order taken [in my analysis]. Nothing of this sort however is intended. The analysis is *formal* and indicates the *logical* "movements" involved in an act of critical thought.[49]

In other words, the five stages do not constitute reflective thought, but rather supply us with a formal analysis of such thought. Reflective problem solving is not a mechanical application of five steps, but is rather a flowing, living activity of the human mind. The steps are nothing but the formal trappings. This is why the Deweyian conception of problem solving is, in many ways, such an inappropriate metaphor for organizational problem solving. The only part of the Deweyian scheme that can be translated into organizational terms is the formal trappings. The "soul" of the scheme is untranslatable. Neither the participant nor the external observer of an organization can regard intelligence or reflection as an X-candidate. Organizations do not have intelligence nor do they reflect; all of us will agree to this, despite the existence of books with titles like *The Mind of the Organization*.[50] Thus the organizational institutionalization of the trappings of thought as norms is simply creating an empty vessel that must be filled by the thinking of real people. And here is the rub—we have no guarantee that the new people entering an institution that seems to be self-renewing or the oldtimers entering new roles in such an institution will be the same sort of thinkers as their predecessors.

CASE I: THE STORY OF GILAD AND YOSSI

It is 1978 and another member of our staff and I are beginning our "drifting in" diagnosis of the Hof Rishon High School, a boarding school, and one of the schools in our Project for the Advancement of Educational Cooperation. The school has a tremendously good reputation in its district and so we are intrigued to see if the reality is like the rumor. First impressions: everyone seems happy. Kids and teachers walk around with relaxed gaits. Talk is animated. Lots of laughter. None of the usual hostility that floats in the air in most high schools. During the first weeks we sit in at a number of faculty meetings of various sorts, run by different people. We note: "This is a textbook case of how meetings should be run." Teachers convey an incredible concern and love for kids. They also feel comfortable with each other. Many views aired. Serious discussions. And what is more, the decisions come to at these meetings in the main are implemented. This we discover by spending some time with the two vice-principals and with heads of departments and seeing how they work.

The one puzzling thing about the school is the headmaster, Gilad. With small, spectacled, blinking eyes, he seems to live in a world of his own. One rarely sees him but when one does he seems to be all alone. During my first day as Gilad's shadow, he sits in his office most of the time and very few people come in. Few phone calls. He sits reading and writing and sometimes we talk. Once we sally out because he wants to play volleyball with a bunch of kids. Twice during the day, meetings are conducted in his office. At both of them he doesn't say very much, but sits seemingly staring into space and doodles.

One's first impressions could be—nice guy, not particularly effective as principal. However, these impressions are almost immediately dispelled for any visitor. At almost every conversation we had with teachers, the one thing that shone through was the incredible respect they all had for Gilad. Then there was the fact that he was always completely relaxed while I shadowed him. This was very unusual. Most headmasters were pretty uptight with us until we got to know them. Also, during those first few weeks I was lucky enough to be present on three occasions when Gilad "went into action." The first of these was at a meeting with the school's board of governors at which one member was suggesting a policy change of some sort. Here I saw Gilad as a political infighter of great shrewdness and force who in a few minutes created a coalition of those favoring his views and thus in the end got the suggestion defeated. The second occurred in his office one day. A young home economics teacher burst into the room on the verge of tears. In her last lesson, the class (of girls) had baked a whole lot of pizza, and she had suggested that some of the pizza be brought to the faculty lounge and offered to the teachers. The kids had refused, saying they wanted to take it back to their rooms, and no matter how much she pushed, they remained adamant. At last they had all marched out of the class in a huff. "I tell you, Gilad, they are impossible. Completely selfish. They don't appreciate what we do for them." With great tact Gilad eventually calmed her down, and in the end, with very little help from him, she began to see the kids' side of the argument too.

The third case was a faculty meeting which, unlike most others I attended, couldn't get off the ground. People seemed to be talking across one another and repeating each other. Of course, Gilad stopped doodling and for one of the few times while we observed at this school, came across as a dynamic, forceful directive chairman of a meeting.

After about four months we reached the conclusion that of all the schools in our project, Hof Rishon's DDAE was probably one of the most developed. And the reason for this was Gilad, who had forged the atmosphere that characterizes the school. This gentle, quiet man was, we decided, that rare animal, a truly democratic headmaster whose respect for people had had a major effect on the willingness of school faculty to take responsibility. Gilad also had avoided the trap most headmasters fall into of becoming bureaucrats and therefore had the time to think about where his school should be going. He also was one of the few headmasters who can be said to have had a vision of that goal, and was trying slowly to move the school in the direction of that vision.

The fault in the school's DDAE resided in one aspect of decision making—the consideration of alternatives. Although everyone was encouraged to express his or her point of view, these all seemed to be taken from a very small universe of possibilities. This was especially marked in the school's pedagogy, which was very traditional. The interesting thing was that there was also evidence that many of the teachers were capable of highly innovative creative work. During each year, the school worked on two special projects. The first was what they called the Jerusalem Project. All students from eleventh grade, together with their teachers, spent four days in Jerusalem at a youth hostel. Divided into small groups, they conducted a series of investigations into various aspects of Jerusalem life and Israeli political life. The second was the Writing Project. For four days classes in tenth grade were canceled and all the teachers, working in a team-teaching format, conducted a program designed to develop skills in writing and library use. A lot of the material used during this project had been designed by the teachers themselves.

The striking fact was that none of the pedagogical ideas from these two projects seemed to be applied in the ordinary lessons at Hof Rishon. This was raised at the meeting in the first year of our project in which we supplied feedback to the school about its DDAE. (Hof Rishon was one of the few schools at which this was done during the first year, as noted in chapter 1). At this meeting, Gilad did not sit on the sidelines, for two reasons. First, as previously mentioned, the school's faculty was not very good at accepting evaluation and criticism; this was true of other schools, also. The participants at the meeting seemed to be floundering, which prompted Gilad to be more active. Second, it was very important, in Gilad's view, that something practical should come from this meeting. Our comments had not really supplied him with any startlingly new insights about his school, but had rather helped him to crystallize or make explicit certain unformulated feelings he had had about the school himself. He regarded our formulation as important, and thus considered it to be essential to push for concrete results. The practical decision that was reached was that during the following year a group of faculty members would work with the project staff in trying to deal with the problem of the traditional pedagogy in ordinary lessons.

We now come to the crucial point in the story. Gilad had to commute a considerable distance to the school daily. A family problem made it imperative that he spend more time at home, and thus toward the end of the year he reached the decision that he could not continue working at Hof Rishon. The new headmaster, Yossi, took over the position at the beginning of the second year of our project.

Yossi is a very different sort of person from Gilad. A large, heavy man with a curling moustache, he is one of those people who looks more comfortable outdoors than in. His academic background is in agriculture, unlike Gilad who came from the humanities. My most animated discussion with Yossi during three years' work occurred when he wanted to buy a second-hand car and discovered I was thinking of selling my car. His reputation in the school (he had been a vice-principal for a number of years) was that of a superb administrator. "If we have any technical or administrative problem that no one can solve, then give it to Yossi. In a few minutes he will come up with the simplest solution and you will ask yourself, 'Why hadn't I thought of that?'"

At the beginning of our second year, Yossi and I planned the implementation of the decision reached at the feedback meeting the previous year. The idea that was eventually adopted, briefly mentioned in chapter 1, was that a group of the most creative teachers in the school would become a sort of school R&D unit. Their responsibility was to learn about, develop, and try out new teaching methods, and with regard to those which seemed to work, to think of ways of disseminating them throughout the school. When I say that Yossi and I planned this together, this is a bit misleading. To a large extent the idea was suggested by me, with Yossi working out its practical applications. Of course, we were always very wary of forcing ideas onto school personnel. In this case, it seems fair to characterize what happened as follows: The rather half-baked development of a decision made the previous year by the school's personnel was initiated outside the school and then fleshed out and made operational by the school principal. What is important to stress is that, at this time, this process was performed with great willingness.

Yossi and I put the idea of a R&D unit to the group of teachers selected (who represented a number of different disciplines — mathematics, literature, Bible studies, physics, biology) and it was greeted with considerable enthusiasm. It was decided that the group, Yossi, and I would meet once a week, and the school timetable was changed in order to create an hour in which we would all be free. I became a secondary figure after the first few meetings. Yossi himself became pretty secondary a short time later. On their own initiative, the teachers developed two team-teaching proposals, one in literature and the other in mathematics. The school had some experience with team teaching from the writing project. However, that experience was related to team teaching of a limited kind, that is, team planning and evaluation without actually teaching together. The R&D group's proposals were on a different level entirely. Here team teaching entailed teaching together as well as planning and evaluating together. In addition, the projects envisioned variable pupil group composition and size.

Yossi decided not to try to implement the literature proposal that year because the literature teacher in the group, who had developed it, was new at the school and was not the head of the literature department. He felt there would be some tension over this and thought (rightly so) that we should wait until the following year. It was decided to try out the math proposal in two ninth grade classes and then compare results with those in the other ninth grade classes, who would thus act as a control group. This meant involving other math teachers because only one of the teachers in the group, Oded, was a math teacher (and head of the department). It seemed to me that Yossi showed great understanding of his faculty's strengths and weaknesses here. Oded was a good teacher but a deplorable head of department, mainly because of a total lack of organizing ability. Yossi realized that without help nothing would ever get off the ground. Thus he, the vice-principal, and the whole of the R&D group gave Oded maximum support on all levels, both in planning the program and during the actual implementation.

Nevertheless, as I impressed upon Yossi, because of the personalities involved in the situation and the fact that this was the first contact of the participants with "radical" team teaching, the school should be satisfied if the experiment just turned out to be less than a complete fiasco. It was in this spirit that the experiment seemed to be conducted. Everyone involved seemed willing to try it, learn from their mistakes, and then try it again.

Actually, the math program wasn't a fiasco; things could have been far worse. At its completion, a fine meeting was held in order to summarize, identify faults, and suggest improvements. It was decided that during the following year the math department would run a revised version of its program, the literature department would try out the program that had been developed that year, and the R&D group would continue meeting and try to develop some new ideas.

Up to this point, the work of the R&D unit seems to exemplify a successful institutionalization of a Dewey-like problem-solving procedure. A problem had been identified[51] (an overly traditional pedagogy), a new school unit had scanned possible ways of broadening pedagogic options, had chosen and developed one such option, had tried it out in practice, had evaluated the results and, on the basis of this evaluation, had suggested improvements and also seemed poised to develop other ideas. Unfortunately, the following year could be called "The Year in Which the R&D Unit Died." First (and this the school had no control over), the national literature curriculum was totally revised, and the teachers were so busy coming to grips with the new curriculum that there was no chance of their also developing a new team-teaching pedagogic approach. Second, the math program never got off the ground, mainly because Oded simply didn't get the sort of support he had enjoyed the previous year. Third, and this is the most important point, Yossi did not succeed in setting up the free hour as he had done the previous year. He continually claimed that he was working on it, but that "this year we are having a lot of technical problems and I don't see how to overcome them." Finally, a one-time meeting was set up by canceling lessons and the group decided that a program should be developed in Bible studies and that Yossi should continue trying to set up time for the R&D group to meet. The group of Bible teachers was never convened and the technical problem of finding time for the R&D group to meet was never solved.

In many other aspects of the school's life, subtle changes took place that year. Other suggestions that required timetable changes couldn't be put into practice and, all in all, the complaint, "We are having a tough year—so many administrative problems" was beginning to be heard more and more. Of course, some of these problems, all would agree, could be described as examples of *force majeure* (for example, a senior staff member suffered a heart attack). However, in most cases, the lack of success in solving the problems referred to above derived from their being seen as of low priority. This had not been the case two years before.

What does this story show? In what way does it illustrate how institutionalizing a Dewey-like problem-solving procedure is insufficient to ensure self-renewal? First, I must stress that I could have chosen far more dramatic illustrations of how changing principals changes schools. In our project, for instance, one school was being examined by a commission of inquiry because of alleged malpractices, and was transformed into almost a model school within a couple of months when a new headmaster came in. However, such an example would not be fair because the first headmaster was simply grossly incompetent. No self-renewalist need be so extreme a holist as to believe that it is possible to create an organization which is *so* independent of the personalities of those who are working in it that it will always continue to function in the same way. All would agree that a gifted principal can transform a school that has been badly run, or that an incompetent principal can destroy a well-run school. The case of Hof Rishon is interesting because it was a democratic school and one would assume that in such a case, the importance of the headmaster would be minimalized. Moreover, both Gilad and Yossi were good headmasters according to the usual sort of criteria, and, what is more, had worked together for many years.

The point is that they were different, and the Dewey metaphor was likely to work well for one of them and not for the other. When Yossi inherited Hof Rishon, he inherited many different norms and beliefs. Some of them were easy for him to adopt. For instance, trust in individual teachers who showed initiative, and encouragement for them to develop their ideas, was something that had occurred during Gilad's time and continued to flourish after he left. I haven't described here some of the very exciting things that occurred as a result of this, but it must be stressed that the death of the R&D group does not imply the death of all school innovation. The problem with the R&D group was that it embodied an idea that required long-range, flexible, tentative, and sustained development and did not promise immediate results. Yossi's cognitive style, if you will, was such that long-range, flexible planning was not very important to him.[52] One of the major thrusts of this book will be to argue that, because of the emphasis in the literature on resistance to change, defensiveness, lack of mutual trust, we have not paid sufficient attention to the fact that simple lack of enthusiasm for an idea, not being "turned on" by a proposal, not being moved by a plan, are major barriers to the implementation of an innovation. When an innovation means institutionalizing problem-solving procedures, then not being "turned on" can lead to one of two results. Either the procedures will die after a time (as happened, after some initial enthusiasm, at Hof Rishon, despite the nonauthoritarian character of the headmaster), or they will become so ritualized that they lose all instrumental significance. Norms of problem solving are never routine norms because they are oriented toward producing something new. Thus they really do exemplify Greenfield's thesis: they require the continual investment of human energy. The institutionalization of the norms is necessary but not sufficient to guarantee their survival.

Before moving on, let me make some of my assumptions explicit, and also counter one objection. First, if as I maintain Yossi did manage to encourage innovative activity that did not fit the Dewey metaphor, then one could ask whether self-renewal and systematic procedures for problem solving are necessarily connected. I will answer this when discussing ill-defined problems.

Second is the question of cognitive style. My presentation of Yossi's cognitive style might suggest that I do not view human nature as infinitely malleable. After all, if human beings were completely malleable, then there would be a way of changing Yossi's cognitive style, which I seem to doubt. To a certain extent I would go along with this characterization of my approach. However, I must stress that we are talking about cognitive style in a very specific way and in a very specific context, and it is not necessarily true that what applies in this case also applies in general. What is specific about this case? My answer is threefold:

1. We are talking about trying to change the style of a middle-aged adult. This seems to me very unlikely.
2. We are not talking about a person learning the ability to think in a certain way. Under certain conditions Yossi is perfectly capable of long-range, flexible planning. Rather, we are talking about long-range, flexible planning learned as a *preferred spontaneous mode of response* by a person with a penchant for short-range, technical planning. It is this that I am skeptical about.
3. We are not talking about learning that comes about as a result of, say, an intensive private therapeutic-like relationship with a teacher, but an on-the-job learning experience (being socialized by certain school norms), which is necessarily far less intensive and focused. It seems to me that even if I am wrong about (1) and (2), (3) acts as a constraint that makes the possibility of changing cognitive style simply illusory.

Third, it could be argued that the R&D unit died because Gilad simply did not bequeath Hof Rishon to his successor very well. According to this argument, he should have seen to it that Yossi internalized the norms of long-range planning or should have opposed his becoming headmaster. I have indicated why I reject the first possibility. And regarding Yossi's being a suitable candidate as Gilad's successor, one should remember that the charac-

teristics of the superb headmaster are numerous and varied. Yossi
may not have had a penchant for long-range, flexible planning, but
he had many other qualities. This is why he is a good if not superb
headmaster.

The Freudian Metaphor

What aspects of the "therapeutic" process used by the consultant should be considered to have contributed to self-renewal?
One possibility is that what is important is the actual knowledge
gained by the organization as a result of the consultant's intervention —·knowledge of factors inhibiting full functioning. Is such
knowledge a reasonable X-candidate? Certainly members of organizations often do conceive of their organizations as having beliefs
and knowledge and therefore one could argue that knowledge of
inhibiting factors could become part of an organization's belief system passed on from one generation to the next. The problem is that,
in most cases, such knowledge is specific to a certain time in the
organization's history (the time of the consultant's intervention). It
is knowledge of factors inhibiting full functioning that were operating when specific people worked in the organization. It certainly is
not clear that such knowledge, if it became part of the organization's "saga," would be of much use to future generations.[53] Of
course, it could be that it was knowledge of such grand folly that its
being purged at a particular time served as a prototype of the dangers of allowing the organization to go in a particular direction.
However, this would be rare.

If the knowledge is not specific to a particular time and group
of persons, and yet is knowledge of inhibiting factors, what sort of
knowledge can it be? One possibility is that it be proverbial knowledge of some sort. This X-candidate is perfectly acceptable from a
conceptual point of view, although common sense would seem to
suggest that it is extremely unlikely that proverbial knowledge
could promote self-renewal in any real sense. If it could, promoting
self-renewal would be a simple, predictable, mechanized sort of
activity. Also it should be realized that the members of the organization who obtained the knowledge originally at the time of the
consultant's intervention obtained it in a special way (through having this knowledge raised to consciousness). It *may* be that the way
the knowledge is obtained is unimportant, but I think that most
consultants would probably see gaining insight as central.

If this is correct, we have a problem. Gaining insight is a

completely unsatisfactory X-candidate. Only people, not organizations, can undergo this process. Not only that, but also insight entails far more than the knowledge contained in maxims or proverbs. Maxims are easily transmitted; insights are not the same sort of thing. They seem indissolubly linked to process — we "gain" them or "get" them. We see a particular situation partially or wrongly, and then we see it differently, more correctly. We have gained insight. If this is so, then insights cannot be passed on in a simple mechanical fashion.[54]

CASE II: THE PASSING ON OF INSIGHT

It is the first headmasters' meeting in our project's second year. Unfortunately, there had been a dramatic change of headmasters at the end of the first year; also, two new schools had joined the project. So half of the headmasters were newcomers. We decided to devote most of the meeting to getting the old-timers to incorporate the newcomers into the group. To make people feel more comfortable, the first hour of the meeting was run by a newcomer to our project staff, which we hoped would add certain symbolic significance to things. He decided to begin the meeting by creating pairs, each made up of an old-timer and a newcomer. After they discussed things for about twenty minutes, the pairs paired up for a further twenty minutes' discussion. Then the quartets got together for the final twenty minutes. To put it mildly, the whole activity was a catastrophe. The main reason for this derived from the behavior of one new headmaster, Zev, who likes things to be clear and well defined. During this hour he continually and vociferously pushed the old-timers to define what they had "got" out of the project the previous year. This, of course, they couldn't do. They all felt they and their schools had benefited in some way but could not define it quickly. The atmosphere became more and more uncomfortable.

Two years later, Aviva, one of the newcomers at this meeting took me aside at the project's final party. She had since become one of the dominant and most productive people in the project, and had really tried to change things in her school. She confided: "David, you know, after that meeting two years ago, I nearly left the project. It was so depressing. The confusion was so total. I, at that time, decided to give it a try for two more meetings. I did and I also got to know F—— and J—— [the two members of the project staff associated with her school] better, began to understand what the project was all about, and the rest you know."

This case illustrates the problem of seeing insight, or becoming aware, as part of self-renewal. Aviva took over a school during the project, and it was thus possible for her to be influenced by our intervention strategy and to gain the same sort of insight her predecessor had gained. But what about the principal who takes over a school after the change-agent-therapist has left? How does that principal gain insight?

One possibility is to see the change agent's task as one of helping the school establish the idea that all involved should continually try to raise unspoken assumptions to consciousness. This is a possibility little discussed in the literature, largely because most consultants have not realized the logical connection between self-renewal and holism. To establish such a norm, one runs into the same difficulties we pointed out with regard to Dewey's five stages. Gaining insight cannot be institutionalized within formalized procedures. However, the problem is less serious in this case because gaining insight, unlike problem solving, is not a continuous or pervasive process. It need not inform all activity, nor all staff members. A school could, once or twice a year, hold a series of meetings devoted to consciousness raising, run by a trained staff member. To a certain extent, the evaluator in our project can be seen as our attempt to create such a role.

There seem to be no problems with this idea. Nevertheless, such a consciousness raiser must:

1. have the skills necessary to help other people in gaining insight;
2. be able to observe the school culture from the outside and thus discover its sacred cows;
3. have the standing in the school to allow consciousness raising to be perceived as nonthreatening;
4. have the ability to *teach* a succesor the skills of helping other people gain insight.

It is a rare person who can fulfill all these conditions, and especially condition 4, so it is extremely unlikely that a school staff will be able to maintain without help people from within its own ranks to fill the role. However, this is unfortunately what is required by the concept of school self-renewal, if therapy is seen, metaphorically, as an organizational process.[55]

CRITICISM OF DEWEY AND FREUD: GOING SLIGHTLY BEYOND METAPHOR

Criticism of Dewey

To date I have criticized the Deweyian metaphor by questioning its applicability to organizations.[56] In addition, the metaphor can be wrong in another way: Dewey may simply have erred altogether in his description of problem solving. If so, using his conception of problem solving metaphorically loses all its credibility. This section is devoted to considering some such criticisms of Dewey's ideas.[57]

Dewey's conception of problem solving and growth derived from his admiration of scientific method.[58] Here we have the main difficulty with Dewey's theory. According to more contemporary theories of scientific growth, Dewey did not understand how science worked. Actually, it would be more accurate to say that Dewey was *usually* mistaken in his understanding of science; it would be too much to hope for complete consistency from such a prolific writer. In most of his writing he is what I would call an evolutionary inductivist. In certain passages, particularly in *The Quest for Certainty,* one can interpret him as saying something else.[59] But these passages are not important here because they form a very tiny part of Dewey's corpus, and also because they have been far less influential.

The modern theorists who challenge the more orthodox interpretation of Dewey's philosophy of science are philosophers like Popper, Kuhn, Lakatos, Feyerabend, Schwab, and Laudan.[60] They stress two crucial aspects of scientific growth:

1. Scientific growth is not cumulative. The history of science gives us many examples of scientific theories that have been replaced by competing theories. In fact, much of the recent thrust in history and philosophy of science is directed to explaining the role of revolutions in scientific progress.
2. Such theories and research traditions function as conceptual systems that determine, at least partially, what we will see, what we will consider as problems, how we go about solving problems, what will count as solutions to problems, and even how seriously failure to solve a particular problem will be regarded.

If these two aspects of the conventional wisdom about science are accepted, then Dewey's evolutionary conception of scientific progress and his five-step model must be rejected as descriptions of how science works. Scientific knowledge grows, not only by perception of an increasing number of connections, but more by substitution of one set of perceptions for another. Scientific problems are usually not solved by scanning a number of alternative hypotheses but rather are only identified and approached through the orientation a particular theory gives us.[61] If so, we can ask, why should everyday problem solving conform to Dewey's model? And if it does not, why should his model be in any way illuminating as a metaphor for how organizations go about or should go about solving problems and renewing themselves?

This criticism of Dewey is too simple. It overlooks, for one thing, a paragraph tucked away in one of Kuhn's lesser-known articles in which he suggests that his description of science probably doesn't apply to engineering.[62] The point is that Dewey would never accept a distinction between science and engineering, and in much of his writing he uses engineering cases as examples of scientific activity. Right or wrong, how does his model fare when applied to engineering-like activity—for example, the development of the computer industry?

A computer can be seen in a vast number of ways, depending on one's conceptual system. However, computer engineers and programmers see the computer in one particular way and see the computer industry as having one relatively well-defined aim—making more and more efficient computers. Of course, the concept of efficiency in this field is continually changing, but this change is not related to conceptual revolutions but rather to the increasing number of factors that need to be taken into account when determining efficiency. Today, for instance, size is an important consideration, but was not twenty-five years ago. All this accords well with Dewey's idea of knowledge growing through the increasing number of perceived connections of an object. Now, if efficiency is relatively unproblematic in the computer world, so also is the identification of problems. This is, of course, how Dewey sees it too. A problem arises when a specific computer or type of computer is judged to be inefficient. Such a judgment can usually be made without much difficulty and without challenge from other members of the profession. How the problem gets solved is again in accordance with the Dewey scheme, and in fact the term "trouble-schooling" expresses perfectly the scanning-like behavior Dewey was referring to. This type of problem solving lends itself to predictable increases in control; thus the ordered and relatively predictable development of the industry seems to fit the Deweyian concept of growth. All in all, the "orthodox" Dewey conception of science seems hopelessly wrong for pure science and yet impressively accurate for applied science.

Let us now return to problem solving in schools. We now see that to the extent that such activity is of an "engineering" nature, the Deweyian metaphor is reasonable (although limited by the considerations already raised). On the other hand, to the extent that problem solving in schools is totally different from solving engineering problems, the metaphor is probably not legitimate. Let us consider three main types of problems that school faculties have to deal with.

The first are *technical problems,* related to the efficiency of the organization, where efficiency is being conceived in a very narrow sense. A good example is drawing up the school timetable. This is usually conceived as a purely logistic problem, slotting people into places and times as efficiently as possible. It is rare that the educational significance or the "hidden curriculum" [63] of these slottings is taken into account. This sort of problem can clearly be seen as having an engineering-type structure.

Second are *human relations problems.* For example, there may exist certain tensions between the headmaster and, say, the teachers of the social studies department. These again are engineering-type problems in the sense that they are easily identifiable; it is clear why they should be resolved; solving them is going to be most intelligently achieved by scanning various possible ways of acting. As a matter of fact, much of the literature on planned organizational change seems to concentrate on such problems and to suggest rather efficient, systematic procedures for solving them.

Third are, for want of a better word, *educational problems.* These are all variants of some sort or other of *the* basic problem of all educational institutions — how can we best provide these particular students with a good education? These are the problems that justify our seeing schools as different from other organizations. School faculty deal with them every day, sometimes on a very specific level — Johnny is causing a lot of discipline problems of late; how should we try to improve matters? — sometimes on a more

general level: how should we best incorporate discovery methods
into our biology lessons? Sometimes they occur on the most general
level imaginable: how free should the climate in our school be?

Can such problems be regarded as engineering-type problems? In most cases they cannot be so regarded, and in fact they are
usually problems of a radically different type. Before arguing this
thesis, I will introduce two special terms: ill-defined problems,[64]
and essentially contested concepts.

I use the term "ill-defined problems" in the sense developed
by Walter Reitman in the field of information-processing models of
cognition. Reitman contrasts ill-defined with well-defined problems, the latter being characterized thus: "With each well-defined
problem we are given some systematic way to decide when a proposed solution is acceptable."[65] An ill-defined problem does not
have such a systematic procedure associated with it. As an example,
Reitman suggests the task of composing a fugue.

Ill-defined problems and the way people go about solving
them, have some very interesting properties. First, let us consider
what defines a problem. The components of a problem can be
viewed as constraints on the problem solution, and therefore on the
problem-solving process. However, in ill-defined problems many
of these constraints are what Reitman calls "open." These are
parameters of the problem which are left unspecified—for example,
in the above example, the length of the fugue is not given. Reitman
proposes that one of the most striking aspects of attempts to solve
ill-defined problems is that the solver closes these attributes in
ways that seem reasonable. Not only this, the solver may change the
chosen parameter values as time goes on and this process of change
is likely to be very jerky and discontinuous.

Another fascinating characteristic of the process of solving
ill-defined problems is that feedback obtained during the solution
attempt may be used in a most "unintelligent" way. For instance,
let us assume the solver "generates a new information structure that
violates the constraints of the problem (as defined), but which
nonetheless appears too interesting or promising in other respects
to throw away."[66] At such points, an attempt is sometimes made to
modify one or more of the antecedent problems and the new structure is not thrown away.

A third important characteristic is that the solution of an ill-
defined problem suggested by a particular problem solver may not
be acceptable to other people (because there is no systematic way
of evaluating a proposed solution). This is significant when we are

concerned with problem solving in organizations. In Reitman's words, "This ambiguity in regard to problem solutions will be intolerable in many organizational contexts, and it will be necessary to make arrangements for communication concerning open parameters and for problem solving facilities capable of resolving any differences with respect to the parameters that may appear."[67]

Reitman maintained that most work on information-processing models of problem solving is limited to well-defined problems, although, in his view, a greater proportion of human energy in the real world is devoted to ill-defined problems. Thus it is significant, if my cognitive psychologist friends are to be believed, that no one has really followed Reitman's lead in developing the theory of ill-defined problems over the last decade and a half. What is quite clear is that the process of solving ill-defined problems is fundamentally incompatible with the Deweyian description of problem solving.

The term "essentially contested concept" derives from the philosophical work of W. B. Gallie. These are concepts that normally surface in fields like aesthetics, political and social philosophy, and the philosophy of religion. Gallie characterizes them thus:

We find groups of people disagreeing about the proper use of the concepts. . . . When we examine the different uses, . . . we soon see that there is no use . . . which can be set up as . . . [the] generally accepted and therefore correct or standard use. Different uses . . . subserve different though, of course, not unrelated functions for different schools, . . . groups, . . . parties, . . . communities and sects. Now once this variety of functions is disclosed we might expect that the disputes . . . would at once come to an end. But in fact this does not happen. Each party continues to maintain that the special function which the term . . . fulfils on *its* behalf or on its interpretation is the correct or proper or primary or the only important function which the term in question can be said to fulfil. . . . Endless dispute may be due to psychological causes . . . or to metaphysical afflictions . . . but . . . there are apparently endless disputes for which neither of these explanations *need* be the correct one; . . . there are disputes . . . which are perfectly genuine; which, although not resolvable by argument of any kind, are nevertheless sustained by perfectly respectable arguments and evidence. This is what I mean by saying there are concepts which are essentially contested, concepts the proper use of which inevitably involves endless disputes about their proper uses.[68]

How are we to differentiate between disputes over essentially contested concepts and disputes that derive from confusion of concepts? Gallie suggests seven conditions an essentially contested concept must meet. First, it must be what he calls appraisive—that is, it signifies or accredits some kind of valued achievement. Second, this achievement must be of an internally complex nature. Third, the achievement must be describable in various ways depending on the way its components are ordered. Fourth, it must be modifiable in the light of changing circumstances and these modifications must be such that they cannot be predicted. Fifth, each party who uses the concept must be aware of the other uses and thus use it *against* the other uses. Sixth, all the uses of the concept must be claimed by the parties to derive from some exemplar or exemplars whose authority is acknowledged by all. Seventh, the continuous competition enables the original exemplars' achievements to be sustained or developed in optimum fashion.

Among Gallie's original list of essentially contested concepts, education does not appear. However, in an extended analysis using Gallie's criteria, Anthony Hartnett and Michael Naish reach the conclusion that education (or, at the very least, "liberal education") is an essentially contested concept.[69] I will not go through their argument here and instead refer the reader to their work, which shows how education fulfils all seven of Gallie's conditions. Suffice it to say that their argument seems very uncontroversial and very convincing.

Dewey, himself would have found Gallie's argument completely unacceptable. Dewey's ideal community, on which he models his conception of the democratic society, is the scientific community as he conceives it. Because scientific method solves problems, its use in social affairs will tend to eliminate controversy. The resolution of some conflict (note, not the compromise between unbridgeable views), may be tentative because scientific method does not lead us to absolute immutable truths, but this is something very different from unending disputes. The use of the idea of education as essentially contested raises the most serious difficulties for the Deweyian metaphor for the following reason: If education is an essentially contested concept, then educational problems will tend to be ill-defined and thus not amenable to systematic problem solving of the Deweyian sort.[70] This seems to me to be the most telling objection to the use of the Deweyian metaphor with regard to school self-renewal and was illustrated time and time again in our project.

Let me stress that my claim that educational problems are ill-defined must not be construed as a reformulation of the Cohen, March, and Olsen conception of organizations as organized anarchies.[71] Their garbage can model has become one of the most fashionable theories in organizational theory and I will return to it in passing when I relate to the notion of loose coupling in chapter 4. I am arguing here for another claim. Cohen et al. maintain that organizations are often characterized by ambiguous goals, lack of knowledge of relevant technology, and transitory participation in decision-making forums. For this reason, choices are often not the result of problem solving and rational decision making but rather simply "happen" as a result of many chance factors. On the other hand, as previously mentioned, the ill-defined problems I am referring to can be solved rationally (although not systematically, in the Deweyian sense) and often this is precisely what happens. I will try to show this with the aid of a case study in which I continue the theoretical discussion; following that, I will make perhaps the most important theoretical statements of this section.

CASE III: RONIT VISITS AMIR

Amir became headmaster of Naharaim Comprehensive High School in Givon in the second year of our project. Within a short time, he transformed his school into a very exciting institution. As was the case with Hof Rishon, the Naharaim School struck visitors as a happy place. Teachers seemed prepared to work hard, take on extra chores, and meet frequently. There are a number of reasons for this. First, Givon is a rather special town whose social characteristics made it easier to achieve the atmosphere that pervaded the school than would have been possible elsewhere. Givon is a small, relatively isolated community of about 15,000 people. Settlement in Givon was not open to anyone; one had to make an application. Those selected tended to be upper middle-class, university-educated, young, and imbued with a pioneering spirit. Many years have passed since then and Givon has become a town like any other where anyone can go to live. But the original population and spirit still influences its character. It is rather pretty, very clean, and still more middle-class than any other development town in Israel. The teachers in its high school tend to be better educated than those in the average Israeli high school, and because of Givon's isolation, school activity fulfils certain social functions for teachers that it does not do in bigger cities.

All this, of course, has nothing to do with Amir, who only harnessed certain of the energies latent in the faculty, in contrast to his predecessor who had managed to encourage the other side of small-town middle-class life—vicious gossip and cutthroat political activity. Amir exhuded trust, warmth, enthusiasm, and a basically nonauthoritarian stance; his faculty responded to that. He also instituted certain structural changes in the school which are the main subject of this case study. He set up compulsory weekly meetings during school hours for all departments. In Israeli high schools this is very rare. Teachers teach a certain number of hours a week and for the rest of the time need not to be present in the school.[72] Most meetings take place after school hours and therefore department heads will usually limit meetings to once a month. Thus Amir's innovation was quite radical and changed the attitude of school staff to meetings, despite the fact that certain meetings were still held after school hours. In Goodlad's terms, dialogue became pervasive.

Later I will discuss the project staff's contribution to school self-renewal at the Givon school. However, in the context of this case study, Amir's structural innovation is important because of its impact outside Givon. At the beginning of the project's third year, Amir presented his story at a headmasters' meeting. He described his structural innovation, which created much discussion and interest. Of the principals, perhaps the one who became most excited was Ronit, the principal of the Pisga High School in Tel Aviv. She mentioned that she would like to visit the Givon school.

Ronit was also a relatively new school principal. Her school is one of the oldest comprehensive high schools in Israel and had itself been very influential. At one time, the principals of all the secular comprehensive high schools in Tel Aviv had originally been teachers at Ronit's school. When she took over the principalship, she essentially appointed a whole new group of vice-principals and department heads who were "her" people. Yet, because of the long tradition of the school as a comprehensive high school, the transition had been relatively smooth and the new people maintained the school's reputation as a tightly run, efficient organization. In Tel Aviv the school has a reputation as one students enjoy going to. This is largely because a great deal of effort is devoted to counseling and, in general, all sorts of extracurricular activities. This pastoral activity always struck me as rather overpowering. The hidden message that the school faculty transmit in a variety of ways to students and to parents is: "We know what is good for you. So let us deal with things, worry for you, decide for you, and everything will be OK." This reminds me of the classic stereotype of the over-powering mama. In many ways this is a remarkable achievement—"overpowering mama" organizations do not usually have over a thousand kids and a hundred teachers.

The teachers at the school tend to be middle-aged and over, and give the impression of being settled and comfortable about their jobs. Although there was an obvious halo effect going, my continual impression when visiting this school was that it was staffed by red-cheeked, chuckly sort of people. You may ask, why did this school join a project specifically devoted to promoting change and self-renewal? There are a number of reasons for this. First, Ronit herself is an interesting combination of opposites. On the one hand, she radiates a placid cheerfulness. On the other, she tends to become very uptight when she feels that she is not part of something happening on the educational scene. There was no possibility that a project like ours could pass her by. Second, the school faculty were not suspicious of universities as are most, and in fact regarded academics with much awe and respect. This made entry into the school a very easy matter. Third, the school pupil population and the demographic makeup of the area in which the school is situated had changed of late. The school had to come to grips with new phenomena—violence within the school, pimps scouting the girls in the school for new "meat," hooligans breaking into the school, and so on. These changes had not resulted in the faculty drastically redefining its role and methods. Yet the changes un-doubtedly worried the staff and I think that there was a vague, undefined hope that by joining our project, they could make the pimps and violence go away.

I have said that the teachers on the whole seemed settled and comfortable. This must not be misinterpreted as indicating lack of staff tensions and conflict. For most of the staff, teaching was seen as work one did "by the book" and not as a mission. For Ronit and some of her senior staff, however, teaching *is* a mission. They were prepared to spend twenty-four hours a day at the school and expected everyone to feel this way. This caused a lot of resentment. In particular, the representative of the teachers' union at the school was vociferous in his objections to the time teachers were expected to spend at the school during the evenings. Ronit and this teacher certainly didn't get on. Ronit regarded him as a smooth politician who was using the school as a stepping-stone to involvement in city politics.

All this is relevant background to Ronit's decision to go with a group of about fifteen teachers from the school (including the union leader) for a day-long visit to Naharaim. On the one hand, she had heard intriguing things about Naharaim that might be relevant for her school. In addition, the fact that Amir didn't seem to have problems with meetings suggested that his solution might help Ronit solve her problem with teacher resentment in general and her conflict with her union leader in particular.

The visit was planned by Amir and Ronit with great care. The Tel Aviv teachers first participated in a tradition at Naharaim known as "Good morning." (Each homeroom teacher spends fifteen minutes with his/her class before lessons start. These fifteen minutes are not used for administrative purposes but rather for something like reading a poem or listening to a piece of music.) After "Good morning," the teachers met with a group of Givon colleagues who told them a little about their school. They then participated in two department meetings. The history department had sat in on a lesson of one of its members and the meeting was devoted to analyzing the lesson. The Bible study department's meeting could best be described as a Bible study group in itself. After these two meetings, the Pisga teachers split up to take a look at some aspect of the Givon school that interested them personally and then everyone met in Amir's office.

It is here, I think, that Ronit transformed this visit into a very special one. Instead of the usual ritualistic question-and-answer session with the host, she requested all present in turn to say what they had found interesting and whether it was transferable to their school. She set a very practical tone. It became clear after a few minutes that she saw this meeting as one devoted to making tentative decisions to be implemented in the Tel Aviv school. The setting, in the office of another headmaster, with the latter and a few of his teachers participating, created a favorable ambience.

Predictably enough, different teachers were impressed with different aspects of the Givon school. Some concentrated on very specific and, I think it is fair to say, trivial details such as the format of class attendance sheets. Others addressed themselves to more general issues and Ronit and one of the vice-principals pushed for discussion of these, especially the question of weekly department meetings during school hours. During this discussion, one of the teachers—Moshe—spelled out with a great deal of insight the implications of adopting the Givon idea. "We have always concentrated on extracurricular activities. Regular department meetings would mean a change of emphasis, a move to thinking more about pedagogy. Do we want that? That is what we have to decide." His input was, in many ways, the pivot for much future development. Essentially, he redefined the problem and thus the discussion.

Finally, it was decided that the idea of weekly department meetings seemed a positive one and that more thought should be devoted to seeing if this (and other ideas picked up during the visit) was practical. In many cases, such a decision could be a signal for burying the whole idea. This did not occur. The discussion continued. Ronit involved our project staff in it as well as the school faculty. At first, it centered mainly on questions of principle—how would the proposed change affect the school? Was it a good idea? As things progressed, the discussions became more practical. The question became: *how* should the Givon idea be implemented? It was felt that in some departments the idea of weekly meetings would simply increase resentment about excessive time devoted to meetings. Thus Ronit sounded out each department head with regard to his or her attitude to the proposed structural change. The heads of approximately 50 percent of the school departments were enthusiastic and it was decided that, at first, only these departments would be involved. These department heads began meeting as a group to plan the implementation and specifically what they would do in these additional weekly meetings. The change was also "timetabled" into the program for the following year.

If self-renewal is conceived as school dialogue, investigation, and thought resulting in positive changes in school practice, then the Pisga school, at this time at any rate, was to a large extent a self-renewing school. The visit and resulting decision invited the school to grow. This it did by allowing the faculty to see school practice in a new light—Moshe's comment in Amir's office was central here—and creating the possibility that certain potentials that had remained dormant would begin to be exploited. The process of self-renewal was linked with problem-solving activity that could be separated out analytically into three different problems with which the school had to come to grips: Have we something to learn from the Givon school? If so, how should we adopt the idea of getting department members to engage in continual dialogue in our school? Finally, how should we reduce tension on the faculty and with the union leader about meetings? Let us consider these three problems in reverse order.

The last was a well-defined problem of human relations. The problem-solving activity associated with it was not very efficient. Without too much thought, the union leader was invited to join the

Tel Aviv "delegation" visiting Givon. But the problem did not go away; the union leader remained unconvinced and mutual resentments were not alleviated.

The second, regarding continued dialogue among colleagues, was a well-defined problem of a semitechnical nature. It was solved efficiently, as far as I can judge, and the way it was solved paralleled (more or less) the Deweyian five stages. The decision to limit the structural change to certain departments was the result of a rational, systematic checking of various possibilities.

However, neither of these was important in this act of self-renewal. The crucial question was: what had we to learn from the Givon school? Coming to grips with it is *the* indication of a process of self-renewal. What can we say about the problem and its solution? First, it is an ill-defined problem, both from the way it is formulated (nothing is vaguer than the idea of "learning something") and also from the essentially contested nature of education (witness Moshe's remark at the meeting in Amir's office). In fact, it is difficult to decide whether it is an educational, human relations, or technical problem, although it should be remembered that the inspiration for the problem was Amir's presentation at the headmasters' meeting and there he had presented his innovation as a part human relations, part educational one.

Second, it was solved rather impressively, not because of the process of solution, but rather because of the solution itself. This is absolutely crucial. As we have seen, many different solutions can be proposed for ill-defined problems, depending on constraints introduced. Not all solutions will be acceptable to everyone. The particular solution arrived at by the school was impressive because it invited the school to grow. The school could have reached other solutions by processes of problem solving that were as intelligent but would not have led to the possibility of growth. For instance, the school could have reached the conclusion that certain differences between the city of Tel Aviv and the town of Givon made it unlikely that procedures used at Naharaim would work at Pisga.

Finally, the way this problem was solved diverges markedly from the Deweyian description of problem solving. It did not derive from some felt difficulty.[73] On the contrary, it was, in effect, invited. The definition of the problem was in many ways the central aspect of the problem solving. Its solution didn't get rid of a difficulty but rather created new difficulties for the school.

In thinking about the Pisga School story, I am reminded of the work of Larry Laudan in *Progress and Its Problems: Towards a*

Theory of Scientific Growth. As Laudan belongs to the nonevolutionary, noncumulative school in the philosophy and history of science, it may be instructive to pursue this analogy. First, Laudan
conceives of science as an activity aimed at solving problems. He
claims that this view has not been explored before in any detail. He
distinguishes between many different kinds of problems (for example, empirical versus conceptual; solved, unsolved, and anomalous)
and suggests guidelines for deciding whether solving a particular
problem is important for a particular theory. (The assumption here
is that no scientific theory can or does solve all the problems in its
domain.) Of special interest is his definition of an anomalous problem: Whenever an empirical problem has been solved by any
theory, then that problem thereafter constitutes an anomaly for
every theory in the relevant domain which does not also serve that
problem.[74]

Theories belong to research traditions, and the rational
acceptance or rejection of a particular theory is linked to evaluating
the progress of the particular research tradition to which the theory
belongs. A research tradition exhibits certain metaphysical and
methodological commitments. Through its history, a tradition will
be characterized by different theories. One theory may be inconsistent with another that it displaces and yet both may belong to the
same tradition. The progressiveness of a research tradition (that is,
whether it is growing or not) depends on its ability to solve important problems. Laudan distinguishes sharply among three measures
of progressiveness. The first is linked to the theories of the tradition
in vogue at the time progressiveness is being evaluated, and the
extent to which they can solve important problems. The second is
concerned with the general progress of the tradition and is determined by comparing "the adequacy of the sets of theories which
constitute the oldest and those which constitute the most recent
versions of the tradition." The third is concerned with the rate of
progress of the tradition and is concerned with "changes in momen-
tary adequacy of the tradition during any specified time span."[75]
One of Laudan's central theses is that these three measures are
independent of each other. For this reason, if we are interested in
general progress (the second measure), it may be rational to aban-
don a research tradition that is progressive by the first measure for
one that isn't very progressive by the same measure, but is the more
progressive of the two by the third measure.[76]

If we substitute "mode of functioning" for "theory" and
"school" for "research tradition," it seems that what happened to

the Tel Aviv school fits the Laudan description rather well. Going to Givon created awareness of an anomalous problem that the Tel Aviv school decided was important enough to demand solution, although the school was by traditional standards quite a successfully functioning one. This required changes that would lead to new difficulties and, in the short run, to reduced effectiveness, but with high probability of long range self-renewal by Laudan's second measure.

This Laudanian way of looking at school innovation is not only applicable to the case of the Pisga School but, because of the essentially contested nature of education, is a pervasive aspect of school life in general. This is as non-Deweyian as one can get.

Before continuing, I would like to relate to one very powerful criticism of the argument presented in this case.[77] The argument is too strong. It applies both to organizations and individuals. However, we all have met individuals who seem to be better at solving ill-defined problems than others. If the quality of an ill-defined problem solution cannot be predicted because of unforeseeable factors, then how can there be good ill-defined problem solvers?

My counter to this is to reject the claim that some people are good at solving ill-defined problems, in the sense that they consistently seem to solve such problems well. First of all, I think that we will find that their ability is nontransferable from domain to domain. For example, we have all met people who can solve ill-defined problems in, say, business, but marry disastrously (choosing a husband/wife being perhaps *the* ill-defined problem par excellence). Second, and this is related to the first point, good ill-defined problem solvers do not consistently suggest better solutions but rather are quicker than most people at picking up feedback about the poor "solutions" they suggest, after setting them in motion. Such people are better at adjusting in mid-flight, as it were.

If I am correct, this is of great significance. Some people are better than others at accepting and using criticism. Also, people can be taught to improve this ability. *However*, the possibility of picking up feedback quickly is also a function of the problem domain itself. Some situations lend themselves to supplying speedy feedback. Others do not. This may well be the reason why good ill-defined problem solvers in business (where getting feedback may be quite easy) may marry badly (where the unwisdom of their choice may not be apparent for a number of years). If we now consider education, I think we can safely say that in education feedback can be obtained only very slowly, simply because education is such a slow process.

Dewey and the Neutrality of Self-Renewal

One of the most central issues that has been discussed concerning Dewey's theory of growth is related to what I called theme 7—growth as an end in itself. By suggesting that educators should not impose their own external aims on the process of education of a particular child, but rather should encourage growth that would realize the child's specific potential, Dewey seemed to be saying that his philosophy was neutral vis-à-vis direction of growth. Much effort has been devoted to showing that, in fact, Dewey's philosophy contains certain tacit values and that such a value commitment is unavoidable.[78]

If this criticism applies to the metaphor of school self-renewal, then this constitutes a most serious criticism. After all, self-renewal is a *reaction* to values externally imposed on schools; if it turns out that self-renewal is just a more subtle form of imposition, this would undercut its central rationale. Unfortunately, I think that the criticism does apply, on three different levels.

The first concerns the bias toward open channels of communication in self-renewal. The ideal of self-renewal that is hinted at in the literature is nonauthoritarian. It encourages open discussion of issues by all faculty, with everyone's point of view being considered important. In some of the literature, one gets the impression that what is being suggested is that open discussion is either logically entailed by the notion of a school solving problems, or else it is the empirical fact that organizations that are efficient problem solvers are characterized by such discussion. However, neither suggestion holds up under scrutiny. Consider the logical claim first. For a school to solve problems efficiently, only a small subset of its faculty need be the designated problem solvers. To be efficient, they need to learn about certain facts and feelings on the part of other members of the faculty. There is no logical basis for the claim that the only efficient way to get at these facts and feelings is through open discussion.

When we turn to the empirical claim, I must stress that the choice of organizations for which empirical evidence is offered, linking problem-solving efficiency and open discussion, is selective. Normally evidence from business organizations or small group research is analyzed and other, rather more difficult sources of evidence, such as political, military, and judicial systems, tend to be ignored.

No, the theory linking open discussion to self-renewal is a *normative* one, and as such indicates a difficulty for the notion of self-renewal. However, as I have said, this is the least problematic level at which lack of neutrality occurs, with only a tenuous relationship to problem solving.

The second level at which non-neutrality operates takes us back to the argument that self-renewing schools have not been shown to be effective. At that point I rejected the argument. What I essentially showed was that, on a conceptual level, if a school is self-renewing, this is sufficient to ensure it will be effective in the long run. However, I did *not* argue that being self-renewing is *necessary* to effectiveness. If there can be many routes to effectiveness, the basis of the choice of the self-renewal route is normative.

Finally, let us consider non-neutrality on what could be called a metalevel. For instance: can a self-renewing school, according to the DDAE criterion, reach the conclusion that the DDAE criterion must be scrapped or changed? Can an organization that is guided by the theory-in-use which Argyris and Schön call model O-II (the theory that enables the organization to double-loop and deutero-learn), reach the conclusion that model O-II is inapplicable to itself? In one sense, the question is linked to a philosophical question of great complexity—can a person rationally decide to be irrational?[79] However, instead of getting involved in that difficulty, let us assume that the non-neutral commitment to rationality is unavoidable and unproblematic. Nevertheless, rationality has many faces; each change strategy geared to promoting self-renewal chooses one face. *This* choice is the problematic one. How undogmatic and unbiased is it? Does it allow the self-renewing school to choose another face? To be honest, in our project, any school that did not "buy" the DDAE ideology was seen by us as a failure and I rather suspect that this trap is one most self-renewalists would fall into.

CASE IV: PROJECT PRESSURE

At the final principals' meeting, Amir, the principal of the Naharaim School, had this to say:

> When I became principal, I was completely inexperienced. One of the first things I felt was the various pressures being put on me—by the Givon community and municipality, by the Ministry of Education. In addition, our school was part of this project. I could have said that as a new principal I have too many other things on my mind and taken the school out of the

project. I decided that would be a pity and went to the first principals' meetings. Also J—— (the member of the project staff assigned to the school that year) met with me a couple of times. The project constituted another source of pressure, make no mistake about it. On the face of it, everything is open but there *is* a line, and subtle pressures to conform to that line. The pressures from the project I found to be diametrically opposite to those I was subjected to by the municipality and the ministry. Because I felt that the project's line fitted in with my personal philosophy of education, I decided to go along with the project's pressure.

Amir not only illustrates the point I have been making but also highlights the fact that one must not exaggerate the external imposition that seems to be latent in the promotion of school self-renewal. There *is* such imposition and we *are* involved in a contradiction, but it would be overly severe to see that imposition as being as limiting and as demanding as the impositions that developed out of the RD&D paradigm.

Criticism of Freud

This section should parallel the last two sections on Dewey in which I criticized the Deweyian metaphor by using criticisms of Dewey's position itself. However, the parallel is not quite complete. In Freud's case, the problem often derives not from Freud himself, but rather from the way he has been interpreted and misinterpreted. Also, it isn't always clear what he actually said. In this section I will relate to a number of such problematic aspects of Freudian theory that create serious difficulties for the Freudian metaphor—resistance (and transference) and repression.

Let us begin with resistance and transference. My point of departure is Freud's paper "Observations on 'Wild' Psycho-Analysis," which has often been the focus in the philosophical literature on Freud. Consider the following celebrated passage:

It is a long superseded idea, and one derived from superficial appearances, that the patient suffers from a sort of ignorance, and that if one removes this ignorance by giving him information (about the causal connection of his illness with his life, about his experiences in childhood, and so on) he is bound to recover. The pathological factor is not his ignorance in itself, but the root of this ignorance in his *inner resistances*; it was they that first called this ignorance into being, and they still maintain it now. The task of the treatment lies in combating these resistances. Informing the patient of what he does not know because he has repressed it is only one of the necessary preliminaries to the treatment. If knowledge about the unconscious were as important for the patient as people inexperienced in psychoanalysis imagine, listening to lectures or reading books would be enough to cure him. Such measures, however, have as much influence on the symptoms of nervous illness as a distribution of menu-cards in a time of famine has upon hunger. The analogy goes even further than its immediate application; for informing the patient of his unconscious regularly results in an intensification of the conflict in him and an exacerbation of his troubles. Since, however, psycho-analysis cannot dispense with giving this information, it lays down that this shall not be done before two conditions have been fulfilled. First, the patient must, through preparation, himself have reached the neighbourhood of what he has repressed, and secondly, he must have formed a sufficient attachment (transference) to the physician for his emotional relationship to him to make a fresh flight impossible.[80]

From the point of view of *seeing* the consultant-organization relationship as a therapist-patient one, this implies that the former be a very lengthy intensive relationship. The consultant must almost be retained on a semi-permanent basis by the organization and only after a considerable period of time and after some rather active intervention by the consultant should raising to consciousness be attempted.[81]

Many organization consultants have taken this tack, perhaps rightly. However, as the length and intensity of the consulting process increases, it becomes less and less plausible to regard the organization as undergoing self-renewal. Fortunately, Freud provides us with a way out of this dilemma, and strangely enough he does this on the page following the above passage. There it seems that the paper was written by two Freuds. The first Freud wrote the famous passage, while the other Freud's contribution is generally ignored because he is a bit of an embarrassment. After most of the paper has been devoted to criticism of a physician who "[bullied his] patient during [her] first consultation by brusquely telling [her] the hidden things he [inferred] from her story," the other Freud suddenly enters and has this to say:

"Wild" analysts of this kind do more harm to the cause of psychoanalysis than to individual patients. I have often found that a clumsy procedure like this, even if at first it produced an exacerbation of the patient's condition, led to a recovery in the end. Not always, but still often. When he has abused the physician enough and feels far enough away from his influence, his symptoms give way, or he decides to take some step which leads along the path to recovery. The final improvement then comes about 'of itself', or is ascribed to some totally indifferent treatment by some other doctor to whom the patient has later turned. In the case of the lady whose complaint against her physician we have heard, I should say that, despite everything, the 'wild' psycho-analyst did more for her than some highly respected authority who might have told her she was suffering from a 'vasomotor neurosis'. He forced her attention to the real cause of her trouble, or in that direction, and in spite of all her opposition this intervention of his cannot be without some favourable results.[82]

Now, if organizational consulting hasn't the problem of a guild like the International Psycho-Analytical Association, and if interventions in organizations never touch such explosive material as the sexual neuroses of individuals, then "wild" psychoanalysis could be conceived as a reasonable metaphor for organizational consulting. This is the other tack that consultants have taken. Consulting then consists in getting a group of people from an organization together for a few weekend sessions, in some secluded hotel, say, conducting intensive workshops, and then saying goodbye. This is sufficiently minimal to count as promoting self-renewal.

Yet I cannot reconcile the two Freuds. Furthermore, if I had to choose between them, the first Freud seems eminently more reasonable.[83]

CASE V: YOCHANAN AND THE "I CARE" GROUP

Yochanan is the headmaster of a school with a very problematic student population. He has been headmaster for quite some time and the first impression that hit me in meeting him was his tiredness. The school faculty also seemed tired. They had, in effect, given up on the kids they taught. In most teacher discussions, the problem of the students' negative self-concepts was brought up, but the irony was that the teachers seemed to have absorbed these negative concepts themselves. Their self-esteem also seemed low. They were uncomfortable about teaching in a difficult school and seemed to think this reflected on them.

Yochanan's relations with his faculty were very different from those he had with pupils. The latter were characterized by warmth and gentleness, but among the adults in the school he stood totally alone. This was one of the few schools in the project in which there existed a clear him/us orientation. There was total mistrust on both sides. He seemed to believe his teachers were out to "get him," and therefore functioned in accordance with the "divide and rule" tactic. This convinced his staff that he was impossible, resulting in a classic vicious circle. Complaining about Yochanan behind his back was an everyday occurrence in which everyone joined, including the vice-headmaster and department heads.

All this was very sad because, in our view, the school was staffed by some particularly talented teachers whose potential was being wasted. Yochanan himself seemed an intelligent man. Unfortunately, he has a boring monotonic voice and tended to be longwinded. This made it difficult for his staff to really hear him, yet his comments at meetings were often constructive.

After the first few months of the project, our staff decided that we must try to help the school to break out of the vicious circle, even if in this case this required us to be a little more active than our ideology prescribed. We discussed a number of strategies and eventually decided that our best bet was the following: we would suggest to Yochanan that a school "think tank" be established. This would consist of Yochanan, a group of teachers willing to participate, and members of the project staff. This group would try to identify problems in the school and suggest solutions to them. We hoped that our presence would defuse some of the existing explosive tensions, that the group would manage to do constructive work, that in this way the beginnings of some mutual trust between headmaster and teachers might be developed, and perhaps the ground might be prepared for some confrontation of the various felt dissatisfactions in the future.

We were not very enthusiastic with this approach. It avoided coming to grips directly with the school's major problem. Essentially, we ourselves were falling in with the school's syndrome. *We* were not sharing openly with the school faculty. Although we felt that the idea of a "think tank" was intrinsically a good one, we had a hidden motive in suggesting the establishment of such a group. Apart from this seeming contradiction, we had misgivings from the ethical point of view because of the manipulative nature of our strategy. Nevertheless, we saw no viable alternative because we didn't believe that Yochanan and his faculty were prepared for a public discussion of their differences.

We approached Yochanan. He certainly wasn't wildly enthusiastic, but was prepared to go along with the idea. A member of our staff then spoke with a number of teachers and obtained their agreement to participate. The group was not necessarily made up of the most bitterly critical teachers of Yochanan, although they were unavoidably critical, seeing as criticism was completely pervasive in the school. The teachers were also a varied bunch — a vice-principal, a pedagogic coordinator, two counselors, a department head, and two "ordinary" teachers. The one thing they did have in common was that they were not totally disillusioned and thus were very enthusiastic about the idea.

The project staff now asked all prospective participants to suggest topics or problems to be raised at the first meetings. The topics suggested by the teachers were teacher morale, definitions of roles and responsibilities, and the organization of the teachers' energy in such a way that it would be effective. Yochanan suggested as topics discipline in the school and the relationship of the pupils to the school. When Yochanan learned of the teachers' topics, he indicated that teachers' feelings did not seem to him a suitable topic for a "think tank."

Clearly, the first meeting was going to be difficult. It took place one evening a few weeks later. According to the project's "line," we indicated that we would not chair the meeting, but rather one member of the project staff would participate simply as one of the group. Yochanan chaired the meeting. It began rather mildly. However, when the question of identifying problems became the topic under discussion, one of the teachers "let rip." She expressed some highly critical comments about the way Yochanan ran meetings in general and this meeting in particular. The result was a tense, argumentative "dialogue" in which all those present contributed. There was much defensive talk and a lot of frustration felt around the table.

The project staff member present was caught off-guard by this development. Because so much was said at the school behind people's backs, he had not expected teachers to interpret the idea of a think tank as an opportunity for confrontation. His responses were of two sorts. He once tried to point out that people seemed to be talking across one another, therefore missing valuable suggestions being made. He also noted that a second school in the project had had a teacher think tank for a number of years and that perhaps this group could learn something from them.

Eventually things calmed down and after a neutral sort of summing up, a follow-up meeting was arranged. The second meeting was held and subsequent meetings the following year. The group was expanded (perhaps as a result of a visit by two members of the original group to the other school with a "think tank"). The activity was even given a special name—the group decided to call itself the "I Care" group. However, at no further meeting was the real problem of the school — the vicious circle syndrome — ever confronted. Yochanan, by his actions and comments during the following months, made it quite clear that he thought the teachers had stepped out of line; that in his view, this was particularly reprehensible because a respected outsider (the project staff member) had been present, and thus the teachers had been washing dirty linen in public; and that all future meetings of the "I Care" group or, for that matter, any other similar group would be run on his terms and in accordance with an agenda acceptable to him. The school continued in the project for another year and a half and then Yochanan decided to discontinue membership.

The project staff went through much soul-searching about Yochanan and his school. Were we to blame? Could we have handled things better? If we had done such-and-such, would things have turned out differently? No doubt we would do some things differently today. However, one of the things we *could* have done I am almost certain would *not* have changed matters at all. A staff member highly experienced in leading group discussions aimed at disclosing conflicts and hidden agendas could have sat in or even conducted the first "think tank" meeting. To believe that such an alternative would have made a difference is simplistic. Yochanan and his teachers were simply not ready to have their vicious circle raised to consciousness. Perhaps if we had worked at this intensively and actively over a long period, we might have effected some changes. However, as I have stressed above, such an approach restructures the organization-consultant relationship in such a way that the term self-renewal becomes inappropriate. I will return to this possibility in chapter 6.

Repression and the Freudian Metaphor

Let us begin by returning to the first of the two lengthy passages quoted from Freud and, in particular, to the following section:

> It is a long superseded idea, and one derived from superficial appearances, that the patient suffers from a sort of ignorance, and that if one removes this ignorance by giving him information he is bound to recover. The pathological factor is not his ignorance in itself, but the

root of this ignorance in his *inner resistances*; it was they that first called this ignorance into being, and they still maintain it now.

It seems to me that this central tenet of Freud's theory is the one that is least emphasized in the popular adoption of his ideas today. Raising to consciousness is deemed valuable in all cases, whereas for Freud, the problematic aspects of the unconscious are those that the patient has, so to speak, driven into the unconscious because they are too painful to deal with consciously. Now it may be that it is all to the good to raise such experiences to consciousness through suitable therapy (although even this is not an uncontroversial claim). However, this tells us nothing about the advisability of raising other matters to awareness. Consider the kind of knowledge that Michael Polanyi has called *tacit knowledge,* for example, the knowledge we have of riding a bicycle.[84] When this sort of knowledge is raised to the level of awareness, *new* problems are created for us that may in fact hinder us more than help us to function effectively. Perhaps becoming aware of the specific actions we perform when bicycling would lead to an accident.

What about the lack of awareness that change agents trying to promote organizational self-renewal are concerned with? It seems very likely that these can often be *seen* more profitably *as* examples of tacit knowledge à la Polanyi than as organizational analogues of Freudian-type repressions. In our project, the most obvious example was the schools' difficulty (mentioned in chapter 1) with feedback. In this case, we saw that self-consciousness about school functioning can create more difficulties than it solves.

Not only does the awareness gained become a problem, but also the process of gaining such awareness can be one that schools have difficulty in dealing with, where the difficulty cannot be seen as parallel to the kind of resistances Freud was referring to. I am reminded of a "confession" made by one of the headmasters at the end of our project about the drifting-in diagnosis of our staff which, remember, was ostensibly geared to *helping* schools. I think his words should be posted on the wall of all school consultants to be looked at whenever they become too sure of their own importance:

> When R—— and L—— [the project staff members who were assigned to this school] started their diagnosis, to be quite honest I didn't know what to do with them. They would arrive and I felt I had to help them, show them things. But I never knew what to show them. It really worried me for a while. I

remember one day R—— arrived and we walked round the
school. We went into the manual training section. R——
struck up a conversation with one of the teachers. He seemed
to be enjoying himself, so with great relief I left him there and
rushed back to my office to work. I had found something for
him to do.

Who Needs Dewey and Freud?

Before concluding, I must ask one final question that in many
ways is *the* question. Perhaps we do not need the Deweyian and
Freudian metaphors at all? Perhaps one can conceive of self-
renewing schools in ways that depart radically from these
metaphors? If that were the case, this whole chapter becomes a
criticism of the actual historical roots of self-renewal but not of
self-renewal itself.

However this is not so. To borrow a famous remark—if Dewey
and Freud had not existed, someone would have had to invent
them. Their metaphors, if interpreted very generally, are essential
components of any theory of self-renewal. Let us reverse the direction of the discussion. Instead of showing how Dewey's and
Freud's theories led to the notion of self-renewal, I will try to show
that the idea of self-renewal implies certain general theses which
are in fact exemplified by the Deweyian and Freudian metaphors.

First to set aside the trivial part of this claim. I have already
argued that the idea of self-renewal is related definitionally to
theme 6 of the Deweyian metaphor—that growth is closely related
to an increasing ability to control one's environment and thus to an
increased capacity for problem solving. The question is, what can
we discover in addition to this? I will consider two aspects of self-
renewal. First, the idea is a reaction to innovations externally imposed on the school. The promotion of self-renewal makes sense
only if we conceive of schools as relatively autonomous institutions.
Now, for any organism (and thus, figuratively, any organization) to
be autonomous, it must be self-conscious, for only through self-
awareness can an organism be considered to be in control of its own
destiny. Self-renewal is thus an idea that almost forces us to adopt
the Freudian notion of consciousness raising.

The second important aspect of self-renewal is more subtle.
The promotion of self-renewal is considered as an example of
planned change. For self-renewal to occur, somebody and some
group of persons outside the schools must be prepared to invest

time, energy, and money into efforts designed to change schools into self-renewing organizations. Their investment is not a blind gamble, but rather time, energy, and money invested in a *plan* whose results are somewhat predictable. If this were not so, we could not be talking about planned change.

Now, any rational plan by an investor for change must be based on one of two (tacit) theories linking the investment to the change: either change is a *mysterious* event which is nevertheless predictable under certain conditions, or it is simply programmable. Let us consider an example of a theory of mysterious but predictable change; investments designed to encourage art are usually of this type. When money is provided to encourage young artists, or special conditions are created for artists to work in, the investor essentially is saying, "We do not understand the marvelous, mysterious way in which great works of art are produced, but we can provide certain external conditions that can help the artist to create. If artists do not have money worries and if their surroundings are congenial and if they can be reasonably certain their art will be seen, heard, or read, then their creativity will be stimulated. Therefore, if we enable this group of young artists to obtain that security and those surroundings, then perhaps our investment will produce some great art." Investors believe they can predict outcomes despite lack of knowledge of mechanism.

In contrast, a simply programmable theory of change links an investment to a result through a specified mechanism. It must be simply programmable because we are talking about *planned* change. The proposed specified mechanism must be capable of translation into a flow chart that is quasi-linear, thus making control possible, and has only a small number of feedback loops, thus limiting complexity.

Now, the promotion of self-renewal in schools involves two distinct stages in the linking of the investment to the desired outcome. The outcome is *not* self-renewal itself, which is surely only a *means* to more innovative, efficient, or effective schools. The two stages are the work of the change agent in helping the school become self-renewing and the process of self-renewal itself. I am here only concerned with the second. The question is, what sort of implicit theory can be allowed for this process? Does self-renewal entail mysterious but predictable change or simply programmable change? I would argue for the latter, because self-renewal is conceived of in terms of increased capacity for problem solving. If self-renewal were dependent on, say, a democratic climate, one could conceive of a theory of mysterious, predictable change linking climate and innovativeness. However, the notion of increased capacity for problem solving seems to invite specification of a process, and this leads naturally to a simply programmable description.

Let us now return to Dewey. Dewey's five steps are a classic example of a description of problem solving that can be translated into a quasi-linear flow chart with but one feedback loop. One could not ask for anything much simpler than that. Thus although the specific details of Dewey's five-stage conception of problem solving are not necessary components of a theory of self-renewal, the Deweyian conception does exemplify something—simple programmability—which is an essential part of any self-renewal theory (including a theory such as that of Argyris and Schön—see appendix B). Furthermore, the two main criticisms of the Deweyian metaphor presented in this chapter—that only the formal trappings of problem solving can be institutionalized and that education is an essentially contested concept, which implies that educational problems are ill-defined and therefore not solved through systematic procedures—are actually criticisms of simple programmability and only happened to be leveled at Dewey because the theories of self-renewal in schools were so clearly based on the Deweyian metaphor.

SUMMARY

In this chapter, I have tried to indicate some of the serious conceptual problems associated with the idea of school self-renewal. This idea derives from the metaphors that I have called Deweyian problem solving metaphor and Freudian consciousness raising metaphor, and the conceptual problems caused by the inappropriateness of these metaphors. School self-renewal entails holism, and a reasonable holistic position prohibits transferring problem solving and consciousness raising from the individual to the organizational level. There are also other difficulties with these metaphors. Educational problems do not lend themselves to systematic problem solving. Consciousness raising, when appropriate, requires intervention that is so extended that the school cannot really be considered to be self-renewing. Also, in many cases, consciousness raising creates more problems than it solves, as Freud himself was aware. Finally, self-renewal, ostensibly a response to the external imposition of solutions onto schools, is itself not completely innocent in this regard.

One thing that has been implied throughout the discussion, is that the conceptual objections to school self-renewal are related to the latter as part of a public policy of planned educational change. I have not argued that there are no cases of schools undergoing self-renewal spontaneously. It is this possibility that I address in the next chapter.

3

Self-Renewal
and Open Belief Systems

The argument I will be presenting in this chapter can be sum-marized very simply:

1. The idea of organizational self-renewal necessarily entails an *open* belief system.
2. All open belief systems have certain properties in common vis-à-vis their *primary* beliefs.
3. The primary beliefs characteristic of schools do not have these properties.
4. Open belief systems change in a specific stipulatable way.
5. School belief systems do not change in this way.
6. Therefore, schools can never be self-renewing organizations.

OPEN BELIEF SYSTEMS

The concept of a belief system has been used in many different disciplines and subdisciplines — for example, in philosophical an-thropology, especially in its concern with the difference between modern scientific thought and nonscientific "primitive" thought; in the philosophy of education; in ethnographic studies of teaching; in political science; in the psychology of attitude formation; and in sociology.[1] I rely heavily on Milton Rokeach's discussion of the term in *The Open and Closed Mind*[2] and Thomas Green's discus-sion in *The Activities of Teaching*[3] because they are, to the best of my knowledge, the most extensive as yet undertaken. Rokeach's analysis has been very influential in many different disciplines, while Green's analysis (Rokeach-based) has the advantage of philo-sophical rigor.

Nobody holds beliefs totally independent of all other beliefs. Beliefs always occur in sets or groups. First, if A believes Q, we will always be able to find a different belief, R, that A must also believe. Green offers the following example: if an American believes some of his ancestors immigrated from Scotland (Q), he must also believe that other people immigrated from Scotland (R). Q and R are related but different beliefs. Second, if A believes Q, he will also believe certain things about his belief; that is, that Q is important or very well established, and so forth.[4]

Thus a person's beliefs are always parts of a belief system. Rokeach has suggested different ways of viewing the organization of a person's belief system, of which we will consider two. First is the degree of isolation of beliefs from each other within a belief system. In many cases, an observer can see that two beliefs are intrinsically related, although the person who subscribes to these beliefs denies the connection. In such a case they must belong to two subsystems of the belief system that are isolated from one another. This clearly emphasizes that the relationship between different beliefs in a belief system are not necessarily logical. In many cases people's beliefs are related psychologically but are logically contradictory.[5]

Second, Rokeach conceives of three layers of beliefs: a central region containing one's core or primitive beliefs, an intermediate region representing one's beliefs about the nature of authority and the people who line up with authority, and a peripheral region representing the beliefs that fill in the details of one's world map.[6]

Of particular interest is the idea of core or (in Rokeach's terminology) primitive beliefs. These include "specific content about the physical and social world, the latter including the person's self-concept and his conception of others."[7] One's primitive beliefs can usually be identified rather easily because they are either totally private or else one is confident that virtually everyone else believes in them. In regard to the latter, "If such a primitive belief could be seriously challenged it would probably be extremely upsetting, because I have never expected it to be a subject for controversy."[8]

Some persons' belief systems can be described as closed, others as open. How can we characterize these properties of belief systems? In the literature, two different tacks have generally been taken. The first may be called a *static* one. An attempt is made to characterize structural properties of open and closed belief systems and also to stipulate certain typical beliefs of these two different systems. Rokeach's work is a good example. He suggests a long list of properties. For example, in open belief systems: (a) the formal content of beliefs about authority is that the latter is not absolute and people are not to be evaluated according to their agreement or disagreement with such authority; (b) the specific content of primitive beliefs is that the world we live in or the situation at a particular moment is a friendly one; (c) there is communication (as opposed to isolation) within and between subsystems.[9] One of the most striking aspects of this static approach is that it often unwittingly lays bare the normative nature of the concept of an open belief system. This is especially clear in considering (b). Belief in a friendly world is a positive quality or value and therefore it is "reasonable" to associate it with openness. However, in many cases one can maintain one's belief that a situation is friendly only by increasing isolation between other beliefs that, if associated, would cause much pain. Nevertheless, despite such considerations, this approach can be very useful.

Second, one can characterize open belief systems as dynamic, following in the tradition of Karl Popper.[10] Openness of belief systems is related to their openness to change. Belief systems are open to the extent that they are receptive to rational criticism. Belief systems are closed to the extent that beliefs are changed only as a result of some change of party line. As Green says:

> When beliefs are held without regard to evidence, or contrary to evidence, or apart from good reasons or the canons for testing reasons and evidence, then I shall say they are held non-evidentially. It follows immediately that beliefs held non-evidentially cannot be modified by introducing evidence or reasons. They cannot be changed by rational criticism. The point is embodied in a familiar attitude: Don't bother me with facts; I have made up my mind.[11]

What are the implications of these two approaches for the concerns of this book? In the section that follows I will discuss the static approach and how this links up with the notion of school self-renewal; then in the next section, the dynamic approach and its relationship to self-renewal will be considered.

SCHOOL BELIEF SYSTEMS AND PRIMARY BELIEFS

Before I can develop the theses, two further ideas or concepts must be explicated.

The Range of Primary Beliefs

I am going to present an idea that is, I think, intuitively clear, but that is extremely difficult to define rigorously. Therefore I wish to use a deliberately vague word — "sorts." In any belief system there are many different sorts of beliefs; it is thus divided up into many different "domains." Now, although Rokeach does not address this point, his analysis implies that in closed belief systems a greater number of domains will have primary beliefs associated with them than in open belief systems; in other words, the *range* of primary beliefs in closed belief systems will be greater than in open belief systems. I suggest this because primary beliefs are those we are not prepared to give up and open belief systems are characterized, at least in part, by their readiness to lay beliefs open to review.

School Belief Systems

The belief system of every adult in a school contains a set of *school-relevant beliefs*—beliefs about educational values, educational practices, about how schools should be administered and how a particular school is, about the people working in the school and about the pupils studying in it, and so on. This set also contains, of course, some beliefs about the content of what is taught in the school. The school belief system will consist of the overlap between the sets of school-relevant beliefs of the majority of adults in the school. It expresses the common knowledge, ideology, and pedagogical theories, what the school staff are trying to pass on to the students and how they think they are doing so. It does not include the school-relevant beliefs of either the students or their parents, which may or may not be similar to those of the school staff. It also ignores the vast number of school-relevant issues about which there is controversy in the school. Most schools have, I guess, a far larger belief system than would seem likely according to the usual accounts of schooling that stress conflict.

Now to the argument: According to the definition of self-renewal we have been concerned with, the belief systems of self-renewing schools must be open, in the static sense at least. This is a conceptual claim. The fact that the range of primary beliefs (that is, beliefs of central importance that need to remain unchallenged for individual or group psychological stability) in open belief systems will be narrow, links up directly with the idea that self-renewing schools are continually questioning aims and methods with a view to improvement. In such schools, very little is unquestionable and this is precisely what is meant by a narrow range of primary beliefs.

We are thus led to the question: Can schools really have only a small number of primary beliefs? I have already indicated that my answer is no, for two reasons. One is relatively straightforward. The second entails a discussion of a number of theoretical anthropological concepts. Let us get the simpler matter out of the way before turning to the more complex second reason.

Means and Ends in Schools

Among the beliefs Rokeach gives as examples of primary beliefs are those directly associated with a person's self-concept. In this he is clearly correct. No healthy person (and open belief systems are supposed to signify psychological health) can continually question the nature of his or her self. If I can be permitted the anthropomorphic approach mentioned in chapter 2, I would argue that no "healthy" organization can continually question its own identity. Therefore every organization's belief system will include certain primary beliefs concerning that identity. However, there are organizations and there are organizations.

Consider the following thought experiment. Imagine you have been told these two stories:

1. A manufacturing firm that makes games branches out and begins to manufacture computer games. Slowly its line of ordinary games becomes less and less important and is eventually dropped. The firm now branches out and begins to make other computer software in addition to games. Over time the computer games become a sideline and are eventually dropped.
2. A certain school that espouses "open education" has been established. The staff believes that kids learn best through play. Play and games and freedom dominate the school curriculum. At some point the school buys a computer that is used as a new resource for play. Kids who want to experiment with it—program it, do calculations, create their own visual displays, and so on. Over time the school has become a totally computer-dominated institution. All instruction is now computer-based. Pupil achievement is continually recorded and monitored by computer because of the staff's commitment to accountability.

Which of these two stories seems more believable? Assuming both are true and that both the firm and the school solved the technical problem of developing the skills necessary to make the various transitions described in the stories — which of the two staffs had more difficulty adjusting to the changes?

Surely, most would agree that the first story is more believable and the school's staff in the second story would have more difficulty adjusting to the changes. Yet both stories are formally (and even substantively, to a certain extent) very alike—an organization concerned to promote a certain goal chooses a means to achieve it, then decides to substitute yet another means thought to be better or more efficient.

Many suggestions could be offered to explain the hypothesized difference. Most of these would contain an implied criticism of schools and their staffs (business people are go-getters, teachers are conservative and unimaginative). My suggestion does not imply criticism but rather stresses an important property of education as a process, which leads us back to primary beliefs. Putting it simply, in schools means and ends are more tightly coupled than in the commercial world, at least on the level of what Argyris and Schön call espoused theory. By this I mean that in educational institutions, far more than in many others, means *necessarily* embody values. For example, teachers may subscribe to group work, not because they believe pupils learn certain specific material better in this way, but rather because they believe human beings should work in groups. Of course, this can also occur in a commercial firm. A particular method of increasing profit may be rejected because it is considered dishonest. Or, to take another sort of example, in the United States an automobile manufacturer could not easily drop this "line" (making automobiles) because, for one thing, automobiles are such very powerful symbols of what America is all about (whereas in Israel, for example, this line was once dropped). Yet in most cases, no particular set of actions focused on achieving the firm's objectives is going to be sanctified. If one course proves inefficient, it will in all likelihood be scrapped; otherwise, the firm's behavior will be regarded as irrational. Thus Robert Merton in "Bureaucratic Structure and Personality" talks of "adherence to the rules, originally conceived as a means [becoming] transformed into an end-in-itself; there occurs the familiar process of *displacement of goals*." [12] This appears in the section of his essay that deals with the dysfunctions of bureaucracy. In schools, however, this is neither clearly dysfunctional nor atypical. This is why the story of a school going from "open education" to "computer-based instruction and accountability" is not particularly believable. It entails more than a change of methods but rather a basic change of values.

The basic values of an organization define its identity and are thus among the primary beliefs of the organization. Therefore, the tight coupling of means and ends in schools will result in a greater range of its affairs being directly tied in with its primary beliefs than in most other organizations. Again, let me stress, we are talking of a continuum and not a dichotomy. What commercial corporations manufacture, produce, or sell *can* embody deeply held values as well as being means to creating profit. However, in schools, by their very nature, this must occur more often.

The Nonevaluation of Instructional Activities

Second, schools tend to have a relatively wide range of primary beliefs for a cluster of reasons derived from certain sociological and anthropological considerations. I am especially influenced by John Meyer's and Brian Rowan's article, "The Structure of Educational Organizations," [13] and to a lesser extent, by another article by Meyer, "The Effects of Education as an Institution." [14]

Meyer and Rowan pose as a central question why educational organizations "take on a great deal of control over the ritual classifications of their curriculum, students, and teachers," and yet do not really control their instructional activities or outputs.[15] By this they mean that tremendous energy is expended in matters like making sure that schools of a particular type offer courses in certain topics that are considered essential in a legitimate school of that type; diplomas of a particular type are only given to students who have taken the required courses; teachers have the necessary diplomas that prove that they have studied those things teachers are required to study. On the other hand, almost no effort is expended in supervising what is actually taught in particular courses and in checking what students have really learned or whether teachers can really teach. (This is presumably why Meyer and Rowan talk of *ritual* classification of curriculum, students, and teachers.) As they put it:

> The resources [schools receive] continue to be focused on the instructional aspects of the system, even though achievement of instructional goals is not measured. . . . It is as if society allocates large sums of money and large numbers of children to the schools, and the schools in turn allocate these funds and children to a relatively un-

controlled and uninspected classroom. All this seems to be done in a great act of ritual faith.[16]

Their article attends to the two aspects of the question more or less separately. Control is imposed on ritual classification because

education functions in society as a legitimating *theory of knowledge* defining certain types of knowledge as extant and as authoritative. It also functions as a *theory of personnel,* defining categories of persons who are to be treated as possessing these bodies of knowledge and forms of authority.[17]

In other words, education is less important as a socializing agency that passes on certain skills, values, and knowledge to students than as an institution that affects society by representing and legitimating both a particular typology of knowledge and a particular social role structure valued by the society. By attending to ritual classifications, schools make these classifications highly visible and imbue them with great potency, thus both presenting and legitimating them.

This aspect of the argument seems very convincing. However, I have problems with the second aspect—the reasons Meyer and Rowan offer for the lack of supervision of actual instructional activity. Putting it crudely, there are four such reasons: (1) Lack of control is more prevalent in the United States than in countries with more centralized educational systems; in the latter, control is achieved through national examinations and/or inspection systems. (2) Control is avoided because it would deflect attention from the ritual classifications which are more important. (3) Control is avoided because in this way teachers are coopted as supporters of the system and the latter's legitimating powers are greatly increased. (4) Control of instructional activities would uncover all sorts of inconsistencies and difficulties.

There are at least three weaknesses in this line of argument. First, I think Meyer and Rowan underestimate the pervasiveness of the phenomenon they are describing. Lack of supervision of instructional activities occurs in centralized systems too, despite national examinations and inspections. These are often empty rituals instigated to pay lip service to the myth of central government's efficacy. Second, at least in reasons 3 and 4, Meyer's and Rowan's explanations do not go far enough. All avoidance of supervision and control coopts those being "let off the hook." All control uncovers inconsistencies. Yet, despite this, in other organizations control is more prevalent. There is something about schools that encourages the relinquishing of control for the reasons 3 and 4 that Meyer and Rowan give, but is not found in other organizations in which these reasons do not justify giving up control. Meyer and Rowan give no hint at what this might be. Third, there is a basic ambiguity in the notion of "instructional activities." On the one hand, these can be conceived very narrowly as those activities geared to teaching the skills and knowledge supposedly necessary for students to be assigned to the correct ritual classifications. On the other hand, such activities can be conceived of as teaching values, teaching the hidden curriculum, and so on. Now, it is never clear which of these two different conceptions of instructional activities Meyer and Rowan are referring to. If it is to the narrow one, then their analysis is probably correct. However, it is then not particularly interesting, because they are simply ignoring most of what goes on in the classroom.

And what if they are concerned with the wider interpretation of the notion of "instructional activities"? In that case, we are led to perhaps the most important criticism of their analysis. They assume that there could be only two reasons for not evaluating X—either X is not considered important or its evaluation is thought likely to open up a Pandora's box. I would argue that on the wider interpretation of instructional activities, there are many other reasons, especially these: First, I may consider evaluation a waste of time because I am almost completely certain of the outcome before I even start; second, I may fear that the act of evaluating X to find out if it contains Y may actually destroy Y. Let us consider each possibility in turn.

A good example of the first reason could be the fact that no playwright would consider it necessary to check every performance of a play by every group of actors to ensure that it is being done properly. This is partially because it is accepted that different performers will interpret a work in different ways. However, there is a much more important and simple reason: *the play has a text.* Any human activity that is performed according to a text, score, or some equivalent, is not going to require external supervision each time it is performed.[18] Now consider teaching. The lecture room next to my university office is always uncomfortably hot, and thus most lecturers using this room leave the door open. Over the years I have been able to observe the behavior of hundreds of lecturers from scores of disciplines teaching a variety of subjects to classes ranging from five to fifty students. On almost all occasions I have seen the following: a lecturer standing talking and/or writing on the board, and students sitting quietly writing. Is it too fanciful to impute this behavioral regularity, to use Sarason's term, to the existence of a "text" which these different "actors" are working with? Or, as Perrow puts it in more prosaic language:

> Think of . . . fully unobstrusive [controls as] the control of the cognitive premises underlying action. . . . The control of premises, while far more difficult to achieve, is even more effective [than direct controls and bureaucratic controls]. Here the subordinate *voluntarily* restricts the range of stimuli that will be attended to . . . and the range of alternatives that would be considered.[19]

Now if this is correct, where do such texts come from in the case of schools? It is too glib to use another theatrical metaphor and link everything back to the "roles" of teacher and pupil within the school's social structure. I have witnessed such astonishingly subtle similarities between teachers in such varied settings, similarities that go so far beyond what is entailed in the role definitions of teacher and pupil that it seems clear to me that something deeper must be going on. To identify this I must digress with an exposition of some aspects of Durkheim's world of the sacred and the profane, and of Geertz's world of Balinese cockfights and what he calls, significantly, "deep play."

Durkheim and Geertz

Over the last decade there has been a gratifying resurge of interest in the work of Emile Durkheim and particularly in his magnum opus *The Elementary Forms of the Religious Life*.[20] The work of Bernstein, Bloor, Douglas, and Schwartz comes to mind immediately.[21] All these authors stress that, despite the fact that the *Elementary Forms* deals with the origins of religious thought in primitive tribes, Durkheim's central thesis is generally relevant to all society and the human mind. Mary Douglas puts this magnificently well:

> Between [Marx and Freud] another intermediate span is necessary that Durkheim's insights were ready to supply: the social determination of culture. It should have become the central critical task of philosophy in this century to integrate these three approaches. If Durkheim's contribution was accepted only in a narrow circle, his

friends have to admit frankly that it was his own fault. When he entered that great debate he muffed his cue. He could have thrown upon the screen X-rays just as disturbing as either of the others. . . . Begging us to turn round and listen urgently to ourselves, his speech would have disturbed the complacency of Europe as deeply as the other two. But instead of showing us the social structuring of our minds, he showed us the minds of feathered Indians and painted aborigines. With unforgiveable optimism he declared that his discoveries applied to them only. He taught that we have a more genial destiny. For this mistake our knowledge of ourselves has been delayed by half a century.[22]

Durkheim was concerned with the notion of a religious attitude. This is *not* characterized necessarily as the belief in the supernatural, but rather as the tendency to classify all things into two classes or opposed groups, which we can designate by the words *sacred* and *profane* (although it has been suggested that *mundane* might capture Durkheim's meaning better than *profane*). How is one to identify the distinguishing characteristics of sacred things? Durkheim rejects a hierarchical explanation (that is, that the sacred is simply superior to the profane) and this leads him to the claim that what is special about the sacred/profane distinction is that it is *absolute*:

In all the history of human thought there exists no other example of two categories of things so profoundly differentiated or so radically opposed to one another; . . . the sacred and the profane have always and everywhere been conceived by the human mind as two distinct classes, as two worlds between which there is nothing in common. The forces which play in one are not simply those which are met with in the other, but a little stronger; they are of a different sort.[23]

This absoluteness supplies us with a visible sign by which the distinction can be recognized:

Since the idea of the sacred is always and everywhere separated from the idea of the profane in the thought of men, and since we picture a sort of logical chasm between the two, the mind irresistibly refuses to allow the two corresponding things to be confounded, or even to be merely put in contact with each other; for such a promiscuity, or even too direct a contiguity, would contradict too violently the dissociation of these ideas in the mind. The sacred thing is *par excellence* that which the profane should not touch, and cannot touch with impunity.[24]

Of course, if this idea is carried to its logical conclusion, we are led to absurdities and Durkheim is aware of this. So at this point he backtracks a bit:

> To be sure, this interdiction cannot go so far as to make all communication between the two worlds impossible; for if the profane could in no way enter into relations with the sacred, this latter could be good for nothing. But, in addition to the fact that this establishment of relations is always a delicate operation in itself, demanding great precautions and a more or less complicated initiation, it is quite impossible, unless the profane is to lose its specific characteristics and become sacred after a fashion and to a certain degree itself.[25]

The reader is probably getting some idea where this last idea leads us vis-à-vis the lack of inspection of classroom activities in schools. However, before forging the link, let us digress further and consider Clifford Geertz's article "Deep Play: Notes on the Balinese Cockfight," an extended and sensitive analysis of an important part of Balinese social life. Through this analysis he shows the interrelationships between Balinese social structure and values, on the one hand, and the cockfight, on the other. The details are not important here; what *is* important is the general question that Geertz poses—what is the significance of cultural forms like the cockfight? He rejects the functionalist answer that the cockfight reinforces social structure and values.[26] In his view we are involved here with social semantics and not social mechanics. In effect, he proposes a new perspective from which to look at cultural forms, that is, to treat them "as texts, as imaginative works built out of social materials." In other words, the cockfight can best be understood by comparing it to art forms in our society and to what the latter achieve for us. In Geertz's own words:

> As any art form . . . the cockfight renders ordinary, everyday experiences comprehensible by presenting it in terms of acts and objects which have had their practical consequences removed and been reduced (or, if you prefer, raised) to the level of sheer appearances, where their meaning can be more powerfully articulated and more exactly perceived. What [the cockfight] does is what, for other peoples with other temperaments and other conventions, *Lear* and *Crime and Punishment* do; it catches up these themes—death, masculinity, rage, pride, loss, beneficence, chance—and, ordering them into an encompassing structure, presents them in such a way as to throw into relief a particular view of their essential nature. . . . An

image, fiction, a model, a metaphor, the cockfight is a means of expression; its function is neither to assuage social passions nor to heighten them . . . but, in a medium of feathers, blood, crowds, and money, to display them; . . . it provides a metasocial commentary upon the whole matter of assorting human beings into fixed hierarchical ranks and organizing the major part of collective existence around that assortment. Its function, if you want to call it that, is interpretive: *it is a Balinese reading of Balinese experience; a story they tell themselves about themselves.* . . . *Enacted and reenacted, so far without end, the cockfight enables the Balinese, as, read and reread, Macbeth enables us, to see a dimension of his own subjectivity.* . . . Societies, like lives, contain their own interpretations.[27]

From our point of view, perhaps Geertz's most important points are contained in the two italicized sentences. Here he makes explicit the dramatic metaphor he is using. It is by being "enacted and reenacted" that the "Balinese reading of Balinese experience" can be seen as a *text*. Let me now try to relate Durkheim's and Geertz's ideas to the problem of lack of control of instructional activities in schools. I would argue that, in an analogous way, schooling is in our society a cultural form that can be treated as a text in which we render to ourselves a reading of some part of our experience ("we" being not only pupils and teachers, but all society). However, the relevant aspect of experience here is, of course, not identical to that of the cockfight for the Balinese. Rather, I suggest that the relevant aspect is our conception of the sacred. Education is not just a theory of knowledge and personnel presented in order to be legitimated, as Meyer and Rowan would have it, but rather a story we tell ourselves about *what being scared means for us.*

Why should we assume a link between education and the sacred? In religious societies (in the conventional sense) the link is self-evident. But even in secular societies there is a sacred domain in Durkheim's sense, and thus the relationship between education and the sacred remains. Schools are the institutions concerned with the passing on of hallowed traditions and the values and knowledge most dear to society. And they are passing these on to the young who are seen in modern society, as in many other societies, as exemplifying purity and innocence.

This view of education makes comprehensible many puzzling phenomena. First, it suggests a source for the texts that determine so many behavioral regularities in schools. As Durkheim points out, the ways in which we can approach the sacred are very limited. We must be very diffident, careful, and respectful. Thus if the trans-action between teacher and pupil is a sacred one, there is not much room for variation in carrying it out. In addition, all adults carry in our heads a memory of the text of that transaction, a memory of a performance with sacred dimensions that we participated in thou-sands of times as children. No wonder that those of us who become teachers tend to reenact the same text rather than adopt the new texts we learn in teacher training. And no wonder that those of us who become parents prepare our children for a similar reenact-ment. For most adults, their years at school are not a vague memory but rather a memory that can and often does force itself into the immediate present.

I am reminded of a conversation I once had with my uncle and his son. He began reminiscing about his high school days. What was so striking was that as his teachers rose up one by one and paraded before him in his memory, he reacted toward these images with the same awe and respect he had felt fifty years before, despite the fact that in the meantime he had become highly successful, owning and managing three flourishing businesses. Also, because both his son and I had studied at the same high school, when men-tioning a teacher's name, he would ask: "Did you have him?" de-spite a time difference of thirty and forty years. His memories of his teachers had a timeless vitality.

Conceiving of education as a text telling us about the sacred also explains our ambivalence toward it. Durkheim tells us the sacred domain is both respected and feared, adored, and kept at a distance. This ambivalence dominates society's and its members' reaction to schooling and education—the low status of the teacher but the outrage when a teacher does something improper; those middle-class parents who send their sons and daughters to violin lessons and ballet classes, and yet themselves never listen to classi-cal music or watch ballet; the bookshelves surrounding the fire-place filled with volumes of the *Encyclopaedia Brittanica*, un-opened but dusted clean.

To what extent is this generally true of all secular societies? Perhaps cultural differences play a role here? For example, is it reasonable thus to link education to the sacred in the United States of the 1980s, with its declining school enrollments, closing of schools and general disenchantment with education? Of course, cultural differences (and economic factors) may make the phenom-enon I have been talking about less important in one country than in another. Certainly a country that flirts with zero pupil growth may be on the verge of finding a new text to tell itself about the sacred. However, before my U.S. readers dismiss my arguments in this way, I suggest they do two things: first, look at the way children and teachers are portrayed on American TV commercials; and, second, consider the fact that in a society in which homosexuality has become widely accepted, there is still discussion (and pretty irrational discussion too) of the gay schoolteacher as a *corrupting influence*.

The most important service of the notion of "education as text about the sacred" from our point of view is to suggest why instructional activities are not supervised. This explanation, I feel, is superior to the one offered by Meyer and Rowan; or, better still, it augments and thus improves upon their explanation. If instructional activities seem to conform to a "text," we have a form of ritual or ceremony (these being conceived, of course, in the broadest terms). Moore and Myerhoff have this to say about rituals and ceremonies:

> And underneath all rituals is an ultimate danger, lurking beneath the smallest and the largest of them, the more banal and the most ambitious—the possibility that we will encounter ourselves making up our conceptions of the world, society, our very selves. We may slip up in that fatal perspective of recognizing culture as our construct, arbitrary, conventional, invented by mortals. Ceremonies are paradoxical in this way. Being the most obviously contrived forms of social contact, they epitomize the made-up quality of culture and almost invite notice as such. *Yet their very form and purpose is to discourage untrammeled inquiry into such questions.*[28]

Thus education as ritual[29] will discourage inquiry, and if the ritual is about the sacred, which is the field of experience par excellence in which tampering is prohibited, then the discouragement will be even more emphatic. This is not necessarily the way things should be, but only the way they are.

How will this discouragement express itself? Inquiry and evaluation can take the form of control and supervision. The Pandora's box that educational systems are wary of opening is not just a "profane" or "mundane" one—containing teacher resentment and the possibility of discovering inconsistencies—but rather one containing the feared consequences of profaning the sacred. For this reason, the behavioral regularities related to instructional activities—the way things are—are never called into question and become the way things should be. Thus Durkheim and Geertz provide an additional explanation for the relatively wide range of primary beliefs in school belief systems, which is why they are so unlikely to be open and, as a result, why self-renewing shools tend to be so rare. This explanation is an example of the second reason for not examining the real meaning of "instructional activity": one does not evaluate X for fear that seeking to find out, say, if X contains Y may actually destroy Y.

In the following section I wish to look at Durkheim's sacred/profane distinction from a slightly different point of view. However, before I do this, two possible criticisms of my argument need to be answered. The first is that the argument is too powerful. If school is a ritual commentary on the sacred, then surely *all* supervision and control would be discouraged. However, what Meyer and Rowan call ritual classifications are very definitely controlled; only instructional activities are not. This would seem to cast doubt on the whole analysis. My answer is that not all supervision and control can be viewed as a contamination of the sacred, as in the case we have been considering. On the contrary, in certain cases, supervision and control *create the sacred aura*. This is precisely what happens in the case of the ritual classifications. These *have* to be made publicly visible in order to be meaningful, and supervision and control are the means for accomplishing this.

Second, taken to its logical conclusion, my argument could be seen thus: If lack of evaluation contributes to the display of the sacred, then it does not indicate malfunctioning. In fact, if schools are to fulfil the semantic function that I have sketched out, it is necessary that they refrain from evaluation. Thus school self-renewal is not an unattainable ideal, but rather an undesirable process that would undermine the school's successful functioning. I am not prepared to take this tack (taken by Meyer and Rowan). There are many different aspects of schooling and the perspective I have developed cannot capture all of these. Some of them could only benefit from continual evaluation. Thus my analysis only indicates certain contradictory features of schooling, or certain tensions that one would somehow hope to resolve (although I am extremely pessimistic about doing so).

Durkheim's Theory and High School Education

The arguments I have presented so far have been equally applicable to all educational levels. The argument in this section is especially relevant to high schools, which are, in most countries, the most conservative part of the educational system, and which were the focus of our own project. I will again be using the Durkheimian conception of the religious attitude and its relationship to the sacred/profane distinction, in this case as it specifically relates to knowledge.

Before connecting Durkheim's ideas to high school education, let me consider them in connection with some classic theories in epistemology. One can divide epistemological theories into two types—those exhibiting a religious attitude to knowledge and those that do not. Whether a particular theory is religious or not depends on the relationship it suggests between that which is thought false and that which is thought true. In "religious" epistemologies, the distinction between the two is absolute. The worlds of the known and the mistaken are sharply distinguished. That which is known cannot become mistaken and vice versa. Also, and this is especially interesting, the *states* of knowledge and ignorance are distinguished from each other; moving from ignorance to knowledge is conceived as a process very similar to that by which Durkheim suggests an object or person can pass from the profane to the sacred domain. This is one aspect of Durkheim's theory I have not yet mentioned, but it is quite central to his account. The passage of an object from one world to the other "puts into relief the essential duality of the two kingdoms. . . . It implies a veritable metamorphosis." Initiation rites, whose object is to introduce young men into the religious life are such that

> this change of state is thought of, not as a simple and regular development of pre-existent germs, but as a transformation *totius substantiae*—of the whole being. It is said that at this moment the young man dies, that the person that he was ceases to exist, and that another is instantly substituted for it. He is re-born under a new form. Appropriate ceremonies are felt to bring about this death and re-birth, which are not understood in a merely symbolic sense, but are taken literally. Does this not prove that between the profane being which he was and the religious being which he becomes, there is a break of continuity?[30]

One example, perhaps the most striking, of a religious epistemology is that of Plato. Plato divides the "universe" into two parts: the world of Forms (the world of truth) and the world of everyday reality. The religious character of the world of Forms becomes apparent immediately from the fact that this is a world of absolute truth. In addition, one must remember the connection that exists for Plato between ignorance and sin. However, the most striking way in which Plato demonstrated his essentially religious stance is in his notion that in order to approach the world of Forms one must be free from the corrupting influence of the senses. This is almost an exact parallel to Durkheim's view of initiation rites. Compare the following two descriptions: First, Durkheim:

> In order to transform youths into men, it is necessary to make them live the life of a veritable ascetic. . . . But abstinences and privations do not come without suffering. We hold to the profane world by all the fibres of our flesh; our senses attach us to it; our life depends upon it. It is not merely the natural theatre of our activity; it penetrates us from every side; it is part of ourselves. So we cannot detach ourselves from it without doing violence to our nature and without painfully wounding our instincts.[31]

Now consider Plato's description, in the analogy of the cave, of the process by which the prisoners are freed from their chains and see the real world for the first time instead of seeing shadows on the wall. (For Plato, this is analogous to the process by which men arrive at truth by freeing themselves from the "chains" of their senses.)

> Then consider . . . the manner of their release from their bonds and the cure of their folly, supposing that they attained their natural destiny in some such way as this. Let us suppose one of them released, and forced suddenly to stand up and turn his head, and walk and look towards the light. Let us suppose also that all these actions gave him pain, and that he was too dazed to see the objects whose shadows he had been watching before. What do you think he would say if he were told by someone that before he had been seeing mere foolish phantoms, while now he was nearer to being, and was turned to what in a higher degree is, and was looking more directly at it? And further, if each of the several figures passing by were pointed out to him, and he were asked to say what each was, do you not think that he would be perplexed, and would imagine that the things he had seen before were truer than those now pointed out to him? . . . Then if he were forced to look at the light itself, would not his eyes ache, and would he not try to escape and turn back to things which he could look at, and think that they were more distinct than the things shown him? . . . But . . . if someone were to drag him out up the steep and rugged ascent, and did not let go till he had been dragged up to the light of the sun, would not his forced journey be one of pain and annoyance; and when he came to the light, would not his eyes be so

full of the glare that he would not be able to see a single one of the
objects we now call true? . . . Yes, I fancy that would need time before he could see things in the world above.[32]

Another religious epistemology is classic inductivism. Again
we have the sharp distinction between knowledge and opinion, two
domains in which different laws are operative. Again, the transition
from the domain of opinion to the domain of knowledge is achieved
by freeing oneself from certain chains. The difference between
inductivism and Plato's approach derives to a large extent from the
fact that the worlds of opinion and knowledge are populated with
different objects and thus the chains are different. Inductive
knowledge is connected with the reality apprehended by our
senses rather than by freeing oneself from these senses. The famous
chains that Francis Bacon suggested—the Idols of the Tribe, the
Den, the Market, the Theatre—are *idols*, and this again emphasizes
the religious attitude he has to the true source of knowledge—
nature itself.[33]

A "secular" epistemology would be one in which the distinction between truth and falsity would be less sharply drawn, where
beliefs considered false at one time could be considered true at
other times, without this entailing that those who consider them
true must discredit those who considered them false, as having
been in the grips of chains of illusion. In other words, such epistemologies would grant that true and false beliefs may have something in common. Most of the epistemologies touched on in the
previous chapter would serve as examples of secular attitudes to
knowledge. Specifically, Laudan's approach and his conception of
research traditions exemplify secularity.

What has all this to do with high school education? In high
schools the function of the school regarding cognitive education
becomes central, whereas in elementary schools many other aspects of education receive equal or often more emphasis. Thus in
high schools the teachers' epistemologies (or, in terms of the concepts I have used in this chapter—the epistemological beliefs contained in the school belief system) are of crucial importance. In
talking of high school teachers' epistemologies, I do not necessarily
mean that these are explicitly formulated espoused theories. Probably most teachers do not consciously espouse an epistemology.
But they do hold certain tacit epistemological beliefs that inform
their actions. In other words, using the Argyris and Schön terminology, they do apply some epistemology as a theory-in-use. Can one

make any generalizations about such teacher epistemologies? *I suggest that they almost invariably display a religious attitude to knowledge.* Before explaining, I will spell out the practical implications of this claim.

For Durkheim, the sacred/profane distinction results in a social division. Society contains two sorts of persons—those who are permitted to manipulate sacred objects and those who are not. We also saw that passing from the latter group to the former requires a process of initiation. In similar fashion, a religious attitude to knowledge creates two sorts of persons—the "knowledgeable," permitted to manipulate and develop knowledge, and those who are not until initiated. The initiation is the process of learning itself, which thus becomes predominantly a process of *passing on knowledge* by the knowledgeable to the novices. Now, because this state of affairs derives from a deeply felt religious epistemology, we can add this cluster of beliefs concerning truth, the prohibition against the uninitiated manipulating knowledge, and the role of the school as transmitter of truths to the list of primary beliefs in the school belief system.

This is of enormous significance. As primary beliefs increase, a belief system is pushed toward further closure. But these particular beliefs are especially potent when they become primary beliefs because they *cause a drastic limiting of educational and pedagogical options.* First, when schools are seen as transmitters of knowledge to the uninitiated, many other possible aims of cognitive education are simply ruled out. For example, developing cognitive creativity can be of no direct concern to schools in which manipulation of knowledge is seen as the prerogative of the initiated.[34] Second, the religious attitude to knowledge sees the act of learning as one of adapting to the (at times cruel) demands of a sacred domain. The innate characteristics of a particular novice are at most secondary, often irrelevant. As a result, any serious attempt at individualizing instruction is inconceivable.[35] At best, the fact that different pupils learn at different speeds and vary in intelligence might be taken into account. But more "radical" notions—that different students, although all studying the same subject in the same class, should perhaps study different topics or perhaps be taught in really different ways—will not seem to be reasonable options. More disturbing, these notions will simply not surface in staff dialogue even when such dialogue is the result of an identified failure of more traditional pedagogy. Furthermore, seeing the pupil as a novice will desensitize the school to most cognitively relevant personal-

ity characteristics. Schools that are capable of developing the most
sophisticated ways of differentiating between different kinds of
discipline problems will see the cognitive side of their pupils' personalities in terms of a simplistic smart/stupid/lazy typology. Of
course, at times, traditional pedagogies and simplistic typologies
may be appropriate. My argument is not another plug for progressive education. Rather, I am saying that the concept of a self-
renewing school suggests that a school should be capable of scanning many options concerning its relative degree of traditionalism
versus progressiveness. A school's religious attitude to knowledge
will lead to limiting itself to more traditional practices and attitudes. Thus Durkheim's sacred/profane distinction not only suggests a reason why the belief systems of all schools cannot be very
open (as I argued in the previous section) but also suggests why the
belief systems of high schools tend to be more closed than those of
other levels of the educational system.

The idea of a religious epistemology in the school belief system is only a useful hypothesis; can it be supported by independent
evidence? Certain suggestive facts lend support to the hypothesis,
although they certainly are not rigorous empirical evidence. First, I
draw on fifteen years' experience with running workshops on
teaching methods for high school teachers and student teachers.
One of the most consistent elements of that experience is the highly
charged reaction of teachers to new teaching ideas which require
that teacher and/or pupils engage in the restructuring of content, or
that teachers individualize instruction by taking into account factors like variation in cognitive style and interest. Teachers do not
simply shrug off the ideas as newfangled but impractical, but also
seem to feel personally affronted by them. And these ideas are not
particularly radical. The same teachers who are prepared to come to
grips with, say, the technology of computer-based instruction will
violently oppose an idea such as that some students will get most
from a history topic by writing a piece of historical fiction while
others will benefit from a careful and rigorous study of historical
documents. The reactions to such suggestions are often so extreme
that it is clear that some rather deep levels of resistance have been
tapped. The idea that a religious epistemology has been violated
suggests what that deep level might be.

Second, many different writers from different countries have
described the image of science, or the epistemology, taught by high
school science teachers in ways that clearly show that, at least in the
scientific disciplines, a religious epistemology in the sense I have

been using the phrase is the predominant orthodoxy. For example, Cawthron and Rowell, in "Epistemology and Science Education," claim:

> In more specific epistemological terms, school science generally projects an image of science which can be called empiricist-inductivist. Although existing in many variants it is basically founded on a conception of scientific method as described by Bacon: A well-defined, quasi-mechanical process consisting of a number of characteristic stages. . . . Each successful verification adds to the stock-pile of objective knowledge.[36]

Third, consider the language of discourse used in high school, such as "to cover the material." This seemingly innocent phrase actually makes sense only within the framework of an epistemology that sees "the material" as made up of important truths which then must be "got into" the pupils' heads. Obviously, such an epistemology is religious as I have conceived of the term.

If one accepts the existence of a religious epistemology, then one must return to the question raised earlier, discussion of which was then postponed—where does this epistemology come from? Here the work of Basil Bernstein on educational *codes* will be particularly useful, specifically his seminal article, "On the Classification and Framing of Educational Knowledge." Bernstein's work is too well known to require an extended exposition, so I will limit myself to sketching those aspects of it relevant to my argument. Bernstein's central terms are "classification"—the degree of boundary maintenance between contents,[37] and "framing"—the degree of control teacher and pupil possess over the selection, organization, pacing, and timing of the knowledge transmitted and received in the pedagogical relationship.[38] These enable us to create a typology of curricula. Of the major curriculum types, the most important is one defined by both strong classification (contents strongly isolated from each other) and strong framing (pupils and teachers have negligible control). This curriculum type is the most typical example of what Bernstein calls a *collection educational code*. Such codes have many interesting properties. First, personal identity becomes strongly linked to subject loyalty, One's identity is largely defined by what one has studied. One result of this is that in the universities the experts in a particular subject constitute a guild jealously guarding their identity. Such a guild has certain power and is interested in maintaining that power. How is this done? Here Bernstein introduces an epistemological postulate: "The ultimate mystery [in any subject] is not coherence but incoherence, not order, but disorder, not the known but the unknown."[39] This secret is only revealed to those who have been socialized successfully, that is, who have entered the guild, and this occurs very late in the educational life:

> Only the few *experience* in their bones the notion that knowledge is permeable, that its orderings are provisional, that the dialectic of knowledge is closure and openness. For the many, socialization into knowledge is socialization into order, the existing order, into the experience that the world's educational knowledge is impermeable.[40]

Translating this into my terminology, and exaggerating slightly to make a point, it is in the interests of university professors to con everyone who is not in graduate school into believing in a religious epistemology. Thus high school teachers will display a religious attitude to knowledge when teaching, either because this is the attitude into which they were socialized (as befitting second-class members of the guild), or else because a collection code encourages one to do this when members of the guild meet the uninitiated.

I was once witness to a most striking example of this second possibility. For research purposes, I sat in on five lessons of a certain high school chemistry teacher who gave a classic demonstration of how to pass on a religious epistemology. In her lessons, the world of chemistry was inhabited by unambiguously absolute truths. During one tea break she began telling me about herself. She was a graduate student in history of science. Her thesis topic was related to the work of Imre Lakatos (whose philosophy of science is a perfect example of a "secular" one). I asked her what she thought of Lakatos's philosophy. On the basis of her lessons, she should have been very critical of his philosophy; however, she was not. She was totally, enthusiastically "for" Lakatos. In her view he was *the* philosopher of science. In other words, the way she was teaching tenth graders totally contradicted her espoused philosophy of science! When I suggested this to her, she was very surprised, although later she came to agree with my impression. This shows that her double standard was not a conscious, cynical act of "public relations," but rather an unconscious set of actions whose form and content were shaped by sociological forces dictated by the collection code of the educational system in which she worked.

Bernstein thus offers us an explanation for the existence of a religious attitude to knowledge. But he does more than this; he also offers us a *theory of change*, or a suggestion as to how the religious attitude could be replaced by another in which, in Bernstein's terms, knowledge is less linked to states of knowledge and is rather linked to ways of knowing. This is perhaps his most important and most pessimistic contribution. Up to this point, after all, the self-renewalist could counter the entire argument thus: "You have shown how things are, how the religious attitude to knowledge limits high schools from becoming self-renewing. But this does not show that self-renewal is impossible in high schools, as you are claiming, but rather identifies sources of resistance to change which the change agent must consider in attempting to promote self-renewal." However, Bernstein effectively renders this argument meaningless by showing that the forces of change would have to come from outside the high schools because the collection code derives from tertiary education's impact and influence[41] (and in later developments of his theory, Bernstein goes further and connects everything to the class structure of capitalist society);[42] and by arguing that, in fact, changes of the collection code at the secondary level are extremely unlikely.

Let us conclude by glancing at Bernstein's own invocation of the sacred/profane distinction (after all, he is one of the best-known disciples of Durkheim).

> A sense of the sacred, the "otherness" of educational knowledge, I submit does not arise so much out of an ethic of knowledge for its own sake, but is more a function of socialization into subject loyalty; for it is the subject which becomes the linch-pin of the identity. Any attempt to weaken or *change* classification strength (or even frame strength) may be felt as a threat to one's identity and may be experienced as a pollution endangering the sacred. Here we have one source of the resistance to change of educational code.[43]

A Pause in Midstream

Before moving on to the case studies and to the dynamic conception of open belief systems, let me briefly pull together the various arguments I have offered so far. The static conception of an open belief system entails the notion that the range of primary (and thus unquestionable) beliefs in the belief system are minimal. I have suggested two reasons why school belief systems tend to have a relatively wide range of primary beliefs. First, on the level of espoused theory, aims and means are very strongly coupled in schools. No organization can continually call into question its own basic aims, and these will always be among its primary beliefs. But in schools, because of the strong coupling, this entails that beliefs about means will also tend to become primary. Second, one of the education system's main functions is to continually display for society its conception of the sacred. This means that schools deal with aspects of society's belief system that are by definition not open to question. Also this display is accomplished through the ritualistic performance of certain types of activities. Teachers seem to be "programmed" to perform according to a specific "text." Ritualistic activity of any sort is again a type of activity that discourages inquiry, and thus we have a further tendency for a school's primary beliefs to involve a greater number of domains of the school's belief system.

Durkheim's distinction between the sacred and profane also enables us to explain specifically why high schools tend to be more conservative than other kinds of schools. They are more concerned with cognitive education than are elementary schools and this cognitive aspect of schooling is informed by a religious epistemology. This again leads to a wider range of primary beliefs.

All this would be of no concern to the self-renewalist if one could show that these properties of education and of schools are not essential defining properties. However, this is precisely the problem. The properties discussed up to now in this chapter all either follow logically from the nature of education itself or are the result of powerful forces from outside the schools. Thus a reduction of primary beliefs, as a result of a self-questioning attitude of self-renewal, is either impossible, regarding some primary beliefs, or else extremely unlikely.

CASES

Although the cases to be presented in this section highlight various aspects of the theoretical discussion, they have one thing in common. In all of them, the contrast between the point of view of the external observer and that of the participants in school culture is central. The external observer is like an anthropologist coming in contact with a foreign culture and at first finding its belief system totally irrational. On one level, the "point" of these cases is to show how, by getting inside these belief systems, one can begin to discover rationality in most strange aspects of school personnel's behavior and opinions.

CASE VI: THE HOLINESS OF FARMING

The Har Galim Agricultural School caters mainly to students from underprivileged backgrounds. Fifty percent of these students, approximately, are from rural settlements and stay at the school as boarders. The other 50 percent are "externals" from the city nearby. During the first year of our project the principal, Aviva, was on sabbatical leave. Our story begins at the beginning of the second year, when she returned. Aviva had the reputation of running things as an enlightened autocrat. A gracious, well-educated, cultured person, she was greatly respected by her staff, but this respect had essentially inhibited almost all drive and initiative on their part. Just about everything went through her office. At the beginning of the second year, she requested that the two members of our staff assigned to her school present themselves at her office before and after every visit. Most autocrats are happy with their lot. Aviva was not. As the project staff and the principals got to know each other better, she became more and more ready to admit that her management style worried her. When other headmasters would tell of how in certain situations they had delegated authority, she always pressed for details, emphasizing that the wanted to learn from them (although she was easily the most experienced principal in the group). To a certain extent, her motivation for supporting her school's joining our project was to learn how to become less autocratic. This was not a pretense; she took it very seriously. During the project, she did many things that must have gone against instincts built up over many years, and I have only the greatest admiration for her.

As mentioned in chapter 1, toward the end of the first year of the project, questionnaires related to the autonomy of teachers in giving grades were drawn up by a committee made up of headmasters and members of the project staff. The Har Galim School was perhaps the school that took these questionnaires most seriously. A committee made up of Aviva, a guidance counselor, four eleventh grade homeroom teachers (in whose classes it was planned that the pupil questionnaires be administered), and the two project staff representatives met three times. At the first meeting the committee familiarized itself with the questionnaires and planned how to get all teachers and pupils to fill them out. At the second and third meetings, the results were analyzed. As a result of conclusions reached, it was decided to draw up a second set of questionnaires specific to the school's situation. Also the coming meeting of all homeroom teachers (a standard monthly meeting at this school) was to address the whole question of student evaluation.

At this meeting, the teachers divided into groups, each discussing a different aspect of evaluation. The three aspects chosen were: changes both in form and content of the standard end-of-term report card, teachers' autonomy in giving grades, and involving pupils in determining grades.

This whole process received very adequate coverage in various issues of the school newsletter. In addition, from the first committee meeting, the teachers had pressed Aviva to stipulate what would be the practical result of the committee's work. She had made it quite clear that she did not view this as a series of meetings devoted to ritualistic teacher talk but rather as a process that would have practical consequences. In this she certainly kept her word. In the short run, the school report card was revised; more fundamental was the introduction in the following year of a rather radical analysis and revision of school policy vis-à-vis involving students in all aspects of "school life," not just in giving grades.

Perhaps most interesting of all was how control of the process moved away from Aviva into the hands of the teachers themselves. At the first few meetings Aviva had been very dominant. Yet already at the general homeroom teachers' meeting the discussions were being chaired by the eleventh grade teachers on the committee. During the following year, this shift became even more pronounced as the activity I have described up to now linked up with the whole idea of a school evaluator.

Again, this school probably took this idea more seriously from the first than any other. Aviva was convinced that internal evaluation was not an activity which could be the responsibility of one person only but rather of a committee, that this committee should be allowed to work in optimal conditions, and that its importance be emphasized throughout the school. Thus a committee of five teachers was appointed (Aviva did not sit on the committee). Arrangements were made for them to meet, together with our two project staff representatives, for a weekly two-hour meeting during school hours. In addition, Aviva demanded that the appointment be ratified by what is known as the "village cabinet." The school is part of a small complex or "village" consisting of a farm, the boarding residences, and the school itself. Each of these is run more or less independently and the village cabinet coordinates activities. The demand for the cabinet to ratify the evaluation committee was of great symbolic significance because, in one sense, this was something purely internal to the school section of the village, and the ratification thus symbolized the importance of the committee on a more global level.

The evaluation committee's prime activity during 1980–81 was to undertake a major evaluation of school policy with regard to student participation in various activities, one in which student representatives were invited to sit in on the committee's work. This involved defining the concept of student participation, discovering and contrasting the various attitudes of staff and students to increased student participation, and making recommendations for further action. Again, this making of recommendations was not a ritualistic activity as far as the committee was concerned. Rather, they saw themselves as a committee with "clout," and one of the few clashes that occurred during the year was over a decision reached by the committee and then vetoed by Aviva. The decision was that the student parliament would prepare and administer the questionnaire to the students about student participation in school activities. When Aviva vetoed this proposal (it is not quite clear why), this caused tremendous resentment. The committee empowered the evaluation chairperson to meet with Aviva and protest the veto; the veto was immediately revoked.

During all this activity, our project staff members' role was very minimal. The original idea of using the questionnaires about grades as a lever for change was theirs, but from then on they remained largely in the background. All felt that Har Galim was one of our successes. Here was a school whose senior staff were committed to change, a school that had adopted the notion of DDAE with great seriousness and seemed to be moving forward steadily. We realized that this growth did not in itself constitute self-renewal in the full sense, because the major test, as I argued in chapter 2, would come at the time that Aviva and/or a significant number of the senior staff would be replaced (after all, during the first year of the project when Aviva was on sabbatical leave, there had been *no* signs of growth). Still, with this proviso kept in mind, Har Galim's organizational learning did seem to be considerable.

But there were limits, and it is these limits that make the Har Galim story relevant to one aspect of the preceding theoretical discussion. At the two-day summer session for the school evaluators before the beginning of the third year, one of the most important topics discussed was that of flaws in school evaluation procedures. We suggested that there were ten very prevalent such flaws. These were: (1) that there is no systematic evaluation procedure; (2) there is no connection between evaluation and decision making; (3) the results of evaluations are reached too late to be of practical import; (4) the evaluation procedures are inadequate from the point of view of scientific accuracy; (5) the conception of evaluation is too narrow from the point of view of its clients, topics, timing, and function; (6) aims are not evaluated; (7) there is no evaluation of plans of action; (8) there is no evaluation of performance (as opposed to results); (9) there is no evaluation of unexpected, unpredicted consequences of actions; (10) the findings of evaluation are not used. Each flaw was explained and the evaluators practiced identifying them with the aid of case studies. The task set the evaluators during the first month of the school year was to evaluate their schools' evaluation procedures and try to identify which of these flaws, if any, characterized them. A disproportionate amount of time was devoted to flaws 6 and 7—evaluation of aims and plans of action—because, in our view, these are perhaps the most important and difficult to identify and change. These are the flaws that show up the school's sacred cows, or, if you will, the school's values and beliefs which, if not evaluated, militate against double-loop learning.

The evaluator from Har Galim, the chairman of their evaluation committee, is Benny. He is a big, good-natured bear, popular in his school both with the kids and the staff. Also he has a good sense of humor, in his case of the dead-pan sort. During the year's meetings with the evaluators he certainly helped make the meetings more fun.

Benny is also a very shrewd, perceptive operator. Thus it came as no surprise that at the first meeting of the evaluators after the summer "marathon" he was one of the two people who had spotted a "sacred cow" flaw in his school's evaluation procedures. This was linked to the school's relationship to agriculture. Israel's history prior to the establishment of the state in 1948 is in many ways similar to that of the American Wild West. The agricultural development of the country by turn-of-the-century pioneers became transformed into a set of dominant values of the society: simplicity, cameraderie, nationalism, and a respect for physical labor. These were strongly linked to the establishment of kibbutzim, probably still the best-known aspect of Israeli society. Against this background it is not surprising that in Israel's early days the elite schools of the country were largely those on the kibbutzim and the special agricultural schools. The latter were boarding schools, situated on farms, whose pupils were largely responsible for maintaining these farms; physical agricultural work was seen as a central part of the school's curriculum. Today Israel is a highly industrialized society in which agriculture is becoming less and less important. The kibbutzim, for example, accommodate only 3 percent of the Israeli population and most have established industries that are usually far more profitable than their agricultural produce. Yet agriculture has not died in the national mythology. It still exemplifies "basic values," and this is reflected in the educational system. Thus even today there exist agricultural boarding schools like Har Galim that are not elite schools anymore but nevertheless continue to represent *the* values of Israeli society. Agricultural work is still central, although most of the pupils in such schools are not going to become farmers when they leave school.

Benny suggested that the emphasis on the importance of agricultural work, the demand that each pupil devote one day a week to working on the farm, was clearly a sacred cow. This was one aspect of school life that simply was not open to evaluation. Farm work was believed to instill the values of physical labor and simplicity; visitors' obligatory first stop on any tour of the school would continue to be the cowshed, and that was all there was to it.

The two project staff members at the school heartily agreed with Benny in his diagnosis. One of them, who is himself a farmer and cannot thus be considered biased against farming, went even further. He claimed that this was also the side of school life which clearly was malfunctioning, and that most tensions within the school derived from it. First, the "one day a week at the farm" rule created the most serious timetable problems. Second, most of the kids did not like farm work and so were being forced into it. They used all subterfuges available to avoid working. So, instead of teaching them simplicity and love of physical labor, farm work was teaching them to become expert con artists.

The evaluators spent much time trying to help Benny develop a strategy for persuading his school to open the issue of farm work to discussion and evaluation. It was clear that this was going to be extremely difficult. Aviva herself made it quite explicit in various conversations: questioning the centrality of farm work in the school's compulsory curriculum was simply absurd. And most of the Har Galim staff agreed with her. Benny admitted that he himself could not shake the belief that farm work was important. He did not see it as an absurd dysfunctional remnant of the past, as our project staff members did, but he understood intellectually what a sacred cow was and realized that sacred cows need to be questioned at times.

The best way to identify the strategy Benny finally settled for is to examine the committee's recommendations at the end of the 1980–81 school year. Of the five central recommendations, the following are of relevance:

a. The school cabinet must appoint new people to the evaluation committee for the next year and ensure that all village sections (for example, boarding school and farm) be represented. . . .

b. As a first step [of what, is not quite clear], a committee to deal with cooperation of pupils with regard to farm work should be established. A representative of the evaluation committee should sit on this pupil cooperation committee.

1. The cooperation committee should deal with farm job assignment under the supervision of the *sadran* [the adult farm worker in charge of job assignment].

2. The farm director should assign an overall work load to each class. The dividing up of the work will be done by the class work committee [that is, by *pupil* representatives].

3. The classes of younger children would be assigned a minimum number of farm work days in order to reduce the number of hours spent at school, because of the apparent surplus of "working hands" in the younger classes.

4. Meetings of homeroom teachers, boarding school supervisors and heads of farm departments should be institutionalized, homeroom teachers and boarding school supervisors being assigned to specific farm departments.

5. Farm work should be seen as an educational activity and not as the exploitation of a work force. Discussions with the pupils before and after work should be held to

explain things. The school should establish in-service training for farm heads with regard to this matter.

These recommendations reflect the kinds of problems regarding farm work discussed by the evaluation committee during the year and how they were formulated; clearly Benny had opted to move forward very slowly and carefully (although, in terms of the other focus of the committee's work—pupil involvement—some of these recommendations reflected the rather extensive changes the school was undergoing). Can one expect these recommendations to result in thoroughgoing questioning of the place of farm labor in the school curriculum? Clearly not. With the possible exception of b. 3, the orientation is entirely one of single-loop learning *with regard to farm labor*—recommendations designed to improve present practice and no more.

However, is it reasonable to hope for anything more? Having distanced myself from the Har Galim School, I now find it absurd to even consider the possibility that Har Galim could remove farm labor from its compulsory curriculum, primarily because of the very strong coupling of means and ends in the espoused theories of schools. The external observer can make the analytic distinction between basic values (the dignity of physical labor) and the means created to promote these values (making every student spend one day a week doing farm work). An outsider can also grant that a school's basic values need not be open to review, yet a school can still have an open belief system. But these values can be achieved in many different ways, and therefore the efficiency of the means chosen should continually be reviewed; if they are inefficient, they should be scrapped. However, a person within the school sees things differently. Despite its dysfunctional aspects, farm labor is as much a part of Har Galim's sense of identity as the commitment to the dignity of physical labor. The two are intertwined.

Once in casual conversation Aviva pointed out that, although she was deriving tremendous benefit from the project staff, she felt they were limited in being outsiders. She then suggested that she hand over her job to the project staff for, say, a week so that they could really get to feel what it is like to be a principal. I answered that precisely by remaining external to the school they could be most useful, that our project was based on the idea of learning from alternate viewpoints, and that I hoped that she and her colleagues could fulfill this role one day in other schools. Today, at least with regard to the farm labor question, I can only reflect on how clever a lady Aviva is.

The following short tale is not related to our project. However, it illustrates so perfectly the notion of education as a display of the sacred that, with the permission of my friend and colleague Walter Ackerman, I will include it. The incident took place in a large comprehensive high school. In Israel, the class is a very important school social unit. Students assigned to a particular class tend to study most subjects together and to stay together for more than one year. Homeroom teachers have far more responsibilities than their American counterparts and the kids on the class committee are likely to have quite a lot of responsibilities, too. In this high school, a class committee came to their homeroom teacher one day with the suggestion that they collect money from all the students, invest it in the stock market, and if by the end of the year they made a profit, they would use it to buy something for the class.

The homeroom teacher raised this suggestion with the school's *hanhalla* (a school cabinet made up of the principal and a group of senior teachers and administrators). The cabinet meeting at which this suggestion was aired was a very stormy one. Many teachers were violently opposed to the idea, and even those who were not stressed the importance of transforming this activity into an "educational" one, which meant that it should be linked to a series of lessons on economics, the Israeli economic system, and so forth. The more vehement opposition was expressed best perhaps by one female teacher who said, "How can we teach the kids A. D. Gordon [an Israeli Thoreau-like thinker of the early twentieth century] and then let them do this?"

There are two fascinating aspects to this little story. First, the class committee had undoubtedly displayed initiative, willingness to work together and for others—all surely admirable qualities that educators devote much energy to trying to develop. Yet the teachers were not impressed by this at all. Second, playing the stock market has become a major national pastime in Israel over the last ten years. Everybody does it. In addition, most of the senior staff at this particular school live in a very plush suburb of their city, and their life style certainly totally contradicts that preached by A. D. Gordon. So, on one level, the reaction of these teachers was irrational, or at least hypocritical. However, if one conceives of education as a display of the sacred and grants that playing the stock market is generally seen as a profane activity, everything fits into place.

CASE VIII: THE PROFANITY OF PUPIL MANIPULATION OF KNOWLEDGE

The Rotford School is a small vocational high school in Jerusalem. It was established many years ago when high schools in Jerusalem were not regional. At that time, any student could apply to any high school and pupils were accepted or rejected on the basis of elementary school scores, ability scores, and usually an interview as well. This situation has changed slightly over the years, but Jerusalem's education system is still only partially regional. Predictably enough, there has developed a pecking order of schools. All Jerusalemites "know" which is the best high school in the city, which is second, and so on. The Rotford School was known as the worst school; in other words, it picked up all the pupils rejected by all the other schools. This meant that it was a classic example of an inner-city school (although such schools in Israel tend to be less problematic and less riddled with violence than those in other countries) whose pupils were not only considered of the lowest ability but also tended to come from lower working-class backgrounds, often from broken or delinquent homes.[44]

When our project staff began sitting in at teachers meetings, one of the first things that struck them was how similar the rhetoric used was to that prevalent in the typical grammar school. For instance, the teachers were concerned because many pupils were having great difficulty with their math lessons. There was mention of inviting some parents and explaining to them that their children might have to be kept back at the end of the year or, in the case of older kids, there would be difficulties in obtaining school-leaving certificates.

This struck us as very strange, not because the teachers were making demands on the pupils but that they seemed really shocked by the poor progress the pupils were making. After all, in a school of this sort, one might be surprised if the kids did well in mathematics. Also because of the known school pecking order, a Rotford school-leaving certificate was clearly at best a formality and, in certain cases, even a certificate of failure rather than success. So why were the teachers behaving as if the kids were studying in a special, say, computer track of an elite school? Why were they teaching in classic grammar-school style? Two possible explanations could be rejected immediately. First, this was not simply a case of the teachers' conditioned reflex—being products of grammar schools and probably trained to work in them, the teachers were simply unthinkingly acting as if they were teaching in grammar schools. There was clear evidence that, in other matters, teachers had adapted rather well. In particular, they dealt with kids with serious discipline problems or problems at home with great flexibility, competence, and compassion. So if teachers seemed capable of responding to the school's unique situation on one domain, why should they have conditioned "grammar-school" reflexes in another? Second, the school pedagogy and curriculum and reactions to these were not the result of directives from on high in the ministry of education. On the contrary, ministry officials had made it quite clear to the principal and teachers that, because of the special character of the school, they would particularly welcome creative and even radical attempts to reach these students.

During most of the first year, the hypothesis we entertained to explain the teachers' behavior and talk was this: the city of Jerusalem, through its educational system, had labeled the pupils in the Rotford School as inferior. Some of this labeling had been transmitted to the teachers, who felt inferior to their colleagues in other schools; here they were, stuck with teaching these "dumb kids." This feeling of inferiority was driving them to keep up with the Joneses. By behaving like teachers in a grammar school, we assumed, they felt that their school might become vicariously a grammar school.

Certain characteristics of the Rotford pupils lent credence to our hypothesis. For example, at the meeting of the school staff in 1978 at which the school decided to join our project, discipline problems were discussed. A number of teachers pointed out that at the end of the previous year, there had been an increased noisiness in the classroom and also kids were sneaking out of school during the school day. Ironically, many of the teachers who pointed this out themselves disrupted the staff meeting by continually whispering to one another, ignoring the headmaster's remonstrations; some of them even sneaked out of the meeting in the middle!

Because of indications like these, we were perhaps less sensitive than we might have been to an interesting contradiction: the teachers' continual insistence that the Rotford School was very different from other schools and that our league of schools might not be overly helpful to them because of this difference. We never really took the Rotford staff seriously in the first year when they argued thus; we thought that they simply were not correct. In all the comprehensive high schools in the league, some of the pupils were like those at Rotford, and one other school was almost identical in pupil population characteristics. So we tended to shrug off their insistence on their uniqueness as a defense mechanism used to avoid learning from others. We saw the contradiction between this idea and their insistence on grammar-school standards and style as another example of how people can live with contradiction.

However, during the second year an incident occurred which showed that perhaps something more subtle was operative here. This incident was the result of certain developments in the principals' meetings during the first year which I did not describe in chapter 1. At one such meeting, a principal complained that the pupils in her school tended to be very passive in the classroom and far too dependent on their teachers. Most of the others grunted agreement. At this time, the project staff's attitude to principals' meetings was that they should themselves exemplify good DDAE, seeing as the project was designed to improve school DDAE. We realized that this was not always possible and that there were going to be discussions where, for all sorts of reasons, flaws in the DDAE process would be apparent. These, we hoped, could serve as future case studies for our group's analysis because all the principals were participants. Any other sort of case study would either be limited to only one of the schools or would be, from their point of view, the analysis of a story. Therefore, we always tried to move discussion in a practical direction. Thus, after a extended discussion of the over-dependence of the pupils, we asked the principals if this issue could not be the basis of some interschool project. Again, after much discussion, a committee made up of two principals and myself was formed and was asked to meet before the next principals' meeting and to suggest how the schools could come to grips with pupil passivity. When the committee met, one of the principals pushed very strongly for a limited, manageable project. Eventually, the following suggestion was made: a group of history teachers from a few schools in the league would design a study unit whose purpose was to improve the pupils' independence in dealing with texts (history was chosen because it is a subject in which texts are central). The material for this study unit would be circulated to principals and history teachers in all the schools in the league for comment. After suggestions were incorporated, the rewritten material would be used by all interested schools in the league and eventually evaluated to see whether it had achieved its short-term goals and more general strategies could be developed from it. This suggestion was brought back to the principals. Eight of them undertook to ask their history departments whether any of their teachers could devote time out of school hours to meetings (and the interurban travel entailed by them) geared to the production of the unit. Eventually, four schools indicated their willingness to send teachers to the meetings (although the teacher from one school subsequently had to drop out).

At the first meeting, the group defined its objective as trying to develop, through a programmed text, the students' ability to identify questions worth asking themselves after reading history. The teachers maintained that with regard to historical material, the following questions were usually the most relevant: What is the main point being made in the text? What is my attitude to what is written — do I agree? disagree? approve? disapprove? Does the historical topic being discussed influence us today? Why did the incident or phenomenon being discussed take place when and where it did? How does the material relate to other things we have previously learned? Does it perhaps contradict certain things or perhaps lend further support to them? Of the effects and results of what has been described, which are long-range and which short-range?

The teachers noted very emphatically that not all these questions are relevant for every text. Different texts invite different questions. Thus slowly the programmed unit became redefined as one in which the students would be asked to read certain texts, indicate which of the six questions they thought should be asked about each text, and on the basis of their suggestions, teachers would give them further explanatory or reinforcing material. The assumption was that certain suggested questions would constitute correct responses to the task, and others would be incorrect. Thus the proposed unit was, in one sense, very traditional—the format of a closed branching programmed text is pretty standard. In another way it was rather radical and innovative, at least in comparison with the typical history unit in Israel—it expected kids to ask questions about what they had learned rather than answer them (weak framing); at least two of the questions it encouraged the pupils to ask (what is my attitude toward this? how does it relate to other things we have learned?) were, to a certain extent, challenges to the sacredness of the written material; it linked history to language learning (after all, what was being proposed was a method of teaching kids to read intelligently), and thus was an example of weak classification, to some degree.

Rotford sent a teacher named Sarah to this meeting. A well-qualified, experienced history teacher, Sarah seemed extremely uncomfortable and ill at ease almost from the beginning of the day's work, and very soon it became apparent why. She said, "I work in a school very different from the other two schools here. Our pupils are culturally disadvantaged kids and also very weak academically. It is absurd to suggest that they could handle material like this." The other four teachers and I tried to point out all the things that are usually pointed out in these sorts of discussions: that there are weak pupils in all the schools, that material like that we were proposing is precisely the kind of material kids like this need more than anyone else because clever middle-class kids are more apt to know how to ask themselves relevant questions when reading historical texts, that the difficulty of the material is mainly a function of how the tasks are formulated and which texts are chosen, that this was planned as an experiment, and so on. All to no avail. Sarah remained unconvinced and, although she participated in the discussion, by the end of the day she could best be described as sulking.

Sarah reported to her principal and other teachers what had taken place. All agreed that the proposed unit was not relevant to their school. The principal phoned me and told me that the school had decided that for this reason it would be silly for Sarah to participate in future meetings. Now, you can't have your cake and eat it. The hypothesis that this is a school that behaves as if it is, vicariously, a grammar school cannot explain this case in which the school was offered a chance to do certain things other schools (including one bona fide grammar school) were doing, and turned it down. There must be something wrong with the vicarious grammar school hypothesis.

Let us try another hypothesis: let us assume that Rotford is guided by a religious epistemology. With this assumption, what seemed totally irrational starts to make eminently good sense. The school's grammar school–like behavior did not derive from imitating grammar schools, but rather from the fact that both Rotford and most classic grammar schools share the same epistemology. Thus when Rotford stressed how different it was from other schools, it was not being inconsistent, but rather was claiming that because of its unique student population it had special difficulties in transmitting its religious epistemology. Sarah's sulks came about because the history unit being developed entailed a strongly secular epistemology. This was what made it a relatively radical proposal, and this was what Rotford could not go along with.

There is of course one obvious problem with this analysis. I

have suggested that just about all high schools have religious epistemologies. If this is so, why were the history teachers from the
other schools prepared to play around with a "secular" unit for
study? Three points need to be noted here. First, one of the five
teachers in the group was a legendary character, generally considered the finest history teacher in the south of Israel, famed for
her innovativeness. She set the tone of the whole discussion. Second, it became clear at subsequent meetings that this interschool
group of history teachers regarded the unit they were preparing as
icing on the cake. It would not change their teaching practices in
any radical way, but was rather something to be used at special
times (as, during the last weeks of term when the official curriculum was completed). This explains the difference between
them and Sarah. In "ordinary" schools where the transmission of
the religious epistemology is going along relatively smoothly, one
can take time off occasionally to play around. In a school in which
the transmission of the epistemology is running into problems, that
time is not so readily available.

The third point is that subsequent events showed that the
written material prepared by the group did run into difficulties in
more "ordinary" schools. At first, everything went according to
plan. The material was given to the principals and their comments
were invited. On the basis of these, slight alterations were introduced in the text. The unit's programmed booklet was then sent to
all schools in the league. So far, so good. However, at this stage, I
was contacted by a few of the more enthusiastic principals, and
with all of them the story was the same: "I gave the material to the
head of our history department. He/she doesn't like it, and I think it
would be wrong for me to push things." In other words the religious epistemology was operative in other schools in the league as
well as at Rotford. (I don't believe they rejected the material because it was inferior. A number of experts on history teaching and
curriculum considered it quite a good example of school-based curriculum development.) So the notion of the league developing a
history curriculum unit on its own fizzled out. This was one of the
reasons for our gradually revising the notion of the principals' meeting as a league executive meeting, where joint projects would be
initiated. We decided that we had perhaps been too ambitious.
More on this in the next chapter.

This is enough to show the religious epistemology at work.
However, let me complete the story by telling you how things
developed in the Rotford School. Because this is a book about the

myths of self-renewal, one would perhaps assume that the story would end in total failure. It did not. Our project staff decided quite early that it was imperative to share with the teachers our puzzlement over their grammar school–like behavior. This was implied by the whole notion of supplying schools with feedback. Second, we thought it possible that showing the school staff how outsiders saw things might lead to their questioning their practices (or perhaps could even lead to their dispelling our puzzlement). So as soon as we felt that we were sufficiently part of the scenery and had stopped being threatening strangers (approximately nine months), we began in informal discussions and, in rare cases, in formal meetings to confront Rotford's teachers and principal with our difficulties. We would point out how classic grammar-school ways of relating to student academic achievement and to the curriculum seemed inappropriate in the setting of their school. It did not square with their emphasis on their school's uniqueness. Neither did it seem to relate to the apparent fact that Rotford students were not coming to grips with the standard curricula being taught them. This was not a sustained, focused activity of our staff but rather something does more or less spontaneously during various school activities and conversations whenever, in our judgment, such confrontation seemed appropriate. Apart from noting our difficulties, we also made it a point to invoke and examine the protocols of meetings of the school staff with ministry officials in order to emphasize how much freedom the school was being given. We also saw to it that the school was made aware of certain experiments with nontraditional teaching methods and curricula in similar schools.

And slowly, very slowly, things began to happen. Slowly a group of teachers began to voice the view that perhaps the way things were done was not necessarily the best way. Let me not exaggerate. They were still not the majority of the teachers, but they were a sufficiently large number that a few departments began serious discussions about the possibility of revising their curricula. This is as far as things had come by the time the project had officially ended — no change yet in practice, but rather significant change in the rhetoric of school discourse.

Yet despite this partial success, this case study again illustrates the impossibility of school self-renewal, for two reasons. First, the change came about because of a dialogue between school personnel and project staff. It is difficult to see how it could have come about without such an insider/outsider sort of relationship. I will have more to say about this in the next theoretical section, where I will argue that schools change most through being part of a more general system of educational talk. Second, consider the amount of energy invested over two years in addressing the problem of the grammar school–like behavior at Rotford, and then consider the "yield." All I can say is that a large minority of the teachers were *beginning* to question school practices; it was unlikely that their questioning would lead to answers that really challenged the basic assumptions underlying practice at Rotford, or that significant answers on the level of discourse would lead to changes in actual practices. And all this took place in a school of the sort that Basil Bernstein argues would move away from collection codes more easily than, say, grammar schools because of the nature of the student population. As I have been stressing, we are dealing with very central, primary beliefs derived from terribly powerful social and cultural forces. It is unlikely that schools can rise above these forces without being helped in a very sustained and extended way.

CASE IX: PROFANITY AND INDIVIDUALIZING INSTRUCTION

Only one aspect of the following story is relevant to the issues I have raised in this chapter, specifically to the idea of a religious epistemology. Nevertheless, my description will go further, for a reason mentioned in the preface. The story gives a good idea of the kind of activities with which schools in our league got involved during our project.

The story takes place during the third year of the project, in the Pisga Comprehensive School, at about the time we visited the Givon school (as described in chapter 2). One of the main protagonists was Ayellet, the school's pedagogic coordinator. In a school whose senior staff was mainly made up of middle-aged teachers, she was the exception. She was about thirty and generally considered the school's rising star. Rumor had it she was being groomed to take over the principalship one day. Rising stars are usually rather flamboyant; she was not. A quiet woman who blushed easily, her three most striking qualities were her equanimity, her passion for innovation, and her strikingly analytic mind.

During this final year of the project, Ayellet asked me, as one of the members of the project staff associated with her school, to help her in her attempts to improve school pedagogical practice. The first thing we had to define was what "help" meant. It immediately became apparent that she wanted me to act as a sounding board for her ideas (cf. chapter 1), and also to speak on new teaching methods at a teachers' meeting she had tentatively scheduled. She had heard that I was good at that sort of thing.

Now, over the last few years I had made it a practice to refuse all such requests, both from schools in our league and outside it. In most cases listening to guest speakers is a ritualistic activity that school staffs engage in in order *not* to deal with their own problems. In this case I agreed to go along with the request, for two interrelated reasons. First, it became apparent that this opening speech Ayellet was suggesting was not just a ritual, but rather part of a general plan—not, I felt, one with much chance of success, but still a plan. Second, I had tremendous respect for Ayellet, so I was pretty sure that if I was right and the plan was faulty, she would realize it immediately and revise accordingly. In other words, I saw my giving a lecture not as an occasion that would allow the school to pass the buck to the external expert, but rather as an occasion which could serve Ayellet and the other members of the senior staff involved in this project as a learning experience. Her plan briefly was: all the teachers involved in teaching tenth grade would meet once every three weeks or so in the evening and try to grapple with *the* problem they faced — the heterogeneity of the classes they taught. My lecture at the first meeting would be a survey of the teaching methods particularly suited to heterogeneous groups of students. I hoped it would motivate the teachers to check their own methods and then to start trying out newer ones. Ayellet hoped that the practical result of my lecture would be that the teachers, within their own subject matter subgroups, would decide to sit in on each other's lessons during the three-week period until the second proposed meeting. Such visits would be discussed at the second meeting.

Although agreeing to go along, I did of course point out that I was a bit skeptical about this plan and I also stipulated that I was not prepared to *run* the first meeting, but to be only one slot in the program. I then raised the problem of numbers. If all the tenth grade teachers attended, then thirty or forty people would be at the meeting, and this was a very large number. After considering a number of alternatives, Ayellet decided to divide the group into teachers of academic subjects and teachers of technical subjects. Each group would meet separately. This in effect doubled the amount of planning and coordination required, but increased the chance of more constructive future meetings.

The academic group was the first to meet. Ayellet began the

meeting by reminding everyone that *the* problem in the tenth grade is the heterogeneity of the classes and then introduced me as "someone we all know who is going to tell us something about the newer methods of teaching such classes." Despite my reservations, I tried to give as interesting a talk as possible, and the reactions and comments of the audience were very similar to those I was used to at the university.

But then things got back to Ayellet and she raised the antiritualistic question: "Well, what are we going to do about all this?" And then things started heating up. Why did Ayellet think there was any problem in teaching heterogeneous classrooms? Why did she think that there was any problem at all in teaching? Things were terrific. The kids were learning. The school's teaching methods were fine. Why had the meeting been called? These newfangled ideas (team-teaching, learning centers, computer-based instruction, and so on) are OK to speak about in a university, but has anyone ever tried them out in actual classrooms?

More or less on this note the meeting broke up. On the level of practical outcomes, it was a complete failure. On the level of ritual, it was partially quite successful because, despite the criticisms being thrown about, everyone seemed to *enjoy* themselves hugely. Teachers seem to like meeting and letting off steam. A few days later, Ayellet and I met and chatted about the parallel meeting with the technical group. Actually, I did very little talking at that meeting. In the main, Ayellet came prepared with an analysis of the academic group meeting and had plans for changing the format of the meeting of the technical group. This chat marks the time when I felt most optimistic about the possibility of school self-renewal during our entire project. Ayellet seemed perfectly capable of diagnosing the failure of the previous meeting and of using the diagnosis as a basis for an improved plan without any help from me. In her view, the meeting had begun badly when she had imposed her definition of the situation — the school having difficulties in coping with heterogeneity—although she remained adamant that in some objective sense this was *the* problem. The teachers had thus been antagonized and had become defensive. From then on, they could only see my lecture as a form of pedagogical entertainment and certainly not as something that need be related to practically. The suggested change of format for the parallel technical group meeting was as follows: Ayellet would begin by asking the teachers to indicate any problem they felt in teaching tenth graders. She was pretty sure that they would come up with exactly the same problem of heterogeneity. She hoped that after discussing this for a while, they would call for some attempt by the school to come to grips with the problem. This was the right time for me to present a brief survey of teaching methods that had been used in heterogeneous classes. From then on the meeting would run like the earlier one.

The meeting took place a few days later and more or less went according to the "script." The teachers did identify heterogeneity as *the* problem, although they didn't formulate it in this way. The way they put it represents one of the classic expressions of a tacit religious epistemology in teacher discourse. "If you teach at the level of the clever kids, the others do not understand, and if you teach at the level of the weaker ones, the clever kids get bored." In other words, as Bernstein puts it, there is no conception of different *ways* of knowing, but rather a *state* of knowledge one wishes to get to. The ease with which pupils can get to this state is the only differentiation among them, and this difference is dealt with by teaching at different "levels." Also, the degrees of freedom in manipulating knowledge are minimal. One can teach either at one "level" *or* at another. That is all. Now, when the classroom situation and its crucial variables are conceived of in this fashion, there is no possible way to solve the problem of heterogeneity. This is why the religious epistemology is so often linked to an elitist social theory that makes it possible to ignore the problem.

At this meeting the one important change in the "script" was instituted by myself, because of the above considerations. Before beginning my survey, I pointed out to the teachers that often when someone is asked to suggest a new perspective in order to solve a problem, the request really is that one suggests a new procedure that does not require any change in the accepted ways of doing things. I stressed that the adoption of any new teaching method that I could tell them about would require that they discontinue certain present practices, and if they were not prepared to do this, then there was little use in my providing them with the survey in the first place. This was probably crucial in setting the discussion within a practical context. The latter part of the meeting was strikingly different from that of the meeting of the academic group, in that everyone seemed to accept that the purpose of the meeting was to reach certain practical suggestions.

Despite this fact, the teachers did very little about putting Ayellet's suggestion of mutual class visits into effect (this again, was predictable) and only after the next meeting did we see signs of actual changes in the classroom. Our main focus here will be on this second meeting. However, before I describe one aspect of it in some detail, let me briefly summarize all subsequent developments.

Ayellet decided the academic group had been so antagonized that it would be a mistake to reconvene the group at that time. At their meeting, a few teachers had been intrigued by the idea of a jigsaw classroom developed by Aronson, and they continued trying to develop this idea.[45] Apart from this, nothing came out of this meeting, but eventually a number of subject matter departments became involved in the change described in chapter 2. Because these departments obviously contained teachers of tenth grade classes, some of the teachers at this meeting did become involved again, toward the end of the year, in ideas related to pedagogical renewal.

My own participation in the continuing work with the technical group was now limited to two very minor activities. First, between each meeting of the group, I met with Ayellet (and sometimes with the principal Ronit too) and acted as a sounding board for their ideas for these meetings. Second, I was present at all the meetings, but usually simply as an observer, both because I felt that this is what our strategy required me to do, and also because the meetings were largely of a workshop nature rather than forums for general discussion.

At the second meeting, Ayellet suggested that the group divide up into subgroups according to teaching subject, and that each subgroup plan a small teaching unit using one of the methods they had heard about at the previous meeting. After further discussion, it was decided that as a start the least revolutionary method—group work—would be tried out. Although none of these teachers had any real experience with group work, there were other teachers in the school who had on occasion worked in this way and the whole idea did not seem too difficult or problematic; the unit being developed was to be tried out in class before the next meeting.

Approximately 60 percent of the teachers did try out the ideas developed at the second meeting. For the others, it became increasingly clear over the next couple of meetings that they were still conceiving of these meetings as self-contained tea, cake, and talk rituals.

At the third meeting, those who had tried out the planned unit reported back to the group. Most of them seemed surprised to have discovered, after initial skepticism, that group work really "worked" in the sense that more kids were actively involved in the lessons than in traditional lecture-discussion lessons. After the reporting was completed, the group again divided up into subject matter subgroups to plan further units.

At the fourth meeting, the group invited the head of the mathematics department to run a workshop on individualized study as a teaching method (the mathematics department had recently adopted an individual study curriculum for ninth graders that had been developed at a national curriculum center). The teachers worked through the mathematical material in order to become familiar with individualized study, and during the second part of the evening raised the question whether similar work was possible in other subjects. The point they made very emphatically was that there is a huge difference between working with ready-made materials and creating one's own material. All agreed that meeting once every three or four weeks was inadequate to really develop any material of their own. This led naturally to the whole issue of meetings during school hours, and this was linked to the timetable changes being planned in the school, as described in chapter 2. Thus at the end of the year, Ayellet's plans for pedagogical renewal with regard to heterogeneous classes became a component of the more general change being implemented with regard to teacher meetings.

Now let us turn to that part of the story for which this is the background. At the second meeting, as mentioned above, the teachers divided up into subject matter groups, each group trying to develop a small teaching unit based on group work. One of the groups was made up of the secretarial studies teachers—two rather matronly ladies and one much younger teacher. They sat in one corner of the room working quietly. At one point, they asked me to come over to help them with a problem. They explained that they had decided on the unit they wished to teach—something about office procedures. They showed me the textbook they worked with and indicated the relevant chapter. I had no experience whatsoever with secretarial studies and so, while they were talking, I continued to page through the book. My attention was divided—which is an important point. They continued to explain their problem. In their experience, the girls studying secretarial skills could be divided roughly into two groups. The first seemed to deal better with material presented inductively (my term, not theirs) such as case studies, discussion of these leading to the formulation of principles. The second seemed to prefer material presented deductively, or principles presented first and then their application practiced by answering the questions at the end of the chapter. The problem? Well, because the class was not going to be taught together but in smaller groups, with tasks being written on pieces of paper and given to each group, should the tasks present a case study or general principles?

Picture the scene. Here I was listening to their explanation and at the same time, paging through the book. So almost without thinking or looking up, I muttered, more to myself than to them: "Well, obviously, you could always let some of the group work with case studies and others with general principles." I then heard silence. I looked up and saw these three women looking at me with what I can only describe as frozen horror. It suddenly dawned on me that my suggestion, which seemed to me so obvious, was for them a stupefyingly radical idea, so extreme that they could only look at me in unbelieving consternation.

Why should this be so? Why should an idea that for an outsider seems self-evident seem so radical to teachers? And make no mistake, this is not a single, exceptional aberration. After this incident, I thought back and recalled hundreds of similar ones, not as clear-cut or as extreme perhaps, but still negative reactions of teachers and student teachers to similar suggestions. Let us immediately discount the more obvious answers one could propose to this puzzle. First, my suggestion was not perceived as threatening, in the sense that it implied that the teachers would have to change their usual teaching patterns. Their reaction was too immediate for that, and it also took place in an artificial workshop atmosphere in which the teachers had already shown, by agreeing to plan group work, that they were prepared, at least in thought, to play around with unusual teaching practices. Second, my suggestion did not simply violate a norm that all pupils must study the same material. After all, teachers seem to have no problem with the idea that weaker pupils study different (that is, simpler) work than their brighter fellow pupils.

It seems to me that the norm being violated is more subtle. Let us analyze my suggestion to the three teachers a little further. Essentially, what is being proposed is the following: all students in the class will study the same topic; some students will get at the topic by way of route A, while others will get at it by route B; those who use A will not afterwards use B, and vice versa; A and B are different but equivalent—neither is a superior route to the topic. It seems to me that the difficulties arise with the last two. Saying that those who use A will not use B, and vice versa, emphasizes a *mutual* exclusiveness, and this is the problematic notion. When teachers allow that weaker students will study simpler material A than the more able ones (who will study B), then, although it is assumed that the latter will never study A, the weaker students will need to study B if they ever are to "really" cover the topic. A and B are *not* seen as equivalent. Thus mutual exclusiveness and equivalence of learning routes are truly radical notions within the context of the standard teacher belief system. They are radical, first, because they directly contradict important components of that belief system and, second, because they violate one of the belief system's basic orientations. The moment mutual exclusiveness and equivalence are allowed, one has stopped being concerned with states of knowledge and is concerned with ways of knowing. As I have tried to show in the theoretical discussion, this would require giving up the religious epistemology, and this is extremely difficult within the context of what Bernstein calls a collection code.

Certainly, within the context of Ayellet's plan, the possibility of this sort of change is totally unrealistic. In this connection, it was interesting to see how none of the units devised by the other subject matter groups at this meeting violated the religious epistemology any more than that of the secretarial studies group. Thus although in one sense certain teachers on the school staff had taken a gigantic stride forward, in another, more fundamental sense the basic categories with which they defined their task remained the same. Could a more active role on my part or perhaps on the part of some other consultant with different skills have changed matters? As we have seen, the theoretical considerations spelled out by Bernstein and Durkheim make this unlikely. Also, of course, such a suggestion leads us back to the same dilemma that we have come up against before—greatly increasing the scope of the consultant's role subtly changes the intervention strategy from one aimed at getting schools to be self-renewing to one in which change becomes an externally initiated and maintained activity. In addition, there are further theoretical considerations that increase my skepticism. These relate to what I have as yet not done; I have devoted much space to explaining how schools cannot and do not change, but have not proposed a theory of how and when they do. And obviously, educational history does show that educational systems do undergo changes. The next section relates to this question of how schools actually change.

CHANGE AND SCHOOL BELIEF SYSTEMS

As we have seen, the dynamic approach to open belief systems stresses their openness to rational criticism, their sensitivity to the "facts." It is clear that the metaphor that inspires this approach is *the growth of scientific knowledge through scientific research* (which, from now on, I will call the *research metaphor*). Just as scientific research sees empirical reality as the ultimate arbitrator of its theories, so open belief systems change by being sensitive to occurrences in the external world—or, better, in the social and physical environment of the "owner" of the belief system (organization or individual). This metaphor may be seen in a tremendously large amount of the work on belief systems and, specifically, the very provocative work in anthropological philosophy that attempts to distinguish between modern and primitive belief systems. Unfortunately, this work seldom adopts Schön's suggestion that we become aware of our tacit generative metaphors. In fact, the assumptions in this field are formulated in ways that actually make it difficult for us to become so aware. The modern mind is defined as more or less scientific in character, or, as Horton and Finnegan put it, rationality and scientific method are more or less equated.[46] It is also usually assumed that modern belief systems are open. The moment this definition and assumption are posited, the research metaphor had been invoked, and all further questions (for example, how open are primitive belief systems? is primitive man really as unscientific as we think? what is unique about the modern world view?) will be formulated in its terms. One of the main thrusts of this section of this chapter will be to question this metaphor.

Openness and All That Jazz

Questioning the research metaphor can best be done by developing an alternative metaphor. The metaphor I choose is taken from the world of jazz music as it exists in the head of a particular jazz fan. Why jazz? Primarily because jazz is an art form I am rather close to. In fact, I *am* the jazz fan I am going to write about. Perhaps another writer would have suggested literature or classical music as a metaphor for capturing changes in belief systems. A lot of the semiotically oriented work in literary criticism which stresses *intertextuality,* and in particular Jauss's *Rezeptionsasthetik,* seems to be making similar claims to those that

I will be making.[47] I would have no quarrel with this, but I think that a strong case can be made for the special suitability of jazz.[48]

I became a jazz fan in the late 1950s. As I became more involved with the jazz of the time, I started to read about the idols of the jazz past like Louis Armstrong, Duke Ellington, Charlie Parker, and I began to listen systematically to their music. On the whole, I found it quite painful, and for many years remained baffled by the critical acclaim these artists had achieved. Yet over the years my appreciation of them and also of those musicians who were the big names when I began listening to jazz has undergone changes, and the mechanisms of change are very significant. Obviously, tastes change as we grow older. However, beyond this, my jazz taste has changed as the result of the continued flow of new music that has reached me over the last twenty years or so. There are two main mechanisms through which this has worked. Let me illustrate the first by discussing my initial lack of appreciation of Charlie Parker. This was very peculiar. After all, he was considered as *the* genius of bop, the dominant style of the 1940s, and in the late 1950s the dominant style was the derivative known as hard bop. However, the essence of the hard bop "development" was to *simplify* the harmonic complexity of bop. For someone raised on the funky jazz of the late 1950s, the dazzling cascading solos of Parker were difficult to come to terms with. Yet two developments eventually allowed me to hear his genius (I deliberately use the phrase "allow me to hear"). These were the entry on the jazz scene of Ornette Coleman and the flowering of John Coltrane. Very soon they became the dominant voices who ushered in the avant-garde of the 1960s, and yet each in his own way captured and highlighted central although different aspects of Parker's greatness. Coleman's music contained a lyrical, yet anguished cry and a marvelous rhythmic looseness that, in my opinion, can be found in the music of but two or three musicians before him — one of them being Parker. Coltrane, on the other hand, at least in the late 1950s, attempted to develop the harmonic complexity of bop in the opposite direction to that of the hard boppers — he tried to create an even more harmonically complex music. Now, like everyone else who listened to jazz in the early 1960s, I listened to Coleman and Coltrane, and thus paradoxically while they were creating the revolution that eventually dethroned hard bop as the dominant style, they enabled me to finally appreciate Parker by reinterpreting him for me.

The second change mechanism is illustrated by the music of pianist Bill Evans, who also became prominent in the very late 1950s. I did not particularly take to his style of playing. Evans stressed the soft, delicate, muted side of jazz. His playing was dominated by subtle use of the pedal, and a kind of pastel harmonic language. To me he sounded like a superior, rather pleasant cocktail pianist. Many other piano styles seemed more attractive and interesting to me. However, over the next ten or fifteen years, slowly Evans's influence became dominant. More and more pianists seemed to be developing the "delicate tradition," until this tradition became *the* style. In the early 1970s the major pianists in the Evans tradition were probably Keith Jarrett and Chick Corea, and they were so important that their music could not be ignored or shrugged off. I myself am an amateur pianist and through all the years of playing until then I had been a most aggressive, percussive player, more interested in the bass than in the treble. At about this time, quite spontaneously, my improvisations began to explore the delicate side of the piano and moved up far more into the treble. Through being enveloped in a certain sound for a decade or so, my personal aesthetic was changing.

Let me now try to draw out of this musical digression those features that make it a useful metaphor for the way belief systems *sometimes* change (like all metaphors, it highlights certain aspects of reality at the expense of others). Some of these features have been indicated explicitly, some only implicitly, but all would occur, I am sure, in the experience of every serious jazz fan.

1. The jazz fan's relationship to different works is not a simple two-valued, good-bad one. One's reaction to music is much more fine-graded. Some pieces are great works of art, others are good, others are so-so, others are pleasant background music, some are uninteresting, some are bad, some are technically superb but emotionally shallow, and so on.

2. From the listener's point of view at least, there are two relevant "systems" of importance. The one is the semiotic, aural system of jazz pieces, records, and performances. The other is the jazz fan's set of reactions to the aural system. There is no external reality beyond the semiotic, aural system that needs to be reckoned with. (I am ignoring things like reviews here.)

3. The development of the system of reactions of the fan is determined in part by one's own taste, but far more important, it develops in response to the internal developments of the semiotic

system of jazz works. This is a bona fide system in which the various works are interrelated.

4. Musical pieces, at least if they are recorded, do not die (as, to a large extent, hit pop records do). They rather enter the tradition that in jazz is institutionally sustained by a very flourishing reissue record industry. The latter ensures that classics of the past are continually being repackaged for new scrutiny.

5. As a corollary of (3) and (4), changing appreciation of works is not a quasi-linear process. In this respect, my Charlie Parker, Bill Evans, and hard bop examples may have been slightly misleading. From them one could get the impression that only one of two possibilities exists for any particular style, musician, or musical composition. Either one goes from liking a style to being unimpressed by it (hard bop), from being unimpressed to being enthusiastic about it (Parker and Evans). However, in fact, vacillating, changing appreciation can continue. For example, form became central in the 1970s, and this has resulted, for me, in a depreciation of Parker's work because, in my view, he had no sense of the overall structure of a piece of music but rather concentrated solely on the form of his own solo within it.

6. As a further corollary, at a particular point in time, certain pieces of music will not be appreciated because of links with other pieces (or styles) in our minds (as, for example, a positive attitude toward hard bop made it extremely difficult for me to appreciate Charlie Parker).

7. New music sometimes enables one to hear such negatively evaluated music in a more positive light by *relinking* it, to coin a term. Old links between pieces are broken and new links are created, and often within the new network a particular work can be heard better. (Parker became acceptable when I delinked his work from hard bop and relinked it with Coleman and Coltrane.)

8. In other cases, our appreciation of a musical style changes because of its insistent presence. It is as if a strange dialect becomes natural to us as we hear it more and more (consider the example of Bill Evans).

9. As Lévi-Strauss once wrote, "I do not aim to show how men think in myths, but how myths think in men, unbeknownst to them."[49] Or, as Culler puts it, "Although [the human sciences] begin by making man an object of knowledge, these disciplines find, as their work advances, that the self is dissolved as its various functions are ascribed to impersonal systems which operate through it."[50] In similar fashion, I would stress the essential passiv-

ity of the listener in the development of one's systems of reactions to a body of jazz music. That music also seems to work impersonally through the listener, to a large extent. Professional musicians may contribute something to jazz themselves, and amateur musicians may contribute too in a small way. The mere listener, whose reactions are largely reflections of external developments, really contributes nothing at all.

10. Openness in this context is not related to openmindedness, but rather to opportunities to hear new music. During much of the 1960s, the body of jazz works in my record collection was relatively closed because jazz records were difficult to obtain in Israel, whereas it became much more open in the 1970s when opportunities to hear and buy jazz music increased dramatically.

As I have said, seeing open belief systems as similar to the jazz fan's "system" of reactions to jazz works can often be more illuminating than seeing them in terms of belief in scientific knowledge. It is not that one metaphor is right and the other wrong, but rather that in certain cases (and, as we will see, school belief systems are one such case) it may be more useful to use the jazz metaphor rather than the research one. Table 3.1 illustrates how the two metaphors make us see open belief systems differently, using the ten features described above.

TABLE 3.1. Metaphors for Open Belief Systems

	Jazz Metaphor	*Research Metaphor*
1. Kinds of beliefs	Beliefs fall into many categories; they have many characteristics, and are not merely true or false.	Beliefs are either true or false; one either believes or disbelieves.
2. Relation of other systems to belief system	The only other important system is the semiotic system of statements that the belief system relates to. The semiotic system varies according to the belief system.	In addition to the belief system there are (a) the semiotic system of statements that the belief system relates to, and (b) the system of natural and social phenomena to which the semiotic system refers (external reality).
3. Reassigning beliefs	Beliefs are reassigned to other areas of the belief system as the result of	Beliefs are reassigned as disbeliefs, and vice versa, as a result of the interaction of

TABLE 3.1. *(Continued)*

	Jazz Metaphor	*Research Metaphor*
	internal developments in the semiotic system.	the semiotic system and external reality.
4. Challenges to beliefs	Beliefs are never absolutely discredited.	Discredited beliefs eventually pass out of the belief system and are forgotten.
5. Mobility of beliefs within the belief system	Beliefs may be reassigned many times.	Beliefs may be discredited, and disbeliefs credited; however, they usually make such a move only once.
6. Accepting new beliefs	Inability to accept some beliefs, at certain times, is natural because of the structure of the belief system at those times that renders incorporation of some new beliefs difficult.	Inability to accept new beliefs—provided they have been empirically proven to be true—is incompatible with an open belief system.
7. Restructuring the belief system	A belief that was once difficult to absorb can be incorporated into the belief system as a result of the incorporation of other new beliefs.	Inapplicable because of (6).
8. Rate of acceptance of new beliefs	Beliefs that were once difficult to accept may slowly come to seem reasonable and acceptable by continually being spoken about.	New beliefs, if empirically proven to be true, must be accepted at once; see (6). Slow acceptance is incompatible with an open belief system.
9. Role of believers in developing their belief systems	Believers play the minimal role of passive reactors to impersonal, external developments in the symbolic realm.	Believers are active in developing very personal belief systems related to their unique physical and social environments.
10. The meaning of openness in a belief system	Openness of belief is a measure of the availability of many channels through which the believer hears about new developments in the semiotic system.	Openness of belief is a measure of the believer's readiness to incorporate new beliefs that necessitate far-reaching changes in the belief system.

Table 3.1 highlights most of the properties of and differences between these two metaphors for open belief systems. Nevertheless, a few further comments are called for. First, the idea in property 1 of the jazz metaphor that there are many kinds of belief, that beliefs are not simply "true" or "false," is, from my point of view, very significant. This is because it incorporates the difference between beliefs we regard as important and those that do not move us (compare the case of Gilad and Yossi in chapter 2, and the following Case XI). It also incorporates the idea of uncertainty about what one actually believes, because a particular statement is not completely clear. Second, it cannot be overemphasized that the two metaphors lead to two different meanings associated with the word "openness" (property 10). The jazz metaphor uses "openness" in the sense of receptivity; the research metaphor links the word to open-mindedness.

Finally, I must note one possible criticism of my presentation of the research metaphor. It could be argued that the metaphor derives more or less from one philosophic source—the work of Karl Popper—and that recent criticism of Popper's position could supply us with a scientific research metaphor with exactly the same properties as the jazz metaphor. For instance, Imre Lakatos has criticized Popper because of his concept of "instant rationality"[51] (see properties 6 and 10 of the research metaphor), and has proposed instead the idea of a research program that is very similar to the notion of a research tradition developed by Laudan (see chapter 2). The point is that such a program or tradition can flourish and decay many times (as befits a radically secular epistemology), and this reminds us of properties 4 and 5 of the jazz metaphor. Then we have the work of Kuhn and his notion of theories being replaced when a scientific community undergoes a "gestalt switch."[52] A whole theoretical area and its associated facts have been perceived in one way and suddenly they are perceived differently. Surely this is similar to the experience of the jazz fan picked out by features 6 and 7 of this musical analogue?

My answer to this criticism is twofold. On the one hand, a metaphor is simply a heuristic device. So even if a Kuhn-Lakatos scientific research metaphor were isomorphic to the jazz metaphor, it would still be necessary to ask which of the two is better to work with. My guess would be that because it derives from an entirely different field of experience, the musical version of the metaphor would highlight the differences between it and the Popperian research metaphor far more easily. However, this leads to the second part of my answer. I am not convinced that a Kuhn-Lakatos scientific research metaphor would be isomorphic to the jazz metaphor. There are obvious similarities, but also subtle important differences, in particular between the notion of a gestalt switch and the process of relinking I have described.

Kuhn distinguishes theoretical and observation statements, and argues that in fact observation statements are never theory-free. What we see is determined by our theories and theoretical assumptions. When one theory is *replaced* by another, the relevant parts of our visual field are restructured. In other words, the gestalt switch describes the changes in the observation statements and is not really applicable to the theoretical changes. The process of relinking differs from this in three important respects. First, it is a process undergone by all parts of the system and not merely by one section of it. Second, it contains no notion of replacement or substitution of certain components of the system. Third, as I have repeatedly emphasized, it relates to the semiotic system as developing internally, whereas the Kuhnian notion is similar to the Popperian one in conceiving of an external reality impinging on and influencing the system.[53]

Thus substituting a Kuhn-Lakatos scientific research metaphor for the jazz metaphor would effect serious changes in the latter, that would prevent it from functioning as I wish it to. However, it must not be thought that no isomorphic (or at least almost isomorphic) metaphors could be created. There is one quasi-isomorph that, when seen in conjunction with the jazz metaphor, may enrich our understanding of how it differs from the Popperian research metaphor. This is political *discourse*.[54]

Political Discourse

The two sources for the ideas to be developed here are Elmer Schattschneider's *The Semisovereign People*[55] and the radical nonestablishment work by Trevor Pateman, *Language, Truth and Politics*.[56] Despite the marked differences between them, they do mutually support each other in moving toward a political discourse metaphor for an open belief system.

Pateman's setting of the discussion is provocative. His concern in the chapter entitled "Impossible Discourse" is with how "people are socialized *out of* certain linguistic and cognitive skills, and in this way socialized *into* a necessary acceptance of particular substantive ideologies and social systems."[57] Control over action can be achieved "by making it impossible for a person to *under-stand* certain sorts of messages."[58] Pateman's radical sympathies make him especially concerned with the difficulty of false con-sciousness. He argues that it is an oversimplification to explain such consciousness as the result of conservative ideologies being transmitted through the schools and the mass media:

> The problem for radicals and revolutionaries is not simply that people have got idea A rather than idea B, but that at least some people lack the means to understand, think with or believe idea B, even when it is presented and argued for in a non-antagonistic way and even when acceptance of idea B would allow people more suc-cessfully to satisfy their material interests than does idea A.[59]

Why do people have such difficulties? One answer suggested is that concepts, in order to be understood, must be organized within the mind as part of a conceptual tree. Let us take Pateman's own example (although in the case study sections of this part of the chapter, I will be presenting what I think are better examples, taken from the field of education rather than from politics). He claims that many propositions and arguments about anarchy are only intelligible within the context of the conceptual tree presented in figure 3.1.[60]

Pateman claims that for many people the word anarchy is not organized within this conceptual tree. In fact, it is not conceptually

FIGURE 3.1.   Pateman's Conception of Anarchy

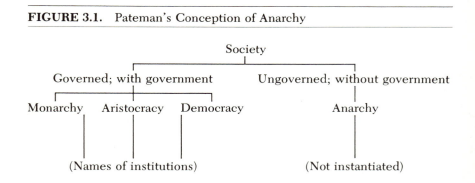

Note: Reprinted with permission of the author, Trevor Pateman, from *Language, Truth, and Politics*, 2d ed. (Lewes, East Sussex, Eng.: Jean Stroud, 1980), p. 131.

FIGURE 3.2. An Alternative Conception of Anarchy

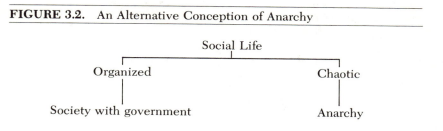

organized at all. For this reason, such people will find discourse about anarchy simply incomprehensible.

My discussion of the jazz metaphor shows that I find this argument very convincing. My only quarrel with it is that Pateman weakens his case by introducing a false dichotomy—he suggests that anarchy is either organized within the conceptual tree he indicates, or not at all. However, there are surely other possibilities. For example, see figure 3.2.

The point is that Pateman's argument works just as well using the conceptual tree in figure 3.2. In both cases, those for whom anarchy is not conceptually organized at all will find much of the discourse about anarchy incomprehensible, and if this second possibility is allowed, his argument is not limited to people with little formal education (as it is quite explicitly in "Impossible Discourse"), but also applies to highly educated people.

Let us treat the issue Pateman raises on a more general level. If my suggested amendment of his argument is accepted, then we can see that the proponents of a particular political position that is generally misunderstood may be best advised to promote their cause by trying first to restructure certain conceptual trees in the general public consciousness. By this I do not mean to advocate the kind of blatant verbal manipulation that Orwell was concerned with in *1984*, and that occurred in Nazi Germany and in East Germany, as analyzed by Mueller in *The Politics of Communication*.[61] I am referring to a restructuring that results from normal political activity in democratic societies. How could or how is such restructuring achieved? This leads us to Schattschneider's *The Semisovereign People*.

One of the central concepts in Schattschneider's book is the notion of a *line of cleavage*. By this he means how people are divided within a particular political universe. The game of politics

FIGURE 3.3. Schattschneider's Political Universe,
with Two Lines of Cleavage

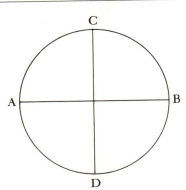

Note: From *The Semisoverign People* by E. E. Schattschneider. Copyright © 1975 by E. E. Schattschneider and The Dryden Press. Reprinted by permission of Holt, Rinehart and Winston, CBS College Publishing.

is often thought to be about the conflicts that take place in the political arena, but instead it is often about the usually hidden metaconflict about where the line of cleavage is to be drawn. Schattschneider illustrates this graphically, as shown in figure 3.3. He goes on to explain:

In this figure, the circle represents the political universe and the lines AB and CD are two possible lines of cleavage. . . . The cleavages shown in the figure are completely inconsistent with each other; that is, a shift from one to the other involves a total reorganization of political alignments. Not only is the composition of each side changed as a result of the shift, but the conflict in the CD alignment is necessarily *about* something different from the conflict in the AB alignment, and the *outcome* of the conflict is therefore different. The political universe remains the same in spite of the shift, but what people can do and what they cannot do depends on how they are divided. Every shift of the line of cleavage affects the nature of the conflict, produces a new set of winners and losers and a new kind of result. Thus a change in the direction and location of the line of cleavage will determine the place of each individual in the political system, what side he is on, who else is on his side, who is opposed to him, how large the opposing sides are, what the conflict is about, and who wins. Since this is the process by which majorities and minorities are made, it may be said that every change in the direction and location of the line of cleavage produces a new majority and a new allocation of power; . . . *the definition of the alternatives is the supreme instrument of power.*[62]

Thus perhaps the best advice one could give to the proponents of a poorly understood political position is: "Try to change the line of cleavage to your advantage." This is not exactly a blueprint for success, but nevertheless a more specific suggestion than restructuring conceptual trees. Of course, in making the suggestion, I am taking Schattschneider beyond what he himself claims. There is no hint in his book that whenever a conflict is about one thing, some other conflict is made impossible because the associated issue becomes difficult to understand. I think this is because of the way Schattschneider conceives of a political universe and the illustrative circles that adorn so many of the pages of his book. "Political universe" seems to be one of the primitive, undefined terms of his system and thus we are left in the dark as to whether the circles indicate people, factions, parties, classes, issues, conflicts, ideas, or some combination of these. I find it useful to regard them as containing ideas, beliefs, concepts, and arguments—what I have called political discourse. When the circles are so conceived, two relationships become apparent: first, the connection between lines of cleavage and restructuring conceptual trees, and second, the connection between the circles of political discourse and the body of jazz music described in my jazz metaphor.

Without making an exhaustive comparison between the jazz metaphor and the political discourse metaphor, I will summarize by saying that it is self-evident that (1), (4), (5), (6), (7), (8), and (9) of the jazz metaphor are displayed by the political discourse metaphor. The only problematic features that do require some comment are (2) and (3), regarding the development of the universe of political discourse as internal rather than being a reaction to external reality, and (10) which defines openness as receptivity. With regard to (2) and (3), I think these are exemplified, to a large extent, in political discourse; however, because our concern is elsewhere, I will not stop to develop this idea. In subsequent sections in which I discuss educational discourse I will make the same cynical claim, and will attempt to justify it there.

The question of openness and closure in the sense of availability is the most problematic aspect of political discourse. The metaconflict over the line of cleavage is in fact conflict over the contents of the agenda of political discussion. Those interested in maintaining an old line of cleavage are interested in preventing new issues from surfacing and are thus for closure. Conversely, those interested in establishing a new line of cleavage are for openness. Political metaconflict is thus a continual conflict *between* openness and closure; no political universe can be characterized as either open or closed.

Comparison of the political discourse metaphor with the jazz metaphor shows that each has certain advantages and disadvantages. Two important disadvantages of the political discourse metaphor are, first, that it is only a quasi-isomorph; it does not capture all features of the jazz metaphor. Second, it is a political metaphor; politics is concerned with conflict, power, authority, force, deception, face-saving, mistrust, bias, distorted communication. Most work on organizational development sees organizations through the prism of such terms, usually conceived as barriers to processes like organizational self-renewal. There is no doubt that this is a perspective that captures much of importance within organizations, but not all. Certain aspects of self-renewal, and certain barriers to it, are missed entirely by the political perspective; I am here concerned with pointing these out. This is one of the reasons I was struck by Pateman's argument. Despite the fact that his book is about politics, he manages to put his finger on a variable—simple, nondefensive, unprejudiced lack of understanding—that must be ignored by the usual political analysis.

Using a political metaphor in a book such as this is thus, in a sense, self-defeating. It seduces the reader into inadvertently smuggling in certain ways of looking at things that are inimical to the very argument I am trying to develop. Yet it does also highlight certain aspects of belief systems that are either missed or less ably concreticized through an aural metaphor. Educational belief systems are concerned with verbal symbols, and thus it may be easier to picture changes within them by comparing the latter to the restructuring of political conceptual trees than by a comparison with the relinkings of an aural system. Even more important, through the notion of a line of cleavage, it alerts us to a pervasive tendency of the human mind—the penchant to think dualistically,[63] in X versus Y terms — which, as we will see, is very marked in educational discourse. For these reasons, I propose the political discourse metaphor as a secondary one to the jazz metaphor. Its job is to fill out and enrich the latter, and by doing this, to capture more aspects of school belief systems.

Change in School Belief Systems

I wish to present three very simple claims:

1. School self-renewal requires that school belief systems be open in terms of the research metaphor, that is, the belief system of a particular school would have to be a semi-isolated system that develops in rational response to its own particular environment, to the school's own students and their successes and failures.

2. As a matter of fact, school belief systems reflect a much larger symbolic system of educational discourse. For simplicity's sake, let us limit ourselves to the system of educational discourse in a particular country (although this is probably in itself a distortion of the facts). This will be made up of all the laws, regulations, and court rulings on education, all discussion of education in the mass media, and all statements and theories about education that in some other way become public.

3. The way the belief system of a particular school actually changes is captured with remarkable accuracy by the jazz metaphor, augmented by the political discourse metaphor. The belief system changes in response to internal developments within the system of educational discourse in a way similar to how a jazz fan's loves and hates change as the jazz corpus changes. One must not exaggerate. This is only a metaphor. At times schools *do* react to their immediate environments (especially during crises),[64] but their belief systems are far more sensitive to changes in their semiotic environments.

At this point, the natural thing to do, I suppose, would be to produce arguments to support these claims, and a little further on I will present case studies that illustrate them. However, I would argue that the really interesting question is how anyone could possibly think or argue that the state of affairs is different from what I here maintain it is. In other words, I think claims 2 and 3 are *trivially* true. To show this, it suffices to point out two aspects of education that I assume are completely uncontroversial. The first is that the whole idea of public education, of laws relating to compulsory education, presupposes that schools are part of a national education system. The second is that almost any book one picks up on the history of education is going to deal with educational change to some extent in terms of the zeitgeist, the history of ideas, the history of public educational controversies and debates, educational fads and fashions. To a certain degree, although not completely, my two claims 2 and 3 are simply new verbal dressing for these uncontroversial facts.

Yet the self-renewalist really does seem to suggest that there exist schools for which my claims do not hold. Even Goodlad, who sees self-renewal in terms of a *league* of schools, is still very far from emphasizing the school as part of a national system. The question then, for me, is: how is it possible that self-renewalists miss the two uncontroversial facts I have pointed out about schools in the above paragraph? (Or at least why do they not refer to them in their writings?)

There are a number of reasons for this:

1. The role of a change agent almost forces one to adopt an ahistorical approach to the organizations one works with. (In chapter 5 I will discuss the forces that shape the change agent role.)

2. We all tend to commit the fallacy of assuming that history, sociology, and politics deal with major issues and events and do not affect day-to-day matters. In the same way as human relations consultants advising, say, a business firm or an army are surely aware that their advice becomes less important during major depressions or wars, but assumes that in "normal" times their contribution can be significant, so educational consultants may assume that when things are running more or less smoothly, then major economic, political, and social forces have no significant effects on their views. This is, as I say, a fallacy. When history, sociology, and politics become invisible, they do not lose their potency.

3. There is an unfortunate tendency in the social sciences for scholarship at the macro-level to work parallel to and independently of micro-level scholarship. In our case, scholarship dealing with systematic features of educational systems seldom bothers to point out the effects of these on the practices and beliefs of individual schools and teachers. Israel provides a marvelous example of this parallelism in the discussion and research over the last fifteen years or so concerning the mid-sixties decision that high schools would "go comprehensive." Much research on the political impact of this decision, on its influence on Israeli social structure and on the plight of the disadvantaged, has been undertaken.[65] However, very little has been written on how this decision affected the way teachers and principals define their situation. However, I would

hazard a guess that it is on this level that the decision has had its most profound effects. A comprehensive high school—unlike, say, a classic grammar school—offers many different options, tracks, and kinds of leaving certificates. Thus the question of *assigning pupils* to the various options becomes a central issue coloring all staff discussion. I will expand on this later. At this stage, suffice it to say that this sort of connection between policy and practice is often ignored.

4. Closely related to (3) is the tendency to assume that talk about education in the public or academic areas seldom actually reaches the schools. Thus we hear the argument that the alternative school movement created much more excitement in university schools of education than in the "field," and that, in fact, there were actually very few alternative schools. Most schools remained unaffected. This argument rests on the assumption that the only way to be affected by something like the alternative school movement is by becoming a convert. However, there are other ways of being influenced that may be just as important. Alternative schools can function as a "definition of the enemy" for traditional schools and thus influence the latter by suggesting what practices will *not* be considered. In other words, issues discussed in public discourse on education can restructure conceptual trees and in this way define and limit options.

5. Again related to (3): one reason why historical and sociological scholarship may elude the educational consultant is the fact that the political dimension in the straightforward sense looms large in much of the educational history and educational sociology literature. By this I mean that power is conceived in the classic sense as being exercised when A participates in the making of decisions that affect B directly, that is, B must comply with the decision.[66] Now, as we have seen in chapter 1, one of the central tenets of the self-renewalist is that the history of education has shown that central authorities have been particularly ineffective in making schools comply with their decisions. Thus it would seem that the history of educational thought and policymaking passes the schools by. However, this conclusion ignores two further aspects of the political dimension which, of late, have received much more attention. First, we have what Bachrach and Baratz have called the second face of power, which deals with A participating in the making of *nondecisions,* or the prevention of certain issues from surfacing, which affects B in indirect but important ways.[67] Then we have the

point brought out by Pateman that policy decisions can result in the structuring of conceptual trees in such a way that certain options will simply not be *understood* by school personnel. This latter possibility is particularly important. As I have mentioned before, this is one of the major reasons why the rational scanning of all possibilities in school staff dialogue is so utopian.

6. There exists a tacit division of labor between those concerned with organizational development and those concerned with the diffusion of educational innovations. This division even assigns these two topics to two different research traditions. Organizational development has been dominated by concepts from social psychology, whereas the diffusion of innovations is usually part of mass communications research.[68] Thus research on planned change has created its own conceptual tree through which research workers approach the subject. The jazz metaphor requires a restructuring of this tree because it suggests that we look at innovation developed from within organizations against a backdrop of ideas diffused from without. In other words, the self-renewalist must begin to be concerned with mass communications phenomena. Such a restructuring is difficult in itself. However, it is made more difficult by virtue of the fact that the diffusion of innovations is, generally speaking, a rather unsophisticated subfield of mass communications research. In most cases, successful diffusion is equated with *adoption* of an innovation. Yet concepts like the zeitgeist suggest that there is another dimension to diffusion. An innovation can have tremendous influence, despite the fact that it is rejected, by successfully diffusing a metamessage concerning, say, the definition of options. Thus, to return to a previous example, the concept of alternative schools as an innovation may not have been adopted, but it may have profoundly influenced educational practice by redefining society's major educational controversies. This way of looking at educational change is not very developed in the mainstream literature of planned change.

7. In similar fashion, a lot of educational scholarship potentially relevant to theories of educational change is itself to blame for being overlooked by change agents, because such scholarship tends to ignore *interissue relationships*. By this, I mean that the impact of an issue on the reinterpretation through relinking of the educational tradition or, in other words, on the restructuring of educational conceptual trees, has not received much attention. Take as an example the situation in Israel in the mid-seventies.

After a decade during which the problem that was defined as the problem of culturally disadvantaged children was *the* issue in Israeli education, for a brief period of two or three years a new major issue surfaced. This was the conflict between the transmission of national values on the one hand and indoctrination on the other.[69] A vast amount of academic energy was invested in analyzing and researching these two issues. However, the material written never linked them together, nor did it show how each in turn defined the structure of educational discourse in Israel at a particular time. In such a situation, how could a change agent have used such material? Essentially in but one way — as a resource. For example, a school faculty struggling with the problem of disadvantaged kids could be introduced to some of the literature on the subject. However, what if one realizes that when public discourse defines *the* issue of education as the problem of the educationally disadvantaged, then this essentially stipulates, for the entire education community, the criterion by which effective schooling is to be judged? What if this labels certain schools, principals, teachers, and curricula as the "good guys" and others as the "bad guys"? When public discourse redefines *the* issue as one of indoctrination versus transmission of values, then the whole educational field undergoes a dramatic change, the labels are moved around, there are new "good guys" and "bad guys" and new criteria for identifying them. In such a case, I suggest that what has been written on these two issues, rather than being seen as a potential resource, is seen as itself a factor determining the directions and limitations of educational change, and as such must be used by the change agent in a completely different way.

8. Perhaps the most important reason why the self-renewalist can continue to use the research metaphor for educational change is that normal historical discourse, although identifying issues and controversies and emphasizing the zeitgeist, fashions, and so forth, tends to mask the fact that the assumptions of such a historical orientation are very cynical and also are in conflict with the research metaphor. On the other hand, our discussion of the jazz metaphor highlights this cynicism and conflict by stressing that change in schools has very little to do with the effects of schooling on its clientele. In this schools are probably very different from many other organizations. For example, Hedberg and Jonsson, whose background is business administration, have developed a theory of how organizational belief systems (which they call *myths*)

change in a Kuhnian fashion, where transitions "emanate from mis-
fits between myths and *perceived realities.*"[70] In schools transitions occur rather because of changes in talk about education.

So we see that there are very good reasons why the literature
on school self-renewal tends to ignore the phenomena captured by
the jazz metaphor. But this of course does not make these phenomena go away. The crucial question is whether things could be different. Could schools become organizations that function as the
concept of self-renewal suggests they should? Could their belief
systems change in a different way? On one level, they clearly could
not. Schools will always remain subunits of a larger educational
system whose clientele is not necessarily, or not only, the pupils in
the schools. Thus if school self-renewal is conceived as being related to independence, it becomes an impossible ideal even in the
most decentralized systems. On the other hand, if school self-
renewal is conceived as related to schools being more sensitive to
their immediate environments rather than as sensitive to educational talk, then I have not produced arguments that this is necessarily impossible. All that I have argued is that this does not often
occur.
Even this might be denied on the basis of present-day research on effective schools. On the face of it, at least, this research
would seem to contradict the claim that *all* school belief systems
conform to the jazz metaphor. It would seem that effective schools
(as measured by pupil achievement in basic skills) do have more of
a commitment to accountability than less effective ones. However,
the question of importance from the point of view of planned
change is: how did the effective schools *get to be* effective? The
self-renewalist would have it that the emphasis on accountability
vis-à-vis basic skills scores is the result of self-initiated inquiry. The
jazz metaphor suggests that, on the contrary, this emphasis is an
expression of the zeitgeist, stressing "back to basics" in present-day
educational discourse. The research on effective schools is still in
its infancy and is basically still concerned with identifying the
characteristics of effectiveness rather than with such process questions. So it cannot really adjudicate between these two approaches.
I can merely present case studies that do show the power of educational discourse and try to show how impossible it would be for
schools to escape this discourse, at least with regard to the specific
aspects of it dealt with in the studies.

CASES

CASE X: THE LANGUAGE OF ASSIGNMENT

During the last ten or fifteen years, the Israeli Ministry of Education has introduced a new set of directives that essentially introduce a new vocabulary into the high schools. Schools can now offer the choice of four different tracks. These are the *Iyuni* (academic) track, the *Masmat* track (a high-level vocational track with great emphasis on the study of electronics), the *Masmar* track (an ordinary vocational track), and the *Masmam* track (a lower-level vocational track). These different tracks were created in order to cater to students with different abilities and interests, and also so that the schools could supply a variety of school-leaving certificates to help place them in the labor market. I have mentioned that going comprehensive profoundly changed Israeli educational discourse and, through this, educational practice. This case study is an elaboration of this point, but I prefer to approach things obliquely, through the story of one person—Yocheved, a counselor at one of the schools in our project. I do this because it is through her story that I began thinking about the influence of vocabulary on school practice.

Yocheved is an elderly gray-haired lady who has been at her school for close to thirty years. She is an old-timer in the best sense of the word; a great concern for her school and her pupils shines out of her. During the first year of our project, Yocheved phoned me and asked if she could talk with me about a problem. The next day we met and she explained her problem. There was a general feeling in the school that the *Masmar* classes were difficult. Both the teachers and the pupils in these classes seemed unhappy. She asked me what the latest research recommendations were regarding placing students in the *Masmar* track. My first reaction was to ask her why she thought there was anything wrong with the way students were being assigned to the track. She looked at me, taken aback: "But I just told you, everyone is very dissatisfied with the way things are at present." I then suggested that I could think of at least one other possible explanation for the dissatisfaction. Perhaps the usual teaching methods of the staff were not applicable in these sorts of classes? (Note, this could not be interpreted as a personal slight because Yocheved was not a teacher but a counselor.) Yocheved became more agitated. She could not understand why I had changed the subject. She had asked me to tell her what the experts said about assigning kids to *Masmar* classes and why I did not just do this? I pointed out that I had not changed the subject but simply backtracked one step in order to ensure that the school's diagnosis of its problem was the correct one (I reminded her of the idea of DDAE); further, I was not sure that there were experts who could give her a simple answer to her question. So instead of not being prepared to help, I was happy to help, and had in fact implied how I could be useful. Perhaps she, I, and a few more teachers might sit down and really go into the question of why students and teachers were dissatisfied with the *Masmar* classes? At this stage she got up, informed me that it was obvious our project was a waste of time, thanked me for speaking with her, and walked out.

After this meeting I phoned the second member of the project staff, Chava Katz, who like me was assigned to Yocheved's school. "Chava," I told her, "I blew it. I succeeded in antagonizing Yocheved and I don't really know what or why it happened." Together we tried to make some sense of the whole incident. Although Chava was not able to help me plan a way of undoing the damage, she provided a most insightful analysis of what had happened. "You didn't take into account that counselors spend most of their time placing kids. Therefore when Yocheved diagnosed the problem as one of inefficient placing, this wasn't a neutral suggestion. It was one that counseling committed her to, one that thus involved her professional identity. Your suggestion to backtrack was *very* threatening."

Actually, time has led me to conclude that we were wrong on two counts. First, Yocheved did not dissociate herself from league activities in her school, and in fact remained one of the most faithful and enthusiastic participants despite the fact that we did nothing overtly to "undo the damage." Second, I now think that Chava's analysis was too narrow. Essentially her proposal was in terms of role theory. The counselor role within the school structure invites counselors to emphasize placement. I would now suggest that the vocabulary of *Iyuni, Masmat, Masmar, Masmam* invites all school personnel to emphasize placement. I say this because, following on the meeting with Yocheved, I began to pay closer attention to the amount of time school personnel devote to discourse using this vocabulary. I soon discovered that such discourse is pervasive. In addition, a great deal of the talk is not only *with* the vocabulary but also *about* it. One sure-fire way of disrupting the agenda at any of our headmasters' (and, afterwards, evaluators') meetings was to say something like, "At our school we do such-and-such with *Mas-mam*." All others present would swoop down, demand elaboration, and then begin commenting. Such a conversation was likely to continue for a considerable period of time, with no possibility of calling the meeting to order. I recall one of our staff members (a teacher with twenty years' experience who had always taught in a special school in which the *Iyuni, Masmat, Masmar, Masmam* vocabulary was inapplicable) stalking angrily out at the end of one headmasters' meeting and saying to me, "If I have to spend another meeting listening to those guys talking about this *Masmat* crap, I am going to go bananas." This talk about the vocabulary also became apparent to me in my capacity as director of our university's teacher training department. I discovered that most of the teachers to whom our students were assigned during teaching practice were devoting a tremendous amount of time to teaching these students the vocabulary. The student was swamped with long explanations, complicated charts, and copies of government regulations.

It could be countered that this concern with the vocabulary associated with tracking simply expresses the fact that these tracks *are* a pervasive feature of the school reality. By restructuring the Israeli education system, creating comprehensive schools with different tracks, the Israeli Ministry of Education had created a new school reality in which questions of placement *were* the central problems the system had to face. I would reject this. I am claiming that the independent variable that determines which problems a school will focus on is not the objective school reality but rather the language in which that reality is described. This is precisely the difference between conceiving belief systems through the jazz metaphor rather than through the research metaphor.

When I began my career as a high school teacher (before the restructuring of the educational system), I taught in a very selective grammar school. What happened when certain pupils attained very poor grades? Objectively speaking, there were a great number of explanations: (1) they were not bright enough to be in the school; (2) they were lazy; (3) they had problems at home; (4) they were being badly taught; (5) the curriculum was poor; (6) certain class friends were a negative influence; (7) they suffered from other problems associated with adolescence. In almost all cases of this sort, the explanations invoked by teachers were (2), (3), (6), or (7). This was enshrined in the stock phrases of the discourse used to talk about such problems. For example, perhaps the most well-worn phrase was, "He isn't exploiting his full potential." What is

particularly interesting from our point of view is that the first explanation, regarding basic aptitude, was very rarely invoked. I would
argue that phrases like "He isn't exploiting his full potential" make
it very unlikely that such an explanation will be offered. *Potential*
is a vague word. Potential is difficult to identify and, even more
important, it takes a long time to discover. Thus when teacher belief systems are dominated by notions like "lack of exploitation of
potential," it is natural to think in terms of "giving the kid another
chance," "letting him try to improve matters," rather than, "He is
just dumb."

Now, consider similar discussion in a comprehensive high
school. Objectively speaking, the same explanations for failure are
possible except that (1) will now be formulated as "He is in the
wrong track." The interesting thing is that in such schools explanation 1 is probably the dominant explanation offered for failure. I
suggest that this is because the new school vocabulary, and the new
teacher belief system associated with it, make it easier for this
explanation to be formulated. The vocabulary of *Iyuni, Masmat,
Masmar, Masmam* is not simply a set of words but rather a conceptual system, an implicit educational theory, a language to think
by rather than just a set of labels for preexisting reality. And, like all
languages, it is semi-totalitarian (not totally so, as an extreme reading of the Whorf-Sapir thesis would have it,[71] but definitely
semitotalitarian)—it invites one to see the world in a certain way
and makes subversion almost unthinkable. In the latter regard, by
the way, I am reminded of a school that decided as an experiment to
create a class in which the normal distinctions did not obtain. It was
called the Non-Track Track!

Let us take this idea of rejection a little further—for, after all, if
school self-renewal were to be possible, it would have to include
continual review by the school of the implicit theories enshrined in
its discourse. Is this possible? Let us assume that through some sort
of consciousness-raising, schools could become aware of their educational language. Let us also assume — although I think it extremely unlikely in most cases—that schools could do this on their
own. In such a case, is it conceivable that a school could decide,
after reviewing the language of discourse of the educational system
of which it is a part, to linguistically excommunicate itself? In most
cases, of course, schools would not willingly opt for excommunica-
tion, but in a sense this is what happens with alternative schools.
However, the process by which it happens—in my experience at
least, and also in at least one famous case in the United States,

described by Smith and Keith,[72]—shows how utopian is the idea of continual language review. Most of the alternative schools in Israel were established in the following way: A teacher or headmaster in an ordinary school saw the light. He/she then *left* the ordinary school in which he/she worked and established a new school. He/she would try not to staff this new venture with ordinary teachers, but with those who had either been trained for some "alternative" type of schooling, or were at least young, inexperienced, and enthusiastic. The "guru" would then take great pains in establishing a new educational vocabulary in his/her school, one that did not contain an implicit theory of education but rather a very explicit one. Great effort would be put into maintaining this alternative vocabulary, precisely because it was an alternative. And so, over time, this vocabulary would become even more rigid and less open to review than the mainstream vocabulary.

CASE XI: CONCEPTUAL TREES AND NOT BEING TURNED ON

If one ordered the educational philosophies of the various headmasters of the schools in our league on a traditional-progressive continuum, probably the two headmasters whose philosophies would fall nearest to the progressive end of the continuum would be Tzila and Amir. Amir we have already met. Tzila is the principal of the Emek Reim School. This is a very famous kibbutz school, generally considered one of the two or three successful open high schools in the country (although the term "open" is a bit misleading and I would prefer to describe it as "openish").

The circumstances by which this school joined our project were rather interesting. All the schools in the project were recommended to us by the ministry (although the decision to join the project or not was left to the schools themselves). As soon as we had received the names of the recommended schools and had visited each for the first time, we began to suspect that to a certain extent we were being offered some of the more problematic schools in the system. This did not bother us particularly. I fully concur with the following sentiments expressed by Perrow:

> In hospital studies, it is my impression that we are seeking refined ways to discriminate between the very best and the next best. . . . I once proposed at a conference of public health officials and doctors concerned with evaluation studies that the government stop funding research of this type and instead develop a simple, rough device that

would distinguish the bottom 20 percent of hospitals from the rest, with a margin of error of 10 percent on each side. This would allow us to pick out the worst 20 or 30 percent of the offenders, and concentrate on improving them rather than improving the best. The government officials and the doctors were appalled. . . . The National Institute of Health, I gathered, was not particularly interested in the worst hospitals.[73]

Nevertheless, we did feel that some sort of balance should be maintained, and so requested that the ministry recommend a few more "good" schools, in addition to those already suggested. One of these was the Emek Reim School. In one sense, this did not really help us, and in fact caused rather serious problems for the project staff member assigned to this school. She would submit to us the most glowing reports on the school's DDAE, on the quality of the people working in the school and on the general atmosphere, and this led her to ask the natural question: "What am I doing here? Does this school really need us?" Of course, as time went on, she did discover reasons for our being in the school, but certainly this question bothered her to quite an extent at first, and so the high quality of the school could be considered problematic.

On the other hand, Tzila's presence at the principals' meetings was very beneficial. She is a strikingly charismatic woman and her contributions often set the tone for discussion in a very positive way. Tzila and Amir are two very dissimilar principals in very different circumstances. Amir's style is more self-effacing. The openness of the Emek Reim School was a school tradition, established by its first principal, one of Israel's most renowned educators. It also derived from the democratic social structure of the kibbutz itself. On the other hand, Amir inherited a very conservative school in which his educational philosophy was an innovation. Also, he inherited a school in which teacher morale was low.

Yet there were a number of important similarities between the two principals over and above their similar educational philosophies. They were both literature teachers and both new principals (although Tzila had much more experience as a school vice-principal than Amir). Both were people who could listen to others and *hear them.* For this reason perhaps, both were remarkably open to the influence of our project staff. In particular, the relationship between Tzila and our project staff member at her school was a very fruitful one. Although the latter was "worried" that the school did not need us, this worry was *not* mutual. From

the first, Tzila saw the project's insights about her school as extraordinarily helpful. She developed great respect for the project
staff member's ability to quietly indicate, by the occasional brief
remark, an important flaw in the way the school functioned. In most
cases, because of Tzila's general tendency to really listen, these
remarks were acted upon. At the beginning, we were worried that
our staff member might be encouraging the school to overestimate
the help that could be obtained from external experts, and thus that
she was developing a dependency relationship which might reduce
school initiative. But it became increasingly obvious that this was
not the case. Rather, the ideas that came from without *in this case*
seemed to be spurring the school on to developing new ideas of its
own, and in this respect the contribution of our staff member
seemed almost a perfect example of the sounding-board function I
have mentioned. In particular, over the years, a very close relationship was established, one that never resulted, however, in the staff
member's being coopted and thus losing her effectiveness.

My relationship with the Givon staff, and especially with
Amir, was in many ways similar. During the third year of the project, almost every Thursday morning I would spend an hour in his
office. Over a cup of coffee, we would chat about his school, his
plans for change, the difficulties he was facing, and so on. As in the
case of the Emek Reim School, there was a lot of mutual respect involved here, which brings me to the specific issue of concern to us.

At one of the meetings with him, Amir raised the problem of
the democratization of his school. As he put it, one of the central
aims was to create a truly democratic institution. He felt that when
it came to the teachers he had succeeded rather well, but with
pupils he saw only failure. The student parliament did not function
well without continual advice and pushing from the teachers. Students' "volunteer" activities in the community were not volunteer
at all, but were the result of subtle teacher pressure. All in all, the
kids seemed not to want to be autonomous, fully participating
members of a democratic school community; this bothered Amir
considerably.

My suggestion (influenced, no doubt, by the discussion
around the history booklet in the first year, as reported in Case VIII,
at which time Naharaim had a different principal) was that the
school staff might be transmitting a double message to the students.
At least, it seemed worth checking out the possibility. All the
examples Amir had given of activities in which democracy was
desirable were examples of extracurricular activities. Yet, 90 per-

cent of school time, students were in the classroom. It may be, I said, that in the classroom the teachers were very undemocratic and did not encourage autonomy. If so, their hidden curricula in the classroom may have contradicted and overwhelmed the democratic messages transmitted outside it. In such a case, it would be understandable why the school was not succeeding in developing a truly democratic, autonomous spirit among students.

Again, let me stress: I made this suggestion in a relaxed, informal, weekly chat with a very open, intelligent principal who knew how to listen. Also, I think my suggestion was not exactly absurd. Of course, that does not make it correct. I am aware, as is surely apparent from previous cases I have described, that I have a tendency to read pedagogical difficulties into just about every school problem. All I am saying here is that my "hypothesis" was sufficiently reasonable to warrant being checked. And yet Amir did not buy it. By this I mean he heard me out, he said, "Mmmmm, that might be," and then he obviously simply put it in that corner of his mind reserved for ideas that do not move him, do not turn him on. Again, he did not reject the idea, he was not defensive about it, he simply was not turned on by it. I found that rather surprising. A principal was bothered about something, someone whom he respected and considered reasonably knowledgeable in these matters threw out an hypothesis to explain his problem — an hypothesis that, if correct, suggested certain lines of action he could adopt — and yet this principal did not really give this hypothesis serious consideration.

As I was puzzling over this incident, something very similar happened at the Emek Reim School. Our impression of the school's functioning was that a great deal of the school's "openness" stopped at the classroom door, and that behind that door (to use Goodlad's famous phrase) some rather conventional, uninspired teaching was going on. This had been raised at the feedback session in which we had presented our diagnosis and the school staff, with great enthusiasm, had reached the conclusion that something must be done about the problem. During the next year or so, our project staff member had had a most frustrating time. Practical decisions to act on this diagnosis had been forgotten. Committees formed to deal with the problem had not been convened because of "practical difficulties." At meetings that had finally taken place, teachers had backtracked and expressed doubts whether anything could or should be done about pedagogical matters.

All this can be explained very conventionally. However, consider the following report of our project staff representative at Emek Reim to the rest of the project staff in the middle of the third year of the project:

> [Tzila and I] talked again about the need to improve teaching at the school and about the strategy that we had formulated to this end last year: a group of teachers from different disciplines who are among the most innovative teachers will meet regularly once a fortnight, and together with me will suggest pedagogical ideas, then at the next stage each member of the group will try to diffuse these ideas further, to crystallize them into a practical plan and to push for its implementation, all this within the subject department to which he/she belongs. . . . In actual fact it didn't work that way: the group met and they raised all sorts of arguments why really the school doesn't need a group like this, and if it does— why them? and why is this not being done within the framework of each department? and what use is it to invest energy in improving teaching when we all know that it is impossible to influence from without and to change people? and how can anyone expect them to devote time to things like this when they are so busy with a thousand other things more important to them? etc. etc. Tzila and I stood firm. We didn't avoid trying to counter all their arguments. But in the face of such lack of enthusiasm nothing could be done. Tzila and I discussed things after this failure. It seems to me that the only reason she felt uncomfortable about what had happened was because she thought that it had upset me. During this conversation it became clear to me that *she herself is not convinced that it is worthwhile investing much energy in developing the didactic aspects of the teacher's work.* The amount of freedom the teacher has to choose and to change is very small and she is also very pessimistic about the possibility of inducing change through external influence (emphasis added).

There would thus appear to be something about pedagogical innovation that makes it problematic even for two principals as committed to innovation as Tzila and Amir. What could this be? The fact that pedagogic change is difficult, as Tzila seems to be saying? Hardly. After all, both she and Amir had been prepared to push for changes in other areas where there also exist many barriers and limitations. Calling pedagogic change difficult is thus, in their case, to label their attitude toward it rather than to explain it.

The explanation I am going to offer is linked to educational discourse in Israel in general and, in fact, to the way such discourse must be expressed in the Hebrew language. I think the source for the problematic nature of pedagogy can be found in the Israeli notion of *mechanech*. This is the name given in Hebrew to the school functionary parallel to the American homeroom teacher. However, this is a bit misleading because, unlike the American situation, the *mechanech* is *the* central figure in the high school structure. As previously mentioned, the class is an important unit within the school in Israel. Pupils in Israeli high schools are assigned to specific classes. A particular class of pupils will study a great number of their subjects together although they will split up for others. Each class has its own classroom, while the teachers do not. The latter move from class to class during the day. In certain schools, a particular group of pupils may stay together as a class for a number of years.

Each class has its own *mechanech*. The *mechanech* is one of the subject matter teachers of the class; a teacher's duties as *mechanech* are officially counted as one-eighth (three hours a week) of a weekly teaching load. As all *mechanchim* know, the time spent far exceeds this. First, the *mechanech* meets with the class for one hour a week, which is known either as the "*mechanech* hour" or the "social hour." The content of this weekly meeting is determined by the *mechanech* and varies considerably from class to class. Some of the more usual options are: discussions of topical issues, guest speakers on various subjects, discussions of class problems—for example, tensions between different groups and pupils within the class or discipline problems with other teachers — or listening to music. In addition, many *mechanchim* often use this hour for announcements, checking absenteeism and other routine chores.

Some *mechanchim* plan the *mechanech* hour by themselves. Others rely heavily on a class committee and in fact devote a great deal of time to developing such a committee. The latter's duties usually cover a great deal of extracurricular activities. The class is to some extent a social unit, and once or twice a year official class parties are held. School hikes are usually organized on a class basis, and in Israel they are extremely important. At least once a year the class (perhaps together with other classes) will go on a three- or four-day hike. In addition, a class may spend two or three days working as volunteers on a neighboring kibbutz, and during the year there will be a number of one day outings as well. All these activities are organized by the class committee together with the *mechanech,* who is the one teacher who will participate in all of them.

The *mechanech* is also the intermediary between the class and teachers who may be having difficulties with the class as a whole or with specific pupils. Teachers feel free to report on these difficulties to the *mechanech* (as long as they are not seen as indicating teaching inadequacies or failings, of course), and expect that the *mechanech* will deal with them. This occurs during the *mechanech* hour, as previously mentioned, or in private conferences with particular pupils.

The *mechanech* is expected to maintain a rather close relationship with each pupil, to meet with them on a one-to-one basis, to visit their homes and to try and help them with problems. If pupils begin slacking at their studies, the *mechanech* will try to get them back into the groove. Toward the end of each term, the *mechanech* calls a meeting of all the teachers of the class to discuss the grades and behavior of each pupil. The *mechanech* is expected to supply the background information on each pupil and, although this is not an official characteristic of the role, to act as a "friend in court" for the more problematic pupils.

At the end of the term, each pupil receives a report card. The card is given by the *mechanech,* who uses the opportunity to give the youngster a pep talk, if needed, or a pat on the back. In addition, twice a year at least, parents are invited to the school and given information about their child's progress. In most cases, parents will meet only with the *mechanech*; however, they may be sent to speak with other teachers.

This peculiar mix of tasks should not obscure the fact that among Israeli educators the importance of the *mechanech* is unquestioned and the role has been described as "the most important function in the process of education." Or, as one high school principal put it: "The *mechanech* is the leader . . . the glue which holds the school together; . . . he must be open, knowledgeable, expert, sensitive." In most schools the *mechanchim,* who constitute about 30 percent of the teaching staff, are clearly the elite group within the faculty. Important management decisions are considered to have been ratified by all the teachers even if in actual practice they have only been approved by the *mechanchim,* who in many schools meet as a group on a regular basis.

In another context, Walter Ackerman and I have analysed the *mechanech* role and have attempted to uncover its hidden logic.[74]

From the point of view of the present discussion, it is sufficient to point out that the *mechanech* is the functionary who is concerned with pastoral care, social education, and character development. And now to reveal one fact that I deliberately have not yet mentioned: the word *mechanech* translates into English as *educator*. Not only this, but also educational discourse in Hebrew distinguishes sharply between teacher and educator. In fact, the notion of a *mechanech* originally developed on the kibbutz schools, the latter being called *Batei Chinuch*—literally, "houses of education" — and not *Batei Sefer,* the usual word used for "schools," which translates literally as "houses of the book"! Any visitor who spends some time in an Israeli high school is almost certain to hear a teacher say something like the following: "I don't deal with education, I am only a teacher." This sentence sounds perfectly natural in Hebrew, whereas in English it does not. A similar idea might be expressed in English as, "I do not concern myself with educational matters, I am only instructing my students." But this is a little forced and, anyway, is very different, because English allows us to say things like, "He isn't a very good mathematics teacher, all he does is give mathematical instruction instead of really teaching." It is almost impossible to express this in Hebrew. Educational discourse in Israel is thus dominated by the conceptual tree presented in figure 3.4.

Figure 3.4 leads us to an explanation of Tzila's and Amir's attitudes. Both of them, because they are innovative and because they conceive of innovation as being related to educational matters, are led by the logic of the language they speak to concentrate on the left-hand side of the tree. A suggestion like the one I made to Amir then becomes problematic. He was interested in something related

FIGURE 3.4.   Basic Conceptual Tree of Israeli Educational Discourse

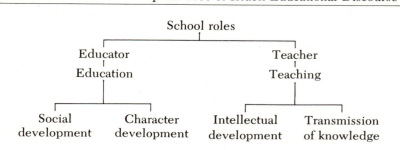

to character development, and I suggested something that is situated on the right-hand branch of the tree. Because we are again not concerned here with an extreme formulation of the Whorf-Sapir hypothesis, which sees thought as totally determined by language, he could *understand* my idea. But because of what I would call a weak version of the hypothesis, he was not turned on by it.

I can offer no *independent* evidence that Tzila's thought about education is shaped by the above conceptual tree. With regard to Amir, there is one very suggestive fact to be considered. As related in Case III, Amir did introduce one major innovation related to teachers rather than *mechanchim*. He introduced the idea that each department would meet once a week during school time. On the face of it, this makes his lack of enthusiasm about my idea concerning the relationship between pedagogy and pupil autonomy even stranger. Yet in terms of the conceptual tree shown in figure 3.4, this is perfectly understandable. His innovation was focused on developing *staff* cohesiveness and thus did not violate this tree. Thus the fact that pedagogic changes, or rather changes that impinged on the teacher role, became problematic only when they were related to educational matters (in the Hebrew sense), does support my hypothesis.

However, perhaps more important is the very strong evidence for the force of the conceptual tree (see figure 3.4) in shaping Israeli educational practice in general. First, we have the astonishing fact that while there is no dearth of research that details the shortcomings in the classroom performance of Israeli teachers there has been no research, as far as I know, regarding the effectiveness of the *mechanech*. Yet there is widespread consensus, in and out of professional circles, that the *mechanech* is the solution to many of the ills that beset schools and that, given the opportunity, is capable of restoring schooling to its preordained place in the forming of the national character. This rather touching faith in the *mechanech*, without a shred of evidence, has become almost a ritual part of public statements about education by senior ministry officials, and only makes sense within the terms of the conceptual tree I have suggested, or at least of some such tree.

Second, let us consider how this conceptual tree has changed in the last decade. In order to do this, let me correct a slight oversimplification of the tree. Up to the early seventies, teaching, in addition to being concerned with intellectual matters and knowledge transmission, was also conceived as being concerned with the transmission of national values—or at least history, geography, and

FIGURE 3.5.   Pre-1970 Expanded Conceptual Tree

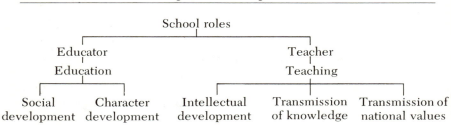

literature teachers were supposed to deal with such matters, which were important but not very important. Thus the tree's fuller structure was as shown in figure 3.5. Then in the early seventies a public debate developed around the question whether the transmission of values was indoctrination or not. Central to this debate was a series of newspaper articles by Sammach Yizhar, a well-known author.[75] Public response to the issue was lively and was not limited to those directly concerned with education. I remember an occasion when I was invited to respond to Yizhar at a lecture on his ideas to a group of air force pilots. Yizhar's contribution did not have the effect he had hoped (he was very opposed to the typical transmission of values in schools, which he saw as limiting the child's autonomy). All he really succeeded in doing was to reaffirm and strengthen the belief that transmission of national values was very important. But he—or rather the debate—did manage to alter the "line of cleavage." As a result of this ongoing debate, I suggest that in Israel today the educational conceputal tree presented in figure 3.5 has changed to that shown in figure 3.6. The reason I say this is that over the last five to ten years a great deal of effort has been invested in trying to *improve* the transmission of national values. New programs have been developed, and these, in almost all cases, have taken these matters *out of the hands* of literature, history, and geography teachers. Today it is the *mechanech,* in the *mechanech* hour and in special short-term projects, who is expected to transmit values.

This highlights two important theses I have argued for. First, the alteration of the "line of cleavage" did not change the basic two-branch structure of the conceptual tree. Rather, it reaffirmed that structure. Because Israeli educational discourse distinguishes between education and teaching, the moment one nonintellectual

FIGURE 3.6. Revised Expanded Conceptual Tree

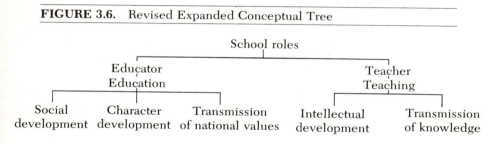

aspect of teaching became really important from the "educational" point of view, it was moved across to the "education" branch of the tree! Thus the "transmission of values versus indoctrination" debate supplies us with strong support for the existence of this tree.

Second, this story suggests what might have been necessary to make Tzila and Amir respond more easily to the idea of pedagogical innovation. I stress "more easily." By the end of the third year of the project, things *had* changed. Tzila had become more committed to pedagogical innovation, and had succeeded in setting up a group of teachers who were trying (this time with far more enthusiasm) to come to grips with this aspect of school life. Amir had begun to think seriously about the possible link between character development and teaching methods and had tentatively begun planning how to address this question the following year. All this came about because our Emek Reim representative and myself continued talking with Tzila and Amir and their school staffs about these issues. This was not problematic because for neither Tzila nor Amir was this set of questions seen as threatening. Essentially what had happened was that dialogue between our project staff and the schools had created a minisystem of educational discourse that influenced school practice by a process similar to that which a more general system would have generated. I will return to the creation of such minisystems in chapter 6. At present, suffice it to say that in this particular case the process by which the school belief systems were changing in response to the minisystems' influence was a very slow one. This brings us back to the question of what would have made the change an easier one.

Let us indulge in some fantasizing. In 1977 Israel Scheffler published an article in the *Teachers College Record* entitled, "In Praise of the Cognitive Emotions."[76] One of the main thrusts of this article was to question the cognitive/emotional dualism so standard in our culture. Now, let us suppose that this article had not been written by an American but by an Israeli, and had been published in an Israeli journal. Let us also suppose that the Israeli was not an academic in the usual sense, but a renowned author like Sammach Yizhar, and that the article was one of a series of articles on the relationship between cognition and what is considered (at least in Israel) as opposed to cognition, for example, character. Let us now try to imagine what would happen if this series of articles caught the public eye. First, this could lead to things like newspaper interviews, or perhaps an appearance with ministry of education officials, a teacher or two, and some professor of education on some TV talk show. Within the context of Israeli political reality, this could well lead to the minister of education setting up a committee to investigate the work of teachers in the classroom vis-à-vis character development, emotional development, and things of that sort. In other words, such a series of articles might result in a profound restructuring of the educational conceptual tree I have been discussing. And if all this had taken place before my first conversation with Amir and our Emek Reim representative's series of conversations with Tzila, I think this case study would have been very different.

This is only a fantasy, but the way the real series of articles by Yizhar influenced educational discourse in Israel shows that this is not an absurd scenario. In fact, my argument in the theoretical section of this chapter was that events of this sort are the most common way of bringing about changes in educational belief systems, and thus changes in educational practice.

Returning to the concept of school self-renewal: could Tzila and Amir have escaped the pervasive influence of educational discourse by themselves? I think not. Universities may not be of much use in the real world, but they do create an enclave where people can develop the philosophical, historical, and anthropological skills needed to question the assumptions of their culture and can find the time to use these skills. People who have to get out and *do* things, and in the final analysis are far more important, are simply unlikely to have the skills or the time to question these assumptions.

4

Self-Renewal
and the Structure
of Educational Systems

THEORETICAL CONSIDERATIONS

All authors hope that the books they are writing have some originality. Certainly much of what I have written in chapters 2 and 3 is original in some sense. However, in this chapter, most of what I present is pretty standard sociological theory and fact about schools and school systems. Except for one section that deals with what I call *implicit power talk*, most of this chapter will review mainstream work in organizational theory and in sociology developed in the early 1970s. This work uses conventional terminology. For instance, it is concerned with power relations, which thus far I have deliberately ignored. It shows quite clearly, I think, that there are serious structural limits to the possibility of school self-renewal.

In addition, I will be making explicit an aspect of the whole problem of school self-renewal which has up to now been only implicit in the discussion. This is the systemic issue. In my original enthusiasm for the promotion of school self-renewal, I saw it as an across-the-board strategy for improving an entire educational system. As we will see, possibilities that make sense when talking about one school in a district become unworkable when the horizon expands to include the entire district. Also, introducing the systemic consideration forces us to compare educational systems. It may be easier to promote something very close to complete self-renewal in one system than in another. It then becomes important to spell out the inhibiting and facilitating properties of educational systems vis-à-vis school self-renewal. Thus I will be using what

Pfeffer and Salancik, in *The External Control of Organizations*, call the external as opposed to the internal perspective.[1]

One further introductory comment: since much of the discussion focuses on educational systems rather than on individual schools, case studies relating to specific schools in our project are less relevant here than in previous chapters. This does not mean that I will not introduce illustrative material from our project, but rather that this material will tend to relate to the general effect of the Israeli educational system on schools and not to particular properties of the project schools.

School Self-Renewal and Professionalism

The idea of school self-renewal conjures up visions of the school staff as a group of people participating very responsibly in group decision making, these decisions being central to the running of the school. In other words, we can conceive of this group of people as highly competent professionals. I stress the word "professionals" because the group decision-making process referred to would seem to exemplify at least four properties generally linked with those occupations called "professions":

1. The decision-making process relates to the provision of a service (education) to clients (the students and perhaps their parents).
2. For the decisions reached to be "good" ones, it would seem that the decision makers (the staff) need to use quite a bit of technical expertise.
3. The decision-making process is largely autonomous, the decision makers being relatively free from the demands and interference of lay persons and/or administrative superiors.
4. The decisions and their implementations are being monitored by peer group control. The staff are a *group* with joint responsibilities.[2]

I am concerned here only with properties 3 and 4, which from now on I will refer to as the *group autonomy* and *collegiality* conditions for school self-renewal. The main question I will be addressing is this: *do the structural properties of schools and educational systems make it possible for school staffs to have such group autonomy and to function with such collegiality?* A lot of mainstream work of the 1970s in organizational theory and in the sociology of teaching indicates quite clearly that the answer is no. I will show this by considering autonomy and collegiality separately.

Can a Teaching Staff Be Autonomous?

There are four necessary conditions for true autonomy, either of an individual or of a group. First, the person or group must be relatively free from direct external control. Second, the person or group must have the ability or talent to make intelligent decisions and implement them. Third, the person or group must want to be free from direct external control. Fourth, the person or group must believe themselves to be free from direct external control (even if I am sitting in an unlocked room I am not free to leave if I firmly believe the door to be locked). Let us consider each of these conditions in turn, with regard to school staffs.

On the face of it, the extent to which a school staff is free from direct external control will vary from system to system. In certain countries (such as the United States, for example) local school boards appear to have great control over what occurs in the schools. In other countries (such as Israel) a central ministry of education seems capable of controlling just about all activity. On the other hand, in countries like England the locus of control seems to reside firmly in the schools themselves. There is certainly something to be said for this way of looking at things. It leads us to certain very reasonable hypotheses and explanations concerning which types of education systems will be more conducive to the promotion of school self-renewal. For example, consider the effort that John Goodlad and I had to expend in creating a league of schools, with the schools' headmasters meeting once a month. Yet as long ago as 1869 the headmasters of the English public schools had established, on their own initiative, the famous and extremely powerful Headmasters' Conference.[3] This seems perfectly understandable when one compares the degree of freedom headmasters have in England with the far more circumscribed freedom of their U.S. and Israeli counterparts.

Nevertheless, the work of theorists like Weick, Dreeben, and Lortie suggests a rather different way of looking at this question of direct external control.[4] They point out that even in those systems in which there seems to be much direct control, in fact external control is minimal. The reason for this is not, as Meyer and Rowan would have it,[5] because the external controllers refrained from exerting their power to avoid opening a Pandora's box, but rather because the structural properties of schools in *all* education systems make it extremely difficult for directives from on high to be simply passed down the line. Two such structural properties are particularly important: first, schools are what Weick calls loosely coupled systems,[6] or what Cohen, March, and Olsen call organized anarchies.[7] One particularly central aspect of the loose coupling of elements in schools is what Lortie describes as their cellular structure of self-contained classrooms.[8] Teachers work as individuals behind the classroom door far from the view of any external authority. This obviously has important consequences vis-à-vis collegiality and I will analyse the notions of loose coupling and cellular structure in greater detail in the section devoted to collegiality. For the present, it is sufficient to point out that the school's cellular structure increases the independence of individual teachers and of the staff as a whole from direct external control. The second structural property of schools is that the products of schooling are intangible and there exists no well-defined teaching technology. For this reason Robert Dreeben maintains:

> Because of the complexity of teaching activities, putting educational policy into effect by passing directives down the line is all but impossible. Difficult as this process is even in industrial organizations that have a far more tangible product and a more clear-cut technology underlying the production process, the directives are even less effective in the schools because the outcomes of educational programs are indistinctly defined and protean in character. Although the organizational charts of school systems indicate clear lines of office hierarchies, this clarity is partly an illusion. . . . Schools . . . cannot be understood simply as the last stop on the transmission line of school system policies. Although principals and teachers are constrained by system-wide directives . . . they also have autonomy. . . . The core activities of classroom management and instruction over extended periods of time cannot readily be governed by rules because of the irregularity and flexibility inherent in these activities. . . . Perhaps the distinguishing characteristic of school systems is the vague connection between policy formation at both the high and middle levels of the hierarchy and its implementation at the level where instruction takes place—the classroom.[9]

It seems then that if the autonomy required by the notion of school self-renewal were simply relative freedom from direct external control, then there would exist no serious structural constraints on such self-renewal. Unfortunately, the three further conditions for true autonomy do not fare as well when subjected to sociological analysis. Consider the ability condition. Put bluntly, for a teaching staff to be truly autonomous, it must be made up of people of relatively high intellectual caliber. When one is talking of one particular school, this condition can obviously be met in certain cases; however, problems arise when one has to consider an entire school system. It seems that the teaching profession is not staffed on the average by persons of particularly high intellectual caliber. To make such a statement is to open oneself to charges of inexcusable arrogance, which is probably why the subject of teachers' intellectual abilities is usually skirted in the literature on educational change. However, ignoring this issue is a classic example of ostrich-like behavior.[10] Dreeben offers an extremely powerful argument why the intellectual caliber of teachers should be low:

> If there is a yearly contingent of intellectually talented college graduates and graduate students, the first question is what occupations they select. If, for example, they spread themselves about equally over the professions, a segment of the talented cohort will fill up the vacancies in a small occupation but not in a large one. Large occupations, simply to fill the available openings, have to fish deeper in the intellectual pool to fill its positions. Teaching is one such large occupation; it comes under particular pressure to find warm bodies to fill classrooms particularly during times of an expanding youth population.[11]

Thus it appears extremely unlikely that the majority of schools could be staffed by a group of intellectually superior teachers, and this would seem to offer an insurmountable barrier to the creation of self-renewing schools. There is, however, a counterargument. It might be argued that the demand that a teaching staff be characterized in its entirety by its intellectual caliber is far too stringent and that it is sufficient for school self-renewal if the staff contains a small elite group capable of change. (As we have seen in chapter 2, the democratic emphasis in the school self-renewal literature is not necessary if self-renewal is conceived of as improved organizational problem-solving ability.) This counterargument is certainly powerful, but it has two flaws. First, the creation of such an elite group is a radical step that contradicts one of the most striking properties of teaching—the fact that it is a mobility-blocked profession. Many theorists have pointed out that the teaching novice and the veteran with thirty years' experience perform almost identical tasks and that teacher "career advancement" is usually achieved by leaving teaching. The implementation of differential staffing arrangements in schools has not been very widespread or successful, and this is probably a sign that this is an extremely difficult change to implement and also that successful implementation might have serious unforeseen consequences. Second, for differential staffing to be an effective counter to Dreeben's "warm bodies" argument, it would have to be implemented across an entire educational system. This means that it would have to be imposed on the schools from without. We thus have the rather paradoxical situation that a move designed to increase staff autonomy requires an act of direct external control to achieve it.

Let us now turn to the third condition for staff autonomy—the *desire* of the staff for autonomy. Central to an analysis of this notion is Dan Lortie's argument concerning teacher conservatism. Lortie conceives of the conservative teacher as unenthusiastic about the new and untried, as approving of existing arrangements and not motivated to press for change.[12] In his view, teaching tends to attract conservative people, or at least people who are conservative about schools. There are two reasons for this: (1) Schools are unique organizations in that new staff recruits have spent most of their lives prior to recruitment in schools. Becoming a teacher is a continuation of something one is very familiar with. Thus Lortie argues that the new recruits consist of a very small group of revolutionaries who were dissatisfied with their school experiences as students, and a very large group of people for whom being a student was a very positive, rewarding, comfortable experience. This second group is likely to approve of present school arrangements. (2) Because of the fact that entry into teaching is rather easy and also because teaching conditions vis-à-vis hours and holidays are also rather easy, compared to the standard nine-to-five job, school staffs are likely to contain a large proportion of married women who see teaching as providing a second income that allows them considerable time with their families. School staffs are also likely to contain some male teachers for whom teaching is a transitory profession. For many in these two groups, teaching is not a profession to which they are highly committed, and thus they are unlikely to welcome changes and innovations that demand commitment.

Teacher conservatism as Lortie analyzes it clearly contradicts the third condition for group autonomy. Teachers desiring group autonomy *want* to engage in serious group discussion and responsible decision making. They expect their actions to be the result of their decisions. They may at times opt for existing arrangements, but they do so because they have decided that in a particular situation these arrangements are best. Conservative teachers, on the other hand, want to continue present arrangements simply because they are familiar and do not confront the teachers with the need to make new decisions.

The question is: could the social forces that encourage teacher conservatism be altered or countered? In the last chapter of *Schoolteacher* entitled "Speculations on Change," Lortie considers three scenarios for change. The first he calls "The Erosion of Tradition." The developments in educational research have created a whole new set of interests—"interests in the process of change itself."[13] This has led to "the institutionalization of the press toward change."[14] Lortie suggests that in the face of these developments it will be difficult to maintain the conservative ethos of teaching:

> The most obvious consequence is that teachers will have to adapt to a context where conservatism, particularly reflexive conservatism, becomes increasingly suspect. This is not to say that teachers will have to accept all the options presented to them; it seems unlikely, however, that a dogged commitment to the past will work if options continue to multiply and norms of rationality take hold. Groups of teachers who openly resist change will run the risk of being labeled "reactionary" and "obstructive"; such conflict may take place in the arena of collective bargaining. Individual teachers may find that the expectations around them gradually shift to new techniques and more frequent innovation. There will be a generalized pressure toward adaptibility.[15]

I do not find Lortie's argument or speculation particularly persuasive. There seems to be no evidence that educational theorists have improved their communication with educational practitioners of late, and this is essential if the interests of the new change-oriented professions were to make themselves felt in the field. In addition, it is not self-evident that the outcome of the clash between the "institutionalization of the press towards change" and the social forces supporting teacher conservatism would be an increase of teacher adaptability. However, perhaps the most serious flaw associated with Lortie's scenario is that we once again encounter the paradox that increasing teacher autonomy seems to require the imposition of external forces.

Implicit Power Talk

The fourth precondition of teacher autonomy—the *belief* in
freedom from external control—will be discussed more extensively
than the others, for two reasons. First, it is least often dealt with.
Second, in certain educational systems, whose properties will be
stipulated, the absence of this belief is probably the most important
structural limitation on school self-renewal. The central concept in
this discussion will be "implicit power talk," which I introduce
through the following example. Imagine a school principal in a
centralized educational system receiving a circular from, say, the
chief history inspector, containing this sort of sentence: "From
1985 all pupils taking the matriculation history examination will not
be able to choose to be examined either on a period of eighteenth-
century history or on a period of nineteenth-century history, but
will all be required to answer at least one essay question on a
period of nineteenth-century history."
      What information does this sentence convey? Obviously, it
supplies the principal with information about a new rule concerning certain activities associated with the study of history in the
school. It also implies that this rule must be obeyed, and in addition
that the chief history inspector has the power in this particular
system to enforce obedience. All this information I regard as true.
However, this sentence (and the fact that it appears in an official
circular, signed by the history inspector) suggests many other
things that are not as obviously true and in certain cases are probably false. For instance, the sentence carries the implication that the
inspector's power to make this rule is uncontroversial, unchallengeable. Or, to take another example, the sentence suggests that
the history inspector has the right to make all rules about history
teaching and is in fact completely "in charge" of history teaching.
Note that these implications are not mentioned openly nor do they
follow logically from what is written. But they will be picked up
unthinkingly by just about every principal and history teacher who
reads the circular. Implications such as these I call *implicit power
talk*. They are contained in discourse initiated by sources outside
the school that have some direct control over school affairs. They
need not appear in a circular as in this example. Official statements
to the mass media, even informal communication with the school,
can also contain implicit power talk. What is important is that such
power talk suggests to the school that the external source has the
power to control certain school activities whereas in fact it does not

(although it controls other activities), and that this suggestion is not made explicitly. The function of implicit power talk is to maintain control of the school through what Perrow calls "implicit controls" (see chapter 3), that is, by encouraging school personnel to believe that they have less autonomy than they in fact have.[16]

Implicit power talk can be extremely effective. It has the advantage of being formulated in a taken-for-granted manner, and, as Schütz, Garfinkel, and Goffman have shown, that which is taken for granted can usually impose its own definition of reality on situations.[17] The claims of power talk, because they are not formulated as claims, tend to remain unchallenged. Also, even when their true nature is recognized, it takes a brave person or someone with considerable knowledge of the system to reject them. This is because implicit power talk comes from a source that does have real power. The dividing line between power claims that the source can enforce and those it cannot is rarely obvious. So ignoring a particular claim may mean ignoring a true claim. People who reject or ignore what seems to them like implicit power talk run the risk of getting into real trouble; most prefer to play it safe.

This does not mean that implicit power talk exists to the same extent in all educational systems, nor does it mean that in those systems in which it is pervasive it is uniformly effective. The fourth condition for teacher autonomy—the *belief* that one is free—unlike the second and the third, and the first, to a certain extent, is not contradicted by structural properties of the sort that necessarily characterize all educational systems. There are contingent structural properties that render implicit power talk more or less effective. At one time I thought the most relevant variable was the degree of centralization of the system, with implicit power talk being more effective in centralized systems. This now seems too crude a measure. We have come to realize that many of the hopes held out for decentralization were rather naive.[18] A far more sensitive variable is the degree of focus in implicit power talk. An unfocused educational system vis-à-vis power talk is one in which a relatively large number of different and competing external sources indulge in such talk. A focused system has very few such sources and possibly only one really dominant one. Implicit power talk will be less effective in an unfocused system because inevitably the various sources will contradict each other at times. This will tend to weaken the taken-for-granted, unchallengeable aura of power talk.

Degree of focus of power talk and degree of centralization are to a certain extent related. A centralized educational system is by definition very focused (provided, of course, that it indulges in implicit power talk). On the other hand, decentralization need not necessarily lead to a lessening of focus. It is conceivable that a local school board can be so powerful that its implicit power talk effectively overwhelms the talk of other potential sources. In such a case, there does not seem to be much difference between a centralized and a decentralized educational system from the point of view of inhibiting school self-renewal.

There is one proviso, however. For the above claim to be upheld, the number of schools controlled by the local source must be sufficiently large to require some degree of bureaucratization of the relationship between the schools and the source. *Implicit power talk is maximally effective in focused and bureaucratized educational systems. It then becomes in fact so effective that the school staff's belief in its lack of autonomy tends to become a self-fulfilling prophecy and its belief in the external source's power tends to become self-perpetuating.* There are two main reasons for this.

First, the structure of power relations in any system directs the thrust to advancement and survival into certain channels. To put it in another way: the way to get ahead or even to avoid being fired is determined to a large extent by what the boss expects one to do; these expectations are often not determined so much by the boss's intrinsic personality but rather by the boss's fulfillment of a leadership role, and that in turn is determined by the kind of organization the boss is head of. In a highly focused educational system, the major external source of implicit power talk becomes a very real boss. If, in addition, the system is bureaucratized, schools will be evaluated by this external source in bureaucratic terms. Efficient rule-following and rule-enforcing behavior is evidence that a school or its staff is functioning well. This means that the staff and particularly the principal will be socialized into becoming typical bureaucratic intermediaries—people adept at displaying such rule-following and rule-enforcing behavior. Over time the system will tend to attract people with such propensities.[19] When this occurs, we have come full circle—implicit power talk has succeeded in staffing the schools with people who do not want autonomy, who feel more comfortable following the rules set down by external authorities.

Second, to best understand the self-perpetuating nature of implicit power talk in certain educational systems, let us consider the following hypothetical case (which, as we shall see, is not so very hypothetical). Assume that those in the upper echelons in the ministry of education in a centralized, bureaucratized, focused educational system decide in good faith to try to increase school autonomy. This does not mean that they decide to completely abolish the centralized structure of the system, but only that they wish to increase the number of areas of activity in which schools are free to do as they please and to reduce the implicit controls operative in the system. One of the most important things the senior officials must do is to replace implicit power talk by implicit and explicit autonomy talk. There are three channels of communication through which this must be done: (a) mediated communication, by which senior ministry officials speak to the schools through officials from the mid-level of the system such as district school inspectors; (b) direct communication initiated by senior officials, by which senior officials make statements to school staffs directly either through the mass media or circulars, or by meeting with them and engaging in face-to-face discussion; and (c) direct responding communication, by which senior officials have to respond to requests, queries, and complaints addressed to them by school personnel.

Ironically, because of the bureaucratized nature of the system, attempts to reduce implicit power talk will in fact tend to reinforce the power talk. This works differently in each communicative context. The problems with mediated communication is that the mid-level functionaries of a bureaucracy have an interest in maintaining implicit power talk.[20] To a large extent, mid-level management positions in all organizations are created as a medium for such talk. There is a danger that when senior officials trust mid-level officials to pass on autonomy talk, the latter will distort the messages and transform them into power talk. This may not be deliberate subversion (although subversion also can occur), but rather a spontaneous misreading of their task.

In addition to such a simple misunderstanding of autonomy talk policy as power talk policy, mid-level officials also have the problem of the "cutoff point." Senior officials do not intend to completely restructure the power relations of the system. There will always be some areas in which the expression of the ministry's direct power is quite appropriate. Senior officials know what these areas are. However, it is difficult to formulate this in terms of general principles. Therefore, mid-level officials have the problem of interpretation. Is this area one in which the schools are now free to do as they wish or not? Inevitably, they are going to misinterpret at times and, considering their position, they are far more likely to err on the side of limiting freedom rather than granting it. Thus once again intended autonomy talk will become power talk. All in all, descriptions of a public bureaucracy's resistance to change seem to apply very well to the situation I am relating here. As Donald Warwick writes:

> Once hierarchy and rules take root . . . many parties become interested in their preservation. Whatever its origins, whatever services it does or does not provide, and whatever the "rational" justification for its continued existence, an administrative agency will usually be able to mount substantial opposition to basic change in its structure or operation. . . . Experience with both large and small reorganizations thus reveals an extrenched resistance to bureaucratic change, and a tendency for amputated limbs to grow back.[21]

The mid-level official becomes a serious source of distortion for upper echelon–school communication channels.

The problem with direct communication initiated by senior officials is that the officials have not the time to sit down and engage in extended dialogue with school staffs. Such dialogue is essential in order to clarify misunderstandings, build new relationships, and construct new common meanings, yet no senior official in a central ministry of education will be able to meet with a particular school staff very often. This is the price paid for efficiency through bureaucratization. Thus most communication will either be face-to-face but brief, or anonymous through the mass media and circulars. In such a situation, it is almost impossible for a senior official to announce to the schools that they are now free, say, to determine their own curriculum and for this statement to be taken at face value. What would be the reaction of school principals who are informed that their schools can now create their own curricula? One hopes that their reaction would be something like this: "Great! The central office has finally realized we are capable of deciding ourselves what to teach." However, remember that these principals have been working in a focused educational system vis-à-vis implicit power talk; very likely the system has successfully inculcated an exaggerated belief in the central office's potency. It is far more likely that the principals' reaction will be of this sort: "The central office keeps on changing the damn regulations! What do they want now? They obviously want me to do something, but blessed if I know what that is! I'll wait until I get further instructions." When one expects to receive instructions and nothing but instructions from the central office, one will read instructions into just about any string of words sent down by that office.

With regard to direct responding communication, senior officials are locked in a double bind, given the constraint that bureaucratized communication with schools is usually brief or anonymous. What should senior officials do when they receive a request, say, to allow a school to use its own curriculum? If they are serious about transforming implicit power talk into autonomy talk, they should refuse to be put in the position of being someone who authorizes requests, pointing out that the school can do as it likes. However, it is just about impossible to say this briefly or by letter in such a way that the school people involved will understand and not perceive this response as rude and insulting. So usually the official falls into the trap of responding. If the policy is to encourage autonomy, the response will probably be to grant the request. But doing this reinforces the official's status as someone with the right to grant such requests, and this ironically reinforces the idea of hierarchy. Once again, the medium is the message. Responding reinforces implicit power talk irrespective of the contents of the response.

The above analysis relates to the dilemmas of the senior officials in a central ministry of education. In this way, I have laid the ground for the analysis of certain of the case studies to follow. The hypothetical senior officials will become real officials of the Israeli Ministry of Education and Culture who have to deal with real dilemmas, double binds, and traps. Yet the analysis is basically valid even when we are talking about local control of schools. If any educational system is focused and sufficiently bureaucratized so that the senior local officials do not have the time to engage in extended dialogue with school staff, the same dilemmas, double binds, and traps are going to surface.[22]

Summary

We see that at least two of the four necessary conditions for group autonomy of school staffs (the ability and the desire conditions) do not obtain in any school system, and a third condition (the belief condition) does not obtain in systems that are focused vis-à-vis implicit power talk. Does this mean that structural properties of educational systems make such group autonomy an impossible ideal? This is probably putting things a bit too strongly. Conceivably, a coming together of certain social forces could change the structure of the teaching profession very profoundly. However, what does seem very clear is that such a coming together could not be the result of the work of change projects of the sort we undertook. The invisible hand of history at the macrolevel would need to be involved.

Collegiality

At first glance, it would seem that if a sociologist wished to indicate *the* central structural property of schools, the choice would vary depending on the perspective of the approach. Therefore, it is interesting that three very different perspectives, mentioned previously, have converged more or less on the same property. First we have the mainstream work in the sociology of teaching, especially that of Dreeben and Lortie, whose concern is with the self-contained classroom. As Dreeben puts it: "Perhaps the most important single property of classrooms, viewed from a school-wide perspective, is their spatial scattering and isolation."[23] Then we have the work of Basil Bernstein in the sociology of curriculum and his stress on two properties of educational codes, one of which is the degree of *classification* that is defined in terms of the strength of boundary maintenance, as previously mentioned in chapter 3. In Bernstein's view, this is linked to the idea of self-contained classrooms. The latter are manifestations of educational codes with strong classification—collection codes—and these, as we have seen, are the most prevalent types of codes.[24] Third, we have the perspective of organization theorists who stress that educational organizations are characterized by *loose coupling*—various entities or events within the organization are responsive to each other but preserve their own identity; their attachment is circumscribed, infrequent, weak, unimportant, and/or slow to respond.[25] Despite the conflicting images conjured up by the words "loose" and "strong," loose coupling and strong classification are clearly related. The difference is that Bernstein, by emphasizing boundaries between contents, is highlighting the "loose coupling" of the subjects in the school curriculum, whereas Weick and other organizational theorists are concerned with a very wide range of loosely coupled elements.[26]

Because we are concerned with teacher collegiality, the sociology of teaching perspective is most immediately relevant here. Teacher collegiality, as I have defined it, and the self-contained classroom structure seem to be at odds. Dreeben puts this very well:

Because they occupy isolated classrooms, teachers work separately from each other for most of the day; . . . they learn very little *at first hand* about what their colleagues are doing and how well they are doing it. . . . This situation contrasts sharply with other occupations with clearly definable work groups . . . where colleagues establish both working and informal relationships with each other. Thus in teaching, those with the most intimate knowledge about the work and its problems, and with the best qualifications to judge it, are afforded few opportunities to come together because of the geographical properties of the workplace.[27]

Yet the convergence of these three sociological perspectives is also very useful to us. It brings into play certain conclusions derived from the other two perspectives. In addition, the convergence invites us to compare the concepts "self-contained classrooms," "collection codes," and "loose coupling," which brings out certain differences between them and raises at least one interesting question.

Let us begin with this latter point. The distinction between loosely coupled and tightly coupled systems is clearly analytic. Real organizations are more or less loosely coupled, and comparison between them is effected by considering a coupling continuum. On the other hand, Bernstein seems to regard collection codes and integration codes (codes with weak classification) as a real dichotomy. Of course, classification is defined as *degree* of boundary maintenance, and this also suggests a continuum. However, the idea seems to be that an educational code is a set of coherent principles, a sort of deep structure of an educational system that generates certain actions and relationships and gives the system much of its meaning. Thus hybrid systems (in which classification is neither particularly strong nor weak) are unlikely to occur in fact, and, when they do, one still should be able to identify the underlying code that is operative. This will be either collection *or* integration.

When we consider self-contained classrooms, this difference between a continuum and a dichotomy is crucial. One of the things that all consultants attempting to promote school self-renewal try to do is to encourage teacher collegiality. Put in terms used by us and by Goodlad in the League of Cooperating Schools project: an attempt is made to make staff dialogue a central aspect of the school's day-to-day functioning. What is more, this seems to be something that is easily done. It may take some time, but it seems that change agents can usually get schools to increase staff dialogue. In our project this was one of the clear indications of relative success. But is this enough? What if one considers teacher isolation/teacher collegiality as a dichotomy? In such a case one has moved from isolation to collegiality only when the school *structure* changes from a self-contained classroom to what is known as a multiunit (that is, team teaching) structure. In other words, getting teachers to engage in dialogue or even occasionally to try team teaching may not be sufficient to achieve true collegiality. It might be necessary to make team teaching a basic organizational principle of the school.

Unfortunately, it seems to me that this stress of dichotomy rather than continuum vis-à-vis teacher dialogue is the correct one. Only in a school with a multiunit structure is teacher dialogue going to deal continually with problems teachers face in teaching specific subjects to specific students in specific ways. Only in such a school does teacher dialogue relate directly to what the teacher does at work. Unless we have that kind of dialogue, the problem of teacher professionalism will not be addressed and the possibility that the school will be engaged in *pedagogic and educational* self-renewal will not be realized. Teacher dialogue in a school with a self-contained classroom structure can help to transform the school into one that is administered democratically. This is probably a good thing, but it is not school self-renewal.

The previous paragraph opened with the word "unfortunately." This needs to be explained. When isolation/collegiality is viewed as two poles of a continuum, success in moving *toward* collegiality is easy to achieve. However, when they are dichotomous, then in order to achieve true collegiality a school must undergo the radical transformation from a self-contained classroom to a multiunit structure. Empirical considerations seem to indicate that this is an extremely difficult thing to achieve in all schools, certainly in large high schools. The original advocates of team teaching in the late 1950s and early 1960s were fully aware of how radical a change they were suggesting. They were proposing and predicting a revolution.[28] However, fifteen or twenty years later, team teaching can be seen as another of those fads that passed across the educational horizon and did not really change the way schools are, except perhaps in the very early grades. As Dreeben puts it: "Self-contained classrooms go back in history at least to the time of Boston's Quincy School built in 1847. They have been remarkably durable."[29]

This does not mean that the advocates of team teaching were wrong in their analysis of the sociological significance of this change. What they underestimated were the forces maintaining self-contained classrooms. In fact, the sociology of teaching perspective has found great difficulty in understanding the central variable (the school's cellular structure) that it itself postulated to capture the nature of teaching. Dreeben admits that the reasons for the durability of the self-contained classroom are "scarcely understood."[30] In an extremely unconvincing explanation, Lortie suggests that the growth of pupil population through the adoption of universal education, and the high turnover that characterizes the teaching profession invited administrators to view schools as "aggregates of classroom units, as collections of independent cells [rather] than as tightly integrated 'organisms.'"[31] However, today geographic mobility seems to characterize people who work in many different types of organizations—business firms, public bureaucracies, the military, universities. Yet the resulting high rate of turnover that characterizes these organizations (or, at least, their local branches) does not seem to have pushed them all in the direction of cellular structure to the same extent.

It is here that the perspectives of the sociology of curriculum and of organizations become useful. The sociology of curriculum *can* explain the prevalence of collection codes and the sociology of organizations *can* explain the durability of loosely coupled structures. These explanations also explain the durability of self-contained classrooms or at least offer a partial explanation. Bernstein, as we have seen in chapter 3, links the existence of collection codes both to the relationship between tertiary institutions of education and the rest of the education system, and also to the impact on education of the class structure of capitalist society. These interconnections are extremely powerful; thus transforming collection codes into integration codes would seem to be possible only if major changes in society in general were to take place.

Organization theory is less concerned with explaining how loosely coupled systems came about than with explaining or describing their consequences. However, such concerns do suggest why organizations that have become loosely coupled remain that way. Take as an example Weick's approach to loosely coupled systems.[32] In brief, his suggestion is that loose coupling can be highly *functional* for the organization. He lists a number of functional aspects of loose coupling.[33] First, it lowers the probability that the organization will have to respond to each little change in the environment. Second, loose coupling allows for local adaption which can be swift and economical. Third, if there is a breakdown in one portion of the system then it will be sealed off and need not affect other portions. Fourth (and this we have already discussed), it limits external control of workers (in our case, teachers) and thus there is more room for self-determination. Fifth, a loosely coupled system is less expensive to run because it takes time and money to coordinate people.

Weick's argument is of great significance in the context of theories of planned change. The important point is that he shows that loose coupling is not simply a dysfunctional aberration that members of the organization are too blind to see, and for this reason is a barrier to change that the change agent must overcome. On the contrary, Weick shows us that loose coupling can increase organizational effectiveness. It now becomes apparent that there are at least two different kinds of effectiveness. The first, associated with loose coupling, is a sort of conservative, minimize-your-losses type of effectiveness. The second, associated with self-renewal, is a more progressive, maximize-your-gains type. We thus now see that projects designed to promote school self-renewal (or, more specifically with regard to the terms I have introduced, to encourage schools to move from a self-contained classroom to a multiunit structure), are not necessarily projects that will transform ineffective schools into effective ones. They may be projects that are simply trying to transform schools that are effective in one way into schools that are effective in another. When seen in this light, not only can it be argued that school self-renewal is not self-evidently a good thing, but also we have a further reason why transforming schools into self-renewing organizations is so extraordinarily difficult.

CASES

Why Principals?

Of the three case studies to be presented here, two relate to principals rather than teachers. This requires explanation, because the focus of this chapter up to now has been teacher professionalism. I discuss principals because, first, our project was set up so that cases involving principals are more readily available. Second, all the case studies relate to implicit power talk, which focuses on authorities above teachers. Third, case studies concerning principals strengthen my point about the effectiveness of implicit power talk. There are approximately 600 high school principals and 13,000 high-school teachers in Israel. Common sense suggests that it is easier for senior officials wishing to transform power talk into autonomy talk to reach the relatively small number of principals rather than teachers. And yet even with the principals I will show that autonomy talk gets distorted back into power talk. My assumption is that this would be even more likely to occur with the teachers. Fourth, and this is the really important point, I take strong exception to the principal-teacher distinction. Throughout this book I have wavered between the use of the American term "principal" and the English term "headmaster" or "headmistress." In my view, this is not simply a linguistic matter. These words express two very different conceptions of the role of the principal/head-teacher. American usage stresses the principal as administrator, whereas English usage conceives of the headmaster/headmistress as a pedagogic and educational leader. Our project was predicated on this English conception.

Historical Background

All the case studies take place against the background of changes in the Israeli Ministry of Education and Culture during the 1970s. Therefore, it is necessary to provide some general historical background about the Israeli educational system.[34]

From 1953 to approximately 1970, the Ministry of Education and Culture epitomized a conception that David Pur and I characterize as "centralization for uniformity."[35] In other words, the ministry was conceived as a department of the state whose job it was to achieve educational uniformity through centralization—uniformity seen as something positive. We choose the year 1953 because in that year the State Education Law was passed. Up to this time there had existed a number of different trends. Each trend was, in effect, a separate school system associated unofficially with a particular political party. Thus, when parents had to choose which school to send their child to, they were faced with a real choice between schools with clearly different aims and philosophical and political bases. The State Education Law, by and large, did away with the trend system and established a national, unified system and a compulsory curriculum.[36] This was a direct outcome of the way statehood was envisioned at that time (it must be remembered that the State of Israel had been established only five years previously). Independent, different trends were reasonable when the people of Palestine lived under the mandatory rule of the British government. However, when mandatory Palestine became the State of Israel, such diversity seemed a contradiction of the idea of statehood. State education was seen as being characterized by uniformity in curriculum, aims (except in the religious domain), and methods, and by a centralized mechanism for putting that uniformity into effect.

The uniformity created by centralization in 1953 was nearly complete at the elementary level but it did not completely characterize high school education at that time. One of the reasons was that, although the elementary schools were and still are state-owned, this has never been the case with the high schools. Some of the latter are privately owned and others are municipal schools. The fact that high school teachers were not employees of the ministry ensured that the high schools would have slightly more of an "open market" character. This was, however, limited because of the national matriculation examination. As it is today, this was set by ministry officials. Pupils' grades on their matriculation certificates are made up of a weighted average of their grades on the examination itself and of the grades given them independently by the school (if they attended what is known as an "authorized" school, that is, one that has been granted the right to give such school grades as part of pupils' matriculation certificates). However, these school grades do not really reflect the schools' right to be autonomous and different. The right to be considered an authorized school is conferred on a school by the ministry if it has "proved itself" over a number of years. How does a school prove itself? In effect, by having a record over those years of a certain percentage of its pupils passing the matriculation examination.

Despite the pressures of the matriculation examination, there did exist a certain variety in the high school system during the 1950s and 1960s, evident in the fact that there were different types of high schools—the difference mainly expressing the various types of pupils that different schools catered to. There were grammar schools geared to prepare students for university education, vocational high schools of different sorts, and also agricultural high schools. However, in the late 1960s legislation was passed, one of whose latent functions was to increase the degree of uniformity in the high schools. This was when, in 1968, the Israeli Knesset (Parliament) voted in favor of the recommendations of a parliamentary commission to reform the education system. As part of this program of reform, it was recommended that comprehensive high schools be established instead of the separate grammar and vocational schools. These comprehensive schools would cater to all or most of the high school population. The main purpose of these comprehensive schools was to facilitate social integration of children from different social classes and ethnic backgrounds.

In actual fact, this recommendation has never been fully implemented. Grammar schools, vocational schools, and agricultural schools continue to exist, although the comprehensive schools have become increasingly important over the years. However, even if the recommendation has only been partially implemented, its symbolic significance is tremendous. Its hidden message is surely that the Israeli education system has but one major problem to contend with (social integration) and one method of solving the problem (comprehensive schooling). This message undoubtedly contributed to the zeitgeist that continued to exist toward the end of the 1960s, according to which uniformity was seen as an essential part of a healthily functioning education system, and the Ministry of Education and Culture was responsible for achieving that uniformity.

Strangely enough, although the 1970s was the decade in which the education system took it upon itself to implement the uniformity-oriented structural reform voted for in 1968, it was also the decade of change within the ministry from a pro-uniformity to a pro-diversity perspective in high school education. There are a number of reasons for this change. First, the impact of the Brunerian revolution in curriculum reached its peak in Israel at about this time.[37] The most important thrust of Bruner's ideas from the point of view of this section is his stress on the need to involve experts from the various disciplines in the preparation of school curricula. As happened in so many countries, this resulted in different universities becoming involved in producing different and at times competing curricula. Because of the high status of the universities, this acted essentially as a legitimation of diversity. Second, at the beginning of the 1970s the romantic critics of education (Holt, Kozol, Kohl, and others) were being widely read.[38] The types of schooling they were advocating clearly did not exist in Israel and thus the idea of creating a few open schools was obviously a response to the spirit of the times, and also clearly legitimized diversity. Third, early in the 1970s it became clear that the uniform reform embodied in the idea of the comprehensive school was more problematic than it had seemed at first. People began to realize that the comprehensive school was good for some pupils and not for others, that it worked in some areas of the country and not in others, and so on. Fourth, and probably more important than anything else, some chance personality factors were vital in changing how the ministry saw itself in the 1970s. The upper-echelon posts in the ministry in general and in the section dealing with high schools in particular were filled, by and large, by some very talented people who sympathized with the more progressive, open ideas in education.

At this juncture, the reader would certainly be justified in expressing considerable skepticism. The claim that for the above reasons the ministry itself could change toward diversity does seem rather unconvincing. One of the seemingly invariable laws of complex organizations is that people in and subunits of such organizations do not voluntarily give up power and control. However, a move from uniformity to diversity within a centralized national education system would seem to be a clear case of the relaxing of control by the central office. Common sense would indicate that this could only come about as a result of powerful pressure brought to bear by some pressure group or other.

The problem is that we have been unable to find evidence of such external pressure, but there is clearly documented evidence throughout the 1970s of ministry-initiated attempts to encourage diversity in the high schools. Of the case studies to be discussed, the most important is the issue of high school autonomy. Between 1970 and 1980, high schools had been granted considerable autonomy. This was formalized in 1980 in a document *The Director General's Circular*—Special Circular A. It gave partial autonomy to the "authorized" schools (those whose grades contribute toward the matriculation certificate), which constitute about 90 percent of all secondary schools, and complete autonomy to what the document referred to as "special" schools, to be defined below.[39]

The document had been prepared by a public committee that worked under the instructions of the chairman of the ministry's Secondary School Committee and included school principals, inspectors, and representatives of local authorities. The recommendations were that the schools should enjoy considerable pedagogic autonomy in order that: (1) each school may initiate, plan, and implement a broadening of its educational and cultural activities in accordance with its own considerations; (2) the school's responsibility for what goes on under its aegis might be increased; (3) the school's dependence on external factors need not unnecessarily hinder its functioning.

Seventeen different areas of responsibility and authority were stipulated. While all seventeen areas would apply to the "special" schools, only fifteen would apply to the fully authorized schools and even fewer would apply to partially authorized ones. The areas of responsibility would include the authority to establish elective subjects, to determine the scope and level of each subject taught in the school, to confirm topics for pupils' extended theses (which could be substituted for examinations), to hire new teachers, to set the regulations for transferring pupils from one grade to the next, the acceptance of the yearly school marks as part of the final mark of the matriculation examination, and so on. Special schools would be granted full authority for the setting of questionnaires for and marking of matriculation examinations.

Thus the upper-echelon officials in the ministry found themselves in the position, sketched in the theoretical section of this chapter, of trying to transform the implicit power talk that had been prevalent for at least twenty years into implicit and explicit autonomy talk. As we will see, they were not very successful.

CASE XII: THE BAD INSPECTOR

Tea break at the Hof Rishon High School: I was sitting at a table with all the economics teachers. They were complaining about the national matriculation curriculum and turned to me for confirmation. Wasn't the ministry impossible? They never allowed deviation. Everyone had to teach the same thing in the same way. I expressed the opinion that maybe the ministry wasn't so bad, that my impression is that ministry policy was to encourage autonomy and flexibility. The teachers looked at me incredulously. Zvi, one of the younger teachers, acted as the group spokesman. "Really, that is what you think? Well, let me tell you something that happened here last year. We developed an idea for our own curriculum and we discussed it with the senior economics inspector. You know what he said to us? He told us to stop playing around! He certainly wasn't prepared to allow us to do anything but teach the standard curriculum. Right, guys?" The rest of the teachers nodded emphatic agreement.

I found this an incredible story, but the teachers remained adamant. They had been rudely refused permission to teach a unit they had developed themselves. This had happened at a meeting they had had with the inspector. They had all heard him. I found all this hard to believe because I knew the economics inspector very well. He was at one time the principal of one of the few open high schools in Israel, and was emphatically "for" diversity and autonomy. I knew that he conceived of his task as encouraging schools to develop their own curricula. So, at the first opportunity, I went to his office, told him what the teachers had said and asked for his comment.

He looked at me blankly for a moment and then suddenly his face cleared, or—perhaps it would be better to say—darkened. "So *that* is how they understood me? Oh my gosh! Do you know what I really said to them? Or, at least, what I thought I said to them? 'Your idea is interesting but you must realize what it involves. Because it is a different approach to economics you cannot play around with it. Either you must prepare your kids for the national matriculation or you must develop your idea seriously and completely, including a proposal for an alternative internal final examination.' Although I didn't say it, I thought it was obvious that I hoped they would choose the second alternative!"

One could not have a better example of how preconceptions (in this case, the belief in ministry power as a result of implicit power talk) can distort one's interpretation of what one has heard. Of course, one can accuse the inspector of responding in an obscure, misleading way, but I think this is really missing the point. No channel of human communication is noise-free. All of us are continually being misunderstood. However, when the communication is ongoing and personal, most of us have developed mechanisms to obtain feedback that helps us spot the cases in which we have misunderstood or have been misunderstood. Bureaucratic communication does not have such mechanisms, and the contact between the inspector and the Hof Rishon economics staff was inevitably bureaucratic and impersonal. A brief face-to-face meeting about once a year is the best to be hoped for considering the number of schools the inspector has contact with.

CASE XIII: DO PRINCIPALS BELIEVE IN THEMSELVES?

In previous chapters I have described certain events that took place at our project's monthly principals' meetings, but I have not as yet discussed them in detail.

The principals' meetings contained or expressed a central paradox of the project. In one sense, these meetings were almost completely controlled by our project staff with the principals acting as passive participants. The agenda was set up at a monthly *staff* meeting that was normally held about two weeks before the principals' meeting. After this staff meeting, each principal was sent a letter describing in some detail the planned agenda for the next principals' meeting. Setting up this agenda was normally a major activity of the staff meeting. We would often devote two or three hours to this, and since the principals were not present, this amount of staff activity symbolizes a great difference between staff members and principals in extent of activity and thought vis-à-vis the principals' meetings.

Another expression of project staff control is that I was almost always chairman of the principals' meetings. In other words, there was a permanent "boss" who was not a principal. In fact, on one occasion when I could not be present and the meeting was run by the principals, the meeting was considered by all to have been very unsuccessful, and many principals expressed the view that this was because the "boss was not around."

These illustrations indicate the very insistent presence of the project staff at those meetings. On the other hand, in another sense the project staff was very passive and very much in the background. There were a number of indications of this passivity. First, although the project staff were the people who set up the agenda for each meeting, they did not regard themselves as the people who determined the agenda. The setting-up process was guided, by and large, by four principles: (1) The agenda for each meeting should reflect the requests and suggestions of principals at previous meetings. In many cases, the lengthy discussion at the staff meetings was related to determining the order in which these requests would appear or resulted from contradicting interpretations by various staff members of what the principals had actually requested. (2) The agenda should always reflect the "logic" of trends that had developed spontaneously at previous meetings. Thus, if at one meeting principals had complained in passing that they had not received feedback, the next meeting should address this issue directly. Or, to take another example, if a principal raised the issue of the distinction between the official school curriculum and extracurricular activity and claimed that there were differences between schools in their relative emphasis on these domains, then this suggested that the next meeting might deal with the question of empirically determining these relative emphases. (3) If any school was attempting some innovation and especially one directly related to its participation in the project, then as soon as possible the principal should be asked to share that school's experiences with the other principals. (4) If at all possible, the general outlines for a particular principals' meeting should be determined together with the principals at the previous meeting. Thus, in almost all cases, the last twenty minutes or so of a particular principals' meeting would be devoted to an attempt to lay out the guidelines that the project staff should use in setting up the next agenda.

To see how the agenda tended to reflect these principles, consider the following letter to the principals prior to a meeting on October 8, 1979:

Shalom,

As decided, the next principals' meeting will take place on —— at the —— School from 9:00 to 2:30.
Agenda for the meeting
a. We will continue the discussion concerning the suggestions[40] from the previous meeting to increase the participation of teachers in the project. We will discuss the advantages and disadvantages of each suggestion and try to reach operative conclusions. The suggestions were:
  1. Creating teacher teams from different schools to address common problems. At first this should perhaps only involve department heads.
  2. Mutual visits of teachers from different schools in the project (perhaps at the beginning the project staff will recommend to a particular school faculty to visit a particular school).
  3. Using the project staff to work with teacher teams in the different schools.
  4. An institutionalized meeting (once a fortnight approximately) of a group of teachers in a school, whose chairpersons would be the principal and someone from the project staff. At this meeting topics related to the project would be discussed. These would be determined by the principal and the project staff representative together.
b. We will discuss the work of the project staff in the schools both with regards to giving feedback and with regards to real help to the schools. The project staff listened with great interest to the "charge" that it was too wishy-washy last year, and intends to bring up some concrete suggestions about this.
c. Ronit will continue to tell us about her problems concerning the position of vice-principal responsible for educational innovations. Avi will tell us about innovations at his school.

See you,
David

A second indication of our passivity was that my role as chairman was generally very low-key. I usually opened every item on the agenda with a few introductory remarks intended to set the scene. These remarks usually reviewed a relevant discussion at the previous meeting, or something of that sort. From this point on, my role was usually limited to acting as timekeeper and determining the order in which participants would speak. In addition, although I was the coordinating chairman of the meeting, a particular discussion was often run by someone else as, for example, a principal who was describing some innovation.

Third, the participation of project staff at the principals' meetings tended to be very minimal. This was not by chance, and in fact was one of the first guidelines laid down in the first year. Staff input would be kept to a minimum and staff members would intervene only in cases in which, in their judgment, the discussion was clearly foundering or being diverted from the kind of topics and processes the project was concerned with (as school innovation, DDAE, cooperation between schools, barriers to innovation). Of course, this was a difficult rule to follow and on occasion the staff slipped up. We would then find ourselves dominating the discussion or adopting a didactic tone and talking down to the principals. However, on the whole the staff did succeed in remaining in the background and were perceived in this way, as Ronit (the principal of the Pisga School) expressed to me:

Apart from those associated with my school, I don't really know the other project staff members even after two years. Until B—— became one of the project members at Pisga, she had been an enigma to me. Now, I realize what a clever sensitive person she is. Or take F——. I don't know, the principals of the schools she is associated with say she is fantastic. But at the meetings she never says a word! I find it very disturbing. If she is so bright, why doesn't she say something? It makes me nervous having these people sitting around like zombies.

One must not exaggerate these indications of passivity. Setting up an agenda always involves a process of selection and emphasis, and is never completely neutral. A low-key chairperson does set the tone for a meeting and partially determines what is going to happen. Even if one's contribution to a meeting is limited to, say, one sentence, one can influence the entire direction of the meeting depending on the sentence and when it is said. Yet the major contribution to the principals' meetings was made by the principals themselves. Moreover, attendance at these meetings was consistently high; many expressed satisfaction with them, and there was a general feeling of cameraderie and "good vibes." It seems safe to conclude that these principals found meeting with their colleagues a rewarding social and intellectual activity.

Therefore, it is rather surprising that the principals felt uncomfortable with the idea of continuing to meet after the official end of the project in 1981. As I have described in chapter 1, we devoted considerable time during the third year to discussing the question of continuation of project activities without the catalyst of the project staff. The principals were extremely reluctant to discuss this matter; discussions were often accompanied by nervous and forced laughter. They doubted that continued meetings without the project staff would work. In Hebrew there is an expression, "to be cooked in one's own juice," which means that something is or is going to be boring and one has entered a vicious circle. This expression was often invoked by the principals: meetings without the project staff would in their view be dull and repetitious. They noted occasions when the project staff had made particularly insightful remarks at meetings as evidence of how important we had been. They repeatedly mentioned their lack of training and knowledge in theoretical matters. Eventually, in a half-hearted fashion, the principals did agree to try out the idea of meeting the following year, but they disbanded after two meetings.

All in all, if one of the aims of the project was to encourage and develop the principals' feelings of self-sufficiency, we had failed rather dismally. The question is, why? Four possible answers come to mind. First, the principals may simply be right; it may be that schools cannot change without some sort of ongoing collaboration with an external agency. This possibility will be discussed in chapter 6. Second, I ran the first two principals' meetings during the first year of the project on the basis of an agenda determined by the project staff. I did this rather unthinkingly; we never considered other possibilities. It may be that this unthinking decision more or less determined what we could achieve during the next three years. Essentially, we had established a norm for running the principals' meetings, one that we did not succeed in changing despite all our efforts throughout the project, and that contradicted the very notion of continued meetings after the project staff had departed. A third reason might be that one of the functions of the principals' meetings was to provide a day's break once a month. Principals are under constant pressure. The project provided an ideal opportunity to get away, to "leave town," to meet with a group of colleagues and spend a relaxing yet intellectually stimulating day in congenial surroundings. It was worth traveling perhaps four or five hours to do this. This was not one of the central aims of our project, but I now see that it was all to the good. However, it is unlikely that people who conceive of meetings as an opportunity to get away will take responsibility for running these meetings. As a last reason: the principals work in an educational system that is bureaucratized, focused, and has been characterized by implicit power talk for many years. This system has convinced school personnel of their lack of autonomy and lack of ability to be autonomous, and has taught them not to seek autonomy. Such a process is not going to be countered so easily by a three-year project designed to promote school self-renewal, considering that the schools remained part of this educational system throughout the project.

Of these four explanations, the fourth is obviously the one that links this example to the theoretical issues addressed in this chapter. I have no way of estimating its relative weight as a factor in determining the principals' unwillingness to continue their meetings. All I can say is that it was not negligible, and the following incident illustrates this.

Toward the end of the first year of the project, it became clear to the principals that taking the project seriously would require setting up regular meetings of teachers, the topics of which would be determined by developments within the project. In the context of the Israeli high school system this was problematic. High school teachers' jobs are defined in terms of weekly teaching hours, as already mentioned; thus regular staff meetings are difficult to set up. A number of principals thought this could be done only if the teachers were paid for the hours in which they were meeting on a regular basis. So they suggested that we invite the head of the high school division at the ministry (the man who had originally invited me to act as his adviser) to the year's final principals' meeting. They would try to convince him to permit the schools in the project to use their budgets to pay the teachers for attending regular meetings.

The final meeting was not the usual full-day affair but rather an evening cocktail party held at a private house a couple of days after the completion of the school year, in other words, in July during the height of the summer heat. Summer evenings in Israel are a blessed relief from the oppressive heat, and this, together with the food, drink, humidity, and holiday atmosphere, all created the special ambience of the evening. It was a relaxed, happy evening, one on which no one could get annoyed, irritated, or insulted about anything. This is probably one of the reasons why the head of the high school division did what he did.

After the usual hour of chitchat, drink, and onion dips, the meeting was called to order and our guest was introduced formally. One of the headmasters explained the problem, and asked if the ministry would allow the schools to pay teachers for participating in project meetings. What we had in effect was an opportunity for a senior ministry official to engage in direct responding communication in a nonbureaucratized environment, and the official used the opportunity to react as he probably would not have done in other circumstances using more formalized communication channels. In essence, he reminded the principals of the ministry regulations about school autonomy, stressed that these regulations allowed the schools to do pretty much as they pleased, and wondered whether the principals needed his permission in the first place.

Because of the surroundings, this reply simply did not come across as abrasive, aggressive, or just plain rude. Thus the context allowed the principals to react as perhaps they would not have in other contexts. Most of them were not happy with the answer, and they made this quite clear. In fact, we were treated to a series of monologues explaining that the ministry had been mistaken to give schools autonomy and that the principals themselves had no desire to be autonomous.

In thinking about this evening, I am reminded of the work of Shimon Reshef, probably Israel's best-known educational historian.[41] Reshef has stressed the changes that schools in Israel have undergone from the mid-1930s (when the thrust toward centralization that culminated in the 1953 Education Act began) to the present. He has also described the character of the schools and their headmasters prior to the thirties. The picture that comes across is of colorful individuals with idiosyncratic educational philosophies, building colorful schools—a sort of preview of the rash of alternative schools that the 1960s and early 1970s produced in the United States and Western Europe. Our principals of the late 1970s lecturing on the danger of autonomy seem like a very different breed.

The moment one makes such a statement, one must follow one of two roads. The first is to bemoan the spirit of the times, the failure of nerve of the new generation of educators. The second is to try to identify and compare the organizational contexts in which the oldtimers and the new breed of principals are situated. The arguments I have developed in this chapter, and specifically the notion of implicit power talk, represent the second alternative.

Toward the end of the 1970s, senior officials in the Israeli Ministry of Education and Culture became increasingly aware that granting high schools autonomy was not enough. To a large extent this new awareness resulted from what they learned from our project. The hierarchical relations between school and ministry officials that obtained because of the centralized structure of the system were now considered to be themselves inhibiting factors with regard to promoting school initiative. Slowly the idea developed of the ministry establishing a nonhierarchical set of relations with a group of high schools. At first this would involve approximately forty schools, but if this redefinition of relations resulted in greater initiative and innovation in these schools, the hope was to gradually increase the number of schools involved. Representatives from two universities were asked to take part in preliminary discussions, and eventually the proposal that crystallized was to establish an Institute for Innovative High School Education in which ministry representatives, two university schools of education, and interested high schools would participate as equal partners.

I will discuss this institute further in the final chapter; here I will give just a few details. At the first informal discussions in which the university and ministry representatives participated, the following tentative guidelines were proposed:

1. The governing board of the institute would be made up of ministry and university representatives plus elected representatives from the participating schools. The executive chairperson of the board would be a rotating position, entrusted in turn to each of the three partners (ministry, universities, and schools) participating in the institute.
2. The institute would contain a number of separate sections or units. The various sections would not be determined fully in advance, but would be developed slowly one at a time after the formal establishment of the institute. Again, all three collaborating partners would be involved in proposing and developing different sections.

3. In order to get some idea of what is meant by a "section," here are a few examples of different suggested sections:
   a. A group attempting to encourage school-based and developed alternatives to the national matriculation examinations (see special schools, already described).
   b. A group attempting to encourage school-based curriculum development.
   c. A teachers' center.
4. In all sections, all three partners would again be represented.

The first few informal discussions logically led to the conclusion that school representatives must be brought in as quickly as possible in order to realize the principle of nonhierarchical relations. The way to do this, it was decided, was to invite about forty principals to a day-long meeting or miniconference with the ministry and university representatives involved. The schools chosen were all involved in innovative projects the ministry was funding or was aware of (including the schools in our project). The agenda for the meeting was planned with great care. The format was as follows: The meeting would open with a presentation of the idea of the institute, its theoretical rationale, historical antecedents, and proposed structure. Then two or three people from the ministry and the university schools of education who had some specific ideas for particular sections of the institute would present their ideas. People would then break up into small groups for informal discussions of the whole concept of the institute. Each group would have two co-chairpersons — one a school principal, the other a university representative, with the ministry officials remaining in the background. Finally, at a plenary session the various groups would report on their discussions. The day would conclude with the principals being supplied with an address and phone number to contact if, after thinking things over and discussing matters with their staffs, they wished to join the institute.

Because I was the adviser to the ministry on high school innovation, everyone—bar one—thought that I should be the person to give the opening presentation. Only I disagreed. Moreover, I objected to the whole idea of an opening address. To my mind it smacked of the same absurdity of education professors lecturing on how bad a teaching method lecturing is. Here we were suggesting a redefinition of the relationship between schools and policy makers, a relationship of equality and mutuality, and the first thing that happens is that the policy makers sit the principals down and tell them how things should be. The rest of the university and ministry representatives involved were not convinced. As they saw it, it was even more absurd to invite a group of people to a meeting and not begin by telling them why you set up the meeting. In the end, I agreed to give the opening talk but made it clear that I would share with the principals my own sense of the absurdity of the situation.

The meeting went off pretty much as planned. The standard of discussion seemed high and the participation of the principals seemed animated and enthusiastic. At the end of the day participants were told to contact me if they wanted to join the institute, or rather, join the group that was planning and developing the eventual formation of the institute.

Then we sat and waited, but the phone calls did not materialize. All those who had been involved were pretty downhearted. We assumed that we had misread signals at the miniconference, that the principals were not interested in an institute. We decided to send out a few unofficial feelers. What we learned in this way is a classic illustration of the self-perpetuating nature of implicit power talk. At least 50 percent of the principals were enthusiastic about the institute and did wish to participate. So why had they not phoned or written me? I think the theoretical discussion earlier in this chapter makes it possible to predict the answer to this question. This was what our unofficial sounding-out of the principals reflected back to us with monotonous regularity with just about every interested principal. It appears that "If you're interested, let us build this thing together — contact us" simply was not interpreted as a message one could act on. The principals had not contacted us because they had been waiting for instructions. As many put it, they had been waiting "to be told what is the next step."

CONCLUDING REMARKS

I began this chapter by saying that what I would be presenting is not very original. In many ways this is the most interesting aspect of the topic of staff professionalization and its relationship to school self-renewal, because what I have been saying is very well known. It is very much part of mainstream organizational theory and mainstream sociology of teaching. It therefore becomes rather puzzling why the literature has by and large ignored the factors stressed in this chapter. In many cases theorists like Dreeben, Lortie, Weick, Cohen, March, and Olsen will simply not be invoked. Occasionally they will be, but the invocation tends to be a ritual bow in the direction of, say, "loose coupling" which is then effectively ignored.

Take *Transforming the School's Capacity for Problem Solving*, by Runkel et al. as an example. It opens with the statement that "some writers have been pointing to the looser side of organizational functioning."[42] March and Olsen, Meyer and Rowan, and Weick are among those mentioned. One gets the impression that the "loose coupling" perspective is being quoted approvingly, but then in the next paragraph one begins to suspect that, in fact, loose coupling is going to be ignored, for Runkel et al. go on: "When we say that getting work done requires coordination and agreement on how to do things, we do not mean that people must swear undeviating commitment to long-term goals, short-term goals, and all the myriad small steps for reaching them. We mean only that there is inevitably some minimal orderliness in what people expect from one another."[43] Very soon this minimal orderliness becomes sufficient to enable the authors to recommend a typical Dewey-like series of rational problem-solving steps. It is then clear that notions like loose coupling have *not* been used to modify the basic OD approach that Runkel and Schmuck and their co-workers developed before the advent of the loose-coupling perspective.

Why should developments in organizational theory and sociology of teaching be ignored? Pfeffer and Salancik offer a partial answer. As I have already mentioned, this chapter, apart from using concepts like "loose coupling," also exemplified what Pfeffer and Salancik call the external or contextual perspective on organizations. This perspective has become part of the received view, at least since Katz and Kahn's classic *The Social Psychology of Organizations*, which stressed the open-system nature of organizations.[44] Yet Pfeffer and Salancik argue that in most cases (and even in the Katz and Kahn book) the predominant concern in work on organizations relates to the latter's internal activities.[45] They suggest two main reasons for this: internal processes are most visible; and we are more likely to attribute causality to individuals rather than to contextual factors.[46]

But this is not enough. I would argue that there is something about the change agent role that invites change agents to ignore certain types of theory that are relevant but detrimental to the idea of planned organizational change. Saying this finally transfers the spotlight from the school to the change agent, thus far a shadowy, rather anonymous figure in our story, but of course in many ways really the central figure all the time. Without the initial intervention of change agents, there is surely no hope that schools will be able to improve their problem-solving capacities. What psychological and sociological pressures do change agents have to contend with? And how do these affect their ability to address both theoretical and practical difficulties associated with planned change? We will analyze their role in chapter 5.

5

Of Mice and Men
THE SELLING OF CHANGE

MICE AND MAGIC FEATHERS

Does self-renewal of schools that are functioning poorly necessarily require the initial help of a good change agent? And if so, is it reasonable to depend on such help? The literature on planned educational change does not really address these questions. It tends to be prescriptive, that is, it suggests what a good change agent needs to do. The implicit assumption here is that the potentially good change agent is around and is clearly beneficial. All that is needed is training.

I question these assumptions. An analysis of the nature of school systems, the change agent's role, and the relationship between them indicates it is likely that change agents discourage rather than promote school self-renewal, and not because change agents are incompetent or badly trained. The interesting problem is: why has the literature tended to ignore this possibility? The terminology developed in chapter 3 provides us with a clue. The belief in the change agent's potential efficacy is usually a primary belief of the change agent/consultant's belief system. The literature on planned educational change is, in the main, written by change agents and consultants. Thus questioning the change agent/ consultant's efficacy is unlikely to surface.

Consider Goodlad's description of what he regards as one of the two major watersheds of his project—the division of the project staff into two groups with two very different approaches to the change agent role.[1] This division, which occurred in the third year of his project, focused on the question of how much help to give the schools. There were those who felt that it was necessary to play the "expert" role and "really help" the schools. Others saw orthodox consulting as a trap that actually limited client growth. It became necessary to decide between these two approaches and the second approach was adopted (or, rather, it was continued, for it had been the underlying approach of the project from the first). As a result, certain members of the staff found they could not continue identifying with the project's aims, practice, and general philosophy, and they resigned. Goodlad graphically describes the tension involved, and the trauma created by the departure of these staff members. He also shows much understanding of the temptation of the expert role:

> This is a common problem in the expert-client relationship and, too frequently, the teacher-student one. Helping others is seductive; personal needs on both sides are fed by the relationship. Growth on the part of the client can be threatening to the helping partner who intuitively sees himself surpassed rather than the client freed. And so, in subtle ways, he may block the client's growth under the guise of helping—thus, ironically, blocking his own growth and restricting his freedom. Soon he is heavy with the chains of an ever-dependent client. One can carry the chains of only a few but can help to set many free.[2]

What is the conclusion that Goodlad reaches as a result of this incident? "The hard lesson, then, was that we had to believe in more than the hypothesis. We had to believe, as well, in the people for whom it presumably applied—all of them."[3] In other words, the project's staff faced difficulties and temptations, and certain of the staff succumbed to them and others did not. However, he seems to believe that succumbing was not necessary. Perhaps with a more carefully selected staff it would not have happened. At least this is the way I interpreted the above passages when developing our project. We tried to take into account the pressures Goodlad refers to. They were pointed out to the staff (who also had read Goodlad's book, of course), and were discussed and we hoped thrashed out almost from the beginning. And yet our staff went through practically the identical trauma to that of the Goodlad staff.

This is extraordinarily interesting; it suggests that we may be dealing with something much deeper than Goodlad imagined. To explore what this might be or, rather, what questions one might ask in order to uncover these deeper issues, let us return to Mary Bentzen's mouse and magic feather principle (see chapter 1) and take this fairy story a bit more seriously this time.

Like all attempts to grasp a particular reality through a metaphor, the story of Dumbo the elephant both illuminates and blinds, captures the reality and distorts it.[4] Chapter 1 used the story to highlight the difference between RD&D and school self-renewal. Let us now consider some of its distortions. First, Dumbo is one of a herd of elephants with one mouse as a friend. We are never told anything of the environment in which they live. However, in fact we are concerned with a whole jungle with its own ecological balance in which there are a whole lot of Dumbos, each needing a mouse. Second, the mouse gets Dumbo to fly by giving him a magic feather. The mouse himself appears to do nothing. But this is absurd. Even when the change agent is truly minimal as a catalyst, he cannot avoid participating in certain school activities. His participation may be extremely low-key, but even then he will be part of some process. So, returning to our mouse, rather than have him simply give a feather to Dumbo, it would be better to have him joining hands (paws? feet?) with Dumbo and flying along with him for a while.

The amended Dumbo story is clearly more clumsy and less picturesque, cute, or compelling. However, it does invite us to ask certain questions we might not have spotted if we had stuck with the original story. Here are four such questions:

1. Once elephants and mice are flying, is there something the mice may possibly do that could cause the elephants to start falling?
2. Are mice perhaps built in such a way that they cannot avoid performing these acts of sabotage?
3. In addition, when mice fly with elephants, are certain ecological forces perhaps brought into play that cause mice to perform acts of sabotage?
4. Let us assume the mice do not sabotage the elephants' flights directly. Nevertheless, perhaps the mice's flying brings into play ecological forces that indirectly cause the elephants to fall?

Let us pose these questions more literally:

1. What can change agents do that subverts school self-renewal?
2. What, if any, are the psychological forces that operate on change agents in ways that increase the likelihood that they will subvert self-renewal? Are such psychological forces inescapable?
3. What, if any, are the structural forces associated with the change agent role that increase the likelihood of subversion of the goal? Are such structural forces inescapable?

4. What the the unintended dysfunctional consequences of competent work by change agents?

One further introductory point: although I have criticized what I called the therapeutic metaphor, I will use it in this chapter. There is a striking parallel between the difficulties faced by change agents and therapists,[5] even if the idea of raising to consciousness has been shown to be problematic in promoting self-renewal. Reflecting on this parallel and also on the very definite differences between change agents and therapists (over and above those discussed in chapter 2) will help us come to grips with some of the above questions.

SUBVERTING SCHOOL SELF-RENEWAL

What can change agents do to subvert school self-renewal? The most obvious way in which change agents' intervention can be counterproductive is by creating dependence. This they can do first simply by their physical presence. Second, they can generate the kind of comfort that Freud described in "Analysis Terminable and Interminable":

> In the course of a few years it was possible to give [the patient] back a large amount of his independence, to awaken his interest in life and to adjust his relations to the people most important to him. But there progress came to a stop. We advanced no further in clearing up the neurosis of his childhood, on which his later illness was based, and it was obvious that the patient found his present position highly comfortable and had no wish to take any step forward which would bring him nearer to the end of his treatment. It was a case of the treatment inhibiting itself: it was in danger of failing as a result of its—partial—success.[6]

Bird formulates this problem of psychoanalysis in more general language:

> One of the most serious problems of analysis is the very substantial help which the patient receives directly from the analyst and the analytic situation. For many a patient, the analyst in the analytic situation is in fact the most stable, reasonable, wise, and understanding person he has ever met, and the setting in which they meet may actually be the most honest, open, direct, and regular relationship he

has ever experienced. . . . Taken altogether, the total *real* value to the patient of the analytic situation can easily be immense. The trouble with this kind of help is that if it goes on and on, it may have such a real, direct, and continuing impact upon the patient that he can never get deeply enough involved in transference situations to allow him resolve, or even to become acquainted with, his most crippling internal difficulties. The trouble, in a sense, is that the direct nonanalytical helpfulness of the analytic situation is far too good! The trouble also is that we as analysts apparently cannot resist the seductiveness of being directly helpful.[7]

The promotion of school self-renewal does not require that the school become "involved in transference situations" (assuming this to be a coherent idea), but certainly school personnel can feel something analogous to the comfort felt by Freud's patient. The following case illustrates this nicely.

Dependence can also be encouraged through the change agent playing the consultant/expert role. This, as we have seen, is the problem Goodlad was particularly concerned with. However, it seems to me that he does not spell out in sufficient detail the distinction between playing the expert role and displaying expertise. This distinction is crucial. After all, one would not wish to claim that in order to promote self-renewal, the change agent must be incompetent. Therefore, competence must be different from playing the expert. What constitutes this difference?

The difference lies in the change agent's presentation of self in relationships with school personnel. First, playing the expert is a special kind of display that carries with it an implicit message that the people one is relating to are *not* experts. It is a display of superiority and power, and is effective because it is expressed covertly. To borrow a term popular in educationl discourse — the change agent's "superiority" is part of the hidden curriculum associated with playing the expert role, and as with most hidden curricula, those transmitting it do so unintentionally.

In contrast, a display of expertise is normally associated with nonhierarchical communication among peers, colleagues, or collaborators. There is an implicit acknowledgement that those to whom one displays expertise are also experts, either in one's own field or in some other aspect of a collaborative venture, and thus are equals.

If this analysis is correct, then whether one plays the expert or displays expertise will not be decided on the basis of conscious rational decisions. Rather, it will depend on the way one feels deep down about the people one is involved with. Putting it simply, the change agent cannot fake it. If one feels superior, then no espoused theory in the world will prevent the expert role from sneaking through.

Let us turn now to the second important difference between playing the expert and displaying expertise. These two stances embody fundamentally opposed presentations of the degree of certainty of expert knowledge. The expert role invites the presentation of knowledge as unambiguous and certain, whereas the display of expertise encourages stressing the fallibility of knowledge. This really is a corollary of what I have said in previous paragraphs. One of the ways experts can express superiority is by stressing the infallibility of their knowledge. It is superior because it is their knowledge. Clients do not have this knowledge. Therefore, if the experts' knowledge is certain, such certainty can only increase their prestige. As we saw in chapter 3 in considering the work of Basil Bernstein, experts in a particular field tend not to disclose to those who have not been socialized into the field that "the ultimate mystery of the subject is not coherence but incoherence; not order but disorder, not the known but the unknown."[8]

Despite the fact that this second distinction between the expert role and displaying expertise follows from the first, I have isolated it as an independent factor. This is because, in addition, it suggests a far more subtle way than the creation of dependence by which change agents can subvert school self-renewal. As I have stressed in chapters 2 and 3, the whole idea of self-renewal makes sense only in terms of a certain view of rationality and of science. One aspect of that view is that we learn from our mistakes. We increase our knowledge and improve our practice by testing our ideas against reality and changing them when they are found wanting. We have the courage to fail. The conception of knowledge as certain is fundamentally opposed to this attitude of mind. Thus when change agents play the role of expert, they transmit a "hidden curriculum" that undermines and contradicts the very norms they are attempting to develop within the organization they are working with.

One further point about the hidden curricula I have been referring to. Like all hidden curricula, they are effective only if they are transmitted consistently.[9] In other words, the displays of self of the change agent will be influential only if they are transmitted in a redundant manner, in the communications theory sense.[10] This will become important later. One must not take the notion of the distinction between the expert role and displaying expertise to its extreme conclusion. Change agents who in general display expertise can occasionally play the expert without this undermining their work completely.

To summarize, change agents can subvert school self-renewal in three ways. First, they can ignore the suggestion one can see posted in the window of a certain travel agency: "Please go away." Second, while staying around they can make things too comfortable. Third, they can play the expert and thus transmit the covert messages that they are superior to their clients, and that there is infallible knowledge. As we will see in the two theoretical sections that follow the next case study, a number of psychological and sociological forces associated with the change agent role encourage subversion of self-renewal. I will concentrate mainly on the third way of doing this—playing the expert—and also, to a lesser extent, on the first — prolonging the intervention. The second — making things too easy—is probably more avoidable but still often occurs. Let us first examine an example of the subversion associated with making things too comfortable.

CASE XV: THE SCHOOL AS FORTRESS

This case illustrates the point that change agents can limit school self-renewal by their physical presence and that they do this even if their presence does generate certain changes. The case probably also illustrates other things, so it is important at the outset to emphasize what it does *not* illustrate. First, in one of the subsequent theoretical sections I will show how change agents can be tempted to prolong their time in schools. In other words, there are cases where "staying around" is clearly a deformation of the change agent's "mouse" role. However, there is no suggestion of such a deformation in the case I will discuss; the change agents did not remain in this particular school too long. In fact, the change agents' actions were very professional and successful. Nevertheless, their presence hindered self-renewal. Second, there is no suggestion that, like Freud's patient, self-renewal could have gotten off the ground if the change agents had delivered an ultimatum announcing that after a certain period of time they would terminate their association with the school. The termination date was known long in advance and this made no difference. Rather, what we have here is an example of how a mouse by helping an elephant to fly just above the trees can ensure that he will not fly above the clouds.

Only in passing does the case address the question of whether it is possible to get elephants above the clouds and, if so, how to do it. Let us now turn to the story.

The schools in our project got to us, or were gotten to in different ways. Yet probably the most usual one, as mentioned in case XI, was for a school to be recommended by a ministry of education official. We had approached various branches of the ministry— those that dealt with different geographical areas or with different types of schools (rural as opposed to urban, for example) — and requested that they supply us with lists of schools which they thought would be interested in innovative ideas. One was the Eliad School, a vocational school in a rather small town near Jerusalem. Most of the teachers did not live in the town but traveled in to work from Jerusalem, which created many problems for the school.

My first meeting with the headmaster Ronen was a strange one. I came to the school to explain the idea of our project, and to see whether the headmaster was interested. If so, I intended to explain that joining the project could be done only if the school staff as a whole agreed. We would then discuss how to explain the project to the teachers and how to organize a teachers' voting procedure. I assumed this meeting would last an hour or two. In fact, it took about ten minutes. During that time I managed to obtain his more or less immediate agreement to join the project, to have the project staff introduce itself at the first school staff meeting a few days before the 1978–79 school year began, and to have the school faculty vote on joining the project at that meeting.

I was bundled out of Ronen's office so fast that afterward, in thinking about the meeting, I could not even recall what he looked like. The only impression that did remain was that, despite the speed with which everything had taken place, Ronen's agreement had seemed grudging and forced. So I regarded the prospect of the Eliad School joining our project with some misgiving. Yet the school had been recommended by a ministry official for whom I had great respect and who knew the schools under his inspectorship inside out. The Eliad School was also a different sort of school from the others we planned to accept (a vocational school in a semirural setting), and the whole rationale of a league of schools was to enable schools that were unlike each other to learn from their differences. Thus we decided that if the school was prepared to join the project, we would accept it.

Unfortunately, none of our project staff was free to attend the first school staff meeting. There was no way we could attend the meeting, and the school could not reschedule it. Should we postpone accepting Eliad into our project until we met with the teachers at a second general faculty meeting, which would take place a few months later? We were not happy with this possibility. The other solution was to accept Ronen's suggestion that he explain our project himself at the meeting and then take a vote. We were not happy with this alternative either, but decided to go along with it. After the staff meeting we phoned Ronen and were informed that the faculty had agreed to join the project.

We have never been able to find out what really happened at that meeting. Certainly when the project staff members assigned to the school began their visits there a few weeks later, none of the school faculty seemed to have the slightest notion which project they represented. This was a bit unnerving, and a very inauspicious start for a relationship with the Eliad School, a relationship that for a year at least was almost totally frustrating.

But I am running ahead of my story. Our project staff's first opportunity to meet Ronen was at the first principals' meeting. This was also an opportunity for me to sharpen my initial blurred impression of him. My impression of Ronen after this principals' meeting is still very vivid. First, he was all jerky nervous motion with energy seemingly continually suppressed. Second, he frowned with slit eyes and thin lips pressed together. Then there were his comments. Many of these could only be described as jeering, condescending remarks. For instance, I opened the meeting with a confession of nervousness, because I saw this meeting as an important beginning to what I hoped was to be a long and fruitful collaboration. Ronen's interjection: "Why are you nervous? We're not!" This itself was ambiguous; it could be interpreted as expressing support, but the tone in which it was said left no doubt that the intention was otherwise. Of course, not all his comments were of this sort, but even the more "academic" ones seemed to transmit the same restless, rather bitter response to the world. Ronen related to ideas like a wolf tearing at meat on a bone.

At first I thought this might be a purely personal reaction, but the staff's reactions were very similar, and the first reports of our two representatives at the school reaffirmed these impressions. Both of them confessed that Ronen simply scared them. They found him forbidding and pugnacious. Also they witnessed a number of incidents which seemed to fit the general picture of Ronen that was beginning to form. For example: One incident occurred at an end-of-term meeting of all teachers who teach a particular class to discuss and finalize grades:

About twenty-five teachers are sitting around the narrow table.[11] Ronen sits at the head. At the opposite end one can't hear much of what is going on. Lots of knitting, gossip, and remarks like "Who are they talking about now?" Ronen's control of the meeting is absolute. He says things like this to the teachers: "Remove those things of yours from the table!" "You are the only person in the room with that opinion." The atmosphere is heavy; there are many bursts of spontaneous talk by the teachers, each new burst silenced immediately by Ronen.

When shadowing Ronen, a project staff member reported:

Two teachers come into Ronen's office to complain about a pupil they suspect has stolen a shirt. Ronen says, "We have no proof, but tell her that if she isn't telling the truth you will send her to me for grilling." One teacher comments, "Good, that should put the fear of God into her!"

Apart from being a little scared of Ronen, our staff members also had great difficulty in getting a real picture of what was going on in the school, for three reasons. First, there were almost no meetings of teachers of any sort. Second, as already mentioned, very few of the teachers seemed to know who our staff were and on whose authority they could ask questions about the school. Third, quite often the following sort of incident would occur. A staff project representative would arrive at the school and either Ronen or the vice-principal would say something like this: "Pity you weren't here yesterday. We had a very interesting meeting. It would have given you a better understanding of what goes on." However, no one had bothered to inform our representative about this meeting.

It seemed to us that the Eliad School was clearly the most problematic school we had. In fact, we were debating about whether we should continue in the school at all. However, at this time, I chanced to meet the ministry official who had recommended the Eliad School to us. He asked for details about the project. I mentioned the monthly principals' meetings. He interrupted, "Tell me, what about Ronen? Does he come to these meetings?" "Sure," I answered. "*All* the time?" "He hasn't missed one yet." The official looked at me in wide-eyed astonishment. "You know, that is amazing. We have practically never been able to get Ronen to any meeting at all!" Ronen is a person of independent means. He was the most highly qualified principal in our project and also taught at a university. So in his case the ministry simply didn't have any clout at all, which was probably one of the reasons that he ignored the ministry and its officials almost completely.

This discussion was extremely illuminating. First, Eliad was obviously the prime example of the ministry's tendency to give us extremely problematic schools rather than schools with some commitment to innovation. Second, if the official was so impressed by the fact that Ronen participated in the meetings, then maybe we should not give up on the Eliad School so quickly.

Yet by the end of the first year we had made no progress. The school was still closed to us to all intents and purposes, with our representatives being deflected deftly from all viable routes to any central aspect of school life. Despite this, Ronen was becoming very critical of the fact that we were not doing anything in his school. We decided we must talk this through with him, to point out that it was impossible for us to assess how the school was functioning because it was not allowing us to see how it was functioning. But the two project representatives approached such a meeting with Ronen with great trepidation. As one of them said, "We may come back from the meeting to tell you Eliad has decided to leave the project."

Actually, probably predictably, the meeting went off very well and in fact proved once again that when things are out in the open, they usually are much easier to deal with. Ronen saw the problem and most of the meeting was devoted to a constructive search for a solution, which was the following: seeing as there were so few school staff meetings and therefore outsiders had difficulty getting a picture of the school, a regular teachers' forum had to be created. It was agreed that this should be a small group (four or five teachers) who would meet with our representatives once a week for an hour. The topic of the meetings was not decided upon. The teachers would be paid to participate (Ronen himself would not participate because he himself and the teachers who were eventually chosen felt that his presence might stifle things).

Meetings of four (and, for a short while, five) teachers with two project staff members remained a permanent feature at the school for nearly two years, and the ebb and flow of this activity during this time is a pretty good reflection of developments in the school as a whole. The activity can be divided into four stages.

Stage 1. The Creation of a DDAE Questionnaire.   One of the first decisions reached was that, because the idea of establishing this group came about because of our difficulties in describing the school's DDAE process, the first task of the group should be to obtain that description. It would not be that of the two external observers, but rather one developed by the four teachers with the help of our staff.

At first, the meetings were devoted to elaborating the whole idea of DDAE and in particular to obtaining the four teachers' estimations of the degree of involvement among teachers in dialogue and decision making. Predictably, they began to realize that estimating is far more problematic than it first appears. Because the group could not agree on either an objective description of reality or what they hypothesized were the subjective definitions of that reality on the part of the other teachers, the group decided to check things empirically through a survey using individual interviews.

Difficulties began to emerge almost immediately, as indicated in the following notes taken by a project staff member:

> [April 1980] In the meantime this business has got a bit stuck; (a) some technical problems arose with these interviews— they [the four teachers] simply haven't got the time; (b) these folks, despite the clear instructions and preliminary planning, simply didn't grasp the technique of interviewing— they are doing all sorts of things that sabotage themselves. (One person passed his private set of instructions to the interviewee and let him react to each point in turn. . . . Another decided that the conversation would be much more exciting if she were to ignore the topics that we had decided upon and just ask the interviewee, "How do you feel about school?" and from his answer she would somehow or other arrive at the material we need.)

The difficulties with interviews led to a partial change of plan. Instead of interviewing, the group decided to draw up a more structured questionnaire that the entire Eliad staff would be asked to complete.

Stage 2. The Response to the Questionnaire.   This stage is captured very well in the following report by one of our representatives:

> We translated the interview into a questionnaire and our group put a copy in the post box of each teacher. And here we are, after quite some time only six teachers out of eighty filled it out. Others were seen throwing it into the wastebasket. The

members of the group were very insulted by this reaction, and discussed things with other teachers, each with those teachers he/she is close to. We now have twenty-four questionnaires filled out and we have even managed to summarize them and reach conclusions in order to get an idea where we are going from here. En route to this achievement one bad thing and two good things (in our view) happened. The bad thing: it became clear that without Ronen nothing moves. On being informed of our difficulty, he went into action full tilt and the questionnaires are being filled out and being sent back. We didn't want it this way. The good things: it became clear that the members of the group are very involved in and committed to what they are doing—both our activity and also what is happening in the school in general. And the other good thing: the trauma the members received as a result of the lack of response of the teachers led to great activity in the staff room. There were many discussions about the school, what can be done in it. In a place like Eliad, it is good to make a few waves.

Stage 3. Planning for the Following Year.   The completed questionnaires were analyzed and, as a result, certain conclusions were reached. Perhaps the most important one was that the teaching faculty felt that contact between and meetings of teachers within the same department were too limited. In order to address this problem, certain organizational preparations for the following year had to be made. For one thing, time would have to be set aside for such meetings. Thus Ronen was told about the group's analysis of the questionnaires before he finished planning the school timetable for the next year, to ensure that the conclusions reached would be taken into account.

Stage 4. The Second Year of Meetings (Third Year of the Project).   The promising developments at Eliad continued, as reflected in the project staff member's notes:

> [December 1980] Our meetings with the teachers continue like clockwork once a week. In our opinion they are getting more and more involved as time goes on. Also more responsible: they are suggesting their own ideas. For instance, they suggested a timetable change that will allow us to meet once a fortnight for a longer meeting, without cancelling the shorter one. Once when we [the project representatives] couldn't make it to a meeting, they arranged a meeting with Ronen in order to report and discuss ideas.

[January 1981] We are working with the group on a topic considered problematic in the school—grading kids. They arranged (without us, together with Ronen) a mapping of various aspects of the problem. Afterwards each one of us took it upon himself to do some homework related to one or two of the aspects. We are now at the stage of reporting to the group what each of us (that is, all six of us) discovered either from reading or from his/her own experience about the problems and possible solutions. The idea is to prepare a document that will act as background material to discussions with various groups of teachers at the school, workshops, in-service courses.

All this shows that our experience at the Eliad School in the second and third years of our project was different from the total frustration of the first. We felt good about the way things were developing. What is more, Ronen seemed to be changing too. Not only were his relationships with our representatives at the school better than during the first year, he also seemed far more mellow and relaxed at the principals' meetings. To a certain extent this was an expression of a real change in his behavior at the meetings. However, it probably also came about as, over time, all the participants — principals and project staff — began to discover different aspects of his personality.

My own "revelatory" experience occurred during lunch at one of the principals' meetings. This took place at a school that took great pride in its home economics track. The tables were set for a high-class banquet and the students waited at table like waitresses at an expensive restaurant. The food was cooked and served attractively, too. I sat next to Ronen. During the meal he delivered a long harangue about how absurd it was to get the kids to act as they were doing, and to cook a meal like the one we were getting. The world paid too much attention to food. The healthiest food is what horses eat. People should eat simply and get on with the more important things in the world. Everyone at the table got involved in the argument. Once I distanced myself from the discussion, I realized how absurd this was. Ronen was enjoying his meal tremendously, eating with great gusto. Was this simply a sign of hypocrisy? I suddenly grasped that this was not it at all. Ronen was arguing because he liked arguing, for the same reasons that I had participated in the school debating society's meetings when I had been a high school student.

Over the next two years, this side of Ronen's personality became more and more apparent. Often he would come out with outrageous remarks. Everyone would begin arguing with him heatedly, and then he would confide in a part-shamefaced, part-amused aside to the person sitting next to him something like, "That isn't quite my position but I had to say it, to put some zip into the meeting; people were falling asleep." In other ways too, the participants discovered that Ronen had a quirky but very real sense of humor, and he became one of the people one could rely on to put all sorts of "zip" into meetings.

So things looked good. This is the time, dramatically speaking, to introduce the "however." Before doing this I would like to point out one further aspect of the good side of the story. Up to now, both the quotations from project staff reports and also my own recounting of the story have tended to stress what happened in the school or what we thought about the school and its faculty at different times. There has been much less information about what *we* did or what the assumptions were that guided us in deciding to do what we did, although such matters are implied in much of what I have recounted.

The work of our two representatives at the school (and, to a lesser extent, the entire project staff at the principals' meetings) vis-à-vis relations with Ronen exemplified five central guidelines of our intervention strategy:

1. *We should let things develop naturally.* The confrontation with Ronen after the first year came about partially because of our frustration coming to a head, partially because up to then we had probably been plain scared, but also — and this is the important point — it only became an option *after* Ronen began expressing criticism that we were not doing anything. In other words, we were assuming that even the activities of the school faculty designed to block our entry set up their own dynamic for change.

2. *Our presence in the school and participation in activities should be very low-key. In cases where this is impossible, we must try to reduce our part in things as soon as possible.* Our representatives were very prominent at first in the weekly meetings with the teachers. But they continually tried to reduce their input and encouraged the teachers to take over more and more of the initiative.

3. *Whenever possible, we should encourage the introduction of a self-evaluatory component into school activities.* Throughout the two years during which our representatives met with the four

teachers, they tried to ensure that what was being done or planned would contain an empirical check of the state of affairs within the school with regard to some relevant matter. At times, this might require them to argue directly for the introduction of such a component; at others a simple question like "Do we know how the other teachers feel about this?" was sufficient.[12]

4. *We should encourage activities that are not necessarily limited in their impact to those participating in them directly and encourage developments that increase such indirect impact.* That the activities undertaken exemplify such indirect impact seems to be self-evident, but how our representatives encouraged this is more difficult to pin down. This is probably one of the most subtle, unconscious, and professional aspects of their work.

5. *We are only human. We like some people more than others and we often are judgmental about people. But when it comes to school personnel we have to try our damnedest to put this aside and find indications that our negative evaluations of them were mistaken. In any event, in contacts with school personnel we should try to transmit as much respect for them as persons as possible.* This does not mean a manipulative, hypocritical, or artificial attitude, but rather a genuine feeling of respect. It is surprising how often, before one of the principals' meetings, someone from the project staff would say something like: "Ronen can't be as bad as we are making out. I am going to sit next to him at the meeting [or sit next to him at lunch or ask for a lift home in his car after the meeting] and try to get to know him better."

So work with the Eliad School is a pretty good example of an intervention which, once it got off the ground after a faulty beginning, developed according to our project's principles and, what is more, the developments seemed to show that the principles work. Now is the time for the "however." My quotations from our project representatives' reports have been very one-sided. Almost from the beginning of the second year of the project, there was a strand of pessimism in these reports. Three very serious problems were identified.

First, Ronen basically had no confidence in or respect for his teachers. At the beginning of the second year of the project, as already mentioned, we requested all principals to fill out a questionnaire concerning their evaluation of their school's DDAE process. Ronen indicated in his answers that at Eliad there was very little dialogue or group decision making. We were very impressed by his honesty and the very realistic, self-critical way he saw things; in our opinion, there were other principals who were less self-critical and realistic in their answers. However, we subsequently discovered that we had misinterpreted him in a very significant way. Ronen was prepared to say that there was very little dialogue or group decision making at Eliad because he thought this was the way things should be. As he told one of our representatives at the school, "You will have your work cut out to convince me otherwise." This attitude never really changed over the last two years of the project. This was apparent from remarks (serious ones, in this case) made at the principals' meetings and, more importantly, from Ronen's reactions to developments in his school. Practical suggestions that arose in the weekly meeting with our representatives and the four teachers were often dismissed with a shrugged: "Oh, that will never work. You can't rely on the people to get involved in such things. They are too busy looking after their own children at home." Or Ronen would agree with a suggestion but never put it into practice; this happened to most of the suggestions that arose at the end of the second year. For instance, the notion of setting up meetings of teachers in the same department never materialized, although it had been worked into the next year's timetable.

The final meeting of the four teachers and our representatives with Ronen at the end of the project illustrates Ronen's attitude perfectly. To quote again from the notes of our representatives:

> Again and again Ronen's total lack of belief in the teachers became obvious, the unwillingness to change anything because "anyway nothing will come of it." The teachers in the group (the women—the men were well-mannered and weak) confronted him again and again with questions like: "Why are you worried? After all, we have time to back off if we see that it really isn't succeeding. What have we got to lose? Why don't you believe in the teachers?" and so forth. And Ronen— amazingly consistent in his inconsistency—changed arguments at the drop of a hat. At one point he brought up the "babies at home argument." When this was countered, he moved on to "How many teachers are there who really can do this well?" and when he received an answer, he moved on to something else.

A second problem was that the four teachers in the group, although very committed to what they were doing at the meetings, simply did not seem capable of producing interesting ideas on their own that would push the school in significant new directions. Whenever our representatives took a completely passive role at the meetings, the ideas that came up did not have much "zip," in their opinion. Of course, judging "zip" is a pretty subjective matter, but I should add that they did not have the same feelings in other schools in which they worked.

Third, probably the most serious problem the school faced was the fact that because most of the teachers commuted from Jerusalem a series of totally counterproductive norms had developed. For example: all full-time teachers' timetables were arranged so that they had two days free a week; staff meetings after school were avoided because everybody left to go back to Jerusalem; most meetings that were held were conceived of as extra work for which teachers should receive extra pay. The net result was that nothing could get organized. Meetings after school were impossible to arrange because everyone disappeared; meetings during school hours were impossible to arrange because a considerable number of the teachers were absent from the school. In those rare cases when meetings could be set up, they were expensive because the teachers had to be paid to attend. The project staff's frustration is illustrated in the following note jotted in June 1981: "It seems that it is impossible to change anything in such a clumsy and petrified (in the archeological sense) organizational context. Any dinosaur would be a ballet dancer in comparison to this organization!" Our representatives did point out to Ronen and the teachers how counterproductive these norms appeared to us, but the school seemed incapable of entertaining the idea that such norms could be open to discussion, criticism, and review.

Thus the Eliad School seems like a very good example of an organization that Argyris and Schön would say is programmed by a Model I theory-in-use. Also, the problems it faces seem very typical interpersonal ones of the sort organizational consultants thrive on. Then why has this case been introduced? And why here rather than, say, chapters 2 or 3? The reason is that Ronen's lack of confidence in his teachers is not an innate trait as I claimed Yossi's cognitive style was in case I, nor are the counterproductive norms primary beliefs sustaining the sacred as I discussed in chapter 3. As to why I introduce the case at all: What we have here is a school that, as a result of a "successful" intervention, is probably less likely to undergo radical revision now than it was before the intervention. The reason is that the intervention resulted in Ronen in particular, and perhaps some of the teachers, feeling more comfortable about their work and work relations, and, in a sense, more fulfilled than they had previously felt. This, together with a few real but minor changes, is what our success amounted to. Moreover, this had been achieved by the end of the second year; during the third year things did not progress further, although there was no regression. Thus I regard the Eliad School case as a metaphoric illustration of what Freud wrote about therapy: "This was a case of the treatment inhibiting itself; it was in danger of failing as a result of its—partial—success."

If so, how could one move a school like Eliad towards a Model II theory-in-use? The Eliad story is not really intended to address this question. Nevertheless, let me conclude by commenting on Argyris's and Schön's claim that they have developed an intervention strategy that does effect such a transformation. Undoubtedly Argyris's book *Reasoning, Learning and Action* produces convincing support for the claim (although he does concede that there is variability regarding people's aptitude for successful double-loop learning).[13] Also, the Argyris and Schön strategy is based on the idea that the learning they are interested in can only begin when people experience decreasing self-confidence and an increasing sense of not being in control. So it is unlikely to lead to the feelings of comfortable well-being that Freud and Bird warn us to avoid.

Yet I do see a problem with their approach in connection with this case. An intervention of the sort Argyris and Schön suggest implies a certain *context* in which it takes place. *Reasoning, Learning and Action* suggests that this context is one of two sorts: a university seminar in which the interventionist is the teacher and the "clients" are the students, or a consulting situation in which the clients have approached the interventionist for help. In these two contexts the implicit understandings and agreements of all the participants make possible the rather directive sort of intervention strategy that *Reasoning, Learning and Action* describes. Are these contexts applicable to the Eliad School? The first is obviously irrelevant, while the second seems to me also to be irrelevant. Remember, we "got into" the school as a research project in which we and a group of schools were to try to improve school practice as a joint venture, with *our* job defined in advance as that of facilitators. This essentially defined or determined our options very profoundly. These options precluded our working as Argyris and Schön do (assuming we had both the competence and the desire to do so). Could we have "got in" as consultants coming to help a school in trouble? I have no evidence one way or the other that would suggest an answer, but intuition tells me we could not have done so.

So let us simply regard the Eliad School case as an illustration of one of the ways in which change agents can subvert school self-renewal — not perhaps the most central way they can do this, but still a fascinating one. Let us now return to the second of the theoretical questions with which this chapters deals, and through this attend to other ways in which subversion comes about.

PSYCHOLOGICAL FORCES INFLUENCING CHANGE AGENTS

Are there psychological forces that encourage change agents to subvert self-renewal? If so, are these forces unavoidable? Let me begin by stating that most, if not all, work roles have certain psychological pressures that influence workers in some way or other. The important task is to distinguish between types of influence. Consider two work roles: that of the trapeze artist in a circus and that of the housewife and mother, traditionally defined. Both have very clear built-in sources of strain. The trapeze artist is performing tasks that are dangerous and no doubt frightening. The wife, at least in recent years, is performing tasks that tend to engender boredom, frustration because they are not self-fulfilling, alienation, and resentment. But here we reach the crucial difference betwen the two work roles. Trapeze artists' fears may take their psychological toll, but aerialists must continue performing daredevil feats. The work will not undergo redefinition. However, when we turn to the wife's work role, the modern history of the feminist movement shows that women's feelings, among other factors, have resulted in a redefinition of the wifely role.

More generally, we can distinguish between work roles whose associated psychological pressures do not undermine the basic stability of the role (the pressures do not result in redefinition of the role) and work roles where the pressures *do* result in role redefinition. This is not an absolute distinction. The influence of psychological pressure is determined, to a certain extent, by the total social context in which it takes place, and this context is historically specific. Yet as a rough-and-ready distinction, the stability of a role can be classified as to the presence or absence of psychological pressure associated with that role. In most cases it is rather easy to decide in which of the two categories a work role should be placed. Often redefining a role to reduce psychological pressure is self-defeating. For example, if trapeze artists were to perform less dangerous tricks, they would lose their audience. Then there are cases in which very obvious opposing forces counter a trend for redefinition. On the other hand, there are cases in which there are no obvious powerful countervailing forces to psychological pressures. This, I believe, is the situation with the traditional housewife role. The one relevant countervailing force—male chauvinism—is one of the reasons for the wife's psychological pressures in the first place, and thus its display is likely to hasten the process of role redefinition.

This possibility (psychological pressures toward role redefinition with no strong countervailing forces is of particular concern to us because it captures perfectly the situation that the change agent is faced with in trying to promote self-renewal. Let us examine the change agent role a little more closely. ("Change agent" in this context refers only to a person engaged in helping an organization to become self-renewing.) Let us imagine the change agent in a number of reasonably typical situations:

Situation 1.   The change agent is wandering around a school during the "diagnosis" stage. He is working in an unstructured way because the conception that is guiding him is that each school is a unique organization, with its own specific culture and problems, staffed by specific unique personalities. On the basis of sitting in on certain meetings, he decides which teachers it would be interesting to interview. These interviews are open-ended but the content of the aforementioned meetings does determine in part what issues he raises in the interviews. These in turn determine his further diagnostic steps. School personnel ask the change agent what he intends to do to help the school become self-renewing. He answers that he cannot say. The actions he takes will be determined by the outcome of his diagnosis. Well, they ask, what are the various options? Which ones will materialize will not be known until completion of the diagnosis, but the possibilities can be stipulated. The change agent answers in a very vague, general way because, he says, the uniqueness of each school's culture makes it impossible to list the universe of possibilities in advance.

Situation 2.   The diagnosis completed in a very large high school, the change agent is now involved in a more active way in promoting school self-renewal. One of the developments is a series of weekly meetings with the principal and certain of the staff. This is the first such meeting, and it is run by the principal. The change agent is very much in the background, although certain steps he took prior to this meeting were certainly the catalyst for setting it up. Also it is clear that until these meetings become a school norm, the change agent will have to attend to ensure their continuation. During this first meeting, thirty minutes pass before the change agent makes any comment. He then makes a very brief one. A teacher to whom he has as yet never spoken looks at him in puzzlement for a moment, and then turns to her neighbor and whispers. The change agent is pretty sure that she is asking her neighbor, "Who is that guy?"

Situation 3.   Imagine a situation very similar to situation 2, a meeting is about moral education, say. This is a topic about which the change agent knows a lot. As the meeting progresses, it becomes increasingly obvious that the teachers and principal know very little about the topic; in fact, in the change agent's opinion, they are simply talking nonsense. At one point he intervenes: "You know, there is a guy at Harvard called Laurence Kohlberg who has developed a special center concerned with moral education. He has produced some interesting material. For instance, there is a book of his called *The Philosophy of Moral Development*.[14] You might find it interesting to read and discuss his ideas." The teachers make a lot of approving noises—"Gee, how interesting"—but not one of them writes down Kohlberg's name or the name of his book. This confirms the change agent's diagnosis that this school faculty does not conceive of the teacher's role as requiring them to read theoretical educational literature.

These three situations exemplify two central psychological strains of the change agent role. Situation 1 points up the change agent's need to display a great deal of *tolerance of ambiguity*.[15] He has no clear idea what he will be doing a few months hence. He cannot even stipulate in any clear fashion the possibilities open to him at that time. And this is not something that occurs occasionally. The need to "play things by ear" is endemic to this role. Not surprisingly, considering the link between school self-renewal and progressive education through the Deweyian metaphor, the change agent promoting self-renewal works in a very similar fashion to the teacher working within the framework of an activity curriculum. Situations 2 and 3 point up the *self-effacement* required of the change agent. He often needs to present himself as a nonperson or, at least, to withhold knowledge that in the short run could benefit schools tremendously. For instance, in situation 3, not only can he suggest Kohlberg as a reference, he could probably also teach a course on moral education himself, and by doing this get the school's deliberations on moral education off the ground.

It is much easier to function in a defined rather than in an ambiguous situation. It is much easier not to be self-effacing. These forces push the change agent toward redefining his role. However, by succumbing to such forces, the change agent almost certainly subverts school self-renewal. Let us consider each force or "temptation" separately.

How can the change agent reduce the ambiguity of situation 1? The most obvious thing he can do is to *structure the situation.* For instance, instead of playing things by ear he can perform his diagnosis with a whole battery of formal questionnaires. These not only constrain and limit his observations, but also allow him to stipulate in advance the universe of possibilities for his more active intervention. (For example: Those schools that obtain low scores on section 2 of questionnaire 5 have problems with interdepartmental communication. These kinds of problems can be eliminated through training exercises 7, 8, and 11, and so on.) The problem with this kind of structuring is that it almost inevitably pushes the change agent toward playing the expert role and the school faculty toward deference to an expert. Playing the expert, as we have seen, subverts self-renewal and thus the change agent's structuring of his work situation must be regarded as counterproductive.

There is a second way of reducing ambiguity that also undermines the change agent's usefulness. This is a more subtle mechanism that may or may not work as I suggest; nevertheless, I will share my thoughts on this matter. Ambiguity can perhaps be reduced through the change agent's adoption of a *stage theory of change.* By this I do not mean a stage-like intervention strategy (for example, distinguishing between a diagnosis and activity stage in our own work), but rather theories that claim that organizations change by going through a linear, stage-by-stage process. For example, in *Changing Schools: The Magic Feather Principle,* Bentzen suggests the following stages: First, the DDAE process is relatively invisible — the staff is unaware of it. Second, the process becomes much more visible. Third, the visibility leads to disequilibrium in principal and teacher role definitions. Fourth, the DDAE process is turned into a critical examination of the changes that the school has made. Fifth, the DDAE process becomes one that signals fully responsible receptivity to change.[16] The details of Bentzen's stage theory are not important here; it is just a convenient example of many, for the literature on planned change is filled with such theories. What is important is what such theories do for the interventionist.

For a student of change, an external observer of school processes, suggesting stage theories of change is perfectly legitimate and perhaps illuminating (provided such theories are seen as simplifications). However, for an interventionist, subscribing to a stage theory would seem likely to encourage further subversion of self-renewal. The moment change agents believe that the changes an organization will undergo are highly predictable and known to them, they will almost certainly approach that organization with the state of mind that encourages the emergence of the two hidden curricula previously mentioned — the expert as superior to the client and the expert as possessor of infallible knowledge.

Let us now turn to the stresses engendered by the requirement for self-effacement. Almost all the ways we have discussed in which self-renewal can be subverted are, unfortunately, ways of reducing these stresses. The relationship is far more direct and obvious than that which obtains between ways of subverting self-renewal and ways of reducing ambiguity. First, by prolonging their stay, by claiming that a school faculty is not yet ready to go it alone, change agents can increase their own sense of worth and importance. Second, by playing the expert role and transmitting the hidden curricula I have indicated, they step out from behind their veil of anonymity.

So, all in all, we see that the change agent role contains within it the potential to be counterproductive with regard to school self-renewal. The question that remains to be answered is: must this potential be realized? This brings us back to the distinction between work roles whose associated psychological pressures do and do not undermine the basic stability of the role. The change agent role seems to me to be of the former type because it does not seem capable of setting in motion powerful forces to counteract the drift away from the original role definition.

Two considerations lead me to this conclusion. First, unlike the trapeze artist's audience, the change agent's clients—the school faculty—have no interest in maintaining the original definition of the change agent role. On the contrary, as Goodlad and Bentzen have amply demonstrated (and as our project also collaborates), schools expect change agents to play the expert role. In fact when they do not do so, *this* creates tension.

The second consideration arises from a comparison of the situation of the change agent with that of the psychoanalyst. As Malcolm puts it:

> The analyst as far as possible confines himself to listening to the patient and (sparingly) offering him his conjectures — which are called "interpretations" — about the unconscious meaning of his communciations. He does not give advice, he does not talk about himself, he does not let himself be provoked or drawn into discussions of abstract subjects, he does not answer questions about his family or his political preferences, he does not show like or dislike of the patient, or approval or disapproval of his actions. His behavior toward the patient is as neutral, mild, colorless, self-effacing, uninterfering, and undemanding as he is able to make it.[17]

This is obviously a very similar sort of self-effacement to that demanded of the change agent, and in fact is probably an even more total one. Consider Brenner's justification for analytic neutrality:

> There are times when his being "human" . . . can be harmful. . . . As an example, for his analyst to express sympathy for a patient who has just lost a close relative may make it more difficult than it would otherwise be for the patient to express pleasure or spite or exhibitionistic satisfaction over the loss.[18]

Psychoanalysts are also faced with the temptation to be less self-effacing, more "human." Yet this does not seem to have caused a drift toward a redefinition of their role. Among the many factors that contribute to this are the artificial, isolated nature of the analytic situation, the power of the psychoanalytic guild, the linking of self-effacement to the esoteric, obscure language of psychoanalysis —a language to which analysts have a strong ideological commitment. However, from our point of view, the most important factor is that the limits of active analytic "intervention" can be couched in the form "Do not do X." There may be controversy regarding a particular X. For instance, many analysts would find Brenner's advice that the analyst should not express sympathy when a patient has lost a close relative a little extreme. Yet the debate with Brenner will be in terms of whether analysts should or should not do this. Herein resides a crucial difference between analysts and change agents. Views regarding the limits of the latter's intervention will be couched in the form of "Do *less* X" or "Do not do X *now.*" Because change agents do not meet the school on a psychoanalyst's couch, they cannot avoid becoming involved to a certain extent in the ongoing activities of the school. Because they are dealing with people whom they are trying to help gain a feeling a self-efficacy within an organizational context, it may be advisable in certain situations, especially at the beginning of an intervention, to lend a helping hand. What this means is that the dividing line between staying around to get things safely off the ground, and staying around because they cannot say goodbye, between momentarily playing the expert because in their professional judgment they should do this, and playing the expert because it is tempting to do so, is very ill defined.

Imagine sitting in on a school faculty meeting at which a change agent is present. For ten minutes of the meeting the change agent effectively takes over and lectures to the faculty. Is this a sign of having succumbed to pressures to redefine the change agent's role? On the basis of this particular meeting, one could not possibly know; such a judgment would depend on much more extensive observation.

But it is precisely this sort of fluidity that ensures that no strong forces will oppose role redefinition. In a situation in which playing the expert and staying around can be justified through rhetoric such as "in my professional judgment," "in this particular case" and so on; and in a situation in which the legitimacy of this justification is difficult to assess, then there will always be those for whom this justification is an (unconscious) coverup of their having succumbed to the temptations to redefine their role.

STRUCTURAL FORCES INFLUENCING CHANGE AGENTS

Are there structural forces that encourage change agents to subvert self-renewal? If so, are such forces inescapable? Change agents do not appear from nowhere. They come from certain organizational contexts or systems that either employ them or have been set up by the change agents as entrepreneurial ventures. These systems maintain certain types of relationships with the schools which the change agents are trying to help, the educational systems of which they are part, and also the change agents themselves. In this section I will argue that these relationships constrain how change agents will work in the schools so as to subvert self-renewal.

One can identify three main contexts or systems from which change agents appear on the scene: Change agents are often research workers, usually from universities, and their intervention is some sort of research project. Another possibility is that change agents are part of a private consulting firm or else are university professors who do consulting on the side. Or change agents are employed as supervisors of sorts by the school system. Each of these contexts raises different issues.

The Research Context

University research workers may be change agents committed to helping schools but they are also university employees, and one of their primary motivations is the hope that this activity will help them in their academic ambitions, for example, gaining tenure or promotion. This means that their activities in the schools are constrained by the university reward structure and specifically by the norms that determine how university faculty obtain things like tenure and promotion. One such norm is obviously that the intervention should lead to something publishable. In itself, this is not particularly problematic. However, when one begins spelling out the further requirements associated with publishing, one does discover some problematic features of the research context vis-à-vis school self-renewal.

For the average research worker, "doing something publishable" implies that research should be done according to the norms that dominate a given specialty. In the case of educational research, as with so much work in the social sciences, this means, among other things, that the research is likely to be guided by what Guba and Lincoln call the scientific paradigm for getting at the truth. Guba and Lincoln see this paradigm as "relying on experimentation as a fundamental technique . . . [and viewing] truth as confirmable; that is, truth is an hypothesis that has been confirmed by an actual experiment." [19]

Of course, change projects are not so much concerned with getting at the truth as with getting something done. Nevertheless, the publishable part of the project, even if it is to some extent a by-product, will inevitably relate to "getting at the truth." What I wish to suggest is that, if this by-product is guided by the scientific paradigm, this will have considerable impact on the "getting something done" part of the project too. The scientific paradigm has associated with it a number of derivative postures about various matters. One such posture is about what Guba and Lincoln call the style of testing hypotheses:

Within the scientific paradigm the style (of testing hypotheses) has been primarily one of *intervention;* that is, the independent and dependent variables are *isolated* and the context is *arranged* so that these variables can account for whatever findings emerge. Such situations [are] often called experimental but [are] probably better termed *contrived.*[20]

The words I have emphasized highlight the problems that the scientific paradigm raises for school self-renewal. First, it is difficult to maintain contrived situations for long periods of time. Thus research projects are likely to remain in schools for far too short a time. Change agents must know how to go away, but they also need to stay awhile! More important, *intervention, isolation, arranging,* and *contriving* are all words that signal active manipulation. The scientific paradigm style of testing hypotheses is antithetical to the notion of minimal catalyst. It rather strongly reinforces the drift toward the expert role.

The paradigm reinforces this role in yet another way. In order to get something published, one must perform a number of actions. Relevant literature must be found and read; field work done; findings processed; ideas thought out and written down; manuscripts typed and put into stamped envelopes. The norms of academic life determine to a certain extent the status of these various actions. Professors usually expect research assistants to find relevant literature for them and expect secretaries to type. However, over and beyond this, the scientific paradigm also ranks these activities. Specifically, this paradigm regards field work as less prestigious than thinking and writing. For this reason, research assistants are often sent into the field, while, the professors remain in ivory towers. The unintended consequence is that that expert role is reinforced, with all the attendant downgrading of the schoolteacher and the school principal.

Apart from the problems raised by the scientific paradigm, university research workers are also constrained by the fact that they need to get their projects funded. In an ideal world, funding would simply be a function of the quality of a research proposal, but we do not live in such a world. Projects have to be *sold.* Thus even in the case of pure research, selling is quite an important "academic" skill that must be learned. However, in the case of interventions whose purpose is to induce change, promotional skills become absolutely central. Not only must people be convinced of the value of certain ideas, but they must also be convinced of the personal competence of the change agent.

How is this all related to the subversive tendencies of the change agent vis-à-vis school self-renewal? My suggestion is that *the problem of how to sell oneself tends to be solved by change agents through their adopting the stance of the expert who does all and knows all*. In fact, they are probably socialized into becoming such people. In order to see this, imagine a change agent trying to convince some funding committee to fund a proposal by telling them that change agents should play things by ear, that they in fact should do very little but should expect the school faculty to do much, and that anyway this way of helping to promote change is perhaps not really likely to work. Judging from my experience, the response to such an approach would be best described as apoplectic. So change agents do not present their proposals in this way. They exude confidence and knowledgeability, they stipulate the steps of their intervention in considerable detail, and they emphasize what they will be doing and not what the school faculty will do. The change agent is the educational salesperson par excellence, as I think is well illustrated in the case study section of this chapter.

This brings us back to the point raised at the end of chapter 4 concerning the strange fact that the work of people like Dreeben, Lortie, and Weick is rarely mentioned or related to in the school change literature. Conceiving of the change agent as salesperson explains this rather well. Salespeople do not devote much time to displaying the flaws in their products. I am not suggesting that the authors of much of the change literature deliberately and cynically hide facts from the public, but that change agents, like all academics, are swamped with theoretical literature; they must select what they attend to. The self-promotional orientation is going to invite them to unconsciously let the ideas raised in chapter 4 pass them by.

The Consulting Context

From one point of view, the economic side of the consulting context may often be less undermining to self-renewal than the economics of the research context. University research workers need to sell their projects but consultants do not always bid for theirs. In many cases, they are approached. When this occurs, consultants need not be as concerned with selling; however, from another perspective, economic factors do set up pressures that encourage the consultant to subvert self-renewal unconsciously.

In order to show this, I must introduce one further consideration about consulting in schools. This derives from the following deceptively obvious pair of claims: schools are rather unique organizations, and therefore, change agents working in schools must be familiar with the school environment. In actual fact, neither of these claims is self-evident. The very existence of a general theory of organizations would seem to belie the uniqueness of the school. The notion of the external perspective, the presumed positive contribution of the naive observer to the understanding of a group's culture would seem to belie the necessity for familiarity with the school setting.

Yet I think there are rather powerful arguments for the uniqueness of schools and the desirability of change agents being very familiar with them. Clifford Geertz's magnificent *The Interpretation of Cultures* will again be of help as it was in chapter 3. Geertz uses Gilbert Ryle's distinction between "thin" and "thick" descriptions. Thin descriptions are simple behavioral ones (for example, rapidly contracting one's right eyelid). Thick descriptions explicate actions in relation to meaningful semiotic structures. It is in terms of such structures that "rapidly contracting one's right eyelid" becomes a twitch or a wink or a parody of a wink.[21] For Geertz, ethnography is thick description:

> What the ethnographer is in fact faced with . . . is a multiplicity of complex conceptual structures, many of them superimposed upon or knotted into one another . . . which he must contrive somehow first to grasp and then to render. And this is true at the most down-to-earth, jungle field work levels of his activity: interviewing informants, observing rituals. . . . Doing ethnography is like trying to read (in the sense of "construct a reading of") a manuscript—foreign, faded, full of ellipses, incoherencies, suspicious emendations, and tendentious commentaries, but written not in conventionalized graphs of sound but in transient examples of shaped behavior.[22]

Ethnography is sometimes very difficult. Why? Geertz's answer is that we often are not familiar with the meaningful structures which would enable us to convert thin to thick descriptions: "What, in [a foreign place], most prevents those of us who grew up winking other winks . . . from grasping what people are up to is not ignorance as to how cognition works . . . *as a lack of familiarity with the imaginative universe within their acts are signs.*"[23]

One would assume that in one's own culture these difficulties would be minimized (although other difficulties associated with overfamiliarity might arise). Yet even here we will be more familiar with some "imaginative universes within which acts are signs" than others. Moreover—and this is the crucial point—some imaginative universes are more difficult for the outsider to gain familiarity with than others. There can be many sources of this difficulty. Two are particularly relevant. First, in some social situations actors may be interested in hiding parts of the imaginative universe which renders their action meaningful. This may in fact be the whole point of what they are doing. Consider, for instance, a lawyer cross-examining a witness. For all sorts of reasons, many of them associated with the drama of the situation, he may wish to obscure his intentions from those sitting in the courtroom (at least for a certain period of time). Often only experienced trial lawyers are going to be able to "read" him. Second, certain imaginative universes may be opaque to external observers because they are part of the actors' tacit knowledge and are thus opaque on the conscious level to these actors themselves.

On both these counts, teaching is an activity that the outsider has great difficulty in becoming familiar with. One reason for this is that the classroom lesson is at least in part a contrived dramatic performance with all the attendant climaxes, denouements, and uncertainties, and the teachers as actors are very concerned to keep it that way and thus hide their imaginative universe. Moreover, the lack of a developed teaching technology is not, as Dreeben would have it, a flaw and a source of criticism. It is simply a reaffirmation of the old claim that teaching is an art. And if this is so, then good teaching will always remain to a large extent a skill characterized by tacit knowledge.

The conclusion this analysis leads us to is that teaching is a supreme example of a profession best understood from within. If we also assume, as I think we safely can, that teaching is an important part of what goes on in schools, then a general theory of organizations (which, by its very nature, cannot very well be concerned with the imaginative universe of teaching) must miss what is truly important about schools. We can also conclude that a consultant who is not familiar with schools as special organizations is not likely to be of much use as a change agent for school self-renewal. There must be special mice who specialize in helping elephants fly. Mice who purport to be able to help elephants, rhinos, and hippos, may get the rhinos and the hippos off the ground, but the elephants are going to remain within the forest.

How does all this link up with the economic side of the consulting context? The link comes from the fact that educational con-

sultants have a very limited potential clientele. There simply are
not that many schools around. In fact, for the average consultant,
the number of potential clients is even less than the above analysis
indicates. Not only must educational consultants specialize in
schools (rather than being prepared to consult in any sort of organization), but also they probably need to specialize in a particular
type of school. In my personal experience, for instance, familiarity
with the imaginative universe of high schools is of very little help
in trying to understand elementary schools.

The moment one's clientele is limited, it is obviously in one's
interest to keep all the clients one has. In this, the consultant's
situation is very different from that of the psychoanalyst. To put it
cynically, psychoanalysts can afford to let their patients get well,
but I am not so sure that educational consultants can afford to let
their clients become self-renewing. So one should not be surprised
to meet consultants of the type I ran into a little while back, who
informed me that he had been a consultant for a particular school
for nearly ten years.

The Bureaucratic Context

Of the three contexts discussed, the bureaucratic context
clearly seems the most problematic. First of all, change agents who
are part of the same educational system as the schools they are
trying to help usually have the major disadvantage of "having
clout." This colors their relationship with the schools. In our project, for example, the principals were often asked by ministry of education officials in what way the project staff representatives in
their schools were different from a sympathetic school inspector.
In answering, some principals would directly invoke the way the
supervisory role militates against a supportive sort of relationship.
They would say that they simply felt more comfortable with our
staff. Others would answer by praising us as people. But surely we
did not have a monopoly on the supportive virtues. The principals
might see school inspectors as being unhelpful as people, but from
an outsider's point of view it seems much more likely that they are
being seen through filters that their role encourages or creates.

The change agent employed by the system has other disadvantages very similar to the ones Wildavsky described in his
classic "The Self-Evaluating Organization." This article examines
some of the consequences of an organization continuously monitoring its own activities. On one level, this means that the entire organ-

ization must be imbued with the evaluative ethic.[24] Yet Wildavsky
shows that structural considerations will lead to certain members
having to deal with evaluation as their special "thing." He then
indicates the pressures such members will have to deal with. They
must, for instance, "obtain the support of existing bureaucracies
while pursuing antibureaucratic policies. They must combine political feasibility with analytical purity."[25] They will have to convince
themselves to live with constant change[26] and worry about security
of employment[27] (assuming that the number of evaluators an organization needs must vary as the organization changes its
activities—at times there will be fewer programs to evaluate, at
times more). Wildavsky argues that this will lead inevitably to the
establishment of a unit of the organization dealing with evaluation,
and that little by little such a unit will gain characteristics of all
organizational entities: it will need to stabilize its environment,
secure internal loyalty and outside support,[28] and make certain that
it does not bear the costs of introducing the changes it advocates.[29]
It will become, in fact, a lobby for evaluation.[30]

The point is that these developments are opposed to the
"pure" spirit of evaluation or, as Wildavsky puts it, they are anti-
evaluative tendencies.[31] Wildavsky's analysis is essentially an attempt to show why a self-evaluating organization is self-contradic-
tory—not in the logical sense, but rather in political terms.

Evaluation is only one part of self-renewal. Yet consider the
idea of a group of change agents constituting a unit within an educational system whose job it is to help another unit of the system (the
schools) become imbued with the ethos of change, problem solving, and evaluation. This is very similar to the situation Wildavsky
addresses. His arguments seem to be directly transferable. The
moment the change agents become an organizational subunit of the
educational system, one that needs to maintain stability and political support, it is difficult to see their activities remaining limited to
being minimal temporary catalysts.

So we see that none of the three contexts from which change
agents usually come is conducive to encouraging the change agent
to promote self-renewal. The one task that remains is to estimate
how permanent the forces I have described actually are.

By and large, none of the arguments presented in this secion
relies on contingent historical factors. One seeming exception is the
argument relating to the economic pressures of the consulting context. These seem likely to be less pronounced in times of educational expansion. Yet surely the difference is not very significant. In

a town like the one I live in—Beersheba—in which there is educational expansion, this comes down to the addition of one or two schools every two or three years. The American experience at present is one of declining enrollments. This comes down to the closing of one or two schools every two or three years in towns of similar size (100,000 people). In other matters this is a profound difference. In terms of consulting clientele it is not.

Another exception, and in this case a real one, is the argument concerning the scientific paradigm and its effect on the research context. Here we may be witnessing changes that could reduce the pressure toward playing the expert role very dramatically. Over the last few years, books like *Beyond the Numbers Game* by Hamilton et al.[32] and *Effective Evaluation* by Guba and Lincoln have heralded the emergence of a new research paradigm that is competing with the scientific paradigm. This new paradigm is "a naturalistic paradigm, relying on field study as a fundamental technique, which views truth as ineluctable, that is as ultimately inescapable. Sufficient immersion in and experience with a phenomenological field yields inevitable conclusions about what is important, dynamic, and pervasive in that field. Ethnography is a typical instance."[33]

This characteristic of naturalistic inquiry is certainly not uncontroversial. However, as Guba and Lincoln go on and list various derivative differences between the two paradigms, it becomes clear that the scientific/naturalistic distinction is very significant with regard to the concerns of this chapter:

> The naturalistic inquirer given his view of multiple realities and the complex interactions that take place between an inquirer and the "objects" of an inquiry, tends to eschew generalizations in favor of "thick descriptions."[34]

> Scientific inquirers take a reductionist stance; that is, they reduce the inquiry to a relatively small focus by imposing constraints both on conditions antecedent to the inquiry . . . and on outputs. . . . Naturalistic inquirers however take an expansionist stance. They seek a perspective that will lead to the description and understanding of phenomena as wholes or at least in ways that reflect their complexity. They enter the field and build outward from wherever the point of entry happens to be. Each step in the inquiry is based on the sum of insights gleaned from previous steps. Thus scientific inquirers take a structured, focused, singular stance while naturalistic inquirers take an open, exploratory, and complex stance.[35]

In brief, the naturalistic posture is the antithesis of the active manipulatory posture of the scientific paradigm.

Naturalistic inquiry and attempting to induce change are not the same thing. Yet the minimal catalyst conception clearly fits the naturalistic posture far better than it does the scientific one. If educational research were to become dominated by the naturalistic paradigm, as Hamilton et al. and Guba and Lincoln are predicting, this would be a truly profound revolution. Not only would it affect research norms, but also it would gradually change the expectations and criteria of those who fund research and planned change projects. In a climate that values open-ended research, it would be much easier to justify open-ended change projects.

Whether the predicted revolution is going to take place or not is something the future will have to tell us. The present situation is equivocal. On the one hand, when *Daedalus* published its celebrated issues on the American school,[36] the preferred paradigm for trying to find answers to the questions asked was the naturalistic one.[37] On the other hand, an influential book like Rutter's *Fifteen Thousand Hours* draws on the most classical scientific research methodologies.[38] Nevertheless, the possibility of a paradigm change does suggest one conclusion we can reach with relative confidence—the research context is the "best" of the three prevalent ones because its subversive tendencies can most easily (although not *very* easily) be minimized.

DYSFUNCTIONAL CONSEQUENCES OF CHANGE AGENTS' WORK

What are the unintended dysfunctional consequences of competent work by change agents? Up to this point, I have mainly been concentrating on the forces that press toward redefinition of the change agent role. In this brief section I wish to take the opposite tack. Assuming the role is not redefined, assuming change agents perform as theories of self-renewal prescribe, perhaps one can still discover dysfunctional aspects of what they are doing. The Ronen case was one such example, but that was associated with the specific intervention strategy. In this section, I wish to consider two dysfunctional aspects of the change agent's activity that are independent of the intervention strategy.

First, the creation of the change agent role adds a further group of auxiliary persons who, like guidance counselors and school psychologists, for example, have entered the teacher's domain. In one sense, this shows a typical process of specialization; compare the similar process whereby a burgeoning number of specialists and scientists have invaded the domain of the family doctor. Such a process usually results in a downgrading of the original profession thereby invaded. Such is the case with the teaching profession. This would not necessarily be a bad thing if it were accompanied by accommodating structural changes in the school (as seems to be the case with the medical profession). However, this does not occur. The invasion of the teacher's domain is far more symbolic than real. To a large extent the classroom remains the central part of the school, where the action is. The introduction of auxiliary professions does not actually displace the focus from the classroom to somewhere else. Rather it just transmits the message to the teachers that they are less competent than certain other personnel who have been trained to deal with certain specific aspects of school life. As we have seen in chapter 4, the notion of school self-renewal requires that teaching become a full profession. Thus we have the paradoxical situation that, regardless of what they do, the very existence of change agents contributes to a process—the proliferation of high-status professions associated with schools, but which do not reach the center of school life—that reduces rather than increases the teacher's professional status.

The second dysfunctional aspect of change agent activity arises from the qualities and qualifications assumed to be required in order to be a good change agent. Often, when making lists of desirable qualities for a particular job role or profession, one falls into the trap of making a list that is either totally trivial (for instance, people in this profession should be nice, pleasant, and sociable) or else could only fit a paragon. In order to avoid this trap, I will limit myself to four "qualities," all of which follow pretty directly from the discussion in this chapter: (1) Change agents should have a high tolerance of ambiguity; (2) They should be self-effacing; (3) They should have many of the predilections of the "naturalistic" inquirer and specifically what Vallance describes in another context as the state of mind attuned to the subtle and irregular qualities of schooling;[39] (4) They should have considerable field experience in schools.

Of the many conclusions one can draw from inspecting these four properties, I limit myself to one: the good change agent was once a teacher and, what is more, was one of what Dreeben calls the talented cohort of yearly college graduates who went into teaching (see chapter 4). Assuming this is so, we can generalize: if the change agents working in the schools of a particular educational system are to do a good job, then most of them should be ex-teachers from such talented cohorts. However, this leads us to another strange paradox. In order to promote school self-renewal, which among other things means increasing school staff's feelings of autonomy, professional pride, and effectiveness, one needs to skim off some of the cream of the teaching profession, remove them from the schools and the profession so that they can help their less talented colleagues become more autonomous, professional, and effective. Seen in this light, the "magic feather" principle begins to seem rather suspect.

CASES

CASE XVI: INSULTS AND WOUNDED FEELINGS

Of all the cases in this book, this is the one in which the distractions from the main point of the story are most powerful. Therefore I wish to point them out before beginning. The distractions I am referring to relate to two extremely serious errors of judgment on my part.

The first error was to accept the school with which this case deals into the project. This was my error because the school was one of the few schools with which I had some previous acquaintance. All my intuitions led to the suspicion that the school and in particular its headmaster would not benefit from a project of this sort. Yet, fearing that these intuitions were simply prejudices, I did not veto the idea of the school joining the project. I think I should have done so. It would have saved everyone a lot of unnecessary frustration.

The second error occurred when the headmaster of the school complained bitterly about the project staff representatives at his school (the reason for which I will explain). As a result, these representatives were replaced by another member of our staff. This was mainly because I thought that the tension that had developed between the headmaster and our representatives was destructive and that the project's aims could best be served by wiping the slate clean. I maintained this position despite the fact that one of the representatives involved disagreed very strongly and in fact advocated that the representatives and headmaster must talk their differences through. In other words, in Argyris's and Schön's terminology, this staff member was proposing a Model II approach to things; I was proposing a Model I approach. Now I see that I was clearly in the wrong. These two errors determined much of the story I am going to tell, and if the purpose of this case were to illustrate consulting mistakes, I would enlarge on them; however, my main purpose is to illustrate the psychological pressures the change agent faces. The story primarily concerns the first two representatives assigned to this school.

The Etz Haim School was an institution catering to rather gifted youngsters, and for this reason it had a very good reputation with regard to student achievement. It also had little difficulty in attracting rather good teachers of the traditional, examination-oriented sort. The school was nevertheless not without its problems. The students and the teachers were not as talented as those of a few years back; Etz Haim was to an extent relying on a past reputation. It also was a rather alienated place—there was very little contact between teachers and a very rigid, authoritarian structure.

At the beginning of the project, Avi, the headmaster, told me that he was very interested in joining our project. However, since he would be on sabbatical during that year, he suggested we postpone serious discussions until the next year. During the last month of that first year, Avi had again taken over the principalship, so I went to see him. We discussed the project for an hour or two. However, this is misleading. I sat in his office for that time, but for most of it other things were going on. People continually entered the office to ask, confirm, request, show all sorts of apparently trivial things. It became clear that everything that went on at Etz Haim passed through Avi's hands. At one point, a department head came to show him a letter he intended to circulate and Avi took up his pen and altered all sorts of things in the letter.

Avi saw our project as one in which a group of external experts would come to help his school in a variety of ways. He showed little interest in the contact with other schools, but questioned me closely about the project staff. Who were they? What university degrees did they have? What experience? and so on. He was not happy with my comment that these formal matters were of little importance in our view, and that the staff were mainly catalysts who would try to play a very low-key role. Nevertheless, the school voted to join the project.

The two project members assigned to the school were R—— and J——. R—— was the youngest and least experienced member of our staff, but she had a most exceptional intuitive ability to "read" people and situations. J—— was a very experienced teacher who had also spent many years training and supervising teachers in various school and university frameworks. Although he had no formal training in psychotherapy, he was extremely interested in and involved with therapeutic ideas and continually stressed the parallels of our work to therapy.

The first meeting between Avi, R—— and J—— raised in the most emphatic way the opposing perspectives of Avi and our staff. They asked Avi to suggest which activities they should sit in on to get a picture of how the school functions. Avi reacted by saying that he did not see why he should do their work for them. Their request was an imposition; he did not have the time for such matters; besides, if they were experts at diagnosing school functioning, they should suggest to him what to look at. At the end of a rather frustrating meeting, the compromise reached was that, at the next principals' meeting, R—— and J—— would present Avi with a list of *possible* ways of getting to know the school and its staff.

This they did, but here we come to a central moment of the story. The written list not only contained suggestions, but also was written in a particular style. The tone was what one could call lightly bantering. There was a hint of sarcasm, a hint that R—— and J—— were obeying "orders" in a situation where "orders" were inappropriate. This was only the very slightest of hints, but it was definitely there. And Avi, who is intelligent and not insensitive to such matters, got the message immediately. He was absolutely furious. He tore up the note without uttering a word, turned his back on R—— and J——, and from then on ignored them.

A week later I was summoned to the school to speak to Avi. Again we spoke for at least an hour or two. He was seriously considering leaving the project. First, he regarded R—— and J—— as grossly incompetent and impertinent. What sort of childish behavior was it to write insulting notes to people? Second, he was very unimpressed with the principals' meetings. He proceeded to tick each principal off on his fingers. So-and-so talks nonsense. So-and-so is an idiot. So-and-so talks so obscurely it is impossible to understand what he is trying to say, and so on. Interestingly enough, in talking about the principals Avi used their surnames, which went against all the norms that had developed in the group over the first year.

During our talk we touched on many different aspects of Avi's criticisms. The most significant is probably related to a list of headmaster types in the project that I suggested. Avi quickly identified himself as of the type that places his body between the project staff and his school. He had readily spotted the problem with this headmaster type: by not really allowing the project staff into the school, he was turning his criticism of the staff as incompetent into a self-fulfilling prophesy. Yet he really was suspicious about their competence. In the end he reached the conclusion that having been an active member of the project for less than two months, he probably needed more time in order to evaluate things.

Despite this perhaps promising conclusion to our discussion, I made the mistake of judging the situation as being too delicate for R—— and J—— to continue as our representatives, so they were replaced by G——. She and Avi seemed to hit it off rather well, and no further incidents occurred during this year, but nothing particularly positive happened either. Avi was one of the two principals whose attendance at the principals' meetings was very erratic, and this did not change throughout the year. Also G——'s job of diagnosing the Etz Haim School's DDAE was not easy because this was another of those schools with very little teacher dialogue, formal or informal. Toward the end of the year G—— supplied Avi and one of the school's vice-principals with feedback (Avi was not interested in having this feedback given to the whole staff). Avi taped the entire feedback session, because, as he later explained, he wanted to analyze the tape to see whether G—— was competent or not. Right up to the end of this year Avi saw the project and its staff as "on trial."

Toward the end of this second year it became clear that for technical reasons G—— would not be able to continue at the Etz Haim School. This could have created very serious problems; however, by this time Avi had revised his attitude toward R—— and J——. Having listened to their contributions to some of the principals' meetings and having heard of things they had done, he decided they were perhaps not incompetent after all. In particular, he had learned that J—— was very knowledgeable in a certain field that Avi considered relevant to the problems at his school and thus expressed interest in involving J—— in a series of activities at the school. This was still relating to our staff as experts rather than as catalysts, but the situation was better than it had been. In any event, Avi's new attitude made it possible for R—— and J—— to be reassigned as project staff members to the Etz Haim School.

A "changing of the guard" meeting was arranged at which Avi, G——, J——, R——, and I participated. The main purpose was to plan how R—— and J—— would take part in school activities in the third year. At one point, Avi referred in passing to the fact that R—— and J—— were not entirely unfamiliar with the Etz Haim School. We now come to a second central moment in this story. R—— interrupted him and in an aggressive tone reminded everyone that the circumstances under which they had stopped associating with the school had not been pleasant. Avi chose to ignore this comment.

Before continuing, I will briefly conclude the story of the Etz Haim School's association with our project. As mentioned in chapters 1 and 4, at the beginning of the third year of our project we raised the question of saying goodbye. Avi volunteered to present a paper at a principals' meeting in which he would make certain suggestions about the nature of the project's continuance without the presence of the "hub" the following year. He took this very seriously, devoting a lot of time to preparing his paper. Unfortunately, the reaction of the principals was not very enthusiastic; after some desultory comment, they began to talk about other things. Again, I was summoned to the school. Avi told me that the reaction of the principals to his ideas had finally convinced him that they simply were not serious, and he had no desire to continue meeting with them. However, he faced a dilemma. The school evaluator he had appointed seemed to be enjoying what he was doing and deriving a lot of benefit from it. Was it possible for him to continue in the project and for Avi to leave? I explained why this was unacceptable—schools joined our project, not individuals. Avi told me he would have to think about things and a week later wrote informing me he had decided to pull his school out of the project.

Let us now turn to the second part of this story—the discussions around the torn note and the changing of the guard incidents among the project staff. At the time of the torn note incident I expressed the opinion that, despite the fact that Avi's reaction had been very exaggerated, there was no doubt in my mind that the note should not have been written as it had. The majority of the other staff members agreed. Yet R—— and J—— were not prepared to accept this. During the next two years, Avi's reaction to their note was repeatedly raised at staff meetings. R—— and J—— always talked about Avi with great anger and hurt, and regarded the torn note incident as justification. His reaction had been absurd; he had no sense of humor; it was irrelevant whether the note should have been written or not. In fact, they saw the slightest criticism of what they had done as evidence that the rest of the staff were being nonsupportive.

The difficulties associated with the changing of the guard incident were even more serious. As we left the school that day, I asked R—— why she had said what she had. Her answer: "I wanted to make it quite clear to Avi that we hadn't forgotten." I said that I could not agree and that the remark had been unnecessary.

A few days later, R—— and J—— phoned me and requested that we meet. R—— and J—— again were very upset and felt that I was being unsupportive. It might seem that the substantive issues raised at this time were irrelevant. This was, after all, a conversation of a boss with two employees who had been criticized for actions they had performed (or rather that one had performed and the other approved of, as later became apparent). It would seem reasonable that all the defenses activated when subordinates are criticized would be operative here and would render any real, open communication impossible. However, our discussion was not by and large a typical win-lose, face-saving sort of affair. J—— and I had known each other for years and were good friends. I think that the problem of the Etz Haim School was the only case where there had ever been any real, serious disagreement between us. I should also stress that the other school in which J—— was working simultaneously was clearly one of our success stories, and he was well aware of my admiration for what he, and R——, also at this second school, were doing. So I think that we managed to identify the real sources of disagreement between us, despite the fact that feelings ran high. These sources of disagreement were not interpersonal ones, but derived from our different conceptions of the change agent role.

R—— and J—— wanted me to explain my reason for disagreeing with what R—— had said at the meeting with Avi. In trying to do this, I went back to R——'s explanation after the meeting: "I wanted to make it quite clear to Avi that we hadn't forgotten." There are two ways of interpreting this. First, R—— might have meant: "I wanted Avi to know because this will help Etz Haim to become a self-renewing school and Avi to be the headmaster of such a school." Or she might have meant: "I wanted Avi to know because he hurt me and it is important *for me* that he know this." If the first were correct, then the disagreement between us was relatively minor; we were just operating with different theories of change. I am skeptical that such remarks have much effect, whereas R—— thinks they might. However, if the second interpretation were the correct one, as I suspect, then the disagreement between R——, J——, and myself was absolutely basic. In my view, one of the crosses change agents have to bear is that the expression of their own personal feelings is only legitimate if such expression *helps the client*. If the expression of feelings is going to hinder the client in any way, then the change agent must put feelings aside. Because change agents are catalysts whose job is to help induce change, sometimes taking the brunt of their clients' negative feelings may help promote change.

R—— and J—— could not agree. In particular, J—— thought I was demanding impossible things from change agents. I pointed out that this is often what transference is all about in therapy. However, this did not convince him. This was one occasion where J—— rejected the therapeutic analogy. As he put it: "Change agents are also people. They also have feelings. They also hurt. Denying this is to deny their humanity. They *should* express these feelings." We were unable to bridge our differences.

Several years' reflection has brought me to conclude that both J—— and I were correct. It seems to me beyond question that any outsider considering Avi's behavior during the time the Etz Haim School was in the project would see that his attacks and criticisms should be taken at more than face value. His criticisms were, at least in part a symbolic expression of problems he was trying to come to grips with on another level entirely. An outsider would also surely agree that until such time as Avi faced up to this other level, there was no chance of any significant changes taking place at Etz Haim. Thus my position: There could be no justification for the change agents getting insulted or angry and expressing anger. On the contrary, Avi's attacks and criticisms should have been understood and accepted for their symbolic significance, and on this level be used as a point of leverage for change within the Etz Haim School.

The problem is that this way of looking at things is valid only in the abstract. J——'s position was in essence a plea not to do this. The crucial incident in the Etz Haim story was not the torn note incident, but rather the meeting of J——, R——, and Avi prior to that incident, when Avi questioned their professional competence. The abstract self-effacing change agent would not be bothered by this. However, J—— and R—— were not abstractions, and they reacted to Avi's implied criticism in a very human, understandable way, albeit not a very professional one. But I argued in the theoretical part of this chapter that, unlike the therapist who has the ready-made language of "transference" and related matters at hand, the change agent is not subject to any strong countervailing forces to the psychological "temptation" to react in so human a fashion.

CASE XVII: SOUL-SEARCHING

The following "case" is simply a highly selective list of un-connected passages from the reports of one member of our staff during the three years of our project. Most of them relate to one particular school, but that is unimportant. The quotations are relevant rather as illustrations of the soul-searching of one change agent with regard to the catalyst/expert dilemma. Some of them show how even a person of great integrity can unwittingly drift toward redefining the change agent role or allow school personnel to redefine that role.

December 1979. To summarize briefly: easy but frustrating to be a facilitator in this school. I will clarify with an example: I told Liora [the headmistress] about the special activities at Hof Rishon (if you remember, she was not present at the principals' meeting where Yossi invited everyone to visit). It seems that Liora had previous contact with a similar project and was extremely skeptical about its efficiency. Nevertheless, she organized a group of five teachers to travel to Hof Rishon for a whole day to see the activities in action. Even when Yossi at the last minute had to change the day of the visit, and it became clear that taking these five teachers out on another day would be very difficult, she remained adamant and they went. A fortnight after the visit, the teachers have already reached conclusions, have made decisions, and are ready to run a similar activity at this school! So the question is: what exactly do they need me for? I ask the same question with regard to the meetings of the literature and language teachers I have been participating in. They were very pleasant and I have been asked to take part in future too, but my help cannot be in creating a *mechanism*—they already have one, alive and kicking. My help cannot be in increasing *awareness* of the need to search for new ideas. The awareness exists and they are searching all the time. I could perhaps suggest some of my own ideas here and there—but then you will all say I am not fulfilling my role as a project staff member but rather am doing consulting. . . . [Report from same month at another school:] Last year G—— met with a few teachers and spoke with them. It is just an insult to us to see how little impact this had in the school.

January 1980. [At the school where Liora is principal:] I am continuing to participate in the various activities I described in the December report. I feel much less inhibited now about contributing something of my own when it seems appropriate (to suggest things; to point out problems, to tell them about ideas from the education literature, to take part more actively in meetings, etc.) than I did last year. I had too many fears of becoming a "consultant," an "expert" (and all our other swear words), of encouraging them to become dependent on me. Sometimes I thought so hard whether I had the right to say something that when I did decide in the affirmative the need to say it had already passed. I checked this business empirically. After a particularly good meeting with Liora and the vice-principal (we meet regularly once a week) at which I suggested a number of things that impressed them, I wished to see what would happen if I didn't turn up at the regular meeting. And so they held the meeting without me, reached decisions, and developed things further. The "pity you weren't here" seemed to me to be just elementary politeness. So there isn't a problem of dependence. Also, Liora has a gift of "catching" ideas of others, adapting them to her needs and converting them to her own.

February 1980. I was present at some interesting activities whose relationship with our project seemed to me to be very unclear. I do not believe that any of these things would not have happened if I had not been present, although maybe they would have developed slightly differently.

November 1980. I was asked to participate in a school-based in-service "marathon" of home room teachers. The second day was devoted to "teachers' remarks when grading pupils' papers." . . . The discussion groups were interdisciplinary and the group leaders were the people in the group I led at the previous in-service "marathon" last year. They even used the materials I prepared then, but they added their own ideas. It was simply great. Such a fine model of work of this sort: the external change agent makes some small wave through the use of his expertise and the teachers *on their own initiative* increase its impact so that it spreads and reaches further and further. And the most important thing: they told me that this changed their attitude entirely to the writing of remarks on pupils' papers. In other words, the in-service course wasn't only interesting with only fleeting impact, but rather was a factor that introduced a basic and permanent change in their behavior. I really believe this was so.

Do you remember our discussion about whether I had done the right thing in acting as discussion leader of a group at that previous in-service marathon and whether perhaps I acted as an expert and thus didn't behave in accordance with the principles of the project? Well, what do you all think now? . . .

Something else happened here: the home room teacher of a special eleventh grade class approached me and asked me to meet once a week with a group of teachers who teach his class, because of difficulties they are having with the kids. We have met twice so far and they tried to describe the difficulties and to define the problems. It became clear they weren't all seeing things in the same way. I suggested the following homework for them: that each one would make the list of students' learning style on the basis of a list of criteria I suggested. . . . They were very enthusiastic. . . . We will see what comes of this. It isn't quite clear to me what they expect of me and whether they won't be disappointed when they discover that I am much less of an expert than they are (with regard to these kinds of pupils).

December 1980. I must say I am seen in this school in very different and strange ways by different people: there is always someone who is opening up his heart to me, even with regard to private matters. . . . Someone asked for advice on how to deal with a problematic class and someone else asked for help with the formulation and editing of something he is writing. It is very peculiar.

January 1981. This has been a frustrating period at the school of waiting for telephone calls from three people and these calls not materializing. I have managed to investigate the problems with two of them. Here are the results: The guy who initiated the meeting concerning the special class decided the effort wasn't worthwhile because he and another teacher aren't continuing with this class next year [!] and so that is over.

The discussion with Liora brought into the open something that wasn't too pleasant to hear and even angered me a bit: she forgot completely that she had to set up a meeting with me and to phone me. It seems she is a bit angry that I don't simply turn up at the school in a regular fashion. As she sees it, I should come anyway, without any special invitation or reason, and then they will always find some way in which I can help. I didn't react because, to be honest, I was taken aback by what she said and I didn't want to say something childish because I felt insulted and afterwards regret it. But maybe she is right? Perhaps in truth that is the only benefit the school can derive from me? . . .

The team of Professor X from the —— University were invited to the school to perform a diagnosis of the teaching problems in the school. . . . I was invited to the final meeting with them at the end of the day. It appears the ladies went to a couple of lessons, saw what they saw, and at the end of the day they said (for 12,000 lire) approximately what I had told them at the feedback session a year ago (for free). Liora kept looking at me, because it frustrated her too. The practical results of the day's diagnosis were very questionable because: (1) the school hasn't the budget to pay external consultants; (2) Professor X's team work specifically on the problems of culturally disadvantaged children. It isn't clear if they will be interested in providing services of other sorts, and it isn't clear if they can really be of use. . . .

Finally they thought of a sort of compromise: someone from the school can be trained by this team and he will then be the convenor of this topic at the school. Liora doesn't really believe that this is practical with regard to Professor X's team. . . . So in the end she suggested to me that I join one of the problematic teaching departments and work with them on their teaching problems. . . . I ask you all to help me decide whether to accept or not. Here are a number of points to consider:

For: The topic interests me personally and I would like to learn more about it. By the way, how is it that in the whole country there is no institution which offers a service of experts on teaching to interested schools? . . .

Questions: Doesn't it make a person feel like grade D material when he/she is approached only because the alternative is too expensive and he costs nothing?

February 1981.   Honestly, must we be satisfied to be catalysts, even of things that are valueless? Is "doing something" really the important issue? Or perhaps if we are investing energy, let's try to make the *best thing possible?* It seems to me that we relate to the school personnel completely differently from the way we relate to ourselves. When it comes to ourselves we criticize, reject ideas, improve suggestions of others, learn from each other, do not hide experience, knowledge, or thought. That is because we see each other as equals. But when it comes to the school people we summon every bit of tolerance, forgiveness, and compromise—that which is generally kept for work with defective children: we encourage them for any effort on their part and pay less attention to the results ("Terrific, sweetie!").

CASE XVIII: PHILOSOPHICAL ARROGANCE

My own academic background, as I have mentioned, is in philosophy of education rather than in organizational theory or social psychology, which is the more usual background of people interested in planned change. When I first began my work as adviser to the Ministry of Education and also with the Project for the Advancement of Educational Cooperation, I started meeting people concerned with change and change projects. Most of them came from a background of organizational theory and/or social psychology. My first reaction was wonder at how different they were from the philosophical types I was friendly with. They also were very different both from the educational radicals I knew (who also were interested in change, albeit from another perspective) and from the members of our own project staff.

At first I could not define what was special about these professional change agent types. Finally I hit on the word that seemed to capture them best and that has figured prominently in the discussion in this chapter — they were salesmen! In fact, the word occurred to me during a period when I was having some difficulty with my life insurance and my change agent colleagues simply reminded me of the insurance salesman I had been dealing with. Their presentation of self, to use Goffman's phrase,[40] was extraordinarily similar—the same unruffled look, the same display of confidence. They even dressed in the same way. At professional get-togethers there did not seem to be the kind of restless "searching for truth" the philosophers were concerned with. Instead, one heard all sorts of expressions of supreme and, I thought, exaggerated certainty—remarks like: "I have an instrument [which always meant a questionnaire] that, if filled out by a school staff, will be able to give you a complete picture of their school's social structure within three days." The language used, as I mentioned in chapter 1, was better suited to Madison Avenue than academia: instruments, targets, clients, client systems, interventions. All these abounded in the language of the professional meetings I attended.

At first, I assumed this was an Israeli aberration. Then I met some foreigners from the "change business." They were exactly the same. I then thought it must be the fact that they came from social psychology and organizational theory, and not from philosophy. Or perhaps it was the corrupting influence of economics, because some of these consultants were obviously making a lot of money.

And then I was asked to present a paper on our project at two conferences, one in Jerusalem at an international conference of psychologists, and the other at a conference concerned with all the change projects in Israeli high schools. This was in the second year of our project, when I certainly couldn't have conceived of myself as writing a book on the *myths* of school self-renewal. I was still very much a true believer.

I suggested to the staff that we all participate and present the papers in a joint fashion. Unfortunately, in both cases, only one member of the staff was able to attend the conference, and she preferred to take a back seat and simply be part of the audience. This was Michal Katz, who I have already credited in chapter 1 with developing a format for supplying the schools with feedback. Michal's background is educational evaluation. She is also a very experienced language arts teacher. Almost from the beginning of our project she began to play the role in our group of resident skeptic and questioner. This was difficult for her. The notion of playing a role is sometimes very misleading. Role players do not see themselves as playing, but are gripped by very genuine emotions and thought. Certainly Michal was not *playing* the skeptic and the questioner, but was truly plagued by doubts and questions. While this did not make life easy for her, it often was of enormous benefit to the project as a whole by helping us to become aware of inconsistencies in our work and of forgotten resolutions and plans.

In this particular case, Michal inadvertently helped me to gain insight into myself and through this to develop some of the ideas of this chapter. At the end of my presentation at the second conference, we talked about how it had "gone over." She commented as follows:

> You know, there is something that bothers me. At the end of your talk there were a few requests for clarification and that was all. No one argued. No one objected. There seemed to be a tacit assumption that this was a great project, a great idea. And then I thought back to your talk at the other conference and also some of the occasions when I have had to explain our project. Never has anyone questioned what we are doing or questioned the validity of our assumptions. But surely we aren't as good as all that! There must be some flaws! And, goodness knows, as a staff we argue a lot! I am telling you, there is something basically misleading about the way we are explaining things.

At the time Michal's remarks seemed interesting, but I did not really follow up on them. However, later it suddenly dawned on me that she could be interpreted as saying that *we were selling our project very well*. From a personal point of view, this meant that I could not continue to maintain the belief that because of my philosophical background I was different from the other change agent/ consultants I knew (and "different" carries the subtle implication of being better). I was as good a salesman as anyone else. It seems it does not matter whether you come from Kurt Lewin or Kant. The need to convince the givers of grants and the schools themselves that you have something good to offer subtly socializes you into presenting a certain stance to the world, one that seems to be clearly counterproductive to what you are trying to achieve.

I could rationalize by claiming that no one raised objections at these conferences because the idea of our project is simply so good. But this whole book shows that objections can be raised. Or I could rationalize by saying that conferences are one thing and working in the schools another; one may be a salesman at conferences, but in the school context one behaves far more circumspectly. However, the fact that until Michal pointed it out to me I was unaware of my salesmanship makes this unlikely. It is far more reasonable to suppose that the subtle *unconscious* behaviors that made me a good salesman at the conferences were present, again unconsciously but still effectively, when I wandered around schools with my magic feather.

CASE XIX: RESEARCH GRANTS AND HOW TO GET THEM

Although this is the second case that does not relate to the Project for the Advancement of Educational Cooperation, I present it because it is almost a perfect illustration of how the behavior of the change agent, working in a research context, is constrained by the need to obtain funding for a project, how this encourages the change agent to be a doer rather than a minimal catalyst.

Pinkas is the headmaster of a large comprehensive high school. He has a reputation for being very energetic, not perhaps the most pedagogically innovative person one could hope for, but very active in the headmasters' union, well respected in the education ministry, innovative in organizational matters. At one point he became dissatisfied with the way in-service training is run in Israel. The idea of teachers going off individually to study summer courses did not seem to bring back much benefit to the school. It seemed to him that school-based in-service training — courses given at the school during school hours and limited to personnel from a particular school — would be much more useful. The question was: what would be taught and who would teach it? Pinkas approached Dr.

Ehud Zahavi, a well-known educator at a nearby university much involved in in-service training, and asked him to run these courses.

Zahavi responded enthusiastically and at this point more or less took over the whole idea, being if possible even more energetic than Pinkas. He proposed, as a start, to give a course on moral and social education to a group of *mechanchim* (described in chapter 3). The course would not be theoretical, but would be oriented toward developing material these teachers could use in their weekly hour-long meetings with their classes. Pinkas had found a way to fund the beginning of this project through ordinary school sources, but it was clear that additional funding would be needed, especially as Zahavi wanted to use the project for research purposes as well.

At that time Zahavi heard that the Israeli Ministry of Education was funding a number of projects designed to promote school self-renewal. He sent in a detailed proposal written with considerable expertise. The reaction of the committee for high school innovation in the ministry was to ask why this project should be considered one concerned with school *self*-renewal. Zahavi replied, again in voluminous detail, that (1) the course he proposed concentrated on the *principles* of constructing units in moral and social education; the teachers who learned these principles would then be able to apply them by themselves in planning future units; (2) the teachers participating would afterward be able to teach these principles to other teachers, both in this school and in others in the area; (3) the program proposed was also a research project. Zahavi would of course publish his results, and these could be used by other schools.

The committee for high school innovation decided it would be necessary to visit the school and see things in action at first hand (the first phase of the project had begun using the funds Pinkas had obtained from other sources). A meeting was set up, eight committee members making the trip.

Imagine the scene: At the school entrance Zahavi is waiting. He greets the committee warmly, reminding those he knows of previous occasions at which they had met. Accompanied by a nonstop bombardment of talk, the committee is ushered into the headmaster's room. Zahavi asks Pinkas's secretary to get some coffee and cake for the visitors, sits everyone down, and introduces the committee to the vice-principal and another teacher. Pinkas is not present.

Zahavi opens up the meeting, explaining again the history and purpose of the project. At various points he calls on the vice-principal and the teacher to confirm things he has said. After about twenty minutes, Pinkas enters, apologizing for being late, but he had been at another meeting. He makes a few general comments about the importance of the project and then asks if there are any questions. One or two members of the committee ask a few questions that are answered by Zahavi. However, almost immediately Zahavi stands up and suggests that questions be postponed until after the committee has seen the in-service courses in operation.

Everyone is led off to a classroom where the observation is to take place. The room is filled with video equipment, tape recorders, cameras "brought specially from the university once a week." The twelve teachers participating in this session wander in and Zahavi begins his lesson. "Lesson" is quite the appropriate word. The teachers are sitting at desks. Zahavi is standing at the blackboard. In typical micro-teaching fashion, one camera is trained on the teacher and the other on the class. The lesson is magnificent. Zahavi is a brilliant teacher. The topic is a certain approach to moral education which the teachers find strange. The discussion is conducted in such a way that the reasons for the teachers' difficulties with the approach are brought to the fore and discussed openly.

The lesson ends. The committee is led back to Pinkas' office. On the way, a teacher passing in the corridor stops Zahavi. She asks, "Who are all these people?" He explains. The teacher turns to the committee: "You must grant Dr. Zahavi this money. I studied with him at the university. It was terribly helpful, but not enough. Without his help it is difficult to get things going. Now we have him here we can really start moving." Zahavi smiles modestly.

The committee, Zahavi, Pinkas, and a number of the teachers who participated in the lesson sit down in Pinkas's office. Zahavi runs the meeting rather like a conductor leading an orchestra. Questions are asked; Zahavi chooses the teacher who will answer it or decides that Pinkas or himself should answer. At one point a member of the committee turns to Pinkas and asks if he has thought what he will do when Zahavi leaves. Zahavi interrupts, irritated. He point out it is too early to expect the school staff to relate to questions like that. The project is planned for a year, perhaps two. He is hopeful that within a year the school will be in a position to answer such a question. The visit ends and the committee travels back to Jerusalem.

During the following three weeks the committee had to decide whether to fund the project or not. This was difficult; on the one hand it was clear that, in terms of the short-range objectives that Zahavi had set himself, this was a worthwhile project enthusiastically supported by a large percentage of the school staff. But when it came to the promotion of school self-renewal, things were not so clear. Many members of the committee were skeptical. However, there were not many self-renewal projects in competition, the sum of money requested was not so large, and Zahavi was driving the ministry of education crazy with an endless stream of phone calls to all and sundry, asking when the decision would be made. At that time ministry policy was to try to be as liberal as possible in supplying grants, provided they were relatively small. So, in the end, a one-year grant was approved. Because of the way Zahavi had formulated the proposal, this money was ostensibly to be used to fund the research side of the project. But the covering letter accompanying the formal approval of the grant stressed that the committee was interested first and foremost in long-term effects on the school vis-à-vis self-renewal.

At the end of the school year, the committee, with great difficulty, arranged a further meeting with Zahavi. Once again, imagine the scene. This time the meeting takes place at Zahavi's university office. Zahavi schedules the committee to meet with him for an hour, and continually checks his watch, saying "I have to rush off exactly at eleven o'clock to a meeting about a new research project I am involved with." He tells the committee with great enthusiasm that he has some fascinating material from the moral education in-service training project that will be published in case study form. What about the effects on the school? Well, he is sure that the course changed the teachers' concepts of moral education very profoundly, and this will surely express itself in their daily work. What about the ideas of the teachers developing their own units and teaching the principles they had learned to other teachers? Well, that didn't quite work out. However, no worry, there is a girl who lives near the school who was a brilliant M.A. student in Zahavi's moral education course at the university, and wrote her thesis on that topic. He has arranged for her to teach a continuation course at the school on moral education next year, both to the teachers who participated this year and any others interested.

6

The Future of Planned Change in Educational Systems

The argument that I sketched in chapter 1 can be formulated with the aid of two syllogisms:

A. *Premises*
1. Schools need to change at times.
2. Change in schools can be planned, at least to a certain extent.
3. Without some help, schools will not engage in such planned change.

Conclusion

External change agents are necessary to help schools to change.

B. *Premises*
1. There are two ways external change agents can help schools to change: (a) through external imposition of changes (RD&D); (b) through developing the schools' capacity to change by themselves.
2. The first option has been shown conclusively by researchers like House and Sarason to be ineffective.

Conclusion

The way to help schools change is through developing their capacity for self-renewal.

However, chapters 2–5 have attempted to show that this latter conclusion is false. If the arguments in these chapters are correct, we are left with two possibilities: the premises of either (A) or (B) are faulty. In this final chapter I will examine these possibilities. In the first section I will address (B), and specifically premise B1. In the second section I will address (A), and specifically premise A2.

ONGOING COLLABORATION

The notions that planned change is either a matter of external imposition, or of developing innate capacities, are psychologically
understandable, as the tour of my own thoughts in chapter 1
showed. However, mistaken. Logically, there is a third possibility.
This I will call *ongoing collaboration* between schools and some
external agency. This possibility is essentially a combination of the
other two. It takes the idea of a continuing relationship from the
RD&D approach which, as we saw, resulted in the development of
organizations like permanent curriculum centers that would infuse
new ideas into the educational system. It takes the idea of collaboration from the self-renewal perspective. Collaboration is a venture undertaken between equal partners with mutual respect for
each other. That respect is at the heart of the notion of self-renewal.

Hybrid solutions are normally created in hopes of maintaining
the good features of all previous solutions and canceling out all
their bad features. However, they often only succeed in exacerbat-
ing the latter. What I propose to do in this section is to examine the
notion of ongoing collaboration both in itself and also in the light of
the difficulties with RD&D and school self-renewal that have been
raised in chapters 1–5. Such an examination should enable us to
decide whether we have a good hybrid or not. However, before
doing this, we will need to put some flesh on the skeletal words
"ongoing collaboration."

Luckily, we do not have to start from scratch. The 1970s and
early 1980s have supplied us with some practical examples of such
collaborations or some blueprints for them. Let us consider a few of
these collaborations. Each one could certainly be described in at
least as much detail as I have used in describing the Project for the
Advancement of Educational Cooperation; however, all I intend
doing is to sketch some of the principal ideas associated with each
example.

Teachers' Centers

The notion of a teachers' center first surfaced in England and
has by now expanded to many other countries.[1] The problem is that
the concept is so general that it includes very different sorts of
organizations. Still, let me indicate characteristics that would apply
to most such centers. Teachers' centers are first and foremost places
where teachers from various schools meet and chat in an informal

atmosphere, the assumption being that this sort of atmosphere encourages freely flowing ideas and gives teachers much support during times when they feel pressured and frustrated. The center and its staff also act as a resource. A teacher will drop in and try to develop a half-baked idea such as, say, using a game to teach a particular concept. At the center there are materials for constructing such a game. Teachers can also be assisted by members of the center's staff who have some talent in designing games and some experience in helping teachers work through their ideas. In many teachers' centers there are also more structured activities—lectures and courses, usually of a very practical nature, in which teachers can enroll. Some centers are located at universities but in most cases their physical setting is on some more neutral ground. The advocates of teachers' centers believe the teachers must regard the center as "their" place and not one that is controlled by some sponsoring organization.

The Harvard Principals' Center

I choose a more specific example, with which I became acquainted in 1982, because, unlike almost all other centers, the Harvard Principals' Center caters to principals rather than teachers. This is a project in which an attempt is being made to create a collaborative relationship between the Harvard Graduate School of Education and principals from the Greater Boston area. The majority of members of the center are either principals or Harvard faculty and students. The main activities of the center, which is housed in the Harvard Graduate School of Education, are lectures, minicourses and workshops, some given by Harvard staff and some —and this is the important point—by principals themselves. Also great care was taken to involve principals from the beginning in setting the guidelines for the center. In other words, despite the fact that the center is housed in a university and has directors who are Harvard faculty members, the principals seem to be equal partners in running the project.

The Institution/School Pairing in Boston

In 1975 a U.S. desegregation court order (*Morgan* vs. *Kerrigan*) matched individual collegiate, cultural, and business institutions in the metropolitan area with individual public schools or public school districts in the city of Boston.[2] These pairings were part of a set of compulsory activities aimed at desegregating a recalcitrant school system. Since the court order, almost one hundred such pairings have evolved, of which those involving academic institutions are perhaps the most significant for our purposes.

Each pairing followed a unique pattern, the schools and institutions involved coming to grips in their own ways with defining the nature of school/institution collaboration. Yet some generalizations can be made:

a. Because these collaborations were the result of a court order, those that involved academic institutions were very different from the usual exploitative relations that obtain when schools and universities "cooperate."
b. A formalized structure and specific institutionalized procedures involving both university and school staffs became essential, if the collaboration was to "happen."
c. The universities were forced to take these pairings seriously and to address themselves first and foremost to the schools' needs and concerns.
d. As far as I can gather, almost all collaborations tended to be *issue-specific.* No talk about general school functioning and problem solving but instead well-defined specific problems (for example, how to improve the curriculum in a particular discipline) formed the basis of each collaborative venture. The problems identified tended to be those the school staff was most concerned with and best suited to what the particular institutional partner had to offer. Thus the institution's staff involved in the collaborative venture tended to be those experienced in the problem area rather than merely the *process* of educational change.

The Israeli Institute for Innovative High School Education

This institute has already been described in case XIV, chapter 4. To briefly recapitulate: the idea here was to establish a nonhierarchic collaboration between university schools of education, the Israeli Ministry of Education and Culture, and certain high schools, in an institute having various sections.[3] Just about every section—both those functioning at present and those planned for future developments—does or will concentrate on developing innovative programs and projects associated with a particular aspect of school functioning. As is not true of most teacher centers and the

Harvard Principals' Center, these activities generally take place at the schools.

One section of the institute not mentioned in chapter 4 is designed in a slightly different fashion. An offshoot of the Project for the Advancement of Educational Cooperation, this section concentrates on external observers performing naturalistic evaluations as to how schools are functioning, their weak points, and the sources of these weaknesses. It is also hoped that in the future these external observers will then help each school to develop plans for self-improvement and/or to decide what other sections of the institute it should participate in.

The Ford Teaching Project

All the previous examples illustrate long-standing or projected ongoing collaborations conceived as such. However, the Ford Teaching Project was planned as a short-term project.[4] Nevertheless, I present it as an example of what ongoing collaboration could mean, because its theoretical rationale made collaboration a very central issue. Another reason for introducing the Ford Project is that it is very well known and a great deal of useful material has been produced by it.

The Ford Teaching Project was concerned with modern curricular ideas developed in the 1960s that embodied what was called inquiry/discovery teaching. Teachers have had considerable difficulty with such curricula since their inception. There are many reasons for this, but two are especially relevant: First, the curriculum designers had underestimated the problems of implementation, and there was no well-developed descriptive theory of inquiry/discovery teaching in the 1960s and 1970s. Of course, a prescriptive theory of such teaching did exist, but no one had devoted the time or energy to analyzing what was involved in trying to implement inquiry/discovery teaching, what were the problems teachers might face, and what were effective ways of resolving these problems. Second, teachers lacked the skills required to diagnose problems accurately and to test remedial strategies.

The project was set up so as to confront both these difficulties at once. The teachers would be initiated into the skills for diagnosing problems and testing remedial strategies, and then they, with the research workers, would collaboratively develop a theory of inquiry/discovery teaching. The assumption here was that in testing theory as opposed to applying it, the teacher is *necessarily* involved in theory development. In addition to addressing these two difficulties, the project had at least one further aim—to engage in a kind of second-order action-research, that is, the development of a theory about how external agencies can best foster teachers' participation in the development of a theory about their own classrooms. This would be the particular interest of the project staff.

To achieve these aims with the forty teachers (from twelve schools) involved, an organizational framework was needed. This framework involved team meetings within each school, institutionalized channels of communication between each school team and the project staff and among themselves, meetings and workshops in which a number of different teams could meet, project staff having access to the teachers' lessons and to private interviews with pupils.

Theories About Ongoing Collaboration

The above are some examples of what I would call ongoing collaborations between schools (and/or school personnel) and other "external" institutions, or at least models of what such collaboration could look like. Many other examples could have been given.[5] Yet although such collaborations are becoming quite prevalent, surprisingly little effort has been devoted to developing a theoretical underpinning to this work. This criticism may seem unjust; after all, each of the examples quoted has some theoretical formulations associated with it. However, they tend to concentrate on explaining the parameters and suggestions specific to a particular type of project. Work on teachers' centers will use concepts and theories current in thinking about in-service training; work on collaborations involving curriculum development will be expressed in terms taken from the curriculum field; work on collaborations involving evaluations will concentrate on evaluatory terminology. There seems to be little work that attempts to analyze the concept of ongoing collaboration in any general way, or proposes a general theoretical perspective from which to answer questions concerning such collaborations.

There are exceptions, of course. One derives from the Boston institution/school pairings, and was developed by Clark Fisher, who distinguishes between three models of pairing relationships.[6] In the One-Way Collaborative Model, the school functions as a laboratory for projects developed by, and largely for, university research workers. Such projects are usually tacked on to the normal functioning of the school, and are never truly integrated into regular school activities. Thus the school does not change in a fundamental way because of the project. Neither does the university, because the project is usually associated with particular individuals rather than being a "university" project. The Two-Way Collaborative Model is described by Fisher as

> a consultive model whereby the school conducts a needs assessment and the institution catalogues its resources, then through a collaborative effort, a matching of needs and resources results. It is characterized by a self-reliant mode, partners in these educational ventures are co-equal, and self-interest is evident on both sides. Attendant programs are built around mutual planning, and an integration of program objectives within the school system's own objectives as well as an internalization of the collaborative into institutional priorities.[7]

The collaboration is between the school and the institution rather than being limited to individuals. The Three-Way Collaborative Model is an extension of the second one in which not only the institution and the school participate, but also all concerned parties, that is, the general community and the parents.

This schema is partially descriptive and partially prescriptive (the three-way model being, to a large extent, a projection into the future). Its strengths lie in its clear distinction between projects tacked on and projects necessitating changes of school and/or institutional structure, and also in its emphasis on the difference between individual and institutional involvement in the collaboration. Its weakness lies in the fact that it does not go beyond a very simple taxonomy. There is an implied assumption that increasing the number of participants and the extent of their involvement is by and large a good thing, but we are not offered a theoretical perspective from which to judge why this should be so.

The second example I wish to present exemplifies a reversal of the advantages and disadvantages of the Fisher approach. It *does* offer a theoretical perspective but ignores some absolutely crucial distinctions. This is John Goodlad's "Networking and Educational Improvement: Reflections on a Strategy." The strategy referred to is that used in the League of Cooperating Schools project, and so the "reflections" go over a lot of the ground covered in *The Dynamics of Educational Change*. Yet there are differences and additions. Consider the following:

One of the most important and least studied aspects of networks is the office referred to here as the hub [what I have called the "project staff"]. It will be recalled that we preordained the mortality of the [hub], on the assumption that there would come a time when it would not be required. *I no longer take this position.* Some such agency as part of a network is essential, I maintain. It should not cease to function but rather should change responsively as the needs of the schools change.[8]

I find this an extraordinary passage. First, Goodlad gives no indication of why he no longer takes this position or rather what caused him to change his mind. Second, the impression given is that this is a rather minor adjustment of the original strategy. However, I would claim this to be perhaps a total reconceptualization of the dynamics of educational change. Instead of self-renewal, we now have collaboration. Instead of the change agent as catalyst, we now have a permanent external agency. Goodlad does not seem to be aware how momentous a change of emphasis this is.

This criticism must be balanced by pointing out the positive features of the "Networking" piece. Goodlad does provide a theoretical framework within which to understand collaboration, or rather he suggests some very illuminating metaphors for collaborations and the dynamics of their functioning. One of these is invoked deliberately and quite extensively; a second is mentioned in passing, and a third only implicitly. Yet all three help us to see the collaboration process with much greater clarity.

The first metaphor is *ecology*. Goodlad had already suggested an ecological model of education in *Dynamics*.[9] But in "Networking" he takes the metaphor further with the terms *ecosystem, synergy,* and *symbiosis*. A school/external agency relationship, or more exactly in Goodlad's case, a *schools*/external agency relationship can be conceived of as an ecosystem in which the various parts can enter a symbiotic relationship, one that will thus result in a synergism—a total effect that will be greater than the sum of the effects when each organism works independently of the other. Goodlad also distinguishes between high-energy and low-energy ecosystems, seeing them as functioning in very different ways. In his view, self-renewing processes require relatively high expenditures of energy.[10]

All this is as yet only the outline of a provocative metaphor and therefore it is probably premature to decide how well ecological ideas capture the essence of ongoing collaboration. The other two metaphors are even less developed. One of these is the idea of an external agency acting as an "alternative drummer," that is, one who beats an alternative rhythm;[11] the other is the implicit metaphor that likens the creation of a network to the action of *massage*.[12] Goodlad does not seem to have realized just how thought-provoking these two metaphors are. Yet it seems intuitively clear to me that developing them could be extraordinarily helpful.

In addition to the examples of Fisher and Goodlad, I would like to mention a contribution that is not really theoretical but probably better described as a research finding. This is one of the better-known findings of the Rand change agent study. Essentially, what was shown in this study was that successful change projects were those in which a process of *mutual adaptation* could be identified.[13] By mutual adaptation the researchers meant that during the process of implementation, both the school and also the external program being introduced underwent changes as a result of feedback links. For such programs to change, the change agents who introduced them would have to be flexible enough to avoid fixating on a particular definition of the desired change. Thus we can say that successful collaborations between schools and external agencies were shown to be those in which both sides were prepared to change and adapt. This can be regarded as an empirical confirmation of Goodlad's insistence on symbiosis.

The Concept of Collaboration

The work of Fisher and Goodlad and the Rand study certainly provide the beginning of a theoretical approach to the notion of ongoing collaboration. But what is missing, it seems to me, is the kind of contribution analytic philosophers are famous (or infamous) for. We need a conceptual analysis of the term "collaboration."

Whereas a full analysis of "collaboration" would require identifying the subtle differences between, say, collaboration, cooperation, and simply working together, I cannot explore these issues here. My analysis will be limited to two conceptual issues related to school/external agency collaboration. In this analysis I will use the terms *collaboration* and *cooperation* interchangeably.

One can distinguish among at least three different senses of "cooperation": the mutual benefit ("you scratch my back, I'll scratch·yours") sense, the coalition sense, and the partnership sense. By "scratch my back, I'll scratch yours" cooperation, I mean that A and B can be considered as cooperating if they agree that A will do something (X_1) for B that B desires if B will do something else (X_2)

($X_1 \neq X_2$) for A that A desires. Typical of this sort of cooperation would be two politicians who agree to vote for each other's bills, where each bill may have importance only for the proposer's local constituency.

Coalition cooperation occurs when A desires something (Y_1), B desires something else (Y_2) ($Y_1 \neq Y_2$), and they realize that Y_1 and Y_2 can best be achieved if they work together. Working together means that A's actions X_1 and B's actions X_2, although different, are interrelated. They can be regarded as components of some more inclusive activity X. Typical of this sort of cooperation is the coalition between two political parties, neither having an outright majority, in forming a government. Here each party has a different ideology, but they agree to form a government together because they feel that by doing this each will be able to promote its own interests best. Government work will be divided between them in some way, such as giving some ministries the responsibility of one party, others of the second party.

Partnership cooperation occurs when A and B have some *common* goal X, and they agree to work together to achieve it. I call this partnership cooperation because a business partnership is probably the clearest example of this type.

As we move from mutual benefit through coalition to partnership cooperation, we also move from Y_1 and Y_2 being different to their being the same, and from X_1 and X_2 being totally unrelated to their being different but related. A superficial conclusion might be that there must be a fourth type of cooperation, where X_1 and X_2 also become identical. Actually, in all but the most trivial cases, this cannot occur. Consider a simple example of cooperation —a wife and husband cooperate in washing the dishes. This will usually mean either that one does half the dishes and the other does the second half, or else one does the washing, the other the drying. In either case, the two collaborators are doing *different* things. There is a division of labor. This is clear with regard to washing and drying, but also applies to the case of splitting work into halves. Here we have two very similar activities, but nevertheless first halves are not the same as second halves. What would we say if the husband washed and dried the dishes, and then the wife did them all over again? In my family, this is not a sign of cooperation but of criticism that I didn't wash the dishes properly. Duplication and harmony do not usually go together. The paradigmatic exception to this would be the case of two people picking up a heavy object together. Here the duplication is necessary, because neither could pick up the object alone. Of course there are such cases, but as the collaborations of interest become more complex and ongoing, such examples become less and less relevant.

When talking about school/external agency collaboration, one can safely say that any stable form of cooperation necessarily entails the division of labor between the collaborators into *different* tasks. This is my first conceptual point about collaboration. It may seem obvious, but most school/external agency collaborative efforts have ignored it. Even when the rhetoric of a project stresses the different sorts of expertise that the school and, say, the university will bring to the collaboration, little is written that stipulates in any detail what the different expertise of the university consists of.

The second conceptual point is this: if we assume that the long-range aims of A and B remain relatively constant, then the form of cooperation that has the best chance of remaining stable is that which I have called partnership. This is enshrined in the words we use; a partnership indicates a more stable relationship than a coalition. However, in addition to linguistic considerations, there are others that also confirm our intuitions. Mutual benefit cooperation and coalitions are dependent for their stability on factors external to the relationship between the collaborators themselves. A's collaboration with B might be advantageous to A at one time, and become a liability at another, as external reality changes. For example, A might discover that of late C has become very powerful, and a possibility exists to collaborate with C provided that the collaboration with B is discontinued.

Partnerships are influenced less by such external changes. As long as both partners continue doing their part of the job satisfactorily, and there are no personal tensions between them, external changes offer few incentives to any partner to dissolve the partnership. Of course, this can occur. A might decide that although the partnership with B is going well, replacing B with C (a new star in B's line of work) could improve things. The point is that such partnership dissolutions need not occur, whereas in the case of a coalition, for example, external changes can make dissolving the coalition almost inevitable. Consider the following example: A, B, and C are three political parties. Elections give A 10 percent, B 49 percent, and C 33 percent of the votes (there are other parties, too). A coalition government consisting of A and B is formed. At the next elections, A, B, and C receive 10, 38, and 43 percent, respectively. Assuming that A's and C's political platforms are not totally at odds, these results will almost certainly ensure that, if A wishes to remain in the government, it will dissolve its coalition with B and form one with C.

Because of this difference between partnerships (as I have been using the term) and coalitions, when a partnership (in the legal sense) dissolves, this is often a sign that at least one of the partners regarded the partnership as a coalition. For instance, when a junior partner in a firm leaves and starts out on his own, this is often a sign that he saw the partnership as a stepping stone, as a means of establishing himself. If so, his goals probably diverge from those of other partners.

The point I have been making—that partnership cooperation is more stable than other forms—is absolutely central to the topic of ongoing school/external agency collaboration. It conflicts very directly with the perspective Fisher and Goodlad have developed. They argue that schools and external agencies can have different goals. Goodlad, in fact, goes even further. He sees such difference as necessary:

> What is required for constructive change is . . . a productive tension between an organism wanting a better condition for itself . . . and an organism whose self-interests are served by assisting in the process. . . . The self-interests of the two parties, *although different,* have something to give to and gain from each other.[14]

In contrast, I have tried to show that if the "self-interests" of the two organisms are not very similar, at the very least the collaboration between them is not likely to be a stable one.

An Attempt at Integration

The groundwork is now over and I can turn to my central task here. The following is the approach I propose taking in this section. Through conceptual analysis I have identified two necessary conditions for stable, ongoing school/external agency collaboration.

First condition
The school and the external agency must not simply duplicate each other's work.
Second condition
The goals of the school and the external agency participating in the collaboration must be very similar.

I will now turn to the problems with RD&D and school self-renewal identified in the first five chapters. I will ask the following questions: Can ongoing collaboration solve these problems? If so, what constraints does this create for the collaboration? This analysis will lead to us identifying an additional five necessary conditions for a stable and beneficial collaborative effort. The one question that will then remain is whether the seven conditions complement or contradict each other.

I will begin with chapter 3, where I dealt with the tremendous difficulty that schools have in subjecting their beliefs about the sacred to scrutiny and empirical check. I also argued that schools' belief systems change according to what I called the jazz metaphor. Educational discourse influences educational practice and such discourse derives from a universe in which the school is only a small part. Can ongoing collaboration with an external agency help schools become aware of and question the sacred beliefs and the conceptual trees that dominate the educational discourse they participate in? The answer is clearly *yes*. This is a task particularly suited to "alternative drummers." However, there is a proviso. *The external agency must be a university or research institute.* The reason for this is not particularly subtle. Identifying and questioning sacred beliefs and conceptual trees are *academic* activities par excellence. And academics are found at universities or research institutes. However, as we will see, this constraint has far-reaching consequences. For the present I will limit myself to formulating it as the third necessary condition for stable and beneficial ongoing collaboration.

Third Condition

The external agency collaborating with schools must be an academic institution.

What then can one say about teachers' centers, which usually pride themselves on being agencies outside the universities, and thus providing a different sort of in-service training from that which university in-service training departments give? My impression is that precisely for this reason the languages spoken by school and center staffs are very similar, and thus the center does *not* act as a different drummer. It provides many terribly useful services that cannot be dismissed out of hand, but it does not help to create a high-energy ecosystem, to use Goodlad's terminology.

Let us now turn to chapter 2 and the question of holism and

its relationship to self-renewal. As we saw, self-renewal implies holism, yet the kinds of things that self-renewal is concerned with (problem solving and consciousness raising) cannot be conceived as norms to be institutionalized and thus perpetuated. The notion of collaboration would appear at first glance to solve this problem. If the change agent can stay around as a permanent institution, holism becomes unnecessary. Whenever gains or growth are squandered due to school staff turnover or staleness, the change agent can once again supply the external "alternative drummer," or energy, and thus try to regain what has been lost. Of course, this effort may not succeed. The staff turnover or staleness may create insurmountable problems. However, the task of the permanent change agent is surely easier than that of the self-renewalist who must try, in a one-time intervention, to create a self-perpetuating structure.

This argument contains a serious oversight, however. Change agents are also not immortal. Therefore, in addition to school staff turnover there will inevitably be change agent turnover. A closer inspection of the above argument shows that it does smuggle in holism, an implicit assumption that the external organization collaborating with the school will be self-renewing. But if this is so, then surely the arguments introduced in chapter 2 will apply to it. All we have succeeded in doing is transporting the locus of the difficulty from one organization to another.[15]

Actually, things are not as bad as that. Transferring the holist assumption to the change agency does improve matters. Take our project as an example. We dealt with ten or twelve schools over the years and thus the problems of turnover in the schools involved ten or twelve principals and approximately seven hundred teachers. We—the hub, the project staff—consisted of one project leader and a staff of five or six people. This drastic reduction in size does reduce or minimize the holist problem. Consider first the staff reduction. A school staff that has to deal with a 50 percent staff turnover in two years, say, is in serious difficulties. We, the project staff, dealt with such a turnover in our ranks almost without noticing that it had occurred. Second, let us compare the change of principals with the change of a project director. For example, when four schools have a turnover of principals, then, if the four outgoing principals had promoted self-renewal (in some sense of the term), it is unrealistic to hope that more than two of the new principals will continue the good work. On the other hand, most universities could find a suitable replacement for *one* research project director without much difficulty.

There is another reason why holist assumptions are less problematic in the hub than out in the schools. Let us return to the Gilad-Yossi case described in chapter 2. There I addressed the argument that the problem with the Hof Rishon School arose because the school search committee chose the wrong successor. Yossi's cognitive style was incompatible with the idea of long range Dewey-like planning and thus he should not have become principal. I rejected this by arguing that the role of principal is a complex one, and the perfect principal must have a variety of essential characteristics. Choosing a good principal (because superb ones are so rare) means choosing someone with *some* but not all of the characteristics of the perfect principal. Yossi had many such characteristics, and certainly was not an absurd choice to succeed Gilad, even if he was unimpressed by long-range Dewey-like planning. However, this sort of dilemma would not arise in choosing a successor for the director of a school change project, for whom the required skills are much more focused, much easier to define. A school principal has to do many things, whereas a project director can concentrate on planning how to help schools change.

There is a proviso, however, that leads us to the next necessary condition for stable ongoing collaboration. The university must take this change agency seriously and consider the position of agency director to be a prestigious one. University folk are very skillful at creating "institutes" and "centers" which on further examination are discovered to be little more than empty shells. Recently I visited an institute with which I had been corresponding and had assumed to be a leading institution in a particular field. I discovered the "institute" to be a one-room, one-person operation (plus half-time secretary) housed in a wooden shack behind one of the university buildings. For a university to be engaged in productive ongoing collaboration with schools, the change-promoting agency should not meet the same fate as this "institute."

Fourth condition

The university must be firmly and extensively committed to and concerned with the change promoting agency it is sponsoring. At the very least, the latter must be equivalent to a prestigious department of the university's school of education.

Now on to chapter 4, and the question of teacher professionalism. Because that chapter dealt with structural limitations to such professionalism, it is too much to hope that school/university collaboration could get rid of all the problems I pointed out. Thus I do not see how collaboration could address Dreeben's argument for the inevitability of the comparatively poor intellectual caliber of teachers. I will not discuss teacher professionalism and collegiality; however, collaboration does offer some hope of reducing the barriers to teacher autonomy associated with teacher conservatism and implicit power talk.

Let us begin with conservatism. Here the work on teacher socialization becomes very relevant. Among the consistent findings over the years is that students studying to be teachers hold views about education that are *relatively* progressive while they are taking courses at the university (in comparison with those of practicing teachers); during their practical training in the schools there is a swing to more conservative views which, as Lortie has shown, then continues through their teaching careers.[16] What this finding shows is: (1) with regard to elementary and secondary education at least, university schools of education hold views that are more progressive than those found in the elementary and secondary schools themselves; (2) these views influence student teachers and thus counteract, to a certain extent, the conservatism these students bring with them (remember, Lortie argues that teaching recruits tend to value the way things *are*); (3) the reality of the schools themselves quickly undoes all the work the universities did; and (4) if we regard the universities and the schools as competing socializing influences on the student teachers, the schools win out.

The fact that the schools win out is not very surprising. After all, the period of pre-service teacher training is *succeeded* by the training the schools themselves give and the more recent socializing force is clearly likely to be more powerful. Also the socialization within the school goes on much longer than that of pre-service training.[17] However, if the schools and the university were engaged in ongoing collaboration, these two considerations would not apply. Therefore there is a good chance that the collaboration would help to counter teacher conservatism.

Of course, things are not quite that simple. There appears to be no evidence that in-service training reverses the socializing trends of the schools toward conservatism, and yet a lot of in-service training does take place at universities. So what is the difference between pre-service and in-service training? The answer, I submit, is that the student in pre-service training is a full-blown member of the university community, a "real" student, whereas the teacher at an in-service course is more or less "passing through." Put in another way, pre-service training is undertaken by people immersed in the university culture. This suggests a further necessary condition for beneficial collaboration between school and university.

Fifth condition

> The university must collaborate in such a way that the school staff enters into the university culture.

I am aware that this condition is formulated in very general terms. In fact, condition 4 can be regarded as deriving from the more general condition 5. The latter could probably be realized in many different ways, and therefore is a more difficult guideline than the previous four conditions. This is not necessarily a criticism, however. Despite its generality, this is an absolutely central constraint on beneficial collaboration. As we will see when I begin to unpack the term "university culture," this is also the most problematic condition.

Turning now to implicit power talk: as we have seen, such talk is only a problem in highly focused and bureaucratized educational systems. In such systems the central ministry or the local education board may object to university/school collaborations and try to undermine them. However, if this does not occur, ongoing collaborations can help counter implicit power talk if two conditions are met. These are rather obvious, and so I will simply introduce them as the next two necessary conditions for beneficial ongoing collaboration.

Sixth condition

> The relationship between the university and the schools must be a nonhierarchical.

Seventh condition

> The collaboration between the university and schools must be personal and nonbureaucratized.

The sixth condition could also have been reached by another route. The considerations that House raised, introduced in chapter 1, also argue for the necessity of a nonhierarchical relationship. So chapters 1–4, together with a conceptual analysis of the term "cooperation," supply us with seven necessary conditions for beneficial ongoing collaboration. What about chapter 5? Certain of the psychological problems that change agents face disappear, as well as the need to be a temporary minimal catalyst. The very notion of ongoing collaboration obviously does this. Another serious problem faced by the change agent working out of a university context is the pressure towards salesmanship because of the need to obtain funding. This is also minimized very drastically by condition 4. If the university is really committed to a permanent change agency situated, say, within its school of education, then the budget of such an agency will depend far less on "soft" money than will a typical short-range research project. This does not get rid of all the problems the change agent faces, but it certainly goes quite a long way toward it.

The Internal Consistency of the Above Seven Conditions

So we see that the arguments developed in this book can be met, to a large extent, by moving from school self-renewal to ongoing collaboration, provided that the collaboration fulfills seven conditions. These are, once again:

1. A school and an external agency collaborating with it must not simply duplicate each other's work.
2. The goals of the school and the external agency must be very similar.
3. The external agency must be a university (or some sort of research institute).
4. The university must be firmly committed to the change agency it is sponsoring.
5. The university must collaborate with the school in such a way that the school staff enters into the university culture.
6. The relationship between the university and the school must be nonhierarchical.
7. The collaboration must be personal and nonbureaucratized.

How consistent are these conditions among themselves? I begin with condition 5, which is the most important one vis-à-vis consistency, because consistency will depend on what academic culture actually is.

It seems to me that three components of academic culture are of special importance here. First, universities are *elitist* institutions. They cater to a select minority of the population; they bestow various degrees according to a clearly defined status hierarchy; they bestow titles on the people who work in them, these titles again forming a status hierarchy; the disciplines taught, studied, and researched within them form guilds which, as Bernstein has shown, attempt to maintain a power base by presenting an image of themselves to the public as "owners" of secret, esoteric, certain knowledge.

Second, within universities two contradictory values coexist in a state of uneasy equilibrium—*individualism* and *the meeting of minds*. On the one hand, university faculty are rewarded for individual contributions to the growth of knowledge. Even in those cases where academics have published articles with other scholars, when one is up for promotion, it is one's own contribution that is going to be assessed. On the other hand, there is much rhetoric concerning the academic community, the community of scholars, invisible colleges, the house of intellect, and so forth. Reviewing other people's books, responding to other people's papers, taking part in symposia — all these are formal activities that university faculty engage in. There are even times when academics get out of their offices and talk to one another and exchange ideas informally!

Third, to use a term introduced in chapter 3, one of the primary beliefs of the academic belief system is belief in theory.[18] In other words, academics consider themselves as committed to research; they believe research contributes to the development of theory and that such development is a good thing. More specifically, when dealing with social scientists, this belief in theory involves the belief that social science theory contributes to practical affairs. In fact, Lindblom and Cohen argue that most social scientists believe that social science research is the only path to authoritative, useful knowledge about social policy.[19]

These three components of university culture make condition 5 extremely problematic. Because of them, condition 5 is likely to contradict conditions 2 and 6 and also the whole notion of collaboration.

Conditions 5 and 2. The problem with condition 2 derives from the last point raised—the commitment to theory and research. The purpose of the collaboration from the point of view of the school is to improve the education it offers its students (I am ignoring hidden motives such as collaborating with a university for prestige purposes.) If the university enters the partnership to promote research interests, then its aims and the school's aims are going to diverge. The partnership will thus be inherently unstable and cannot be the basis for ongoing collaboration.

My views here are so different from the received view on this matter (as represented by Goodlad and Fisher, for example) that I must address two predictable objections to my position. It might be objected that theory and research, even when they appear to be totally divorced from practical matters, eventually lead to useful applied knowledge and thus, according to this argument, both the school and the university faculties involved in a collaborative venture have the same aim—the improvement of practice. However, the belief that pure research will lead to useful practical knowledge is at most a tenet of ritual faith; I know of no evidence for it. On the contrary, one would be hard pressed to find much of what goes on in schools that relates to recommendations derived from research. It is not so simple to translate theory into practice. For instance, John Wilson has argued that the types of approaches that constitute the field of educational theory today—if you will, the state of the art—ensure that practice cannot rely much on theory.[20] I have argued that most theory is at odds with the teacher's perspective.[21] Lindblom and Cohen maintain that people solve many problems in other ways than with the aid of social science research (for example, with common-sense knowledge or direct action), and indeed in many cases such solutions are far better than anything social science could have suggested.[22] All in all, most educational research workers do not seem to realize how extremely problematic and complex the relationship between theory and practice really is.

A further answer to the above objection is that if research workers are correct and their research is really useful for practice, they seem not to have persuaded those engaged in practice that this is so. The mistrust of educational practitioners for theory is notorious. Thus a collaboration predicated on the idea that the university partner's contribution will be to theory and research (and at best will contribute to practice only indirectly) seems unlikely to get off to a good start. Finally, even if the far-off consequence of present research is to help improve practice, most research workers would be less than honest if they maintained that this consequence was what motivated them in undertaking the research. As with most scientists, their primary interest in a particular research question is intrinsic. Within the academic context this is quite admirable, and by saying this I am not criticizing research workers. All I am pointing out is that their personal aims in collaborating with a school are different from those of the school faculty.

A second objection to my view that a university/school collaboration is not likely to be fruitful is that most of the examples of collaboration given in this chapter prove empirically that I am mistaken. In fact, the Goodlad project and our own project also might be construed as evidence favoring collaboration. In the case of our project, one of the principals wrote me as follows:

> I have been thinking a lot about the lack of contact between theory in the university and practice in the schools. The problem lies in both directions. The latter don't ask and search, the former doesn't answer. It seems to me that of all the forms of cooperation our project was supposed to promote, this was the strongest and most significant.

Thus our project and many of the other cases mentioned in this chapter would appear to constitute examples of successful collaboration.

I can best answer this argument from direct experience with our project; however, all I have read concerning the other examples leads me to believe that similar problems characterize them also. My counterarguments are fourfold. First, our project lasted three years. I do not believe one can extrapolate confidently from a project planned for a limited, defined period in a discussion of ongoing collaboration. Second, the research focus of our project was on educational change. This is perhaps a special case. It is more difficult to differentiate between the school's interests and the research interest when the latter is concerned directly with improving school functioning than when it is concerned with, say, the psychological mechanism that ninth graders use in learning certain kinds of concepts. Third, for most of our project staff, research was either secondary to the primary task of helping the schools, or was of no interest whatsoever. This leads to the fourth point, which is perhaps the most important: the relative lack of interest in research and the limiting of research interests to the topic of educational change occurred because our project did not conform to conditions 4 and 5. Let me expand on this.

Of the project staff, I was the only member who was a tenured senior faculty member of a university department of education. In addition, although at the time of this project I was chairman of the teacher training department, the project was not an official department project. It was in many ways my own private "baby," for which, through personal initiative, I had obtained funding. Most of the project staff were taken on specifically to work on this project and had no other contact with the university. Those who did had part-time teaching assistants' posts. Although I reported on the project to the tenured faculty on a few occasions, probably only one or two other members of our department really knew what this project was all about. If, for some reason, I had had to leave the project, it would probably have folded immediately without anybody being much the wiser; alternatively, the university would have had great difficulty in replacing me because it had no clear idea of the nature of the project or any official ideological commitment to it.

Contrast this with another project that was going on at the same time. A certain high school had approached our department and indicated it was prepared to open its doors to research projects and help from the department. It is of course curious that a school should have done this; my impression is that there were hidden agenda operative here. However, the most important thing is that in our department the word got around fast, and quite a number of senior faculty expressed interest in doing certain research. One acted as a coordinator of sorts, and for a while four or five mini-projects were going on in that school, a state of affairs that exemplifies conditions 4 and 5 far better than our project. University involvement was semiofficial; more members of the senior faculty were involved, and thus university culture was involved to a far greater degree. One of the inevitable results was that faculty members with no direct interest in improving or changing the functioning of this school and, in fact, with no knowledge of high schools whatsoever, engaged in research at the school simply because this was a heaven-sent opportunity to find suitable subjects for experiments and manipulations in which they were interested. Predictably enough, the moment a research project was completed or, in certain cases, the moment a project ran into some difficulty, the faculty member concerned simply withdrew from the collaboration. My argument is that condition 5, and the associated condition 4, make this pretty well inevitable. The moment a collaboration conforms to conditions 4 and 5, research workers of this sort are going to be tempted, and legitimately so, to get a piece of the action, school and university aims are going to diverge, and the collaboration will become unstable.

Conditions 5 and 6. The tension between nonhierarchic collaboration and university culture derives from the university's elitist orientation; I assume that this does not require elaboration. The only other point that might be worth further comment is that we can supply some empirical confirmation of the difference between a circumscribed collaboration that does not fulfill condition 5 and an extensive ongoing collaboration that does. Again, our project can serve as an example of the former. As we have seen throughout the many cases described in this book, the relationship between the school faculties and our staff was emphatically nonhierarchic. This was one of the rather fine characteristics of the project. Contrast this with the whole activity of pre-service teacher training, in which universities and schools work together in an ongoing fashion, because the universities need the schools as sites for student teaching. Also condition 5 clearly pertains here, because this training is part of the ordinary teaching of students which is one of the university's defined official tasks.

Let us consider pre-service training a little more closely. Note that there are university faculty members who supervise the part of the pre-service training that takes place in the schools. This supervision is conceived in a variety of ways depending on the teacher training program at a particular university. Yet one generalization will apply in almost all cases: these faculty members form a special group within the teacher training department, defined as those whose expertise is in practical didactics. They are usually differentiated from those faculty members who teach more theoretical matters — educational philosophy, psychology, and sociology, for instance. What is interesting is that almost inevitably two things occur: The students consider the "practical guys" to have been more useful to them than the theoreticians. Nevertheless, despite the students' preference, the "practical guys" are lower-status faculty within the university hierarchy and are generally looked down upon by the theoreticians. If the latter cannot forego hierarchy within the university when it comes to their relationship with the "practical guys," there is not much hope of their being able to do so in relationships with the even more practical guys—school faculty and principals.

Condition 5 and Collaboration in General. There are two levels at which condition 5 seems likely to undermine the notion of collaboration. The surface level relates to the second component of condition 5—the tension between individualism and the idea of a community of scholars. In those academic institutions in which individualism is dominant, we have the ironic situation that schools are asked to collaborate with an institution which itself finds collaboration problematic.

The deeper level at which collaboration is undermined relates to university culture in toto. In chapters 3 and 4, I dealt with Bernstein's argument that university culture is a major creator of what he calls collection codes. Such codes discourage collegiality within school faculties. Surely it is reasonable to suppose that this lack of enthusiasm for collegiality within schools might spread to other sorts of collaboration, with other institutions. Thus the university culture may undermine collaboration indirectly by contributing to the creation of the norms that maintain self-contained classrooms.[23]

Is Collaboration Impossible?

Should we conclude from this analysis of condition 5 that stable, beneficial, ongoing collaboration between schools and external agencies is impossible? It certainly seems so. On the one hand, there are powerful reasons why the external agency should be an academic institution. On the other, academic culture seems to contradict many of the essential conditions for a positive collaboration.

This is probably too pessimistic a conclusion. All academic institutions are not identical. I see no reason why a particular university's culture (both with regard to the individualism/community of scholars issue, and also other things), belief system, and norms cannot be different from those I have sketched out. Nevertheless, I have observed that most university environments conform to my generalizations. Yet there can be institutions that, if they are lucky to have deans of their education schools who are committed to improving education at all levels, *can* create viable collaborative efforts. But such collaborations are not the rule. This chapter has pointed up certain sociological patterns that militate against such across-the-board collaborations. Thus any general national educational policy that relies on such collaborations is likely to lead to rather spotty results.

There is another reason why school/academic institution collaboration cannot be the basis for a general educational policy. Put very simply, the number of academic institutions in any geographic area is usually small. For this reason it is unrealistic to count on academia being able to "cover" the entire elementary and secondary education system. At best, positive collaborations between all the academic institutions in a particular education system and a limited number of schools is all one can hope for.

This then is my conclusion: as a general policy, ongoing collaboration is doomed to failure. As a strategy for creating interesting and productive enclaves within an education system, such collaboration is a very viable and encouraging option provided that attention is given to the seven necessary conditions sketched out in the previous section.

IS PLANNED EDUCATIONAL CHANGE POSSIBLE?

This book began by describing the road to commitment and then continued along the long road from commitment to skepticism. There have been very few deviations from this pessimistic route on the way, excepting the possibility discussed in the previous paragraph of creating productive enclaves. The time has come, therefore, to face squarely the possibility that the entire journey was misguided, and that I have been traveling along the wrong road. This is what is entailed in questioning what I called syllogism A in the introduction to this chapter — leading to the conclusion that schools require the help of external change agents—and specifically in questioning the premise that change in schools can be planned.

Although it is hardly a conclusion to call for further research in order to reach a conclusion, that is what seems most appropriate at this point. Therefore I will avoid a direct answer to the question: "Is planned educational change possible?" I can only hope that some of the definite answers to questions and some of the new ways I have suggested for looking at planned change that are scattered throughout the book will provide a balance to the "suggestions for future research" conclusion.

What I propose to do is to gather together and examine more closely some of the hints that appear in previous chapters that it may be impossible or unimportant or misguided to try to plan changes in schools. In this way I will produce (and criticize) a list of arguments against planned educational change that I will augment with further arguments. All in all, I will address six arguments.

The first is what I referred to in chapter 2 as the radical argument. It is perhaps best known as the correspondence principle and was introduced by Samuel Bowles and Herbert Gintis in *Schooling in Capitalist America*.[24] Put simply, the correspondence principle maintains that social relations within the school reflect the structure of labor relations within capitalist society. Expanding this idea, we can argue that the important things that happen in schools are reflections of properties of the society at large. If this is so, important changes within schools will only occur as a result of profound general social changes. Planned educational change divorced from a wider context is thus laughably irrelevant. Instead of sending change agents into the schools, we should send agitators onto the streets to help usher in social revolution.

In chapter 2, I rejected this type of argumentation by pointing out that deciding whether planned educational change is laughable or not is an empirical question. One must not reject the strategy of working within the system out of hand. Yet my experiences with working within the system, described in this book, have not been very encouraging. Must we then accept the radical thesis? I think not, and for reasons derived from the radical literature itself. Ironically, it has been the radical Marxist theorists themselves who have found the holes in the correspondence principle. One of the best-known arguments against the principle derives from the work of Michael Apple and Paul Willis.[25] They argue that Bowles and Gintis have an overly passive conception of the recipient of education, that is, the student, and they offer powerful empirical reasons for rejecting this conception. In their view, students often rebel against the hegemonic impositions of the ruling class through schooling. If this is so for students, I see no reason why it cannot apply just as much to the school staff. Of course I am then considering a different "rebellion" from the one Apple and Willis are concerned with. I am also using their work in a way they would probably not be happy with. Yet I do not think I am distorting their argument. I accept, as they do, that human beings are not simply passive receptacles of external social forces. This rejection of a total social determinism undermines the first argument against the possibility of planned educational change. If human beings control their own destiny to a degree, they can plan their own education systems.

The second and third arguments are very similar and will be dealt with together. The second is Meyer's and Rowan's thesis that schools are actually very effective organizations provided one realizes that their function is not so much to teach but rather to provide society with the display of a particular theory of personnel and knowledge. The third argument is my own, that schools tell us about the sacred. Both these arguments seem to suggest that planned change is unnecessary because the present situation is satisfactory, although in chapter 3 I express reservations about this conclusion with regard to my own argument.

In addition to what I wrote in chapter 3, there seems to me to be a far more important flaw in this line of argumentation. Essentially we are being seduced into committing two classic functionalist errors. First, we are making a value judgment when we claim that an institution is performing well, rather than simply identifying that institution's objective function. Thus anyone who accepts either the argument of Meyer and Rowan or my analysis—yet who believes that schools should not be displaying theories of personnel and knowledge, nor should they be telling us about the sacred—cannot dismiss planned change as unnecessary.

Second, even when value controversies have been settled, identifying the satisfactory functioning of an institution is always specific to a particular time and place. It is never universally valid. The fact that schools today tell us, say, about the sacred, does not ensure that they will do this tomorrow. And so the suggestion that planned change is unnecessary is, at best, a claim that is valid in a particular situation, but not invariably.

The fourth argument against planned change has not been mentioned previously. It derives from Charles Lindblom's and David Cohen's *Usable Knowledge*. This book argues for similar theses to those Michael Cohen, James March, and Johan Olsen, and Karl Weick presented when talking about organized anarchies and loose coupling.[26] Lindblom and Cohen are critical of the assumption of most social scientists that problems are solved through rational, analytic procedures. This sometimes does occur, but often problems are solved in other ways that we do not usually call "solving" but, on inspection, prove to be as effective as rational analysis. One of these they call "interactive" problem solving, that is, "to undertake or stimulate action—usually interaction—so that the preferred outcome comes about without anyone's having analyzed the given problem or having achieved an analyzed solution to it."[27] Some examples they give of interactive problem solving are coin tossing, mugging (for the mugger it is a way of implementing a solution to the problem of inadequate income), and voting in an election.

Lindblom and Cohen go on to criticize the notion of "*the* decision maker."[28] We often assume that there exists an identifiable decision maker whose decision will determine the solution to a particular problem. However, this is reasonable only if the problem is being solved analytically. In most cases of interactive problem solving, there is no single decision maker. Outcomes are achieved through the uncoordinated decisions and actions of many different people and groups. It would be more reasonable to regard these outcomes as "happening" than as the result of "*a* decision."

Clearly the notion of planned educational change derives from an analytic view of problem solving and is predicated on the assumption that there is *a* decision maker, or group of decision makers, and thus Lindblom's and Cohen's thesis is, in some ways, an argument against planned change. The problem is that it is not completely clear in what way their thesis is against such planning. Does their book imply that educational planning should simply be abandoned, because educational policy is, by and large, the result of interactive problem solving? Or perhaps it implies that educational planning should be continued, but that the planners should have very modest estimates of the extent to which their plans will be implemented?

Let me be more concrete about the difference between these two approaches. In the first section of this chapter, I suggested that ongoing collaboration between universities and schools could have important positive effects on the schools, provided that seven conditions were fulfilled. I then showed that university belief systems are so constituted that it is extremely unlikely (but not impossible) that these seven conditions could form a consistent system. Imagine the official policy makers of a particular educational system trying to make sense of this. Two options seem to be open to them. First, they could argue: "Well, we can call on the universities and schools to collaborate, but that is about all we can do. Most of the schools and universities will ignore our call. A few will pick up on the idea and of these some will create viable ways of collaborating." This approach is perfectly rational, but hardly an example of planned educational change.

A second approach might be: "We must invest a great deal of money in encouraging university/school collaboration. Not only that, we should use a group of change agents whose job it will be to try and encourage schools and universities to enter such collaborations and to try and ensure that the schools and universities adapt in ways that conform to the conditions necessary for constructive positive collaboration. We should be aware in advance that in most cases we are not going to succeed. At best we are going to create a number of productive enclaves. This is all we can hope for, but it is worth the money, time, and energy we would be investing." Again, perfectly rational, and this time the approach can be regarded as exemplifying planned educational change.

Both these approaches can be seen as following from Lindblom's and Cohen's argument. Which is better? Which will lead to a greater number of productive enclaves? As far as I can see, Lindblom and Cohen do not offer an answer to this sort of question.

Certainly it would be worthwhile having some relevant research data to help us to decide. I am not aware of any such data and thus my first "proposal for further research" would be to generate some.

The fifth and sixth arguments are in some ways rather similar. The fifth derives from the second part of chapter 3, whereas the sixth is presented here for the first time. In chapter 3 I argued that schools change in ways that conform to the jazz metaphor. Educational discourse, the language in which it is formulated, the conceptual trees on which it is based, determines educational practice to a large extent. The point is that educational discourse functions as a semiotic system which, to paraphrase Lévi-Strauss, men do not think in but rather the system thinks in men.[29] In other words, those who use the discourse do not usually have rational control over it, but rather the parameters of the discourse operate through them. This seems to make the rational planning of educational change clearly irrelevant. This is the fifth argument.

The sixth argument returns to the notion of the "hidden curriculum," which I have mentioned in passing. Since Philip Jackson coined the term in *Life in Classrooms*,[30] it has become one of the most popular, ill-defined, useful, and useless terms in the educational literature. In other contexts I have discussed the hidden curriculum in great detail.[31] Only two aspects of it are relevant here. First, I will define the hidden curriculum by following Jane Martin, whose article "What Should We Do with a Hidden Curriculum When We Find One?"[32] is one of the most serious attempts at conceptual clarification of the term. A hidden curriculum will consist of those school learning outcomes that are either unintended by the teacher or are intended but are not openly acknowledged to learners in the school setting.[23] The important point about this definition is that it conceives of the hidden curriculum as being related at least in part to things teachers are unaware they have taught. Second, most writers on the hidden curriculum would agree with Benjamin Bloom who claims that the hidden curriculum is a more pervasive and thus a more efficient curriculum than the manifest curriculum.[34]

These two points about the hidden curriculum lead to the following conclusion: perhaps the most important aspect of schooling from the point of view of student learning is unrelated, by and large, to the conscious planning of the school's teaching staff. This again transforms the idea of planned educational change into a questionable undertaking. Here then is the sixth and final argument against planned educational change.

The fifth and sixth arguments and the strategies for countering them have at least three things in common. First of all, as we have seen, both are special cases of the more general argument that there are many central aspects of schooling that do not seem to be the result of rational decision procedures, despite my rejection of complete social determinism. Second, there is a similar gap in our knowledge concerning both educational discourse and the hidden curriculum. In neither case do we have an empirically based theory of change. We do not know how either educational discourse or the hidden curriculum changes, or how such changes affect educational practice. We do not even know whether a theory linking such changes to practice in a predictable way is theoretically possible or not. The notion of the jazz metaphor is a promising start, with regard to educational discourse at least. But it is only a start. Its formulation in this book is certainly not sufficiently detailed to allow us to talk of a developed theory of change. I would regard the attempt to build on the jazz metaphor and to build a similar theory vis-à-vis the hidden curriculum to be an absolutely top-priority research task.

The third point related to both the fifth and sixth arguments is the question of consciousness raising. Although teachers are generally unaware of the central parameters of the educational discourse they are part of, the conceptual trees associated with the discourse, or the hidden curriculum that they teach, *they can be made aware of these matters*. The question then arises: how would this new awareness affect things? Would teachers be more in control of the discourse through which they speak? Would it result in their being capable of changing the hidden curriculum they teach?[35] These empirical questions are of huge import. As far as I know, no one has ever addressed them.

Why are the research agendas suggested in the last two paragraphs so important? The answer, I suggest, is that until such research supplies us with answers to the questions I have raised, there is no way of answering the really basic question—is planned educational change possible? Arguments 5 and 6 are undoubtedly the strongest arguments against planned educational change. The answers supplied by the two research proposals above will decide whether these arguments can be countered or not. If we were to know, for example, that making teachers aware of the assumptions behind educational discourse and of the hidden curriculum they teach would result in the school staff having more control over their teaching, and if, in addition, we knew that control over discourse and hidden curricula resulted in predictable changes in school practice, then the notion of planned educational change would be given a new lease on life. Planning would once again became viable and important, and new theories and strategies of planned educational change would be needed and could be formulated.

On the other hand, what if we were to discover that consciousness raising had no effect on the extent to which teachers were in control of their discourse or of the hidden curricula they taught? Or what if we were to discover that control over discourse and hidden curricula did not result in predictable changes in school practice? In my view, either of these possibilities would deal a death blow to the notion of planned educational change.

Appendices
Notes
Bibliography
About the Author
Index

Appendix A

A COMPARISON OF THE PROJECT FOR THE ADVANCEMENT OF EDUCATIONAL COOPERATION AND THE LEAGUE OF COOPERATING SCHOOLS

The difference between two educational change projects can derive from at least six different sources:

Theory
> The two projects might be based on different theories of change.

Personalities
> The projects might be staffed by very different sorts of people with totally different styles of creating and maintaining contact with schools.

Accidental events
> To a certain extent, a project's development will be the result of accidental happenings related to the specific schools, the project staff, or the milieu in which the project takes place.

Initial constraints
> Not all the parameters of a project that were determined at the beginning derive from the theory of change on which the project is based. All sorts of extra constraints enter the picture. Some of these are part of the situational givens the change agents have to accept whether they want to or not. Others are the result of decisions by the project staff, decisions that do not follow (nor contradict) the theoretical assumptions of the project, but will nevertheless affect the activities undertaken very profoundly.

Crucial decisions during the project

In every project, certain situations will develop into central choice points. At such points the project can go in one of two or more directions, and the choice will profoundly affect further developments. In such cases the various options are usually all consistent with the basic theory of the project. Unfortunately, often such crucial decisions are made without the project staff realizing at the time how significant the decision is going to be. Then only after the fact do they become aware how a decision has in fact introduced new constraints into the project.

Cultural and structural differences

Every project takes place within a certain cultural milieu and within an educational system with certain structural properties. These affect the outcomes of certain actions undertaken by the project staff, and also limit the actions open to the staff.

In comparing the League of Cooperating Schools with our own Project for the Advancement of Educational Cooperation, I will refer only in passing to the first three sources just named. The theoretical differences should not be too marked, since we saw our project as based on the same assumptions as those of the Goodlad project. We may have been wrong and may have misinterpreted Goodlad, although that seems unlikely. With regard to personality differences, I cannot say, never having met any of Goodlad's staff except Goodlad himself. In addition, I am not sure that this source of difference is of much general interest.

Accidental events did constrain both our projects. For instance, our project took place during three years in which Israeli high school teachers were involved in a series of very serious labor strikes, which from the point of view of the project staff were accidental events. Because according to general opinion the teachers lost most of their battles in these strikes, the mood of teachers in the country was very "down" during these years. This surely affected the possibility of inspiring teachers to get involved with change. However, in terms of general lessons learned from our experience, it is of no importance, as is true of all accidental events.

The other three sources of difference between our projects are of more general interest. Let us begin with initial constraints. One such constraint is the length of the change project. Goodlad's project continued for five years, ours for only three. In fact, this is not quite an initial constraint, because at the beginning we spoke of three to five years. However, almost immediately it became clear that funding for the project would cease after the third year. Is the difference between three and five years important? What is the optimal length of a project of this sort? It is impossible to answer these questions. Certainly during the third year some members of our project staff thought that we needed more time. But then others would point out that in all likelihood the same would be said in the fifth year if we continued for another two years. One interesting point is that one school that changed rather profoundly joined the project in its second year and thus was with us for only two years. On the other hand, this school joined an organizational structure which had been in existence for a year. So, all in all, I cannot say whether the difference in length of our two projects was significant or not. This difficulty is of course predictable on the basis of the discussion in chapter 5 about the psychological pressures on change agents to redefine their roles.

A second initial constraint on our project was the decision to work with high schools, as opposed to elementary schools as Goodlad did. This is absolutely crucial. Not only are high schools more conservative as a rule than elementary schools, they are also more compartmentalized, larger, and thus more loosely coupled. For this reason interventions in high schools raise certain problems that do not exist in elementary schools. For instance, it is possible for the change agent to be involved with the principal and a group of teachers of a school without other teachers even being aware that this activity is going on. In other words, the problem of *dissemination* becomes crucial. At times I strongly disagreed with the way certain principals and project staff members interpreted the notion of dissemination. In my opinion, they conceived of it as passing on *news*. If a teacher did not know that an activity was taking place, this was considered a sign of failure. On the other hand, I see dissemination as being concerned with passing on the *spirit* of the project. If a teacher becomes caught up in, say, a new set of norms of problem solving and evaluation, it seems to me unimportant whether that teacher is aware that these norms are the result of the school being involved in a change project or not.

Another constraint that limited us without our predicting where it would lead was the question of the geographic location of the staff members. Our project accepted the assumption of Goodlad that schools should come from different districts so that the league could become an organization cutting across normal lines of authority. I am not sure we were correct in doing this, for reasons I will return to. However, we created a league that covered about half the state of Israel. In such a situation the question arises: should staff members be chosen so that their geographic spread covers the league, or should they be chosen so that all live in close proximity to the university in which the project is housed? We (or rather I) chose the first possibility. As far as I can gather, Goodlad chose the second. This led to some interesting differences. Our staff members could reach the schools to which they were assigned relatively easily because, in most cases, the schools were very close by. In many cases it was possible simply to drop in. This gave us a great deal of flexibility. Yet when it came to project staff contact and meetings, we soon realized we had created an organizational nightmare. Apart from the principals' meetings (and the evaluators' meetings in the third year), the staff could meet together only once and occasionally twice a month for a day-long meeting. So communication between the staff members became a problem. We tried to overcome this partially by working as couples wherever possible. This did help, but still each couple worked more or less on its own.

So our choice had its advantages and disadvantages. The League of Cooperating Schools project seems to have had precisely the opposite advantages and disadvantages. It is difficult to say which setup is superior. Perhaps a third hybrid possibility can be found.

Let us now turn to crucial decisions during the project. Here I cannot do much more than repeat three examples earlier referred to. Goodlad mentions the conflict between interpreting the role of project members as catalysts versus active consultants. This arose in the third year of his project, when the decision was to opt for the catalyst interpretation. Strictly speaking, this is not an example of the sort I am referring to, because this was a choice point at which one of the two choices was clearly at odds with the theory of change on which the project was predicated. Still, it was a decision that had profound effects on the way the project developed afterwards.

One example from our project was the "decision" that project staff should set up the agenda for the principals' meetings. This was in my view wrong, although we have no way of knowing what would have happened if we had taken the alternative path.

A second example from our project was our decision to suggest the establishment of the role of evaluator in each school. With regard to this aspect of our work, there is no doubt in my mind that we needed more time. Yet there is also no doubt that here we stumbled upon something that should be tried and developed further in other projects. Some of the most interesting achievements and most fascinating questions for future research derived from the idea of an evaluator role. Consider the following questions (some of which were mentioned in chapter 1, but not really answered satisfactorily):

1. Who should be the evaluator? In some schools a vice-principal, usually the principal's right-hand assistant, was chosen. In others a guidance counselor, in others just an ordinary teacher. In our limited sample, to our surprise, the evaluatory ethic usually progressed best when the evaluator was a vice-principal, which seems to contradict the different drummer notion. Much more research needs to be done on this.
2. Should the evaluator work with a permanent school evaluation committee or not?
3. Should the evaluators of a group of schools work *as* a group (that is, choose common evaluatory tasks and then compare notes) or should each one concentrate on things specific to the school?
4. What should the "curriculum" of a training course for evaluators consist of? Do they need instruction in classic evaluation methodology? Perhaps the fact that these are internal evaluators (who will thus be evaluating ongoing school activity rather than the controlled environments set up in research projects) renders classic evaluation techniques useless?

Before moving on to the final group of differences between our project and the Goodlad one, I will mention one further crucial decision that Goodlad discusses with regard to his project. This was the decision to change the format of the League journal or newsletter from a more academic to a more folksy, school-based one. Unfortunately, we never succeeded in getting such a newsletter going, but Goodlad's conclusions and suggestions about this are still of general relevance.

I now turn to the cultural and structural differences between the United States and Israel and their educational systems that affected the two projects. I will deal with one cultural difference and one structural one. The cultural difference relates to a culture's response to travel. In projects concerned with "massaging" a group of schools into a league, this is an absolutely central variable. The difference between the States and Israel can be stated very simply: for Americans, interurban travel for business reasons has a positive or, at worst, neutral connotation, whereas in Israel it has a negative one. To a certain extent this is the result of purely physical considerations. American roads are superb, automobiles are larger and thus more comfortable than in Israel, and then there is good old reliable Howard Johnson's. In Israel there is an efficient and incredibly cheap public transport system, but still interurban travel means sweat, crowding, noise, and bumpy roads. However, these two different responses probably also tap into the far deeper level of dominant myths, symbols, and images in both societies. Spelling these out would constitute a fascinating research project. What is important here, however, is that in Israel massaging a league into existence conflicts with the basic national antipathy to interurban travel. Of course, people do commute and travel in Israel. But whenever one learns that one will have to attend a meeting in another city, one's first reaction is to groan. This may seem like a trivial thing, but I suggest that it transforms a league of schools into an inherently unstable and fragile organization.

The structural difference between the American and Israeli educational systems is obvious: the U.S. system is decentralized, whereas Israel's is centralized. From the beginning we suspected that this might render inapplicable many aspects of the theory of change Goodlad proposed. Our suspicions were justified. Centralization creates at least three problems for a league of schools:

The "Unbreachable" Hierarchy Lines.   Even when one chooses schools from different districts, one cannot really cut across the ordinary lines of hierarchy, because the different districts are really simply organizational subunits of the same system. Thus factors like implicit power talk cannot be countered effectively. One's league is never really an organization with countervailing norms and discourse. All schools in the league are, by definition, a subset of the same organization.

School Selection.   A specific aspect of the above problem is that the selection of schools becomes problematic. Goodlad approached a number of school districts and asked each one to select one school to take part in the league. Obviously in such a situation it is unlikely that a district will deliberately nominate its worst school. However, when all schools are part of the same system, then very poor schools *are* going to be nominated. Local pride becomes pretty well irrelevant. An action research project is conceived as one whose purpose is to help schools, so systems might be tempted to give the project the schools that need the most help.

Here I will briefly fill out the story of the three schools that left us by their own choice during the three years of the project. Two of these have been described. The third case was a well-known open high school whose headmaster was an ideologically committed believer in open education but who was himself very autocratic in his management style. He was convinced that his school's ideology was the final answer to education's problems and was contemptuous of all people who disagreed with him. I am not simply expressing a personal opinion. In any event, this school's participation in our project was nominal from the beginning. The headmaster expressed no interest whatsoever in obtaining feedback and his appearances at the principals' meetings were very rare. They usually occurred when the agenda offered a possibility for him to present at length his school's ideology about something. To just about everyone's relief I think (including the principals and the four project staff members who had, at various times, been assigned to this school), the headmaster decided to resign from the project at the end of the second year.

My feelings about this case and the other two "impossible" cases we tried to deal with are ambivalent. On the one hand, I have quoted approvingly Perrow's argument that we should try to help the most problematic organizations and not those that are already doing quite well. On the other hand, problematic schools demand tremendous investments of energy and time, and the chances of success of any sort are almost nonexistent.

During the year of my writing this book an unpredicted situation increased my ambivalence. Two members of our staff became the staff members of the section of the Institute for Innovative High School Education (described in chapter 6) that was to perform naturalistic evaluations for schools. During this year they were scheduled to do this in approximately fifteen schools. Due to a drastic cut of Israel's education budget, the institute's budget was also reduced, and finally only four schools could be dealt with. Thus, purely by chance, the two staff members were forced into a situation where they had to select four out of fifteen schools. They decided to choose four schools that appeared capable of using such an evaluation and appeared open to receiving it, too. Over the years, the staff members had developed a great deal of expertise in broadly capturing the essentials of a school very quickly and their

choices were apparently good ones. This means that these schools
were *not* the most problematic schools in Israel.[1] Because of this,
the staff members seem to have been extremely successful with
these schools in terms of the objectives of this section of the institute. Is this better than trying valiantly but mainly unsuccessfully to
help really problematic schools? I don't know. In any event, it is
clear that this dilemma surfaces much more readily in centralized
educational systems than in decentralized ones.

The Lack of Variety Between Schools.   Theoretically, comparing
schools, there are at least three sorts of variables one could concentrate on. First, there are very obvious variables over which the
school staff has ostensible control. Take, for instance, teaching
methods. The teaching methods prevalent in a particular school
clearly determine much of what goes on; two schools with different
dominant teaching methods will be obviously different, that is,
even an untrained observer will sense the difference between
them; the staff can adopt whatever teaching methods they like (at
least in principle). Second, there are subtle variables over which
the staff has ostensible control. Consider organizational climate.
Probably only a trained observer would readily spot the difference
in organizational climate between two schools, yet climate is
clearly determined to a large extent by the actions of the staff. Third,
there are very obvious variables over which the staff has very
little control. For example, the character of the neighborhood in
which a school is situated is an important determinant of who goes
to the school, and this will determine much of what happens in it.
Yet the staff cannot simply move the school to wherever it wants to.
From the staff's point of view, physical location is a given.

   Although one could concentrate on any one of these three
kinds of variables, in practice it is the first and third kinds that are
noticed. In a centralized educational system, the variance between
schools vis-à-vis the first sort of variable is far smaller than in a
decentralized system. The reason for this is that, despite the ostensible control the staff has over these variables, the implicit controls
of the centralized system ensure a great deal of uniformity. Thus a
school's staff tend to concentrate on the third sort of variable when
comparing themselves to another school. Remember these are variables over which the staff do not even have ostensible control. So,
in terms of these sorts of variables, schools can learn very little from
other, different schools. On the contrary, contact with such schools

is seen as at best interesting for its curiosity value, at worst a waste of time.

This is one of the most important problems we faced when it came to all the activities designed to "massage" the schools in our project into a league (trying to start a newsletter, to organize school visits, and so on) and thus we came to the conclusion, as mentioned previously, that this aspect of Goodlad's project was not easily importable into our educational system.

Appendix B

THE SIMPLY PROGRAMMABLE NATURE OF ARGYRIS'S AND SCHÖN'S THEORY OF CHANGE

A linear flow chart is shown in figure B.1. The nodes A, B, C, D, E, F, G, and the arrows can be ordered in a straight line. All the arrows point in the same direction. At each node (except for A and G) one arrow leads to the node and one from the node. No node has more than one arrow leading to it and also no node has more than one arrow leading from it.

Figure B.2 shows a quasi-linear flow chart. The difference between this flow chart and the previous one resides in the feedback arrows from E to C and from F to B. Because of these, not all the arrows are in one straight line nor do they all point in the same direction (the feedback arrows' directions being, not opposed to the general flow, but different from it). However, the nodes all remain in one straight line and no node has more than one nonfeedback arrow leading to it or from it.

The first flow chart describes a predictable process. Because of the similarities between the flow charts, we can say that the second also describes a process that is more or less predictable. It will also arrive at F unless either C D E C or B C D E F B is a vicious circle.

FIGURE B.1. A Linear Flow Chart

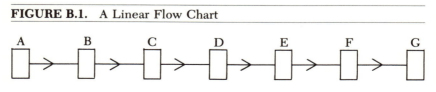

FIGURE B.2. A Quasi-linear Flow Chart

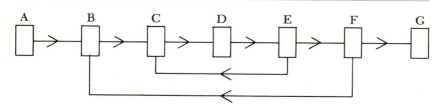

In Argyris's and Schön's *Organizational Learning: A Theory of Action Perspective* there appears a flow chart describing Model O-II learning systems.[1] At first glance nothing would seem to be less like a quasi-linear flow chart. The "program" has two major branches and feedback loops at just about every node. However, in an article by Argyris called "How Learning and Reasoning Processes Affect Change," there appears another version of this flow chart.[2] This second version captures the essence of the first and it is not an oversimplification, although it certainly is a simplification. I reproduce it in figure B.3 almost exactly, except that I use rectangles to signify each node, whereas Argyris does not always do this, and I name certain nodes that Argyris does not name in the diagram.

Argyris explains this figure thus:

Single-loop learning occurs when matches are created or when mismatches are corrected by changing actions. Double-loop learning occurs when mismatches are corrected by first examining and altering the governing variables and then the actions. Governing variables are the preferred states that the individuals strive to satisfy when they are acting.[3]

We see that in this version of the flow chart all nodes are in one straight line excluding the "Match" node, so that with this one exception, this is a quasi-linear flow chart. Again, like a quasi-linear flow chart, the process will reach the "Match" node unless either the single or the double loop is a vicious circle. Thus the Argyris-Schön theory is capable of being translated into a flow chart that is *to all intents and purposes* quasi-linear and has a small number of feedback loops. It is thus *simply programmable*, which is what I argued in chapter 2.

There is another interesting point to note about the Argyris-Schön theory. Consider the components of the single loop:

FIGURE B.3. Flow Chart Adapted from Argyris

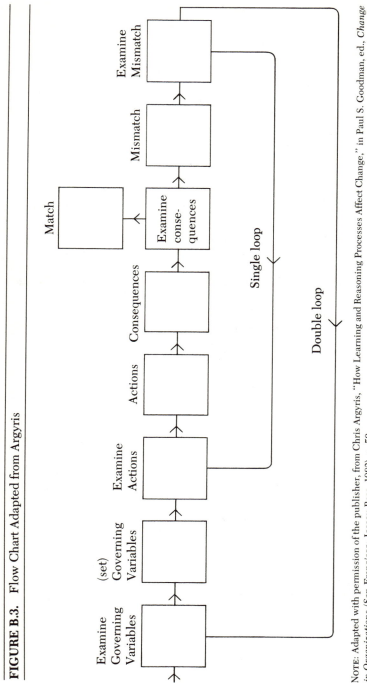

NOTE: Adapted with permission of the publisher, from Chris Argyris, "How Learning and Reasoning Processes Affect Change," in Paul S. Goodman, ed., *Change in Organizations* (San Francisco: Jossey-Bass, 1982), p. 50.

mismatch, examine mismatch, examine actions, act, produce consequences, examine consequences. This is clearly simply a reformulation of the classic Dewey five-step problem-solving process. So we see that the simpler of the two types of learning processes that Argyris and Schön postulate is classically Deweyian. The more complex learning type, double-loop learning, introduces the further complication of examining governing variables. It is thus more complex than the Deweyian five-step process, although it must be stressed that Dewey does deal with reviewing governing variables in other contexts of his philosophy. Also, the double-loop learning that Argyris and Schön are concerned with is only a little more complex than the Deweyian five-step process. In other words, even the one theory of change examined in chapter 2 which seemed to escape the Deweyian metaphor, only does so in a very partial sense.

Notes

Chapter 1. The Road to Commitment

1. Apart from works I will be referring to directly in the text, I found the following helpful: Richard O. Carlson et al., *Change Processes in the Public Schools* (Eugene: Center for the Advanced Study of Educational Administration, University of Oregon, 1965); Center for Educational Research and Innovation (CERI), *Case Studies of Educational Innovation,* vols. 1–4 (Paris: OECD, 1973); Neal Gross, Joseph B. Giacquinta, and Marilyn Bernstein, *Implementing Organizational Innovations: A Sociological Analysis of Planned Educational Change* (New York: Basic Books, 1971); Jerald Hage and Michael Aiken, *Social Change in Complex Organizations* (New York: Random House, 1970); Matthew B. Miles, ed., *Innovation in Education* (New York: Teachers College Press, 1964).

2. Ernest R. House, *The Politics of Educational Innovation* (Berkeley, Calif.: McCutchan, 1974); Jerome S. Bruner, *The Process of Education* (New York: Vintage Books, 1963).

3. House, *The Politics of Educational Innovation*, pp. 220–21.

4. Ibid., p. 210.

5. Ibid., pp. 223–25.

6. Robert Chin and Kenneth D. Benne, "General Strategies For Effecting Changes in Human Systems," in *The Planning of Change*, 2nd ed., ed. Warren G. Bennis, Kenneth D. Benne, and Robert Chin (New York: Holt, Rinehart and Winston, 1969), p. 34.

7. Seymour B. Sarason, *The Culture of the School and the Problem of Change* (Boston: Allyn and Bacon, 1971).

8. Paul Berman and Milbrey W. McLaughlin, "Implementation of Educational Innovation," *Educational Forum* 40, no. 3 (March 1976): 361. This article is a summary of important findings from the Rand study. Title III programs are those funded under the 1965 federal Elementary and Secondary Education Act Title III Innovative Projects.

9. Shevach Eden, *Implementation of Innovations in Education* (Tel Aviv: Ma'alot, 1977).

10. Ronald G. Havelock, *The Change Agent's Guide to Innovation in*

Education (Englewood Cliffs, N.J.: Educational Technology Publications, 1973).

11. Quoted in Mary M. Bentzen, *Changing Schools: The Magic Feather Principle* (New York: McGraw-Hill, 1974), p. 3.

12. John I. Goodlad, *The Dynamics of Educational Change* (New York: McGraw-Hill, 1975); Bentzen, *Changing Schools*.

13. Richard A. Schmuck et al., *Handbook of Organizational Development in Schools* (Eugene: Center for the Advanced Study of Educational Administration, University of Oregon, 1972), and *The Second Handbook of Organizational Development in Schools* (Palo Alto, Calif.: Mayfield, 1977).

14. John Eggleston, "School-based Curriculum Development in England and Wales," in *School-Based Curriculum Development*, CERI (Paris: OECD, 1979), pp. 85–86.

15. Bentzen, *Changing Schools*, pp. 65–66.

Chapter 2. Conceptual Problems: The Problem-Solving and the Therapeutic Metaphors

1. Ludwig Wittgenstein, *On Certainty* (New York: Harper and Row, 1972), p. 44.

2. Samuel Bowles and Herbert Gintis, *Schooling in Capitalist America* (New York: Basic Books, 1976), p. 274.

3. Two typical examples of research on effective schools are: Wilbur B. Brookover, *School Social Systems and Student Achievement: Schools Can Make a Difference* (New York: Praeger, 1979); Michael Rutter et al., *Fifteen Thousand Hours* (Cambridge, Mass.: Harvard University Press, 1979).

4. Of course, this is assuming that the school does not have characteristics $x_1, x_2, \ldots x_n$. If it does have these characteristics, then it depends what "not worthwhile" means for the faculty. If it means that the desired educational objective is seen by them as not worth expending the effort to achieve, then the research linking it to $x_1, x_2 \ldots x_n$ is still irrelevant. On the other hand, if they see it as something undesirable, then the research does become relevant—the faculty must try to change the school in such a way as to get rid of $x_1, x_2, \ldots x_n$.

5. This is only if we conceive of self-renewal as improved problem-solving ability. However, almost all writers on school self-renewal smuggle in a further characteristic—the self-renewing school is democratic. I will have more to say on this later on. At this juncture, it is sufficient to point out that this characteristic of self-renewal might contradict effectiveness. Effective schools may be those that are undemocratic. As a matter of fact, this does seem to be a common finding in research on effective schools.

6. Donald A. Schön, "Generative Metaphor: A Perspective on Problem-Setting in Social Policy," in *Metaphor and Thought*, ed. Andrew Ortony (Cambridge: Cambridge University Press, 1979), p. 256.

7. The notion of metaphor in general, and its relationship to thought in particular, have been studied with great interest of late. Apart from the article by Schön and the collection of articles in which it appears (ibid.), I found the following very helpful: Mark Johnson, ed., *Philosophical Perspectives on Metaphor* (Minneapolis: University of Minnesota Press, 1981); George Lakoff and Mark Johnson, *Metaphors We Live By* (Chicago: University of Chicago Press, 1980); Paul Ricoeur, *Interpretation Theory* (Fort Worth: Texas Christian University Press, 1976); Paul Ricoeur, *The Rule of Metaphor* (Toronto: University of Toronto Press, 1977); Israel Scheffler, *Beyond the Letter* (London: Routledge and Kegan Paul, 1979).

8. To a certain extent it would be more comprehensive to talk of a therapeutic metaphor in general. I explain why I nevertheless call this a Freudian metaphor later in this chapter.

9. John Dewey's most extensive discussion of habit is in *Human Nature and Conduct* (New York: Modern Library, 1930).

10. John Dewey, *Logic: the Theory of Inquiry* (New York: Henry Holt, 1930), pp. 104–05.

11. John Dewey, *The Middle Works* (Carbondale: Southern Illinois University Press, 1978), 6:236–37.

12. John Dewey, *Democracy and Education* (New York: Macmillan, 1964), p. 150.

13. Ibid., p. 340.

14. The influence of Darwinism on John Dewey is very clear in *The Influence of Darwin on Philosophy* (New York: Henry Holt, 1910). See also Richard Hofstadter, *Social Darwinism in American Thought* (Boston: Beacon Press, 1955).

15. Dewey, *Democracy and Education*, pp. 41–53, 139–51.

16. Ibid., p. 51.

17. Kenneth D. Benne, "Deliberate Changing as the Facilitation of Growth," in *The Planning of Change*, ed. Warren G. Bennis, Kenneth D. Benne, and Robert Chin (New York: Holt, Rinehart and Winston, 1964), pp. 230–31.

18. Richard A. Schmuck et al., *The Second Handbook of Organizational Development in Schools* (Palo Alto, Calif: Mayfield, 1977), p. 293.

19. Philip J. Runkel et al., *Transforming the School's Capacity for Problem Solving* (Eugene: Center for Educational Policy and Management, University of Oregon, 1979), p. 48.

20. Schmuck et al., *Second Handbook*, p. 3.

21. Matthew B. Miles, "Planned Change and Organizational Health: Figure and Ground," in *Managing Change in Educational Organizations*, ed. J. Victor Baldridge and Terrence E. Deal (Berkeley, Calif.: McCutchan, 1975).

22. It is interesting that Dewey sees life itself as a process of self-renewal, and that this is what distinguishes living organisms from inanimate objects; cf. Dewey, *Democracy and Education*, pp. 1–4, 9.

23. Katherine C. Mayhew and Anna C. Edwards, *The Dewey School* (New York: Atherton Press, 1966).

24. Seymour B. Sarason, *The Culture of the School and the Problem of Change* (Boston: Allyn and Bacon, 1971), p. 3.

25. Ibid., p. 64.

26. Dewey, *Middle Works*, 6:237.

27. Gregory Bateson, "Minimal Requirements for a Theory of Schizophrenia," and "Social Planning and the Concept of Deutero-Learning," *Steps to an Ecology of Mind* (New York: Ballantine, 1972). See also Paul Watzlawick, John H. Weakland, and Richard Fish, *Change: Principles of Problem Formation and Problem Resolution* (New York: W.W. Norton, 1974).

28. Chris Argyris and Donald A. Schön, *Organizational Learning: A Theory of Action Perspective* (Reading, Mass.: Addison-Wesley, 1978), p. 3.

29. For example, Carl R. Rogers, *On Becoming a Person* (Boston: Houghton Mifflin, 1961).

30. Historically speaking, Ronald Lippitt is one of the central figures in the development of the group dynamics tradition. The book that probably symbolizes the link between group dynamics and OD best is Ronald Lippett, Jeanne Watson, and Bruce Westley, *The Dynamics of Planned Change* (New York: Harcourt, Brace and World, 1958).

31. R. Bruce Raup, Kenneth D. Benne et al., *The Improvement of Practical Intelligence* (New York: Harper and Row, 1943).

32. Charles W. Morris, *The Pragmatic Movement in American Philosophy* (New York: George Braziller, 1970).

33. In a sense, the entire Freudian corpus is relevant here, and especially the case studies. I will limit myself to Sigmund Freud, *Collected Papers*, vol. 2 (London: Hogarth Press, 1924), papers 26, 31, 32, 33, 34; *Collected Papers*, vol. 4 (London: Hogarth Press, 1925), paper 6. In addition, I found the following useful: Harold P. Blum, "The Curative and Creative Aspects of Insight," *Journal of the American Psychoanalytic Association* 27, supplement (1979): 41–70; Antony Flew, "Psycho-Analytic Explanation," Stephen Toulmin, "The Logical Status of Psycho-Analysis," and Richard S. Peters, "Cause, Cure and Motive," in *Philosophy and Analysis,* ed. Margaret McDonald (Oxford: Blackwell, 1954); Alistair C. MacIntyre, *The Unconscious* (Atlantic Highlands, N.J.: Humanities Press, 1958); Peter B. Neubauer, "The Role of Insight in Psychoanalysis," *Journal of the American Psychoanalytic Association* 27, supplement (1979): 29–39.

34. Argyris and Schön, *Organizational Learning*, p. 38.

35. Ibid., p. 39.

36. Schmuck et al., *Second Handbook*, p. 191.

37. Ibid., p. 190, emphasis added.

38. Mary M. Bentzen, *Changing Schools: The Magic Feather Principle* (New York: McGraw-Hill, 1974), p. 91.

39. Ibid., p. 109.

40. John I. Goodlad, *The Dynamics of Educational Change* (New York: McGraw-Hill, 1974), pp. 101–02.

41. One exception is: Louis M. Smith, John J. Prunty, and David C. Dwyer, "A Longitudinal Nested Systems Model of Innovation and Change in Schooling," in *Organizational Behavior in Schools and School Districts*, ed. Samuel B. Bacharach (New York: Praeger, 1981).

42. For example: Thomas B. Greenfield, "Reflections on Organizational Theory and the Truths of Irreconcilable Realities," *Educational Administration Quarterly* 14, no. 2 (Spring 1978): 1–23; "Organizational Theory as Ideology," *Curriculum Inquiry* 9, no. 2 (1979): 97–112; "The Man Who Comes Back Through the Door in the Wall: Discovering Truth, Discovering Self, Discovering Organizations," *Educational Administration Quarterly* 16, no. 3 (Fall 1980): 26–59.

43. Thomas B. Greenfield, "Organizations as Social Inventions: Rethinking Assumptions About Change," *Journal of Applied Behavioral Science* 9, no. 5 (Sept./Oct. 1973): 559.

44. Ibid., 561.

45. The classic articles on holism versus methodological individualism appear in John O'Neill, ed., *Modes of Individualism and Collectivism* (London: Heinemann, 1973).

46. Ernest A. Gellner, "Explanations in History," in ibid., p. 253.

47. Greenfield, "Organizations as Social Inventions," p. 556.

48. There would appear to be a possible alternative to (c) which I will call (c'): most members of the organization are selected *because* they accept the set of sentences mentioned in (a). In other words, one appears to be able to maintain self-renewal through staff *selection*. However, (c') assumes that there exists within the organization a group of *selectors*. Over time these must also change, and the new selectors must continue to select new members of the organization who accept the set of sentences mentioned in (a). Thus the old selectors must see themselves as obligated to getting new selectors to accept the sentence "Members of our organization should believe . . . and should be selected on this basis." However, *this sentence will be one of the sentences in (a)*! So (c') collapses into (c).

49. John Dewey, "An Analysis of Reflective Thought," *Journal of Philosophy* 19, no. 2 (1922): 29–30, emphasis added.

50. Ben Heirs and Gordon Pehrson, *The Mind of the Organization* (New York: Harper and Row, 1977).

51. It must be admitted that without the school's involvement in our project, the first stage—perplexity, confusion, and doubt—would probably not have arisen. The perplexity was, in a sense, *imported* by us, or rather by our supplying the school with feedback. Up to that point, the problem we addressed had been but a vague, worrying idea in the head of one person—Gilad. However, after it had been imported, it became a part of the reality the school had to contend with.

52. The pioneer work on cognitive style is Herman A. Witkin et al., *Psychological Differentiation* (New York: John Wiley, 1962), pp. 67–70.

See also Kenneth M. Goldstein and Sheldon Blackman, *Cognitive Style* (New York: John Wiley, 1978).

53. Cf. Burton R. Clark, "The Organizational Saga in Higher Education," *Administrative Science Quarterly* 17, no. 2 (June 1972): 178–84.

54. Cf. Israel Scheffler, "Philosophical Models of Teaching," *Reason and Teaching* (London: Routledge and Kegan Paul, 1973), pp. 71–76.

55. Here the metaphor also becomes extremely shaky. In Freudian consciousness raising there is always an analyst. However, the possibility under discussion assumes that a part of the "patient" becomes the analyst.

56. The criticism does not apply to Dewey's own attempts to translate his ideas to the social level. Dewey was *not* a holist, as becomes clear in scrutinizing his social writings. See, for example, John Dewey, *The Public and Its Problems* (Chicago: Swallow Press, 1954). See also Gail Kennedy, "The Process of Evaluation in a Democratic Community," *Journal of Philosophy* 56, no. 6 (March 1959): 253–63.

57. Cf. Lowell Nissen, *John Dewey's Theory of Inquiry and Truth* (The Hague: Mouton, 1966); Israel Scheffler, *Four Pragmatists* (London: Routledge and Kegan Paul, 1974), pp. 204–06, 236–39, 247–55.

58. John Dewey, "Science and the Future of Society," in *Intelligence in the Modern World: John Dewey's Philosophy*, ed. Joseph Ratner (New York: Modern Library, 1939).

59. John Dewey, *The Quest for Certainty* (New York: Minton, Balch, 1929).

60. The work of Feyerabend, Kuhn, Lakatos, and Popper is conveniently juxtaposed in Imre Lakatos and Alan Musgrave, eds., *Criticism and the Growth of Knowledge* (London: Cambridge University Press, 1970). With regard to Laudan and Schwab, see Larry Laudan, *Progress and Its Problems* (Berkeley: University of California Press, 1977); Joseph J. Schwab, "The Teaching of Science as Enquiry," in *The Teaching of Science*, ed. Joseph J. Schwab and Paul F. Brandwein (Cambridge, Mass.: Harvard University Press, 1966).

61. However, in order to show that this is but one side of Dewey, consider the following passage from *The Quest for Certainty:* "If one looks at the course of science, we find a very different story told. Important conclusions of science are those which distinctly refuse to be identified with anything previously known. Instead of having to be proved by being assimilated to the latter, they rather occasion revision of what men thought they previously knew" (pp. 184–85). Yet on the following page Dewey writes: "What has been said does not imply that previous knowledge is not of immense importance in obtaining new knowledge. . . . Inferential inquiry is continuous, one phase passes into the next which uses, tests and expands conclusions already obtained" (p. 186).

Or, to take another pair of examples, again from *The Quest for Certainty:* "The formulation of ideas of experienced objects in terms of measured quantities . . . does not say that this is the way they *must* be thought, the *only* valid way of thinking them" (p. 135, emphasis in original). This seems to accept the notion that conceptual systems determine what we see. Yet in another passage Dewey writes: "If doubt and indeterminateness were wholly within the mind . . . purely mental processes ought to get rid of them. But experimental procedure signifies that actual alternation of an external situation is necessary to effect the conversion. A *situation* undergoes . . . transition from problematic to settled, from internal discontinuity to coherency and organization" (p. 232, emphasis in original). This does not seem to square with the passage immediately preceding, even if the phrase I deleted in the final sentence of the last quote is "through operations directed by thought."

62. Thomas S. Kuhn, *The Essential Tension* (Chicago: University of Chicago Press, 1977), p. 237.

63. I will be using the notion of a hidden curriculum elsewhere, going into greater detail in chapter 6.

64. A similar notion to that of an ill-defined problem is Lindblom's concept of "incrementalism." For example, see David Braybrooke and Charles E. Lindblom, *A Strategy of Decision* (New York: Free Press, 1963).

65. Walter R. Reitman, "Heuristic Decision Procedures, Open Constraints and the Structure of Ill-defined Problems," in *Human Judgments and Optimality*, ed. Maynard W. Shelly and Glenn L. Bryan (New York: John Wiley, 1966), p. 282.

66. Ibid., p. 307.

67. Ibid., p. 303.

68. W. B. Gallie, *Philosophy and the Historical Understanding* (London: Chatto and Windus, 1964), pp. 157–58, emphasis in original.

69. Anthony Hartnett and Michael Naish, *Theory and the Practice of Education*, vol. 1 (London: Heinemann, 1976), pp. 79–82.

70. The distinction between technical, human relations, and educational problems is useful, but not absolute. There *are* borderline cases. Louis Smith has suggested an interesting such case to me in conversation. The superintendent of schools in the district in which the "Kensington" school which he and Keith described—Louis M. Smith and Pat M. Keith, *Anatomy of Educational Innovation* (New York: John Wiley, 1971) — developed a policy handbook. This contained a list of all formal educational decisions in the district. There also existed a formalized procedure for replacing old decisions in the handbook with the ones that supplanted them. This handbook was still in use fifteen years later. It began as a solution to a *technical*, bureaucratic problem of keeping track of decisions. However, according to Smith it has been used extensively as a resource for addressing and clarifying *educational* problems (in my sense of the word). Predictably, because this handbook is partially a solution to a technical problem, its existence has ensured that many educational problems in this district are well-defined ones (at least as they are conceived by the people involved).

71. See Michael D. Cohen, James G. March, and Johan P. Olsen,

"People, Problems, Solutions and the Ambiguity of Relevance," in *Ambiguity and Choice in Organizations,* 2d ed., ed. James G. March and Johan P. Olsen (Bergen: Universitetsforlaget, 1976).

72. An official commission known as the Etzioni Commission, whose task was to examine the status of teachers and their working conditions, recommended drastic changes with regards to this aspect of teacher working arrangements. This occurred during the 1980–81 school year. To a certain extent these recommendations have already been put into effect, and as a result teachers need to spend more time at school. Nevertheless, we are a far cry from the optimal situation where teachers are at school throughout the school day.

73. Cf. Richard L. Daft and Selwyn W. Becker, *The Innovative Organization* (New York: Elsevier North-Holland, 1978), pp. 131–36.

74. Laudan, *Progress and Its Problems,* p. 29.

75. Ibid., p. 107.

76. Ibid., p. 111.

77. This is Donald Schön's argument.

78. Cf. George R. Geiger, "Dewey's Social and Political Philosophy," in *The Philosophy of John Dewey,* ed. Paul A. Schilpp (Evanston, Ill.: Northwestern University Press, 1939), pp. 366–67.

79. Joseph Agassi, "Rationality and the *Tu Quoque* Argument," *Inquiry* 16, (1973): 395–406.

80. Sigmund Freud, "'Wild' Psycho-analysis," *Standard Edition of the Complete Psychological Works of Sigmund Freud*, vol. 11 (London: Hogarth Press, 1957), pp. 225–226, emphasis in original.

81. Strictly speaking, in terms of Freudian theory, raising to preconsciousness must come first. However, as I have stressed, the Freudian metaphor is highly selective in its use of Freud.

82. Freud, "'Wild' Psycho-analysis," p. 227.

83. Even the first Freud is empirically questionable. See Seymour Fisher and Roger P. Greenberg, *The Scientific Credibility of Freud's Theories and Therapy* (New York: Basic Books, 1977).

84. Michael Polanyi, *Personal Knowledge* (London: Routledge and Kegan Paul, 1958).

Chapter 3. Self-Renewal and Open Belief Systems

1. Apart from the works I will be referring to directly, see Barry Barnes, "The Comparison of Belief Systems: Anomaly versus Falsehood," in *Modes of Thought,* ed. Robin Horton and Ruth Finnegan (London: Faber and Faber, 1973); Louis M. Smith and William Geoffrey, *The Complexities of an Urban Classroom* (New York: Holt, Rinehart, and Winston, 1968); Robert E. Lane, *Political Man* (New York: Free Press, 1972); James T. Borhek and Richard F. Curtis, *A Sociology of Belief* (New York: John Wiley, 1975).

2. Milton Rokeach, *The Open and Closed Mind* (New York: Basic Books, 1960).

3. Thomas F. Green, *The Activities of Teaching* (New York: McGraw-Hill, 1971).

4. Ibid., p. 41.

5. Rokeach, *Open and Closed Mind*, p. 34.

6. Ibid., pp. 39–40.

7. Ibid., p. 40.

8. Ibid., p. 42.

9. Ibid., p. 56.

10. Cf. Karl R. Popper, *Conjectures and Refutations* (London: Routledge and Kegan Paul, 1963).

11. Green, *Activities of Teaching*, p. 48.

12. Robert K. Merton, *Social Teaching and Social Structure* (New York: Free Press, 1957), p. 199, emphasis in original.

13. John W. Meyer and Brian Rowan, "The Structure of Educational Environments," in *Environments and Organizations*, ed. Marshall W. Meyer (San Francisco: Jossey-Bass, 1978).

14. John W. Meyer, "The Effects of Education as an Institution," *American Journal of Sociology* 83, no. 1 (July 1977): 55–77.

15. Meyer and Rowan, "Structure of Educational Environments," p. 79.

16. Ibid., p. 91.

17. Meyer, "Effects of Education," p. 66, emphasis in original.

18. The notion of conceiving social actions as a text has become an important strand in social science theory today. This strand is reviewed in Clifford Geertz, "Blurred Genres: The Refiguration of Social Thought," *American Scholar* 49, no. 2 (1980): 165–82. A central book in this tradition is Paul Ricoeur, *Hermeneutics and the Human Sciences* (Cambridge: Cambridge University Press, 1981). I also found helpful Israel Scheffler's "Ritual and Reference," *Synthèse* 46, no. 3 (March 1981): 421–37. A text need not necessarily be related to a dramatic performance. So the notion of social action as text is slightly different from the notion of social action as drama. Nevertheless, there is much similarity between these two ideas. The "social action as drama" approach in the social sciences is presented well in James E. Combs and Michael W. Mansfield, eds., *Drama in Life* (New York: Hastings House, 1976).

19. Charles Perrow, *Complex Organizations* (Glenview, Ill.: Scott, Foresman, 1972), pp. 150–51, emphasis in original.

20. Emile Durkheim, *The Elementary Forms of the Religious Life* (New York: Free Press, 1965).

21. Basil Bernstein, *Class, Codes, and Control*, vol. 3 (London: Routledge and Kegan Paul, 1977); David Bloor, *Knowledge and Social Imagery* (London: Routledge and Kegan Paul, 1976); Mary Douglas, *Purity and Danger* (London: Routledge and Kegan Paul, 1966); Barry Schwartz, *Vertical Classification* (Chicago: University of Chicago Press, 1981).

22. Mary Douglas, *Implicit Meanings* (London: Routledge and Kegan Paul, 1975), p. xx.

23. Durkheim, *Elementary Forms*, pp. 53–54.

24. Ibid., p. 55.

25. Ibid.

26. By rejecting the functionalist answer, Geertz is not rejecting the notion of a function. He is, after all, talking about what art forms *achieve for us*. His new perspective amounts to suggesting new sorts of functions of a semiotic nature, rather than the usual functions invoked by classic functionalism.

27. Clifford Geertz, *The Interpretation of Cultures* (New York: Basic Books, 1973), pp. 443, 444, 448, 450, 453, emphasis added.

28. Sally F. Moore and Barbara G. Myerhoff, eds., *Secular Ritual* (Amsterdam: Van Gorcum, 1977), p. 18, emphasis added.

29. Cf. Madeleine R. Grumet, "In Search of Theatre: Ritual, Confrontation and the Suspense of Form," *Journal of Education* 162, no. 1 (Winter 1980): 93–110.

30. Durkheim, *Elementary Forms*, p. 54.

31. Ibid., p. 351.

32. Plato, *The Republic* (London: J. M. Dent, 1976), p. 208.

33. Francis Bacon, *Novum Organum*, bk. 1, secs. 38–44. There is great irony in the fact that Bacon, who symbolizes the beginning of modern science's overthrow of religion, should have smuggled so religious a posture into his scientific attitude.

34. Some people hold that, in order to be creative in a particular domain, one must first immerse oneself in that domain's tradition. Thus, developing cognitive creativity might be an *indirect* concern of schools which see knowledge manipulation as limited to the initiated. In other words, such schools might claim that their initiating of the students into the "truths" of various disciplines is preparing them to be creative one day (after they leave school perhaps?).

35. One might argue that Plato is an exception. The Socratic dialogues do seem to be based on the idea that Socrates always begins where his companion in a discussion *is*, and thus that Socrates is taking his companion's personal characteristics into account. However, it is difficult to know whether this is just a literary device or whether Plato really was concerned with individual differences. The test would be to examine the Platonic Socrates in a classroom situation (that is, involved in a conversation with many different "pupils") rather than in a dialogue. This we cannot usually do. In many of the dialogues there are more than two characters, but in these, the different characters are usually dealt with serially rather than in a true classroom situation. The closest Plato comes to a classroom is, in my view, in *Phaedo* in the interplay between Socrates, Simmias, and Cebes. However, this still is not close enough to count as "individualized instruction." One thing one can say about Plato — in the analogy of the cave, quoted in note 31, there is no sense of the different

prisoners perhaps being brought up out of the cave *in different ways*. Also, the curriculum he suggests for the education system of his republic is emphatically a compulsory one, with no suggestion that different students of the same class might need to learn different things in different ways.

36. E. R. Cawthron and J. P. Rowell, "Epistemology and Science Education," *Studies in Science Education* 5 (1978): 33.

37. Basil Bernstein, "On the Classification and Framing," *Class, Codes, and Control* 3:88.

38. Ibid., p. 89.

39. Ibid., p. 97.

40. Ibid., pp.97–98, emphasis in original.

41. Basil Bernstein, "Class and Pedagogies: Visible and Invisible," *Class, Codes, and Control* 3:137, 148.

42. Basil Bernstein, "Aspects of the Relations Between Education and Production," *Class, Codes, and Control*, vol. 3.

43. Basil Bernstein, "On the Classification and Framing," *Class, Codes, and Control* 3:96.

44. It is irrelevant here which theory is invoked to explain this real or apparent relationship between scholastic achievement and home background, working-class culture and language, labeling, capitalistic hegemony, and so forth. See Basil Bernstein, *Class, Codes, and Control*, vol. 1 (London: Routledge and Kegan Paul, 1974); Noell Bisseret, *Education, Class Language, and Ideology* (London: Routledge and Kegan Paul, 1979); William Labov, "The Logic of Nonstandard English," *Georgetown Monographs on Language and Linguistics* 22 (1969): 1–22, 26–31.

45. Elliot Aronson et al., *The Jigsaw Classroom* (Beverly Hills, Calif.: Sage, 1978).

46. Horton and Finnegan, eds., *Modes of Thought*, p. 17.

47. Hans R. Jauss, "Literary History as a Challenge to Literary Theory," in *New Directions in Literary Theory*, ed. Ralph Cohen (Baltimore: Johns Hopkins University Press, 1974).

48. I have been greatly influenced by what I regard as the best history of jazz yet written: Martin Williams, *The Jazz Tradition* (New York: Mentor Books, 1971).

49. Claude Lévi-Strauss, *The Raw and the Cooked* (New York: Harper and Row, 1969), p. 12.

50. Jonathan Culler, *The Pursuit of Signs* (Ithaca, N.Y.: Cornell University Press, 1981), p. 33.

51. Imre Lakatos, "Falsification and the Methodology of Scientific Research Programmes" in Imre Lakatos and Alan Musgrave, eds., *Criticism and the Growth of Knowledge* (London: Cambridge University Press, 1970), pp. 154–77.

52. Thomas S. Kuhn, *The Structure of Scientific Revolutions* (Chicago: Chicago University Press, 1962), p. 85.

53. One approach to scientific research which does come quite close to the idea of the jazz metaphor is Alisdair MacIntyre, "Epistemological

Crises, Dramatic Narrative and the Philosophy of Science," *Monist* 60, no. 4 (October 1977): 453–72.

54. Although I do not refer to his work directly, the approach of Murray Edelman is obviously very relevant. See *Political Language: Words That Succeed and Policies That Fail* (New York: Academic Press, 1977).

55. Elmer E. Schattschneider, *The Semisovereign People* (Hinsdale, Ill.: Dryden Press, 1975).

56. Trevor Pateman, *Language, Truth, and Politics,* 2d ed. (Lewes, East Sussex, Eng.: Jean Stroud, 1980).

57. Ibid., p. 122, emphasis in original.

58. Ibid., emphasis in original.

59. Ibid., pp. 124–25.

60. Ibid., p. 131.

61. Claus Mueller, *The Politics of Communication* (New York: Oxford University Press, 1973).

62. Schattschneider, *Semisovereign People,* pp. 60–61, emphasis in original.

63. Cf. Robert Hertz, "The Pre-eminence of the Right Hand: A Study in Religious Polarity," in *Right and Left: Essays on Dual Symbolic Classification,* ed. Rodney Needham (Chicago: Chicago University Press, 1973).

64. Louis M. Smith, John J. Prunty, and David C. Dwyer, "A Longitudinal Nested Systems Model of Innovation and Change in Schooling," in *Organizational Behavior in Schools and School Districts,* ed. Samuel B. Bacharach (New York: Praeger, 1981).

65. For example, Abraham Minkowitz, Dan Davis, and Joseph Bashi, *An Evaluation Study of Israeli Elementary Schools* (Jerusalem: Hebrew University School of Education, 1977).

66. This approach is often associated with Robert A. Dahl; see "The Concept of Power," *Behavioral Science* 2, no. 3 (July 1957): 202–03.

67. Peter Bachrach and Morton S. Baratz, *Power and Poverty* (New York: Oxford University Press, 1970), pp. 3–16, 39–51.

68. See, for example, Everett M. Rogers and F. Floyd Shoemaker, *Communication of Innovations: A Cross-Cultural Approach* (New York: Free Press, 1971).

69. Cf. Sammach Yizhar, *On Education and Education for Values* (Tel Aviv: Am Oved, 1974).

70. Bo Hedberg and Sten A. Jonsson, "Strategy Formulation as a Discontinuous Process," *International Studies of Management and Organization* 7, no. 2 (Summer 1977): 100.

71. Cf. Benjamin L. Whorf, *Language, Thought, and Reality* (Cambridge, Mass.: MIT Press, 1956).

72. Louis M. Smith and Pat M. Keith, *Anatomy of Educational Innovation* (New York: John Wiley, 1971).

73. Charles Perrow, "Three Types of Effectiveness Studies" in *New*

Perspectives on Organizational Effectiveness, ed. Paul S. Goodman and Johannes M. Pennings (San Francisco: Jossey-Bass, 1977), pp. 99–100.

74. David Gordon and Walter Ackerman, "The Mechanech: Role Function and Myth in Israeli Secondary Schools," *Comparative Education Review* 28, no. 1 (Feb. 1984): 105–15.

75. These were reproduced in an expanded form in Yizhar, *On Education.*

76. Israel Scheffler, "In Praise of the Cognitive Emotions," *Teachers College Record* 79, no. 2 (Dec. 1977): 171–86.

Chapter 4. Self-Renewal and the Structure of Educational Systems

1. Jeffrey Pfeffer and Gerald R. Salancik, *The External Control of Organizations* (New York: Harper and Row, 1978).

2. Cf. Robert Dreeben, *The Nature of Teaching* (Glenview, Ill.: Scott, Foresman, 1970), pp. 6–40; Myron Lieberman, *Education as a Profession* (Englewood Cliffs, N.J.: Prentice-Hall, 1964).

3. See Jonathan Gathorne-Hardy, *The Public School Phenomenon* (Harmondsworth, Middlesex: Penguin Books, 1979), pp. 110–11.

4. Karl E. Weick, "Educational Organizations as Loosely Coupled Systems," *Administrative Science Quarterly* 21, no. 1 (March 1976): 1–19; Dreeben, *Nature of Teaching;* Dan Lortie, *Schoolteacher: A Sociological Study* (Chicago: University of Chicago Press, 1975).

5. John W. Meyer, and Brian Rowan, "The Structure of Educational Environments," in *Environments and Organizations,* ed. Marshall W. Meyer (San Francisco: Jossey-Bass, 1978).

6. Weick, "Educational Organizations."

7. Michael D. Cohen, James G. March, and Johan P. Olsen, "People, Problems, Solutions and the Ambiguity of Relevance," in *Ambiguity and Choice in Organizations,* 2d ed., ed. James G. March and Johan P. Olsen (Bergen: Universitetsforlaget, 1976).

8. Lortie, *Schoolteacher,* pp. 13–17.

9. Dreeben, *Nature of Teaching,* pp. 45–48.

10. Cf. David Gordon, "Teacher Training and Ostriches," in *Educational Administration and Policy Making,* ed. Ephraim Ben-Baruch and Yoram Neumann (Herzlia, Israel: Unipress, 1982).

11. Dreeben, *Nature of Teaching,* p. 163.

12. Lortie, *Schoolteacher,* p. 30.

13. Ibid., p. 216.

14. Ibid., p. 217.

15. Ibid., p. 219.

16. Charles Perrow, *Complex Organizations* (Glenview, Ill.: Scott, Foresman, 1972).

17. Cf. Alfred Schutz, "Equality and the Meaning Structure of the Social World," *Collected Papers II: Studies in Social Theory* (The Hague:

Martinus Nijhoff, 1964); Harold Garfinkel, *Studies in Ethnomethodology* (Englewood Cliffs, N.J.: Prentice-Hall, 1967); Erving Goffman, *Behavior in Public Places* (New York: Free Press, 1963).

18. Cf. Mario Fantini and Marilyn Gittell, *Decentralization: Achieving Reform* (New York: Praeger, 1973).

19. Cf. Michael B. Katz, *Class, Bureaucracy, and Schools* (New York: Praeger, 1971).

20. Cf. John W. Tuthill, "The Repeal of Parkinson's Law," *Intellectual Digest* 3 (April 1973): 34–35.

21. Donald P. Warwick, *A Theory of Public Bureaucracy* (Cambridge, Mass.: Harvard University Press, 1975), pp. 155–56.

22. Again, although he is not quoted directly, Murray Edelman's analysis of political language is directly relevant to all I have written in this section; *Political Language: Words That Succeed and Policies That Fail* (New York: Academic Press, 1977).

23. Robert Dreeben, "The School as a Workplace," in *Second Handbook of Research on Teaching*, ed. Robert M. W. Travers (Chicago: Rand McNally, 1973), p. 468.

24. Basil Bernstein, "On the Classification and Framing of Educational Knowledge," *Class, Codes, and Control* (London: Routledge and Kegan Paul, 1977), vol. 3. Bernstein's point is clear when considering interdisciplinary team teaching. This contradicts strong classification by definition. However, what about teachers from the same discipline working together? Logically, this does not contradict strong classification, although, as a matter of fact, this type of team teaching rarely occurs in collection codes.

25. Weick, "Educational Organizations," p. 3.

26. Ostensibly, conceiving of educational organizations as loosely coupled contradicts the point made in chapter 3, that means and ends are tightly coupled in schools. However, in chapter 3 I was referring to the tight coupling of means and ends at the level of espoused theory, whereas here we are more concerned with the level of theory-in-use.

27. Dreeben, *Nature of Teaching*, p. 52.

28. Cf. Judson T. Shaplin and Henry F. Olds, eds., *Team Teaching* (New York: Harper and Row, 1964).

29. Dreeben, "School as a Workplace," p. 464.

30. Ibid.

31. Lortie, *Schoolteacher*, p. 16.

32. Weick, "Educational Organizations."

33. In actual fact, Weick lists more positive functions of loose coupling than those I mention, and also for each positive function he points to a parallel dysfunction. However, this list is not completely satisfactory because Weick uses the words "function" and "dysfunction" loosely. In certain cases he is simply pointing out a positive benefit (or negative consequence, in the case of a dysfunction) in terms of the running of the organization. In others, he is pointing out a consequence that is positive or

negative in terms of a value system. In yet other cases he is referring to function in the narrower and, for us, more important sense of a consequence, which sets in motion certain forces that press toward maintaining the system as a loosely coupled, stable one. Of the seven functions he mentions, five are of this latter sort, and these are the ones I list in the text. Of the seven dysfunctions mentioned, only one is a "real" dysfunction, that is, a consequence which sets in motion certain forces which tend to destroy or disrupt the working of the system. This is Weick's fifth dysfunction— loosely coupled systems will repair defective subsystems less efficiently than tightly coupled systems.

34. Cf. Aharon F. Kleinberger, *Society, Schools, and Progress in Israel* (Oxford: Pergamon Press, 1969).

35. The material in this section was originally presented in slightly different form as part of David Pur and David Gordon, "Conservatism and Centralization in School Systems—The Case of the Israeli High Schools," in *Educational Administration and Policy Making,* ed. Ben-Baruch and Neumann. At the time this section was written, Pur was chair of the Pedagogic Secretariat of the Israeli Ministry of Education and Culture.

36. In one sense, the trend system still exists because the State Education Law does distinguish between religious and secular schools and also between schools for Hebrew-speaking and non–Hebrew-speaking students. However, the majority of studies in the curriculum of these various types of schools are common to all of them. Also the officials responsible for these different schools all belong to the same ministry of education and culture.

37. Jerome S. Bruner, *The Process of Education* (New York: Vintage Books, 1963).

38. John Holt, *How Children Fail* (New York: Pitman, 1964); Herbert R. Kohl, *The Open Classroom* (New York: New York Review Book, 1969); Jonathan Kozol, *Death at an Early Age* (Boston: Houghton Mifflin, 1967).

39. *Director General's Circular,* Special Circular A: The Secondary School (Jerusalem: Ministry of Education and Culture, August/September 1976).

40. I should stress that these were not suggestions made by our staff, but rather the principals themselves.

41. Cf. Shimon Reshef, *The Labor Movement School System in Pre-State Israel* (Tel Aviv: Hakibbutz HaMeuchad Press, 1980).

42. Philip J. Runkel et al., *Transforming the School's Capacity for Problem Solving* (Eugene: Center for Educational Policy and Management, University of Oregon, 1979), p. 4.

43. Ibid.

44. Daniel Katz and Robert L. Kahn, *The Social Psychology of Organizations* (New York: John Wiley, 1966).

45. Pfeffer and Salancik, *External Control of Organizations,* p. 6.

46. Ibid.

Chapter 5. Of Mice and Men: The Selling of Change

1. John I. Goodlad, *The Dynamics of Educational Change* (New York: McGraw-Hill, 1975), pp. 126–34.
2. Ibid., pp. 154–55.
3. Ibid., p. 155.
4. Cf. George Lakoff and Mark Johnson, *Metaphors We Live By* (Chicago: University of Chicago Press, 1980).
5. Janet Malcolm, *Psychoanalysis: The Impossible Profession* (New York: Knopf, 1982).
6. Sigmund Freud, "Analysis Terminable and Interminable," in *The Standard Edition of the Complete Psychological Works of Sigmund Freud*, vol. 23 (London: Hogarth Press, 1964), p. 217.
7. Brian Bird, "Notes on Transference: Universal Phenomenon and Hardest Part of Analysis," *Journal of the American Psychoanalytic Association* 20, no. 2 (April 1972): 285–86.
8. Basil Bernstein, "On the Classification and Framing of Educational Knowledge," *Class, Codes, and Control* (London: Routledge and Kegan Paul, 1977), 3:97.
9. Cf. Benjamin Bloom, "Innocence in Education," *School Review* 80, no. 3 (May 1972): 343.
10. On redundancy, see Wendell R. Garner, *Uncertainty and Structure as Psychological Constructs* (New York: John Wiley, 1962).
11. In certain subjects students are tracked. This is the reason for the large number of teachers involved with one class.
12. During the third year of the project, this encouragement of self-evaluatory components within school activities should have been the task of the school's internal evaluator (see chapter 1). Unfortunately, the person chosen by this school as evaluator was totally unsuitable, did not take her role seriously, and, at the end of the year she was fired.
13. Chris Argyris, *Reasoning, Learning and Action* (San Francisco: Jossey-Bass, 1982).
14. Laurence Kohlberg, *The Philosophy of Moral Development* (New York: Harper and Row, 1981).
15. Cf. Else Frenkel-Brunswick, "Intolerance of Ambiguity as an Emotional and Perceptual Personality Variable," *Journal of Personality* 18 (1949): 108–43.
16. Mary M. Bentzen, *Changing Schools: The Magic Feather Principle* (New York: McGraw-Hill, 1974), pp. 92–104.
17. Malcolm, *Psychoanalysis*, p. 38.
18. Charles Brenner, "Working Alliance, Therapeutic Alliance and Transference," *Journal of the American Psychoanalytic Association* 27, supplement (1979): 46–47.
19. Egon G. Guba and Yvonne S. Lincoln, *Effective Evaluation* (San Francisco: Jossey-Bass, 1981), p. 55.
20. Ibid., p.74.

21. Clifford Geertz, *The Interpretation of Cultures* (New York: Basic Books, 1973), p. 7.

22. Ibid., p. 10.

23. Ibid., p. 13, emphasis added.

24. Aaron Wildavsky, "The Self-Evaluating Organization," *Public Administration Review* 32, no. 5 (September/October 1972): 511.

25. Ibid., p. 510.

26. Ibid., p. 513.

27. Ibid., p. 514.

28. Ibid., p. 517.

29. Ibid., p. 513.

30. Ibid., p. 515.

31. Ibid., p. 517.

32. David Hamilton et al., eds., *Beyond the Numbers Game* (New York: Macmillan, 1977).

33. Guba and Lincoln, *Effective Evaluation*, p. 55.

34. Ibid., p. 58.

35. Ibid., pp. 70–71.

36. "America's Schools: Public and Private," *Daedalus* 110 (Summer 1981); "America's Schools: Portraits and Perspectives," *Daedalus* 110 (Fall 1981).

37. Three observers with naturalistic orientations were asked to visit a number of schools and then write portraits of them. The portraits, by Sara L. Lightfoot, Philip W. Jackson, and Robert Coles, consist of seven articles, and constitute the major portion of the second issue of *Daedalus* devoted to the schools: "America's Schools: Portraits and Perspectives," pp. 17–143.

38. Michael Rutter et al., *Fifteen Thousand Hours* (Cambridge, Mass.: Harvard University Press, 1979).

39. Elizabeth Vallance, "The Hidden Curriculum and Qualitative Inquiry as States of Mind," *Journal of Education* 162, no. 1 (Winter 1980): 138.

40. Erving Goffman, *The Presentation of Self in Everyday Life* (Garden City, N.Y.: Doubleday, 1959).

Chapter 6. The Future of Planned Change in Educational Systems

1. See, for example: Sharon Feiman, ed., *Teacher Centers: What Place in Education?* (Chicago: Center for Policy Study, University of Chicago, 1978).

2. Cf. Maida A. Broadbent, *School/Institution Collaboration: Issues and Concerns* (Boston: College and University Co-Ordinators, The Cultural Education Collaborative, Tri-Lateral Council for Quality Education, Inc., 1980).

3. Since this passage was written, the Israeli Ministry of Education and Culture has run into considerable difficulties in funding this institute. In effect, the whole idea has been put in cold storage. Only two sections of

the institute are functioning, as independent units, and there seems to be no chance of this situation changing in the near future. Nevertheless, I present the idea of the institute here, because the purpose of this section is to *illustrate* the *notion* of collaboration.

4. Cf. John Elliot and Clem Adelman, "Teacher Education for Curriculum Reform. An Interim Report on the Work of the Ford Teaching Project," *British Journal of Teacher Education* 1, no. 1 (January 1975): 105–14.

5. Michael Fullan has reviewed some examples. See *The Meaning of Educational Change* (New York: Teachers College Press, 1982), pp. 180–92.

6. Clark N. Fisher, cited in Broadbent, *School/Institution Collaboration.*

7. Ibid., p. 10.

8. John I. Goodlad, "Networking and Educational Improvement: Reflections on a Strategy," Unpublished, 1977, p. 33, emphasis added.

9. John I. Goodlad, *The Dynamics of Educational Change* (New York: McGraw-Hill, 1975), pp. 163–65, 201–22.

10. Goodlad, "Networking and Educational Improvement," p. 45.

11. Ibid., p. 8.

12. Ibid., p. 11.

13. Paul Berman and Milbrey W. McLaughlin, "Implementation of Educational Innovation," *Educational Forum* 40, no. 3 (March 1976): 352–53.

14. Goodlad, *Dynamics of Educational Change*, p. 163, emphasis added.

15. Goodlad is well aware of the problems associated with the "hub" being self-renewing. He writes of the dangers of *cooption* of the hub.

16. See, for example, Robert F. Peck and James A. Tucker, "Research on Teacher Education," in *Second Handbook of Research on Teaching*, ed. Robert M. W. Travers (Chicago: Rand McNally, 1973).

17. See David Gordon, "Teacher Training Institutions and Schools: A Case of Limited Cooperation," in *Cooperation in Education*, ed. Shlomo Sharan et al., (Provo, Utah: Brigham Young University Press, 1980).

18. Ibid., p. 330.

19. Charles E. Lindblom and David K. Cohen, *Usable Knowledge* (New Haven, Conn.: Yale University Press, 1979), pp. 40–53.

20. John Wilson, *Educational Theory and the Preparation of Teachers* (Windsor, Berks.: NFER Publishing Co., 1975).

21. See David Gordon, "Theory and the Teacher's Perspective," *Journal of Philosophy of Education* 14, no. 1 (June 1980): 31–38.

22. Lindblom and Cohen, *Usable Knowledge*, pp. 10–29.

23. It may be that a move from the scientific to the naturalistic paradigm of inquiry will change this state of affairs. Naturalistic inquiry, because it is expansive rather than reductive is likely to be more interdisciplinary in orientation than scientific inquiry, and this undermines collection codes, by definition.

24. Samuel Bowles and Herbert Gintis, *Schooling in Capitalist America* (New York: Basic Books, 1976).

25. Michael W. Apple, "The Other Side of the Hidden Curriculum: Correspondence and the Labor Process," *Journal of Education* 162, no. 1 (Winter 1980): 47–66; Paul Willis, *Learning to Labor* (New York: Columbia University Press, 1981).

26. Michael D. Cohen, James G. March, and Johan P. Olsen, "People, Problems, Solutions, and the Ambiguity of Relevance," in *Ambiguity and Choice in Organizations*, 2d ed., ed. James G. March and Johan P. Olsen (Bergen: Universitetsforlaget, 1976); Karl E. Weick, "Educational Organizations as Loosely Coupled Systems," *Administrative Science Quarterly* 21, no. 1 (March 1976): 1–19.

27. Lindblom and Cohen, *Usable Knowledge*, p. 20.

28. Ibid., p. 33.

29. Claude Lévi Strauss, *The Raw and the Cooked* (New York: Harper and Row, 1969), p. 12.

30. Philip W. Jackson, *Life in Classrooms* (New York: Holt, Rinehart and Winston, 1968).

31. For example, see David Gordon, "The Aesthetic Attitude and the Hidden Curriculum," *Journal of Aesthetic Education* 15, no. 2 (April 1981): 51–64; "The Immorality of the Hidden Curriculum," *Journal of Moral Education* 10, no. 1 (1981): 3–8.

32. Jane R. Martin, "What Should We Do with a Hidden Curriculum When We Find One?" *Curriculum Inquiry* 6, no. 2 (1976): 135–51.

33. Martin's similar definition appears on p. 144, "What Should We Do?"

34. Benjamin Bloom, "Innocence in Education," *School Review* 80, no. 3 (May 1972), p. 343.

35. Is not a hidden curriculum of which the teachers are aware a contradiction in terms? Not quite, for two reasons. First the definition of the hidden curriculum I have been using allows teachers to be aware of their hidden curricula provided the latter are not acknowleded to the learners. Second, one must distinguish between being aware of the hidden significance of an action *while* performing it, and *before and after* its performance. I have argued elsewhere that teachers can be aware of the hidden curricula associated with certain actions before performing them, and thus can take these curricula into account in planning future action. However, *while performing these actions* it is impossible to devote attention to hidden curricula. See David Gordon, "The Concept of the Hidden Curriculum," *Journal of Philosophy of Education* 16, no. 2 (1982): 187–98.

Appendix A.

1. The opposite is also not true. They did not deliberately choose schools without problems!

Appendix B

1. Chris Argyris and Donald A. Schön, *Organizational Learning: A Theory of Action Perspective* (Reading, Mass.: Addison-Wesley, 1978), pp. 142–43.

2. Chris Argyris, "How Learning and Reasoning Processes Affect Change," in *Change in Organizations*, ed. Paul S. Goodman (San Francisco: Jossey-Bass, 1982), p. 50.

3. Ibid., p. 49.

Bibliography

Agassi, Joseph. "Rationality and the *Tu Quoque* Argument." *Inquiry* 16 (1973): 395–406.

"America's Schools: Portraits and Perspectives." *Daedalus* 110, special issue (Fall 1981).

"America's Schools: Public and Private." *Daedalus* 110, special issue (Summer 1981).

Apple, Michael W. "The Other Side of the Hidden Curriculum: Correspondence Theories and the Labor Process." *Journal of Education* 162, no. 1 (Winter 1980): 47–66.

Argyris, Chris. "How Learning and Reasoning Processes Affect Change." In *Change in Organizations*, ed. Paul S. Goodman. San Francisco: Jossey-Bass, 1982.

———. *Reasoning, Learning and Action.* San Francisco: Jossey-Bass, 1982.

Argyris, Chris, and Donald A. Schön. *Organizational Learning: A Theory of Action Perspective.* Reading, Mass.: Addison-Wesley, 1978.

Aronson, Elliot, et al. *The Jigsaw Classroom.* Beverly Hills, Calif.: Sage, 1978.

Bachrach, Peter, and Morton S. Baratz. *Power and Poverty.* New York: Oxford University Press, 1970.

Bacon, Sir Francis. *Novum Organum*, book 1.

Barnes, Barry. "The Comparison of Belief Systems: Anomaly versus Falsehood." In *Modes of Thought*, ed. Robin Horton and Ruth Finnegan. London: Faber and Faber, 1973.

Bateson, Gregory. "Minimal Requirements for a Theory of Schizophrenia." In *Steps to an Ecology of Mind.* New York: Ballantine Books, 1972.

———. "Social Planning and the Concept of Deutero-Learning." In *Steps to an Ecology of Mind.* New York: Ballantine Books, 1972.

Benne, Kenneth D. "Deliberate Changing as the Facilitation of Growth." In *The Planning of Change*, ed. Warren G. Bennis, Kenneth D. Beene, and Robert Chin. New York: Holt, Rinehart and Winston, 1964.

Bentzen, Mary M. *Changing Schools: The Magic Feather Principle.* New York: McGraw-Hill, 1974.

Berman, Paul, and Milbrey W. McLaughlin. "Implementation of Educational Innovation." *Educational Forum* 40, no. 3 (March 1976): 345–70.

Bernstein, Basil. "Aspects of the Relations Between Education and Production." In *Class, Codes and Control,* vol. 3. London: Routledge and Kegan Paul, 1977.

———. "Class and Pedagogies: Visible and Invisible." In *Class, Codes and Control,* vol. 3. London: Routledge and Kegan Paul, 1977.

———. *Class, Codes and Control,* vols. 1, 3. London: Routledge and Kegan Paul, 1974, 1977.

———. "On the Classification and Framing of Educational Knowledge." In *Class, Codes and Control,* vol. 3. London: Routledge and Kegan Paul, 1977.

Bird, Brian. "Notes on Transference: Universal Phenomenon and Hardest Part of Analysis." *Journal of the American Psychoanalytic Association* 20, no. 2 (April 1972): 267–301.

Bisseret, Noell. *Education, Class Language, and Ideology.* London: Routledge and Kegan Paul, 1979.

Bloom, Benjamin. "Innocence in Education." *School Review* 80, no. 3 (May 1972): 333–52.

Bloor, David. *Knowledge and Social Imagery.* London: Routledge and Kegan Paul, 1976.

Blum, Harold P. "The Curative and Creative Aspects of Insight." *Journal of the American Psychoanalytic Association* 27, supplement (1979): 41–70.

Borhek, James T., and Richard F. Curtis. *A Sociology of Belief.* New York: John Wiley, 1975.

Bowles, Samuel, and Herbert Gintis. *Schooling in Capitalist America.* New York: Basic Books, 1976.

Braybrooke, David, and Charles E. Lindblom. *A Strategy of Decision.* New York: Free Press, 1963.

Brenner, Charles. "Working Alliance, Therapeutic Alliance and Transference." *Journal of the American Psychoanalytic Association* 27, supplement (1979): 137–57.

Broadbent, Maida A. *School/Institution Collaboration Issues and Concerns.* Boston: College and University Co-Ordinators, The Cultural Education Collaborative, Tri-Lateral Council for Quality Education, 1980.

Brookover, Wilbur B. *School Social Systems and Student Achievement: Schools Can Make a Difference.* New York: Praeger, 1979.

Bruner, Jerome S. *The Process of Education.* New York: Vintage Books, 1963.

Carlson, Richard O. et al. *Change Processes in the Public Schools.* Eugene: Center for the Advanced Study of Educational Administration, University of Oregon, 1965.

Cawthron, E. R., and J. P. Rowell. "Epistemology and Science Education." *Studies in Science Education* 5 (1978): 31–59.

Center for Educational Research and Innovation (CERI). *Case Studies of Educational Innovation,* vols. 1–4. Paris: OECD, 1973.

Chin, Robert, and Kenneth D. Benne. "General Strategies For Effecting Changes in Human Systems." In *The Planning of Change,* 2d ed., ed.

Warren G. Bennis, Kenneth D. Benne, and Robert Chin. New York: Holt, Rinehart and Winston, 1969.

Clark, Burton R. "The Organizational Saga in Higher Education." *Administrative Science Quarterly* 17, no. 2 (June 1972): 178–84.

Cohen, Michael D., James G. March, and Johan P. Olsen. "People, Problems, Solutions, and the Ambiguity of Relevance." In *Ambiguity and Choice in Organizations*, ed. James G. March and Johan P. Olsen. 2d ed. Bergen: Universtetsforlaget, 1976.

Combs, James E., and Michael W. Mansfield, eds. *Drama in Life*. New York: Hastings House, 1976.

Culler, Jonathan. *The Pursuit of Signs*. Ithaca, N.Y.: Cornell University Press, 1981.

Daft, Richard L., and Selwyn W. Becker. *The Innovative Organization*. New York: Elsevier North-Holland, 1978.

Dahl, Robert A. "The Concept of Power." *Behavioral Science* 2, no. 3 (July 1957): 201–05.

Dewey, John. "An Analysis of Reflective Thought." *Journal of Philosophy* 19, no. 2 (1922): 29–38.

———. *Democracy and Education*. New York: Macmillan, 1964.

———. *Human Nature and Conduct*. New York: Modern Library, 1930.

———. *The Influence of Darwin on Philosophy*. New York: Henry Holt, 1910.

———. *Logic: the Theory of Inquiry*. New York: Henry Holt, 1930.

———. *The Middle Works*, vol. 6. Carbondale: Southern Illinois University Press, 1978.

———. *The Public and Its Problems*. Chicago: Swallow Press, 1954.

———. *The Quest for Certainty*. New York: Minton, Balch, 1929.

———. "Science and the Future of Society." In *Intelligence in the Modern World: John Dewey's Philosophy*, ed. Joseph Ratner. New York: Modern Library, 1939.

Director General's Circular. Special Circular A: The Secondary School. Jerusalem: Ministry of Education and Culture, August/September 1976 (in Hebrew).

Douglas, Mary. *Implicit Meanings*. London: Routledge and Kegan Paul, 1975.

———. *Purity and Danger*. London: Routledge and Kegan Paul, 1966.

Dreeben, Robert. *The Nature of Teaching*. Glenview, Ill.: Scott, Foresman, 1970.

———. "The School as a Workplace." In *Second Handbook of Research on Teaching*, ed. Robert M. W. Travers. Chicago: Rand McNally, 1973.

Durkheim, Emile. *The Elementary Forms of the Religious Life*. New York: Free Press, 1965.

Edelman, Murray. *Political Language: Words That Succeed and Policies That Fail*. New York: Academic Press, 1977.

Eden, Shevach. *Implementation of Innovations in Education*. Tel Aviv: Ma'alot, 1977 (in Hebrew).

Eggleston, John. "School-based Curriculum Development in England and

Wales." In *School-Based Curriculum Development*, CERI. Paris: OECD, 1979.

Elliot, John, and Clem Adelman. "Teacher Education for Curriculum: An Interim Report on the Work of the Ford Teaching Project." *British Journal of Teacher Education* 1, no. 1 (January 1975): 105–14.

Fantini, Mario, and Marilyn Gittell. *Decentralization: Achieving Reform.* New York: Praeger, 1973.

Feiman, Sharon, ed., *Teacher Centers: What Place in Education?* Chicago: Center for Policy Study, University of Chicago, 1978.

Fisher, Seymour, and Roger P. Greenberg. *The Scientific Credibility of Freud's Theories and Therapy.* New York: Basic Books, 1977.

Flew, Antony. "Psycho-Analytic Explanation." In *Philosophy and Analysis*, ed. Margaret McDonald. Oxford: Blackwell, 1954.

Frenkel-Brunswick, Else. "Intolerance of Ambiguity as an Emotional and Perceptual Personality Variable." *Journal of Personality* 18 (1949): 108–43.

Freud, Sigmund. "Analysis Terminable and Interminable." In *The Standard Edition of the Complete Psychological Works of Sigmund Freud*, vol. 23. London: Hogarth Press, 1964.

———. *Collected Papers*, vols. 2, 4. London: Hogarth Press, 1924, 1925.

———. "'Wild' Psycho-analysis." In *The Standard Edition of the Complete Psychological Works of Sigmund Freud*, vol. 11. London: Hogarth Press, 1957.

Fullan, Michael. *The Meaning of Educational Change.* New York: Teachers College Press, 1982.

Gallie, W. B. *Philosophy and the Historical Understanding.* London: Chatto and Windus, 1964.

Garfinkel, Harold. *Studies in Ethnomethodology.* Englewood Cliffs, N.J.: Prentice-Hall, 1967.

Garner, Wendell R. *Uncertainty and Structure as Psychological Constructs.* New York: John Wiley, 1962.

Gathorne-Hardy, Jonathan. *The Public School Phenomenon.* Harmondsworth, Middlesex: Penguin, 1979.

Geertz, Clifford. "Blurred Genres: The Refiguration of Social Thought." *American Scholar* 49, no. 2 (1980): 165–82.

———. *The Interpretation of Cultures.* New York: Basic Books, 1973.

Geiger, George R. "Dewey's Social and Political Philosophy." In *The Philosophy of John Dewey*, ed. Paul A. Schilpp. Evanston, Ill.: Northwestern University, 1939.

Gellner, Ernest A. "Explanations in History." In *Modes of Individualism and Collectivism*, ed. John O'Neill. London: Heinemann, 1973.

Goffman, Erving. *Behavior in Public Places.* New York: Free Press, 1963.

———. *The Presentation of Self in Everyday Life.* Garden City, N.Y.: Doubleday, 1959.

Goldstein, Kenneth M., and Sheldon Blackman. *Cognitive Style.* New York: John Wiley, 1978.

Goodlad, John I. *The Dynamics of Educational Change*. New York: McGraw-Hill, 1975.

————. "Networking and Educational Improvement: Reflections on a Strategy." Unpublished, 1977.

Gordon, David. "The Aesthetic Attitude and the Hidden Curriculum." *Journal of Aesthetic Education* 15, no. 2 (April 1981): 51–64.

————. "The Concept of the Hidden Curriculum." *Journal of Philosophy of Education* 16, no. 2 (1982): 187–98.

————. "The Immorality of the Hidden Curriculum." *Journal of Moral Education* 10, no. 1 (1981): 3–8.

————. "Teacher Training and Ostriches." In *Educational Administration and Policy Making*, ed. Ephraim Ben-Baruch and Yoram Neumann. Herzlia, Israel: Unipress, 1982.

————. "Teacher Training Institutions and Schools: A Case of Limited Cooperation." In *Cooperation in Education*, ed. Shlomo Sharan et al. Provo, Utah: Brigham Young University Press, 1980.

————. "Theory and the Teacher's Perspective." *Journal of Philosophy of Education* 14, no. 1 (June 1980): 31–38.

Gordon, David, and Walter Ackerman. "The Mechanech: Role Function and Myth in Israeli Secondary Schools." *Comparative Education Review* 28, no. 1 (February 1984): 105–15.

Green, Thomas F. *The Activities of Teaching*. New York: McGraw-Hill, 1971.

Greenfield, Thomas B. "The Man Who Comes Back Through the Door in the Wall: Discovering Truth, Discovering Self, Discovering Organizations." *Educational Administration Quarterly* 16, no. 3 (Fall 1980): 26–59.

————. "Organization Theory as Ideology." *Curriculum Inquiry* 9, no. 2 (1979): 97–112.

————. "Organizations as Social Inventions: Rethinking Assumptions About Change." *Journal of Applied Behavioral Science* 9, no. 5 (September/October 1973): 551–74.

————. "Reflections on Organizational Theory and the Truths of Irreconcilable Realities." *Educational Administration Quarterly* 14, no. 2 (Spring 1978): 1–23.

Gross, Neal, Joseph B. Giacquinta, and Marilyn Bernstein. *Implementing Organizational Innovations: A Sociological Analysis of Planned Educational Change*. New York: Basic Books, 1971.

Grumet, Madelaine R. "In Search of Theatre: Ritual, Confrontation, and the Suspense of Form." *Journal of Education* 162, no. 1 (Winter 1980): 93–110.

Guba, Egon G., and Yvonne S. Lincoln. *Effective Evaluation*. San Francisco: Jossey-Bass, 1981.

Hage, Jerald, and Michael Aiken. *Social Change in Complex Organizations*. New York: Random House, 1970.

Hamilton, David et al., eds. *Beyond the Numbers Game*. Basingstoke:

Macmillan, 1977.

Hartnett, Anthony, and Michael Naish. *Theory and the Practice of Education,* vol. 1. London: Heinemann, 1976.

Havelock, Ronald G. *The Change Agent's Guide to Innovation in Education.* Englewood Cliffs, N.J.: Educational Technology Publications, 1973.

Hedberg, Bo, and Sten A. Jonsson. "Strategy Formulation as a Discontinuous Process." *International Studies of Management and Organization* 7, no. 2 (Summer 1977): 88–109.

Heirs, Ben, and Gordon Pehrson. *The Mind of the Organization.* New York: Harper and Row, 1977.

Hertz, Robert. "The Pre-eminence of the Right Hand: A Study in Religious Polarity." In *Right and Left: Essays on Dual Symbolic Classification,* ed. Rodney Needham. Chicago: Chicago University Press, 1973.

Hofstadter, Richard. *Social Darwinism in American Thought.* Boston: Beacon Press, 1955.

Holt, John. *How Children Fail.* New York: Pitman, 1964.

House, Ernest R. *The Politics of Educational Innovation.* Berkeley, Calif.: McCutchan, 1974.

Jackson, Philip W. *Life in Classrooms.* New York: Holt, Rinehart and Winston, 1968.

Jauss, Hans R. "Literary History as a Challenge to Literary Theory." In *New Directions in Literary Theory,* ed. Ralph Cohen. Baltimore: Johns Hopkins University Press, 1974.

Johnson, Mark, ed., *Philosophical Perspectives on Metaphor.* Minneapolis: University of Minnesota Press, 1981.

Katz, Daniel, and Robert L. Kahn. *The Social Psychology of Organizations.* New York: John Wiley, 1966.

Katz, Michael B. *Class, Bureaucracy and Schools.* New York: Praeger, 1971.

Kennedy, Gail. "The Process of Evaluation in a Democratic Community." *Journal of Philosophy* 56, no. 6 (March 1959): 253–63.

Kleinberger, Aharon F. *Society, Schools and Progress in Israel.* Oxford: Pergamon Press, 1969.

Kohl, Herbert R. *The Open Classroom.* New York: New York Review Book, 1969.

Kohlberg, Laurence. *The Philosophy of Moral Development.* San Francisco: Harper and Row, 1981.

Kozol, Jonathan. *Death at an Early Age.* Boston: Houghton Mifflin, 1967.

Kuhn, Thomas S. *The Essential Tension.* Chicago: University of Chicago Press, 1977.

———. *The Structure of Scientific Revolutions.* Chicago: Chicago University Press, 1962.

Labov, William. "The Logic of Nonstandard English." *Georgetown Monographs on Language and Linguistics* 22 (1969): 1–22, 26–31.

Lakatos, Imre. "Falsification and the Methodology of Scientific Research

Programmes." In *Criticism and the Growth of Knowledge,* ed. Imre Lakatos and Alan Musgrave. London: Cambridge University Press, 1970.

Lakatos, Imre, and Alan Musgrave. *Criticism and the Growth of Knowledge*. London: Cambridge University Press, 1970.

Lakoff, George, and Mark Johnson. *Metaphors We Live By*. Chicago: University of Chicago Press, 1980.

Lane, Robert E. *Political Man*. New York: Free Press, 1972.

Laudan, Larry. *Progress and Its Problems*. Berkeley: University of California Press, 1977.

Lévi-Strauss, Claude. *The Raw and the Cooked*. New York: Harper and Row, 1969.

Lieberman, Myron. *Education as a Profession*. Englewood Cliffs, N.J.: Prentice-Hall, 1964.

Lindblom, Charles E., and David K. Cohen. *Usable Knowledge*. New Haven, Conn.: Yale University Press, 1979.

Lippitt, Ronald, Jeanne Watson, and Bruce Westley. *The Dynamics of Planned Change*. New York: Harcourt, Brace and World, 1958.

Lortie, Dan. *Schoolteacher: A Sociological Study*. Chicago: University of Chicago Press, 1975.

MacIntyre, Alisdair C. "Epistemological Crises, Dramatic Narrative, and the Philosophy of Science." *Monist* 60, no. 4 (October 1977): 453–72.

———. *The Unconscious*. Atlantic Highlands, N.J.: Humanities Press, 1958.

Malcolm, Janet. *Psychoanalysis: The Impossible Profession*. New York: Knopf, 1982.

Martin, Jane R. "What Should We Do with a Hidden Curriculum When We Find One?" *Curriculum Inquiry* 6, no. 2 (1976): 135–51.

Mayhew, Katherine C., and Anna C. Edwards. *The Dewey School*. New York: Atherton Press, 1966.

Merton, Robert K. *Social Theory and Social Structure*. New York: Free Press, 1957.

Meyer, John W. "The Effects of Education as an Institution." *American Journal of Sociology* 83, no. 1 (July 1977): 55–77.

Meyer, John W., and Brian Rowan. "The Structure of Educational Environments." In *Environments and Organizations*, ed. Marshall W. Meyer. San Francisco: Jossey-Bass, 1978.

Miles, Matthew B. "Planned Change and Organizational Health: Figure and Ground." In *Managing Change in Educational Organizations*, ed. J. Victor Baldridge and Terrence E. Deal. Berkeley, Calif.: McCutchan, 1975.

Miles, Matthew B., ed. *Innovation in Education*. New York: Teachers College Press, 1964.

Minkowitz, Abraham, Dan Davis, and Joseph Bashi. *An Evaluation Study of Israeli Elementary Schools*. Jerusalem: Hebrew University School of Education, 1977.

Moore, Sally F., and Barbara G. Myerhoff, eds., *Secular Ritual*. Amsterdam: Van Gorcum, 1977.

Morris, Charles W. *The Pragmatic Movement in American Philosophy.* New York: George Braziller, 1970.

Mueller, Claus. *The Politics of Communication.* New York: Oxford University Press, 1973.

Neubauer, Peter B. "The Role of Insight in Psychoanalysis." *Journal of the American Psychoanalytic Association* 27, supplement (1979): 29–39.

Nissen, Lowell. *John Dewey's Theory of Inquiry and Truth.* The Hague: Mouton, 1966.

O'Neill, John, ed. *Modes of Individualism and Collectivism.* London: Heinemann, 1973.

Ortony, Andrew, ed. *Metaphor and Thought.* Cambridge: Cambridge University Press, 1979.

Pateman, Trevor. *Language, Truth, and Politics,* 2d ed. Lewes, East Sussex, Eng.: Jean Stroud, 1980.

Peck, Robert F., and James A. Tucker. "Research on Teacher Education." In *Second Handbook of Research on Teaching,* ed. Robert M. W. Travers. Chicago: Rand McNally, 1973.

Perrow, Charles. *Complex Organizations.* Glensview, Ill.: Scott, Foresman, 1972.

———. "Three Types of Effectiveness Studies." In *New Perspectives on Organizational Effectiveness,* ed. Paul S. Goodman and Johannes M. Pennings. San Francisco: Jossey-Bass, 1977.

Peters, Richard S. "Cause, Cure and Motive." In *Philosophy and Analysis,* ed. Margaret McDonald. Oxford: Blackwell, 1954.

Pfeffer, Jeffrey, and Gerald Salancik. *The External Control of Organizations.* New York: Harper and Row, 1978.

Plato. *The Republic.* London: J. M. Dent, 1976.

Polanyi, Michael. *Personal Knowledge.* London: Routledge and Kegan Paul, 1958.

Popper, Karl R. *Conjectures and Refutations.* London: Routledge and Kegan Paul, 1963.

Pur, David, and David Gordon. "Conservatism and Centralization in School Systems—The Case of the Israeli High Schools." In *Educational Administration and Policy Making,* ed. Ephraim Ben-Baruch and Yoram Neumann. Herzlia, Israel: Unipress, 1982.

Raup, R. Bruce, Kenneth D. Benne, et al. *The Improvement of Practical Intelligence.* New York: Harper and Row, 1943.

Reitman, Walter R. "Heuristic Decision Procedures, Open Constraints and the Structure of Ill-Defined Problems." In *Human Judgments and Optimality,* ed. Maynard W. Shelly and Glenn L. Bryan. New York: John Wiley, 1966.

Reshef, Shimon. *The Labour Movement School System in Pre-State Israel.* Tel Aviv: Hakibbutz Hameuchad Press, 1980 (in Hebrew).

Ricoeur, Paul. *Hermeneutics and the Human Sciences.* London: Cambridge University Press, 1981.

————. *Interpretation Theory.* Fort Worth: Texas Christian University Press, 1976.

————. *The Rule of Metaphor.* Toronto: University of Toronto Press, 1977.

Rogers, Carl R. *On Becoming a Person.* Boston: Houghton Mifflin, 1961.

Rogers, Everett M., and F. Floyd Shoemaker. *Communication of Innovations: A Cross-Cultural Approach.* New York: Free Press, 1971.

Rokeach, Milton. *The Open and Closed Mind.* New York: Basic Books, 1960.

Runkel, Philip J., et al. *Transforming the School's Capacity for Problem Solving.* Eugene: Center for Educational Policy and Management, University of Oregon, 1979.

Rutter, Michael, et al. *Fifteen Thousand Hours.* Cambridge, Mass.: Harvard University Press, 1979.

Sarason, Seymour B. *The Culture of the School and the Problem of Change.* Boston: Allyn and Bacon, 1971.

Schattschneider, Elmer E. *The Semisovereign People.* Hinsdale, Ill.: Dryden Press, 1975.

Scheffler, Israel. *Beyond the Letter.* London: Routledge and Kegan Paul, 1979.

————. *Four Pragmatists.* London: Routledge and Kegan Paul, 1974.

————. "In Praise of the Cognitive Emotions." *Teachers College Record* 79, no. 2 (December 1977): 171–86.

————. "Philosophical Models of Teaching." In *Reason and Teaching.* London: Routledge and Kegan Paul, 1973.

————. "Ritual and Reference," *Synthèse* 46, no. 3 (March 1981): 421–37.

Schmuck, Richard A., et al. *Handbook of Organizational Development in Schools.* Eugene: Center for the Advanced Study of Educational Administration, University of Oregon, 1972.

————. *The Second Handbook of Organizational Development in Schools.* Palo Alto, Calif.: Mayfield, 1977.

Schön, Donald A. "Generative Metaphor: A Perspective on Problem-Setting in Social Policy." In *Metaphor and Thought,* ed. Andrew Ortony. Cambridge: Cambridge University Press, 1979.

Schutz, Alfred. "Equality and the Meaning Structure of the Social World." In *Collected Papers, vol. 2, Studies in Social Theory.* The Hague: Martinus Nijhoff, 1964.

Schwab, Joseph J. "The Teaching of Science as Enquiry." In *The Teaching of Science,* ed. Joseph J. Schwab and Paul F. Brandwein. Cambridge, Mass.: Harvard University Press, 1966.

Schwartz, Barry. *Vertical Classification.* Chicago: University of Chicago Press, 1981.

Shaplin, Judson T., and Henry F. Olds, eds. *Team Teaching.* New York: Harper and Row, 1964.

Smith, Louis M., and William Geoffrey. *The Complexities of an Urban Classroom.* New York: Holt, Rinehart and Winston, 1968.

Smith, Louis M., and Pat M. Keith. *Anatomy of Educational Innovation.*

New York: John Wiley, 1971.

Smith, Louis M., John J. Prunty, and David C. Dwyer. "A Longitudinal Nested Systems Model of Innovation and Change in Schooling." In *Organizational Behaviour in Schools and School Districts,* ed. Samuel B. Bacharach. New York: Praeger, 1981.

Toulmin, Stephen. "The Logical Status of Psycho-Analysis." In *Philosophy and Analysis,* ed. Margaret McDonald. Oxford: Blackwell, 1954.

Tuthill, John W. "The Repeal of Parkinson's Law." *Intellectual Digest* 3 (April 1973): 34–35.

Vallance, Elizabeth, "The Hidden Curriculum and Qualitative Inquiry as States of Mind." *Journal of Education* 162, no. 1 (Winter 1980): 138–51.

Warwick, Donald. *A Theory of Public Bureaucracy.* Cambridge, Mass.: Harvard University Press, 1975.

Watzlawick, Paul, John H. Weakland, and Richard Fish. *Change: Principles of Problem Formation and Problem Resolution.* New York: W. W. Norton, 1974.

Weick, Karl E. "Educational Organizations as Loosely Coupled Systems." *Administrative Science Quarterly* 21, no. 1 (March 1976): 1–19.

Whorf, Benjamin L. *Language, Thought, and Reality.* Cambridge, Mass.: MIT Press, 1956.

Wildavsky, Aaron. "The Self-Evaluating Organization." *Public Administration Review* 32, no. 5 (September/October 1972): 509–20.

Williams, Martin. *The Jazz Tradition.* New York: Mentor, 1971.

Willis, Paul. *Learning to Labor.* New York: Columbia University Press, 1981.

Wilson, John. *Education Theory and the Preparation of Teachers.* Windsor, Berks.: NFER Publishing Co., 1975.

Witkin, Herman A., et al. *Psychological Differentiation.* New York: John Wiley, 1962.

Wittgenstein, Ludwig. *On Certainty.* New York: Harper and Row, 1972.

Yizhar, Sammach. *On Education and Education For Values.* Tel Aviv: Am Oved, 1974. (in Hebrew)

About the Author

David Gordon is a Senior Lecturer in the Education Department, Ben-Gurion University of the Negev, Israel. He is also managing director of ALITA, an educational consulting agency sponsored by his university, and has served as an adviser to the Israeli Ministry of Education and Culture on high school innovation. He has had numerous articles published in professional journals and books. His Ph.D. degree is from Hebrew University in Jerusalem.

Index